FRONT-LINE THEATRE.
Putting up a play-bill of the Yaroslavl " Volkov " Theatre in
A Fellow From Our Town.

[*Frontispiece.*

ACTORS CROSS THE VOLGA

A Study of the 19th Century Russian
Theatre and of Soviet Theatres in War

by

JOSEPH MACLEOD

London

GEORGE ALLEN & UNWIN LTD

FIRST PUBLISHED IN 1946

312775

PRINTED IN GREAT BRITAIN AT
THE UNIVERSITY PRESS
ABERDEEN

AUTHOR'S PREFACE

WHEN the public has indicated its interest in a first book on a new subject, it rightly tends to be critical of a successor. The author was surprised and pleased by the welcome given to *The New Soviet Theatre* in 1943. He is all the more conscious of the faults in this book. The critical reader, if he or she takes it as a history, will feel that it has no middle, or perhaps that the middle is contained in the earlier book, and that this is clumsy. But this is not a history. It is a study of Soviet theatres in war.

The extraordinary vigour of the Soviet theatres in war, however, cannot be understood without some knowledge of the pre-Revolutionary background, the nineteenth-century Russian theatre ; and as far as the author is aware, there are no books in English (and those few in Russian are practically unobtainable) on this subject. An absorbing subject ; and one which is treated herein too sketchily.

Nor is the main body of the book a complete history, but again only an interim report. A transmission. A channel, through which information may circulate. The details had to be culled from many sources ; they were bewildering in their prolixity ; and the task of setting them in order, of getting them in due perspective, had to be done spasmodically, in leisure hours which became fewer and fewer as the work progressed. Nor have the writing of the final chapters and the revision of the whole been made any easier by the intermittent arrival of flying bombs, which meant keeping the sources and the growing manuscript in a place of safety away from the desk at which the writing was done.

If therefore there are inconsistencies, redundancies, repetitions, mistakes in detail, if the writing flags or the path seems to disappear in the undergrowth, the author begs for clemency. It seemed to him that the need for a full understanding of our Soviet Allies' culture and evaluation of life (such as best a theatre can give) grew more urgent as victory drew nearer, and he hastened to finish his task as a contribution to that understanding, without which no peace in the world can be permanent, but our twenty years' friendship may be wrecked by misconstruction.

TO

KIT

IN RETURN FOR THINGS FOREGONE

AND FORGONE

CONTENTS

Part One

OLD WORLD, EARLY NINETEENTH CENTURY

Part Two

OLD WORLD, LATER NINETEENTH CENTURY

Part Three

THE WAR, FIRST ASPECT

Part Four

THE WAR, SECOND ASPECT

Part Five

NEW WORLD

LIST OF ILLUSTRATIONS

And Art made tongue-tied by Authority
—SHAKESPEARE

Part One

OLD WORLD: EARLY NINETEENTH CENTURY

CHAPTER I

IMPERIAL THEATRES

A BIRD'S-EYE VIEW

It is the year 1850. Imagine that we are flying at a great height north-ward over the Black Sea, the shores of which for centuries have been visited by little boats of various shapes, trading between East and West. We are approaching the land, land that stretches West for one and a half thousand miles, North for one and a half thousand miles, and East for something like four thousand.

To our left a great river approaches from due West, entering the Black Sea not so very far from where Ovid comforted himself with his *Tristia* mournfully in exile. This river, the Danube, connects many of the countries, and several of the capitals, of the European civilisation to which we belong, with this strange land below us. Cutting through the grey plains from the north come three more great rivers, the Dnieper, the Don and the Volga, not all flowing into this Black Sea, but all bulging eastwards, as if the people on the inside of the bulge were pressing in that direction, or as if water, obligingly lending itself to the disposition of man, had thrown up three lines of ramparts against the unpredictable East. And far to our right is the reply of the unpredictable East, a similar rampart bulging back against us, the Ural River. Impossible not to imagine from the very geography that here is not a No-man's-land between Athens and China.

It is not a land we know well. Even the air is filled with the unfamiliar. From the steppes rise bustards, evil-looking, bald spectres, more like night-mares than birds, which bump along the ground like overladen aeroplanes before they can take off. The eagles in the mountains are not the eagles we know. Even the little homely birds, singing a few yards from the soil, are of unexpected colour. Thrushes are black or grey.

And the people, too, are different from what we have come to call European. True, there are a few cities which have houses and public buildings of architecture in a recognisably Italian-origin style, though an altered one. In St. Petersburg (which is commonly called Peterburg), and Moscow, and Odessa, there are more than a hundred thousand of a city

9

population.[1] Four other towns have half that number ; some twenty have a quarter. And in these there are well-to-do people who do not depend on the land directly for a living, merchants, doctors, and the like, who use handkerchiefs and crowd their rooms with knick-knacks and furniture, whose wives and daughters study the French fashions and wear much lace. In these towns there are a few schools ; but most children of the well-to-do are taught at home by foreign governesses and tutors. The rest are not taught at all.

Peter the First's window on Europe has been dimmed and shrouded with lace curtains and the police. The harsh reign of Nicholas the First is coming to an end. Pushkin is dead ; Lermontov is dead ; Byelinsky, the great critic and thinker who located and directed the new Russian literature, died two years ago, thereby cheating the police on their way to arrest him. Gogol is still alive ; Ostrovsky, in his twenties, is making his mind up ; Turgenyev, Dostoyevsky, and Tolstoy are young men not yet on their feet, though in two years Turgenyev is to be arrested, and Dostoyevsky taken out for execution and then sent to Siberia in partial reprieve. Cultured people are proud of these writers, who are putting Russian among the European literary languages ; but cultured people are few, and confined to the towns.

In the countryside, where the overwhelming majority of people live, there are few villages, no hamlets. People live in small townships of a thousand or more.[2] This is partly for safety, against wolves and robbers and the drunken sons of the nobility ; and partly because they belong to the nobles, body and soul. They work for them in a feudal way, for no wages. They spend their spare time winning just enough food for their families to exist upon from strips of ground which also belong to the nobles. Even the craftsmen, blacksmiths, wheelwrights, locksmiths, belong to the nobles. They buy off their personal duties by annual payments while they learn their craft or practise it.

You would think from this that the nobles would be rich. And many of them are, fabulously so. These go travelling in Europe, drink wine, speak French. They plant trees to shelter their houses in the open plains.[3] But to be sent for long periods to their homes is a punishment. They do not like Russia, they do not understand the language. Their families have been noble so long that fortunes tend to split up and titles to be less a family rank than a class badge. An English traveller records that already there exist at the same time some three hundred Prince G——s.[4] Younger sons and cadet branches are not necessarily rich. They have to take posts under the Emperor, in the Army or as *chinovniki*.

The *chinovniki* are very numerous. They spread all over the huge space of land below us. They are badly paid, perhaps because what was right for the Tsar to pay in the Middle Ages must obviously still be right for him to pay, and anything else would be wrong ; and new posts must be graded accordingly. But the *chinovniki* have positions and dignities and uniforms to maintain (they get into trouble if they do not) ; so they take bribes. Big ones for important officials, just a rouble or two for the lesser, who cannot claim nobility. The social scale is strict. There are fourteen degrees of *chin*, and each has its appropriate form of address, from " Your Honourable " to " Your Privy Councillor " or, if the official is a Baron, " Your Brilliancy ".[5] Plainly, here we are nearer to China than to Athens. And the resemblance is continued in the strictness of the financial scale. The lesser *chinovnik* must hand on a big enough share of his takings to his superior, just as he must address him with humble enough respect, or unpleasant consequences will follow. And so, though he may be taking quite a handsome amount each year, he is never very rich ; and his energies are just as much consumed in winning a living for his family as those of the serfs all round him.

He may even not be exempt from personal violence. A station-master on the post-chaise system that links the townships together may have kept his horses few, to save expense. Now several parties of travellers have arrived simultaneously, each bribing him to give them priority. Who will win ? The knowing traveller, the young noble. He will kick or beat the station-master till he gets double priority. Cynically, the whole system was summed up in the popular saying : " God is high and the Tsar is far ".

Mercifully, travellers are few. That is what strikes us first about this vast land, the absence of much movement from place to place. Where people are born, there they die. They are not allowed to do much else. Indeed the network of *chinovniki* is partly intended to keep the people static. If an owner allows a serf to leave, there will still be his papers to scrutinise and object to. If the serf cannot bribe the official, he cannot leave. And little is the money a serf can save.

Landowners going in coaches to and from their estates ; fashionable persons passing to and from watering-places . . . but otherwise the only motion appears to be that of inspecting officials (visits rare and dangerous to all in the neighbourhood) or officers going to the east. All the time officers go east, or return from the east on furlough. All the time there are wars in the east, nobody knows what for. A cynic may say it is to train the troops for a real war against Turkey. But at least this provides careers for younger sons. And it draws bad characters from the townships, where they might spread ideas. Ideas and a bad character necessarily go together.

Five years ago, for instance, guerrilla troops of the people of Dagestan cut to pieces a Russian column that was trying to beat into submission the grand Highland chief Shamil. Shamil is going from power to power. Soon he is to order that his own mother should receive a hundred lashes for proposing terms that savoured of compromise, and fifty of those lashes from filial piety he will take on his own back. Such inflexibility takes a lot of fighting ; and indeed it can only be defeated by upper-class cunning. What will break Shamil will be the return of his own son from captivity, turned into a Russian officer type. That is progress, as it is understood in Court circles.

In general the Tsar is not interested in progress. As our traveller observes with much foresight, Europeans have not yet connected East and West by cutting a canal through the Isthmus of Suez, though he sees that this cannot be long postponed. The Tsar, by the geographical position of his dominions, could have the monopoly of the mid-nineteenth-century carrying trade between the continents. Steam is already at his disposal. Macadam, four years dead, has shown Europe how to make roads. A single canal, 56 miles only, between Volga and Don would make a water link. But this is not dug. There are a few steamers on the great rivers, but they are the property of foreign firms, mostly British. In the main, traffic is by small boats that drop the anchors of larger ones a few hundred yards ahead, on which the larger ones haul themselves up the stream by a windlass of horses or men.

The only railway of any importance is between Moscow and Peterburg, drawn on a map by the Tsar with a ruler, and avoiding all the commercial centres on the way. The one daily passenger train takes twenty-two hours.

There are few roads, mostly rides through the forests, or trails across the steppes marked by white posts with tufts of straw on their tips, or posts striped black and white if it is a post-road. Travellers sit on planks suspended on wheels without springs, or are bumped and bruised in tarantasses that hurtle down ravines and over hillocks. Goods go to fairs by ox-waggon or camel-cart, of wood or wicker. Heavy taxes are paid on all goods that enter the country. Thus home-made things are kept dear, benefiting the owners of the men and women who make them. The Tsar himself, however, has plenty of money. His idea of a rich country is himself owning rich possessions.

Some of the nobles, though, are interested in progress. By hearsay they are in touch with the West. An inventor on the Volga has heard of steamboats and seen a steam engine. He designs one for his boat and installs it, not as a means of propulsion, but as an adjunct to the windlass. He adds expense, but saves no time. No invention is allowed to be publicised until official examination has passed it as useful.

Most ' educated ' people are thus kept on a bare margin of life. Life to them in their country isolation is a thing of lonely pleasure, like hunting, whether of wild boar or pretty village girls. Their social delights are limited to negotiating advantageous marriages for themselves or their children. Their financial problems, if they have money, are complicated by seasons in the capitals. We cannot expect them to be much interested in truthful portrayals of life on theatre stages. And most have an even narrower margin. Having little to do but suffer in a world where nobody knows the reason for anything that happens, they do not wish to see similar suffering mirrored by actors. And the stagnation of the countryside does not allow them even the escape to a dream world on the stage. They can dream only in fumes of tobacco or *mahorka* indoors (for they will be fined for smoking out of doors), or by getting mercifully drunk on vodka indoors or out of doors. For the Tsar has no interest in tobacco manufacture, but he has in the consumption of vodka. Oliphant tells us that the Russian peasant is not offensive when he is drunk. He will be beaten if he is.

That is the broad picture we see below us, as we fly above the countryside within the furthest rampart, the River Volga. What goes on beyond that rampart is wild and unknown, and none of our business.

Audiences in Moscow

In the big towns it is different. There are theatres in Peterburg and Moscow and Odessa. Good ones. People are proud of them. As early as the end of the eighteenth century Sandunov, the first comic genius of the Russian stage, has made such a hit that a memoir writer who has seen the same part played in Paris suggests Molière himself would have been delighted with Sandunov's Scapin, because he became the character in gesture and action before he opened his mouth.[6] That implies something of actor and audience. For there are audiences to be had.

We have Byelinsky's description of the Moscow audience in early days.[7] " In the Petrovsky Theatre in Moscow ",* he says, " gather people of different classes, different degrees of education, different tastes and requirements. Here you will see merchants with beards and merchants without beards, and students, and people who live in Moscow because they are happy living there and it is their habit to live where they can be happy. Here you will see fashionable tail-coats and yellow gloves, striking *vengerki* † and an overcoat and old-fashioned *capotes* with collars, and short winter coats and bear-fur coats, hats and peaked caps and everything but nightcaps, bonnets with ostrich feathers and little caps with bits of hare fur, and

---

* The Maly Theatre in Moscow was sometimes called the Petrovsky Theatre, because (like the Bolshoy) it was situated in the square known as Petrovsky Square, Theatre Square, and after the Revolution, Sverdlov Square.

† Short Hungarian jackets.

2

heads in embroidered shawls of silk or calico. Here you will see people
for whom *Filatka and Mirosha* ★ is an entertaining and interesting piece,
and people for whom the repertoire of all Europe does not provide too
great riches ; people who want to hear nothing but Shakespeare ; people
for whom a Gogol comedy is the height of perfection, and people to whom
a Gogol comedy means no more than crude farces do, even when these
lack any sign of talent ; people who see in the dramas of Mr. Kukolnik †
exemplary compositions, and people who see in them nothing but tedium.
In short, in the Moscow theatre public there are almost as many tastes and
opinions as there are figures comprising it, and it is no rarity to encounter
the most subtle and cultured, the most refined taste side by side with the
most crude and banal ; no rarity to overhear from your neighbour on
one side the most intelligent, and on the other the most nonsensical, comment.

" Even people possessed of the same degree of education do not in
Moscow speak with the same voice in one and the same words, because
in Moscow every man would have his own outlook on things, his own
judgment of them. Tragedy or a pathetic play they prefer in Moscow,
and value higher than comedy or vaudeville. This is understandable.
For comedy you need a more refined public than for tragedy, since the
latter concerns the sufferings and feelings of humanity, even unconscious
ones, and awakens these powerfully even in souls that are fast asleep, whereas
the former requires for appreciation people who have grown up in a mature
civilisation, requires an Attic subtlety of taste, an observant mind, able to
catch each nuance, each scarcely perceptible stroke. In Moscow tragedy
is liked by merchants with beards and merchants without.‡ And no
wonder. For in great part they are people who are not lightly moved,
who yield only to very strong feelings. . . . If they decide to go to the
theatre, then give them Mochalov (whom they call Muchaláwf). For
him many of them will pay on his benefit night a hundred, two hundred
roubles or more for a box they could pay less than fifteen for. They like
Mochalov, and like to tell their friends, stroking their beards, long before
the night and long after, ' I paid such-and-such for Mochalov's benefit '.
A purely Moscow trait, which you don't encounter nowadays in Peterburg."

★ *Filatka and Mirosha, Partners :* a vaudeville in two acts by P. Grigoryev. The
slow-witted Filatka serves as a soldier in place of his brother. At first he is a coward ;
then he grows brave.

† " This Kukolnik ", says K. Waliszewski, " was a poor playwright and worse
novelist ; " adding a word about his " Inflated rhetoric and pompous patriotism ".
When taken to task for writing to order, Kukolnik replied, " I'll play the part of
an *accoucheur* to-morrow, if I'm so directed ".

‡ This represented a difference of outlook. Some of the newly rich tried to
look and behave like gentlemen, others looked and behaved like mujiks. Both types
combined in a subscription of 3,500 rubles for Mochalov to have a holiday abroad ;
and the day he died all the Moscow shops shut for grief.

AUDIENCES IN PETERBURG.[8]

In Peterburg, Byelinsky explains, there *is* such a thing as a " theatre public ". It has no heterogeneous classes, everyone is in " the service ", meaning, of course, they are officials of some kind. It has a single taste. It never contradicts itself. It is always perfectly assured. It is an *individuum*, properly dressed, well-to-do, not demanding very much, not giving much away, afraid of extremes, very like the respectable classes in France and Germany, says Byelinsky. It is perfectly at home in the Alexandrinsky foyer, so much so that it doesn't welcome strangers there, so strangers seldom go. Strangers go to the Mihailovsky Theatre, unless they don't know French, in which case they don't go anywhere. So the Alexandrinsky public is homogeneous. If it applauds, everyone applauds, even if they don't want to. Accordingly, actors and authors all play for safety, doing only what they know pleased last time. And the audience never tires of calling its favourites, once they are its favourites. Karatygin they will give fifteen calls in an evening ; but nobody else. And it applauds perpetually, not from extravagance, but because it is perfectly satisfied with all the plays it is given.

We must examine this Peterburg audience more closely. In 1832 there were nearly half a million people in Peterburg. One-quarter were peasants, one-quarter house and personal servants, one-tenth officials, one-tenth soldiers and their families. There were only about forty-two thousand aristocrats, and a little more than that number of merchants and middle-class professional people. But the theatres were supposed to be for the aristocrats only.

There was the Bolshoy, which gave Italian operas and ballets and very occasionally plays. *Woe from Wit* had its first performance here in 1831. There was the (Peterburg) Maly, where at first there was no gallery and the aristocrats rented their boxes for a period of years. Only in 1819 the Third Circle had been turned into a gallery seating 180, and the aristocrats ceased to be alone. Rude, rough, uneducated merchants invaded their sacred premises. The Maly was demolished in 1832, just as a new theatre building was completed opposite it.

This was the famous and still extant Alexandrinsky Theatre. It was designed by Rossi, and contained the latest scenic ingenuities from Paris. It was named for Alexandra, wife of Tsar Nicholas. It was illuminated with a thousand oil lamps. And a specially hand-picked audience glittered in the light of them at the opening performance on the last day of August. They heard first the overture to an old opera called *Ivan Susanin*,* by Kavos.

* Not to be confused with Glinka's opera, *A Life for the Tsar*, which is nowadays called *Ivan Susanin*, as was originally intended before the Tsar altered the title.

They watched then a patriotic tragedy by Kryukovsky, which bored them. They brightened to the ballet divertissement " A Spanish Wedding ", by Blash.

Drama bored them, though they always gave an ovation to the Karatygins. It bored them because they did not understand Russian very well. When they wanted a play, they would go to French plays at the Mihailovsky Theatre. Yet they crowded out the Alexandrinsky Theatre when it gave ballet, as it generally did. One of the reasons why there were few plays to attract them, was that the Imperial theatres were administered by an official called Gedeonov, who knew nothing about theatres, and like most of his class at that time, never opened a book of any kind if he could avoid it. After all, mere eyesight can enjoy a dancer, but to follow a tragedian or a wit demands the use of the head. Gedeonov's administration consisted largely in seeing that interviewers filled in their requests correctly in the proper form of words. He would then scrawl " NO " across the application. So regularly and successfully did he do this that he remained in office for twenty-five years, his rules a sore trial.

However, in 1836 the ballet was transferred in a body to the Bolshoy Theatre, and the Alexandrinsky Theatre was left with a second-rate orchestra, faded curtains and an old stock of costumes. The noble audience went with the ballet, though they used to come back on benefit nights for the Karatygins or Sosnitsky, Vera Samoïlova, or Asenkova.

(Poor, sweet-faced, honourable Asenkova ! She rejected the insulting advances of the cynical young Guards officers ; and they in revenge one night shouted such filthy words at her from their boxes that she fled weeping into the wings, and, trapped by their cruelty (for the stage was her only means of honourable livelihood) worried herself into a decline, and died of tuberculosis before she was 25.)

The population of Peterburg was changing. Merchants, business men, master-craftsmen, and the more intellectual of those in State service, were multiplying fast. When the nobility deserted the Alexandrinsky, these came to it, bringing their wives and families, putting on white gloves to show they were " good style ". It was the same story as our eighteenth-century London audience told. But these were more full-blooded and rough. They wanted emotional, exciting plays.

The management gave up comedies from the French, smart dialogue, literary traditions, and tried to find good Russian plays to suit them. There were no good plays.

The audience liked Asenkova as a male impersonator in vaudeville better than as Ophelia. Vaudevilles were all the rage, as they had been in Beaumarchais' time in France. They were written in rhyme, with plenty

of song and dance. The music was often compiled by the prompter.*
Frequently the author would state what popular tune his words were
intended to fit. The Parisian model, as written by Scribe and Balzac,
was followed. Dances were French too, the can-can, the polka. Some
of these entertainments were elegant and graceful, but the majority were
cheap : either love-scenes in romantic settings with dirty *double-entendres*
in the dialogue, or plays of manners with smuggled satirical double meanings
at the expense of the *chinovniki*.

They liked the Samoïlovs too in melodrama—also Parisian in origin.
They liked Lyadova in operetta. But most of all they liked the Karatygins
in lush patriotic drama, at which they could stamp their feet and cry
" Bravo ! " or " Forah ! ".

The patriotic drama was a deliberate invention of Tsar Nicholas himself. He was a suspicious, anxious man, afraid of uprisings, oppressed by
the nightmares of tyrants. He knew that the rising middle class sided with
the mujiks and masses rather than with the aristocrats ; and if they were
faithful to the monarchy, of which he was never sure, it was only for protection against the aristocrats. He knew nothing about the theatre, but
realised its importance when the merchants crowded to it with their families.
He gave instructions that the theatre was to be used for the " political
education " of the middle classes. At first this was done through the
censorship, the famous Department III. But in 1848, when crowned heads
were falling over all Europe, he became yet more distrustful, and read every
play himself before it was licensed, banned authors like Schiller and
Beaumarchais absolutely, and demanded a yet more specifically patriotic
repertoire. Anything that was likely to evoke applause for its independent
views by the " non-privileged classes " (that was the phrase actually used)
was to be cut forthwith.

The playwrights Polevoy and Kukolnik obliged. Kukolnik said,
" Love of the Fatherland, the Tsar and the Holy Ones is by itself the one
and only (but so wholly rich and bounteous) theme of popular drama ".
And he concocted plays called *The Hand of the Almighty Saved the Fatherland*,†
Prince Mihail Vasilyevich Skopin-Shuisky, or topical plays like *The Naval
Occasion at Sevastopol* in 1854, wherein after all had expressed their love for
their country from different angles, there was a final demonstration and
hymn sung in the audience.

* He at least would have some stage sense. At this time music was written for
plays by professional musicians, but with no regard whatever to stage requirements.
The stage manager often chose for serious dramas passages from opera or instru-
mental works. Gautier expected a new comedy form to evolve from the vaudeville.

† This caused a sensation in 1834 because all its five acts had sets designed by the
same painter ; but the event remained the exception. Usually painters were asked
to supply only single scenes, A Trip By Rail to Tsarskoye Selo, or The Wreck of
the Frigate " Medusa ". These would be duly applauded.

Polevoy followed suit. He liked having groups of plain, simple folk on his stage, to shout " Forah ! Forah ! " when the goodness of the Tsar was mentioned. He confessed that the theatre for him was only " an indulgence, a relaxation after real work ".

But this kind of authorship had its pitfalls. Grigoryev intended a roaring patriotic success in *The Russians at the Approach to the Turkish Frontier*, only to have it banned. As Nicholas observed, " At the present time, when warlike actions are not noted for any brilliant successes of importance, Grigoryev's play savours somewhat of advertising the past ".

In general, of plays like *Russian Saints*, *A Russian Wedding at the End of the 16th Century*, or *The Best School is the Tsar's Service*, Byelinsky said that the society they depicted was as much like Russian society as it was like Arabian.

The Early Nineteenth-Century Theatre in Russia and Britain

The standard of performance in both Peterburg and Moscow was amateurish. Mishaps were frequent. In a performance in 1831 of a five-act tragedy, *The Bandit of the Bohemian Woods*, adapted from Byron (presumably his *Werner*), the castle collapsed in the last act, and in the general panic the wife of the actor Bryansky, seeing him apparently dead, shrieked out his little name " Yasha ! ", after which it was solemnly announced that owing to the collapse of the castle, the play could not be concluded. And this is only one of many recorded that summer.[9]

In other words, the theatre was not taken *seriously*. Shakespeare was popular, certainly, though less for his poetry or understanding than for his stage effects. But in any case, you cannot judge a theatre period by the number of Shakespeare performances given. Even in the lowest years of British theatrical history (not far removed from the one we are now discussing in Russia), as Allardyce Nicoll has shown,[*] many of Planché's ultra-popular burlesques depended for their effect on the audience's memory of Shakespearean phrases, and he further quotes Colman the Younger (who died in 1836) as saying that a modern audience would not allow of any further meddling with the text of Shakespeare. Yet at the same time he quotes Leigh Hunt in 1807, " Any man . . . will find that his chief entertainment has arisen from the actors, totally abstracted from the authors ". (*Ibid.*, p. 50.)

The same might be said of almost any country in our view : France, Italy, Spain, Germany, America, in all these the stage has become a place for sight and sound more than for the experience of life. In London especially. In London the old audience of aristocrats had left the theatre entirely. Even the merchants did not come often. The new class of

---

[*] *A History of Early XIXth Century Drama*, Vol. I, p. 90.

manufacturers were too busy making money. Only the miserable mob came, clambering into the critics' favourite places in the pit, clamouring for cheaper and cheaper seats. The managers build bigger and bigger theatres. The actors have to shout. Playwrights adopt a simplified, poster-like technique. Characters become types, wit becomes clowning, elaborate stage machinery with real fire and real water attract wider and bigger and noisier audiences.

This mob asserts its will. Kemble bows to it over prices. Kean has to beg its pardon. Madame Vestris, pioneer of the Little Theatre, gives it the light fare it wants.[10] Manager after manager, even the blarneying Elliston, has in the broader issue to submit. And what the public boos, he dare not announce for further showing, for fear of physical violence. This, even though the patent theatres of Covent Garden and Drury Lane are administered, like the Imperial theatres of Russia, under the Crown, with the monopoly of all written plays.

This wild, uneducated mob did not want literary plays ; they did not want to think. They wanted thrills. The thrill of a good tune, of apparent death in a waterfall, of a city in flames, of a fine woman declaiming glorious meaningless words. Bradlee Watson has shown how Shakespeare to them was a thrill as good as a prize-fight, with speech a series of " points " and plot a series of punches. And even Shakespeare had to be given progressively more sumptuous settings as each manager vied for public support. And, deeper, because this mob were themselves in the power of the wicked beyond hope of escape, they insisted in their excitement on good being triumphant, and their hisses against the villain meant much more than just helping the play along.

In Russia it was not quite the same. As Lunacharsky neatly puts it, in the Imperial theatres " the Tsar and his courtiers held the ballet and opera pretty firmly in their hands ; but the drama fluttered there like a captured bird ".[11] And despite the *chinovniki* a continual war went on, especially in Moscow, between reactionaries and liberals. As proof of this, Lunacharsky cites some of the plays done : *Hernani* and *Ruy Blas*, by the feared Republican Victor Hugo ; *Intrigue and Love*, with its savage attack on the cruelty and crime of the ruling class, and *The Robbers*, in which even the good are overcome by the evil of the times ; Goethe's political prison drama *Egmont;* and the human plays of Shakespeare. These, he argues, are not the fare a reactionary tyrant would choose for his subjects, unless he had to ; but more and more of the intelligentsia were coming to the Moscow theatre, and they wanted truth on the stage.

In progressive theatres, truth on the stage and truth in life must go together. If therefore there is a feeling for liberation, a broadening, enlarging, forward-looking move in life outside, the theatre too must broaden,

enlarge and look forward.   Otherwise it will be a mere convention, apart
from life.   Therefore a theatre anxious to improve itself artistically, must
in such a community throw in its lot with those trying to improve life
outside.   And conversely : reactionary and official governors will wish
to suppress any tendency to " human " drama, because that is interested in
the individual, the unique, the independent dignity of man, which threatens
the artificial, schematised society those governors help to maintain.

The Moscow theatre never went chasing after spectacle.   " It shrank
from didacticism as from fire."   The word was the thing.   " The Maly
Theatre serves the word."   And it was by attending to the words, the
truth and the implication of what they were saying that Maly actors and
actresses like Shchepkin, the Sadovsky family, Yermolova, and the rest of
the Maly great ones, built up a tradition of theatrical truth or realism
that obtains to this day, though it has continually altered with altering times.

All over the world this realism was creeping on the stage.   In England
and Scotland a series of intelligent actors or actor-managers, Kemble,
Bannister, Planché, Macready, Charles Kean, Phelps, Irving, and along another
line Madame Vestris, Charles Matthews, the Bancrofts, each broke down
a further convention.   Each tried to equate the truth of what was done
on the stage with the truth of the lives of the audience.   In France Antoine
fought the diction and stance and remoteness of the Comédie-Française ;
in Germany the Meininger company and Moissy fell into naturalistic faults
in countering tragic bombast ; in Italy Salvini and Rossi and Duse set their
stars in the heaven but as a guide to their steps on the ground.   The Fourth
Wall was no modern invention.   Leigh Hunt used the term in 1807.[12]

So it was in the Maly Theatre in Moscow.   But at great cost.   Truth
might be wanted by increasing numbers of audiences ; authors like Gogol
and Griboyedov, Suhovo-Kobylin, Potehin, Ostrovsky, Tolstoy, might
write truthful and broadening plays, showing real people frustrated by a
false environment : but if that environment was created and kept by
Tsarist officials, and these officials ruled the theatre, then a stout heart and
a clear head were required of author and actor.   Improvement in art
became dangerous.

Moscow Plays

Let us first consider what the authors had to reform.   What sort of
plays did the Maly actors have ?   It is true there were Shakespeare's *Othello*
and *King Lear*.   But in very inferior translations.   There were feasts of
fine words by Racine and Corneille and Voltaire.   But the majority of
plays were fustian.   Kukolnik's tragedy, *Skopin-Shuisky*, may be taken as
an important play of the time, seeing that it had its *premières* simultaneously
at the Alexandrinsky in Peterburg and the Maly in Moscow.

It represented, as we may guess from what has already been said about this author, humility toward the Powers-that-be as a high duty and the Church as the base of all good government. Bolotnikov, the leader of a crowd of oppressed and rebellious peasants, was shown as a thief and a brigand, having as his sole purpose burning, slashing, and destroying, for the mere sake, it is to be supposed, of the pleasure given by such exercise. Attached to him, by chance of course, is the hero of the tragedy, Prokopiy Lyapunov. He begins to reproach himself with his " misdeeds " and with keeping company with a " dishonourable mujik ". The action proceeds by murders, and the development of character by monologues. Thus Lyapunov :

> Pardon me, O my sword, long my companion,
> E'en in the storm unselfish friend wert thou !

And faithful to the poisoned prince Skopin-Shuisky, Lyapunov throws through the window to the raging mob below (now getting ready to shout " Forah ! ") the doctor who had compounded the fatal draught ; and snarling

> Drink under the knife of Prokopiy Lyapunov !

he compels Yekaterina Shuisky, who had administered it, to drink the dregs. And so on. Lermontov went to this play. He sat in the theatre and listened, and looked.

> At last amid applause the curtain fell.
> A friend came up to me and said with scorn :
> " Well, brother ! Pity ! So poor Skopin's dead.
> But, you know, really he was never born."[13]

In Russian drama there were two main influences : the Comédie-Française and the Sturm und Drang. Voltaire's *Mahomet* did give sublimity, if nothing else, to theatre evenings, though Napoleon reading it on St. Helena said, " It is astonishing how ill all his dramas are adapted for reading. When criticism and sound sense are not cheated by pompous diction and scenic illusion, they immediately lose a thousand per cent." [14] Ozerov's plays did not even provide sublimity. His range of theme was wide, *Oedipus in Athens*, *Ossian*, *Dmitry of the Don* . . . he chose any hero, ancient or modern, for Comédie-Française treatment.* And Comédie-

---

* Dmitry Donskoy was a fourteenth-century rallier of the Russians against the Tartar hordes, as Alexander of the Neva rallied them against the Teutonic Knights. Ozerov's play, however, was intended not as history but as fulsome praise of his own monarch. Both heroes have recently come to favour, in a Socialist-realist light, in Soviet films and plays. V. A. Ozerov (1770-1816) wrote better in French than Russian. His plays kept the Classical Unities and clichés, following Sumarokov (1718-77) whose Frenchified Slav heroes had been impersonated by Italian actors. Pushkin said, " I don't like Ozerov—not from jealousy but from love of art ". See Б. Варнеке: „История русскрво театра xvii-xix всков", 3rd edtn. Искусство, 1940, pp. 26-7. Though a sentimentalist, Ozerov was not without righteous indignation.

Française treatment the actors gave his plays. Dmitrevskoy (1733-1821) studied every nuance of elegant diction for its possible effect. " Effect ", says a memoir-writer, " was the soul of Dmitrevskoy." " Semyonova ", explains the same writer, " sang." [15] Semyonova (1786-1849) was, roughly, the Russian Siddons. And the same held good of Shusherin Plavelshchikov, and the other prominent actors whose careers ended in the first half of the nineteenth century.

In plays derived from the German school, however, though there was still much literary style, there was a great deal more action. And many were written in prose, coming nearer to the spoken word. Declamation was neither so easy nor so suitable. Its full power is kept for ends of scenes, building up to a dramatic phrase, which can be delivered in an attitude, and a dramatic exit made, often with the attitude maintained while moving into the wings.* Vociferous applause leads to a return on-stage and a bow, which renews the applause, which renews the bow, which renews the applause, and so forward with the action suspended till player and applauder are satisfied and quiet ensues for the next passage.

Such a dramatic exit is a gift not only to the actor, but to the author too. When a situation has got beyond his control or ingenuity, and no further action is possible, the author can always fall back on the stage direction, *Rushes wildly out*, which enlivens the scene, solves the problem, and even creates in itself a new situation for the characters remaining on the stage.

Even the best of such plays approximates to melodrama. The standards are those of stage not life, where dramatic exits seldom solve any problems, indeed as a rule they intensify them. But such were being written and performed all over Europe at this time, because they gave actors chances to display their manipulation of voice, limb and body, and they excited the audience to applause (hence the phrase, " clap-trap "), and that was what the audience had come for. They can be examined in the products of Lessing, Kotzebue, and the earlier plays of Schiller. *The Robbers* (1781) made Schiller famous ; and both it and *Intrigue and Love* are more popular in the Soviet Union to-day than they have ever been in our countries. They are an astonishing blend of theatrical tricks and deep human understanding. Careful production can partially evaporate the former and distil the latter ; but such production was out of the question, even if anyone had thought of it, as long as dramatic exits were demanded by the actors.

For the actor was supreme. In so far as there was any producing, it was done by the stage manager ; but his powers were chiefly confined to reading the play to the assembled company before the first rehearsal, alluding

---

* A relic of this custom can sometimes be seen in Shakespeare productions to-day in Britain, when Harry V or Hotspur marches off with his right hand clenched above his head, his left gripping his sword, and his body inclined forward.

to each character by the tone of his voice if he was able ; at rehearsal, to organising entrances for convenience or by tradition ; and in performance to seeing that each player was ready in the wings at the right moment. An even more valuable service done by this official was to keep the peace between rival stars, male or female, and to soothe the temperaments of single ones.   In this respect in most countries his modern successor resembles him.

THE SUPREMACY OF THE ACTOR

Rehearsals were few.   Martynov (1816-60), a Peterburg actor of real ability, was by no means the only star who owed his first appearance to the fact that he happened to be hanging about the stage door when the lead was incapacitated and, knowing the lines by heart, was able to speak them in character without ever having been on the stage ; as a consequence of which he received an ovation and an engagement.   But such lack of rehearsal was nothing strange even to Mrs. Siddons, who reveals that when she first played Lady Macbeth, she retired to study the part *on the night preceding her first appearance in it,* and was so overcome by the horror of the play that she fled panic-stricken up to bed without daring to undress, " drying " embarrassingly the next day as a result.[16]   But though she mended her ways immediately, the strictures she brings upon herself refer only to the lack of study, not the lack of rehearsal.

Each actor was the be-all and the end-all of his or her own performance. The author wrote for this, and the audience paid its tribute for it.   " Service " in the Imperial theatres was not well paid, though in Peterburg at least there was a pension paid after twenty years.[17]   Nor were benefit nights too frequent.   But prominent persons in the audience lavished gifts on their favourites.   So it was essential that nothing should be allowed to tarnish the player's reputation as an artist, neither an inferior part, nor one that did not cause the audience to applaud, nor an insult from a rival, nor a harsh word from a patron.   A financial premium was thus set on temperaments as well as on conservative plays.

Aspirants to a stage career in Peterburg were trained in a special school. That is to say, instruction could be given in opera-singing, ballet-dancing, orchestra, scene-painting, stage machinery and even props-making and carpentry, but very little attention was paid to acting, which was a personal thing, and either you could act or you couldn't.   Admission to this school was permitted by a governor, who was a *chinovnik.*   Usually the pupils were children of actresses or servants, or very rarely of the bourgeoisie. The governor saw to it that applicants were of the right type.   Those who were of the right type, but had no stage gifts, were given small parts or reserved for the chorus, thereby further enhancing the isolation of the

stars. And as the same governor had the right of admitting players to the
living quarters, the majority of stars used to give him expensive presents
at New Year, Martynov being so notable an exception that a memoir
writer mentions the fact.[18] So the vicious circle was kept entire. The
star of Moscow, though an individualist, was kept humble by the pressure
of public opinion and self-important by that of his own ; the star of Peterburg was dominated directly by the presence of the court officials. But
in both cases the domination was ultimately an economic one, the structure
of things and people.

So if there was to be any reform, it was to be expected in Moscow
rather than in Peterburg ; and though there was a tentative movement in
the latter through Yakovlev (1770-1817) it came to the former with more
power and fruitfulness in the author Gogol (1809-52) and the actor
Shchepkin (1788-1863).

How Reform Came to the Maly

Semyonova married a Senator Prince, and after his death even appeared
on the stage again, though in her own household. The majority of players
were of much less ambitious social position and attainment. Shchepkin
was a manumitted Ukrainian serf. Yakovlev was a merchant's son and
had no education whatever.[19] "This actor", wrote F. Koni in 1851,
"revealed a new element to the audience.[20] Before his time genuine feeling
was not known to the actor. All was subordinated to a single exuberant
declamatoriness, warmed with artificial heating. Yakovlev was the first
to understand that for an art this would not do . . . and he contrived to
wed himself to the character he was representing, grafted its feelings on his
own, and was always moved so naturally on the stage that he spontaneously
moved his audience." He could do this even in Ozerov ! So it was not
unnatural that in his person Hamlet or Othello really stirred Russian audiences

But re-interpretation of classics by actors is never enough for a reform
of the theatre generally. Single improvements must be swamped in the
mass of "theatrical" plays. Before actors could develop the psychological
or realistic side of their art, they had to have new matter in the plays
themselves.

Authors were springing up with a new interest in living people and a
deep concern to write the truth about them. If these authors had come to
their maturity, there is every possibility that the Russian theatre in the
'forties would have been famous in history, despite the stranglehold of
the chinovniki. For the actual duration of a "new theatre" is unimportant.
Many of the world's finest theatrical periods lasted little more than a generation. But unhappily these authors all died young, and with little written
for the stage.

The realism of Lermontov (1814-41) can be best judged by comparing his *Masquerade* with Schiller's *Intrigue and Love*. Both contain as a climax a lover poisoning the woman he loves ; but whereas in the latter it is done as a part of the action, as a result of intrigue, melodramatically, as we would say, in the former it is a psychological necessity, the inevitable result of the life of the poisoner. Lermontov, like Pushkin, died as the result of a quite unnecessary duel. Griboyedov was assassinated in 1829 at the age of 34 on a diplomatic mission in Persia, but his *Woe from Wit*, a bitter satirical study in disillusion amid the vices and deceits of society, was not printed till 1833. When Gogol died, in 1852, he was only 43, and had big schemes he did not live to carry out. But between 1832 and 1837 he had written two full plays and some half-dozen one-act sketches which gave the Russian theatre the chance it was waiting for. Another full-length play, *The Order of Vladimir, Third Class*, concerned a *chinovnik* who went mad through disappointed ambition. Gogol realised it would never pass Department III, and had abandoned it even after the disappearance of the " patents " which held up dramatists for many decades.

What can the British stage offer to parallel this striving for realism, even though doomed ? Edward Fitzball, Bulwer Lytton, Sheridan Knowles ? Their works are available to the reader to-day only with difficulty. Even the celebrated drama, *The Lady of Lyons*, cannot be seriously compared with any Gogol comedy. For anything like a parallel we must wait for T. W. Robertson in the 'sixties and 'seventies. Even then *Caste* (1867) is scarcely up to *Revizor* for either intellectual point or deep realism in the behaviour of people.

In both these plays society is shocked by the intrusion of an unwelcome figure : a small town, to which comes a young impecunious adventurer mistaken for a Government Inspector ; a titled family, whose heir and hope marries a girl from the London slums.

Of the two, one might expect the former to be a literary, schematic thing, with stock types dependent on situation, as a derivative of the *capa y espada* plot, and the latter to be a subtle study in personal relations. In fact, the opposite is true. In *Caste* the development of the plot is a literary convention : the husband, a young officer, is ordered off to India and is reported killed only to reappear without warning in the last act alive and well. His mother is a stock figure of a Grande Dame, and her speech is theatrical. The young wife's father is a fun-figure of a nineteenth-century working man, always drunk. Her sister's " young man ", who is a plumber, even talks in the jargon of his trade like the comic relief character of all melodramas from " Monk " Lewis onwards. It is true there are no dramatic exits. These are replaced by end-of-act tableaux : Act I, Entrance of father-in-law to be, very drunk, as hero says " My wife ! " ; Act II, Young wife falls fainting in hero's arms as his mother buckles on his sword to go to the wars ; Act III, Hero's mother bends over cradle booming " My grandson ! " as father-in-law falls off chair drunk, and comic aristocrat examines him through eyeglass. This is a purely theatrical end. The social implications of real life which have been raised (but avoided) throughout are abandoned in a sentimental and particular reconciliation. Life ends with the curtain's fall.

In *Revizor*, on the other hand, the social implications are pointed throughout. The play ends with a tableau. The real inspector has arrived. This is not only a deliriously funny situation. You cannot witness it and not think of the lives of all these little provincials and their wives, their hopes and plans for advancement dashed, their consternation at having wasted so many bribes (money not being plentiful) on an impostor, their forebodings about what the real inspector will say of their past errors. In fact, life goes on after the play is ended, and so therefore does the author's social implications in creating that life. This is true satire.

But also each step in the developing action is due to these lives. Not only are they real people, but their positions in the play are due to their characters. There are no stage effects for the sake of stage effect. And when the Mayor's wife closes the First Act by leaning out of the window screaming instructions till the curtain falls, the dramatic exit, as stage punctuation, is doomed. This is true drama.

Certainly, Gogol wrote only with the means at his disposal. This was the theatre of the aside. But he did not use the aside to tell the audience something he couldn't otherwise explain ; he uses it to sharpen the moment by a pointed word. A present-day actor could cover each aside with his facial expression alone. This is true theatre.

What is more, though the tone is funny, the characters are so well-rounded that we are not surprised to hear of Shchepkin's effect as the Mayor. His little tubby figure, though comic in official uniform and top boots (like so many eminent actors down the ages Shchepkin was a little man), did not prevent him from reducing the audience to tears.[21] He was now 48 years of age, and destined to live another quarter-century, having an influence on the theatre of his time almost comparable with Garrick's. Davydov, for instance, who died as recently as 1925, is said to have been a faithful copy of Shchepkin in the Mayor, even in small details.

This influence was all the stronger with the passing of the old-style actors, Mochalov, middle-aged in 1848, Karatygin at Peterburg in his early fifties, in 1853. The latter objected to the new ideas of Shchepkin, and expressed his objections in Blimpish vaudevilles. Mochalov's antipathy was more a matter of temperament. He had always depended on inspiration. He started in " Classical " tragedy, but soon made his name in

Shakespeare, especially as Hamlet, "a living, actual, concrete Hamlet", said Byelinsky, "but not Shakespeare so much as Mochalov, because he deliberately added to Hamlet far more strength and energy than could exist in a man who finds himself at war with himself and is crushed under a burden too heavy for him to bear, and also because he gave him far less grief and melancholy than Shakespeare's Hamlet should have". Mochalov was terrific but erratic ; a true romantic.

Shchepkin united the effectiveness of Karatygin with the inspiration of Mochalov. But above all, he knew life. It was said of him that he was at home in the Court equally as in the cottage ; and that was his secret. He wanted to put the life he knew on the stage. Gogol gave him the means to do so. Between them, the Maly Theatre became the home of a realistic and serious stage art, a "temple" of art, a place where actors were aware of their responsibilities, a base for an organic development which though from time to time it has been slowed up, has not stopped in a hundred years.

Shchepkin had his feet firmly on earth, and was able to defeat the *chinovniki*. They might rule all the actors in the kingdom, but he had been a serf, and knew how the world had to live. He did not forget his humbler brethren. Here is a scene recorded by Herzen, the great Russian political philosopher, whom in self-exile in London Shchepkin visited to persuade him to come home.

"The Directors of the Moscow theatres* had stopped certain payments due to the actors as bonus. The time for hearing complaints arrived, and the actors chose Shchepkin to go to Peterburg as their advocate. The Director at that time was the well-known Gedeonov. Gedeonov opened by flatly refusing to distribute the sums that had accrued, on the grounds that the books were being checked and could not be recovered.

"Then I must trouble the Minister", stated the actor.

"An excellent idea ! I will report to him, and you'll get a refusal."

"In that case, I'll file a petition to the Tsar."

"What good will that do ? Inflicting squabbles like these on his Imperial Highness ! As your superior, I forbid you."

"Your Excellency", said Shchepkin, with a bow, "these sums belong —and in this even you would agree—to actors who are badly off. They have entrusted me with the advocacy of their rights. You have refused me and threatened the refusal of the Minister. I wish to petition the Tsar —you forbid me as my superior. There remains one last channel. I will give the whole question to *The Bell*."

* Besides the Moscow Bolshoy and the Moscow Maly there was a third Imperial theatre in Moscow, the Summer Theatre in the Petrov Park, counterpart to the third "patent" house in London, the Haymarket, licensed for the summer months only.

(Now this was a periodical edited and printed by Herzen in London, which, like *The Week* to-day, found its way to many ministerial desks ; one of the earliest examples of an " underground press ". Its effect on Gedeonov was immediate. Herzen goes on :)

" You're out of your mind ", yelled Gedeonov. " Do you know what you're saying ? I'll have you arrested."

(Then he changed his tone.)

" But listen, I'll excuse you. You spoke in the heat of the moment. To cause a commotion about trifles like these . . . aren't you ashamed ? Come to the office to-morrow, and I'll see what can be done."

Next day the money was assigned to the actors, and Shchepkin went home.

Such was the leading actor of the Maly Theatre. For if Moscow was under a remoter control than Peterburg, it was a paper control, and that, in matters of artistic performance, is even more deadly. Nevertheless it was from Moscow that the first free air blew.

But these are only two tiny dots on the landscape below us. Still keeping our date in 1850, let us now go to the little towns. We cannot yet venture very far. Never beyond the third rampart, the Volga. We are still in Russian Russia. Dipping down to the little towns. Dim little, dull little, stuffy little towns, but with such strange yearnings for Theatre.

CHAPTER II

SLAVE THEATRES

THE GREAT FAIR AT NIZHNY-NOVGOROD [1]

Where the River Oka joins the Volga there is a hill, studded with white walls and crowned with golden onions. Across the Oka a bridge of boats connects the town with what looks like an early nineteenth-century anticipation of a World's Fair. Indeed much of the accessible world has come here; that can be seen in the mass of shipping on both rivers: square, over-painted, and ornate vessels, with wooden huts on deck from the windows of which peep sly Oriental maidens over cargoes of cotton, Persian shawls, Georgian rugs, pelts, dried fruit; strong, clumsy boats out of Siberia with loads of iron and tea; craft of all rigs and sizes moored alongside Western ships that have brought knives from Sheffield and manufactures from the heart of Europe.

This is a real Fair. Villagers from hundreds of miles, merchants from the chief towns of Russia, meet here to make their annual fortune or buy their annual stock. A cosmopolitan crowd. It mills in the streets, which are narrow and muddy. It spends its money wisely, or recklessly, or cunningly, for six weeks of the moiling year. It splashes mud everywhere, from Russian boots or wheels, on gaily coloured embroidered robes. Uncouth drunken creatures stagger and fall in the mud, lashed by the knouts of Cossacks, stationed like policemen here and there.

This is the Fair for six weeks in the year. But Nizhny is not always like this. There is a quiet, tasteful shopping centre, a fashionable coffee-house, where a military band plays every afternoon; there are white cottages nestling in dark green clumps of trees; there is the Governor's Residence over the Bazaar. Nizhny has a social life. There are big estates in the neighbourhood. And for entertainment there is a Theatre. There has been since the time of Napoleon.

This theatre had a wide auditorium made out of a wooden building and seating a thousand. Moscow prices, increased during the Fair . . . partly to deter undesirables, and partly because its noble owner was not above profiting from the bigger demand for seats. Performances every night during the Fair at eight o'clock, and every seat taken. Thrice weekly during the winter.

There were boxes for the nobility and gentry; the richer merchants crowded into the *fauteuils*. But both classes were eager to be entertained. They did not mind much what the play was, or the opera, or the ballet (for there might be any of these). Every performer got a curtain-call at the close, one after the other all down the cast, because there was none that had not pleased somebody. And once, when the company happened to contain two Moscow actors from a non-Imperial theatre, though they called themselves " Court Actors "—Mr. Kondakov and Mr. Lisitsyn— their ovation was tremendous from the Moscow merchants in front.[2]

But this had little theatrical significance ; for both Moscow actors and Muscovites in front were, in a sense, evacuees. They had fled from their place of business at the approach of the *Grande Armée* in 1812, and were living as best they might in " reception " areas, though we should note that they have not crossed the Volga. They could not carry on their business beyond it.

The scenery is said to have been tolerable at this theatre. Lighting, as yet, was by tallow candle. The standard of acting was not high, because in their enthusiasm the audience was ready to overlook any faults, and the stage knew this. The merchants had no time for culture and the aristocrats were only passing theirs. But the actors, who were they ?

SLAVE VALUES

The actors were slaves belonging to Prince Shahovsky,[3] whose company arrived each July and stayed till the end of the Fair in early autumn. Actors, singers, orchestra, all belonged to him in the same way as their relations belonged who worked his land or served in his house. In number they equalled the company of an Imperial theatre—for the Prince owned many " souls "—and were sorted like horses for drama, opera, and ballet.

The girls were kept almost under lock and key like jewels. They were guarded, rigorously, by old women, " *Mamushki* ", selected by the Prince as " reliable ". They were delivered, like private letters, in a carriage to the rehearsals in the mornings, and again to the performances in the evening ; and again brought back in a carriage, like a confidential answer, after the show. And both at rehearsal and at performance the *Mamushki* watched them in the dressing-room till the stage manager called them to the stage ; and in the wings watched another *Mamushka*, called a " watch-woman ", who never let them out of her sight, and stopped them saying a single word to any male actor beyond what was written in the script.

This jealous supervision, out-Spanishing the duennas, was motivated by no high concern for their morals as mere morals. The Prince owned them and did not wish his property damaged, whether a horse with a turn for speed, a house with a fine façade, or a pretty serf-girl with a voice.

In 1851, at Tambov, a rich landowner called Mossolov was running a theatre with such a company, and one of his best actors, Sasha Kozakov, had a passionate and complete *affaire* with an actress who was his master's mistress also. The master had Kozakov flogged when he found out, and threatened to flog him to death if he persisted. But he did persist ; and the master, sending the actress off to serve as a dairy-maid, gave orders for Kozakov to be horse-whipped. But Kozakov escaped and ran away.

On the road he fell in with a strolling player who had made good and was on his way from Vladimir to Moscow, to play in *Hamlet* at the Maly. Kozakov joined his company, became a fine and famous comic actor, and Rybakov bought him his freedom. Rybakov refused a permanent engagement at the Imperial Theatre with the proud artist's equivalent of Anselm's *Nolo episcopari :* ' I don't want to be a *Chinovnik* '—and off he set again for the provincial theatre.

The fate of the slave-players was not often such, however. When the girls were about 25, they were married. Perhaps one should say, mated. The Prince would send for Masha, and ask if she liked Stepan ; then he would send for Stepan, and ask if he had any objections to Masha. And so they were married, by the usual custom of kennels or stables. Whether the mating took place if they couldn't bear each other might depend on how the Prince was feeling that day, though he would know, of course, that a marriage of incompatibles would not improve the acting of either partner.

This particular prince, Shahovsky, seems to have been a man of some honour and feeling, though. He had his preferences among his players, but never what the *Mamushki* called his " favourites " among the girls. On the whole he seems to have tried to be a father to his company. He knew them all by name. Indeed he would change their names, for he disliked vulgar ones ; and if a new-comer had a vulgar name, she was entered in the list and called by a more elegant one, Akulina or Fevronia.

These slaves were taught to read, because that was useful for an actor ; but not to write, because that might lead to trouble. Every morning, too, the Prince himself gave the girls lessons in elocution and deportment, so that they could impersonate great ladies on the stage. And before he presented the world with his company's rendering of *Woe from Wit*, he even sent the principals, male and female, to Moscow to pick up what they could by studying the Imperial players.

The young slaves thus developed as artists with a false bubble round their souls. They could cleverly ape the manners of a world they could never know. But inside they remained the same, playthings of the world they aped. How could their acting be profound ? But as it was just to divert, it did not matter.

Nevertheless, slaves though they were, they won respect and rewards for their cleverness. There were benefit nights for the leads ; and members of the audience, moved or intrigued by any special performer, would send up gifts. These gifts were current coin, barterable for other things. And a benefit night was more valuable then that it became later in the century, when gas-light, or author's fees or heavy taxation, or all three, reduced the actor's share by about a half.

The benefit night was carefully cosseted and prepared beforehand. The beneficiary would hire a cab and drive from door to door with as much pomp as he or she could assume, selling tickets for as much more than the usual price as the customer was willing to pay. Few could resist a professional charmer of either sex standing on their doorstep, slave or free ; and the big sums sometimes realised were due as much to the actor's personality off the stage as to his abilities on it. This " gold-ticket " practice, of course, was not limited to Nizhny-Novgorod, nor to Russia. It held good in our own British theatres for centuries, though Macready tried in 1820 to stop it by his refusal of more than the ordinary price for any ticket.[5]

A humiliating business ! One of the actresses has left us an account of it :

> " They never ask you to sit down ; but out into the hall pours the whole multitudinous family, standing and staring at you from head to foot as if you were some wild animal. The head of the house takes the playbill, and starts making sundry comments on the choice of play, casting, and so on. In the end you're lucky if he says kindly, ' All right ! Anything to oblige. Give me a box ! ' . . . Glory to God that that custom went out of use of its own accord in the early sixties ! "[6]

Even Shchepkin in Moscow had to follow it. Being a famous man, he got into the living-rooms, but even then he records one householder, when he heard the purpose of the visit, ringing for the servant to take Shchepkin through and see that he got a cup of coffee.

When a slave was once trained and had proved his ability, he became a valuable property. For a man, wife, and six-year-old daughter who could dance the Cachucha and the Tampech, the price was a whole village and 250 souls.[7] But as they still belonged, body and soul, to their owners, even the most gifted artists were liable without any appeal to corporal punishment. Shepelev's theatre at Vyksa (in the Vladimir Gubernya) was unique in being the only provincial opera apart from those in cities like Odessa and Riga. When Afanasyev was in charge of it, he relates with pride,[8] he released his subordinates from this liability, merely putting them into detention, or fining them, when they misbehaved. He begs the reader of 1890 not to be surprised, because municipal theatre managements had had actors beaten or musicians transferred to looking after the stoves, as late as the eighteen-forties. At which time Berlioz was a theatre musician in Paris, and Verdi was conducting his own operas in Milan.

THE COMING OF THE PROFESSIONALS

So as yet actors were of small importance. The first thing in a town was to have a theatre building.

In Penza, which lies between the Volga and the Don, there were three theatres before there were plays to act or a company to act them. " Just as ", remarks one ironic writer, " from the time of Peter the Great we had universities, academies, high schools, when as yet there were neither teachers nor pupils." Ultimately these three theatres were occupied by a company that played only opera and Italian music, by a second company of serfs belonging to a *chinovnik* (" his whole household ", observes the same writer, " from the janitor to the groom, and the housemaid to the laundry-woman ". These played both comedies and tragedies) ; and a third curious company which was only good for comedies " with or without songs ". This last was headed by a free actor, not a serf. He had been picked up somewhere by the management, and was of great value as he knew his job as well as a slave could. The management was a middle-aged woman, daughter of an aged Prince who had come to end his days in that neighbourhood, but being unable to live at home she married an old bear of another nobleman, who bored her so much that she bought a tumbledown wooden house in Penza and turned it into a theatre.[9]

Kaluga. A pretty little town in a pine wood on the high left bank of the Oka, some hundred miles out of Moscow to the south-west. Many well-known families of rank lived nearby, and at the end of the eighteenth-century it was decided to build a theatre, with a club attached. Clubs were beginning to become fashionable. A local *littérateur*, Baturin, was placed in charge of both, and of a publishing venture as well. The appointment was made by the deputy Governor . . . with the Governor-General's consent, of course, since Kaluga was the chief town of both Tula and Kaluga districts. The club was to be used for routs, masked balls, assemblies. It was justified, Baturin says, on the ground that it would increase trade and bring money into the town ; and the Governor-General had no objections to this.[10]

But Baturin took his task seriously. He himself translated Riccoboni into Russian. Luigi Riccoboni was an Italian theatre manager who travelled in the first half of the eighteenth century through Italy, Spain, France, Holland, Flanders, Germany, and England. He published his impressions of the theatres in these countries, together with an " Essay on the Art of Acting", and a not so valuable comparison between " Ancient and Modern Drama ".* Baturin placed a copy of his translation in the rehearsal room, so that the company could improve their performances by applying Riccoboni's precepts.

" At first ", recalls Baturin, " my actors' pride was offended : it seemed

---

* These were all translated into English and published in London in 1741. He was much impressed by the *naturalness* of English acting in comparison with Italian and French ; and this, fourteen years before Garrick's first appearance !

odd to them that a person not himself an actor could show them how to
work on their parts and correct their acting. However, they soon came
to see how useful the directions I gave them were ; they began to feel the
difference in acting by rule of thumb (рутиною) and a knowledge of true
theatre art. Only one actress, who had come from a Moscow theatre
and thought thereby she was better than the rest, despised, or rather failed
to understand what was written in the handbook. . . . And seeing that she
was possessed of neither the goodwill nor the intelligence to understand
my correction of her acting, I did not compel her ; with the result that she
remained for ever the same bad actress she had always been."

On this paragraph two interesting reflections may be made. First,
the word рутина has already appeared as a term of criticism in Russian
theatre circles, and an attempt is being made to get rid of the fault in the
interests of fresh, supple acting. Secondly, already there are signs of the
coming change, by which free actors filter into the slave companies, and
middle-class managers (with almost a tendency toward production) among
the noble owners. This is the softening-up, without which no attack on
the established system could be made by any lone artist.

Differences of class were observed rigidly to begin with. Kostroma,
on a landscape-painter-loved reach of the Volga, north-east of Moscow,
was a town picturesquely planned during the eighteenth century in the
form of a fan. In 1812, to serve the many Moscow evacuees, there had
come to Kostroma a troupe from the Moscow Imperial Theatre, shedding
theatrical and cultural light on the neighbourhood. The lesson had been
not forgotten. By the 'forties the Kostroma Theatre had become famous
in the provinces and even in the metropolitan Press. From this elegant
little town comes evidence in a playbill. Opposite the characters are set
the serfs' names, Andrey Volkov, Malanya Naïdenaya ; but opposite a
character played by a free man is set the imposing Г. Василев, *Mr.* Vasilyev.
This change meant that instead of those curious, unstable performances
of slaves trained by amateurs, there began to appear professional players
paid and managed by professionals, an arrangement beginning to resemble
the nineteenth-century provincial theatres in other countries, but with a
more local interest and character here, perhaps. It meant, further, that
theatres would cease to be such direct servants of the nobility, who might
be expected to attend less and less frequently as they lost control of the
actors ; the merchants and manufacturers would take their places, and the
populace at large would perhaps get a chance to slip into the cheaper seats
no longer taken by the middle classes. Finally, it meant a higher standard
of performance by the individual actor, as knowing more about the society
he was impersonating.

Not that the standard of the nobles' slaves was always low. On the

contrary, in two places at least it would seem to have been remarkably
high. The two places were Kazan, the capital of the Tartars—if so conquered a remnant of the world's conquerors can be said to have had a
capital—and Oryol.

Kazan, downstream from Nizhny-Novgorod, another bastion of our
outer rampart, was in those days growing to a city the size of Cambridge
to-day. It stood on a hill in the midst of a great plain, crowned like so
many provincial cities, by its Kremlin. The Tartars were Moslem, and
the countryside was therefore dotted with mosques, and the women wore
Oriental shawls over their faces, when they remembered to ; but they were
not very strict followers of the Prophet, nor were the men, though dignified,
very civilised.

Kazan was famous for two things : its embroidered leather work,
valued all over Europe ; and its University, at which among its weed-grown
gardens Tolstoy was at this moment being educated, and later Lenin was
to follow him. Zinin the chemist and Lobachevsky, the creator of non-
Euclidean geometry, were professors at Kazan University ; and both
chemistry and mathematics kept Kazan high among the Universities of
the world.[11] But it goes without saying that it was not for the Tartars
that there was a theatre here. It was for the students, the University folk,
the semi-intelligent people that gather round a University for various
reasons. They—and it—were Russian.

An audience slightly above the average in intelligence will call actors
from a distance. So it was not surprising that Moscow actors like
Plavilshchikov visited Kazan, and stayed there. They did not play in very
interesting plays. In a society where the eyes and ears of all follow the
monarch's will, people who live in the country are either disappointed
people or frustrated people, or without ambition. Local pride is of such
things as a street paved with the soft novelty of wood blocks. So they are
not likely to have so absorbed an interest in life that they want to hear a
great dramatist's comment upon it, nor will they admire the mere skill of
impersonation. Voltaire's *Mahomet*, *The Clemency of Titus*,* Ozerov,
will be an entertainment grand enough for them.

But in University circles there is youth, eager for knowledge of the
world, quick to appraise skill, unsatisfied by being passive. Students
provide interesting amateur theatre if they have the stimulus of a good enough
professional one. And that is the chief gift of Kazan to theatrical history.
The professionals there stimulated the amateurs to serious work.

---

* A drama by the Italian poet Metastasio (1698-1782), from which Mozart took
the libretto for his last opera. At Kazan the drama was played without Mozart's
music.

An Early Stanislavsky

In Oryol, on the other hand, which had no university, we find perhaps the best of the slave theatres, belonging to Count Kamensky, who was director as well as owner. A friend of the Count's, who visited his theatre in 1817 records [12] that the scenery was " charming " (that, of course, was all the background was designed to be as yet), the music " agreeable " (for even in those days a play with no music was poor entertainment), the costumes " tidy " (this is high praise for the time), and the general effect " seemly ". From the very restraint of his choice of adjectives we feel we can trust this observer. But we also get a quite clear impression of the show. There is a guiding hand behind this, somebody of taste, somebody who almost has the idea of uniting all the elements of theatre into one. A male Madame Vestris. A timid feeler, that will one day grow into a Meininger, a Stanislavsky. What of the company ?

The company was giving two plays the night our observer went, a drama and a short piece. In the latter the Count's own household serfs were playing. " They were not very diverting " is the comment. The former was given by actors recently acquired. The count was said to have given the sum of 500 peasants for them, or in the elegant financial diction of the day, " five hundred agricultural souls ". They were better than the others, the account goes on, " but still not actors. The Abbot and the Dumb Man were better than the rest. The women were all bad."

Next day at a rehearsal for a forthcoming production, he was impressed by the count's abilities. " I fancy the Imperial management in Moscow could not have staged it better. Everything was arranged here with a lavish hand. But as for the play itself, I've never seen anything like it. A mediocre composition, very indifferently realised."

So the Count was in advance of his own company. He tried to get the company to memorise their parts so well that they could dispense with a prompter. He came down very heavily on anyone who " dried ". He attended to all the business himself, even " front-of-house " work, even down to the dispatch of complimentary tickets, of which he kept a note in a book in his own hand.

His audience was a keen one, but not from the highest circles. The highest circles came only to mock at his show. Indeed once there arrived a corps commander, a divisional commander, several generals, and society ladies, including a countess. The ladies began laughing. Kamensky noticing that their laughter was not caused by any comic shafts in the dialogue, ordered all the oil lamps but one to be put out. The theatre filled with oily smoke. Kamensky stopped the show, and never sent them complimentary tickets again, not even though the corps commander was a baron. Evidently a man of feeling for the theatre. He would have been of great benefit to the Russian theatre at the other end of his century.

SIBERIA

Such were characteristic of the slave theatres. But they exist only inside the third rampart. Russian society itself does not venture further. There is nothing but wildness and conquest beyond. Let us, however, who can look back from the security of history, make the journey east, to the land of chilled hearts and frozen bodies. Let us make it in the company of Eve Felinska, sadly speeding into exile, separated from her children, in 1839. She was a Pole, of a rich and literary family, who had founded schools for her serfs, and perhaps sheltered a patriot or two, and who will be saying which was the greater crime in the eyes of the Tsar ? [13]

With two other unhappy ladies, watched but not much assisted by a sergeant, she crossed the Volga at Kazan, having come from Kiev and Tula by sleigh in the bitter weather before spring. Her accurate eye noted everything, in spite of her wretchedness : how the Tartar men in their loose robes resembled the gaberdined Jews of Poland, how there were six races in the Tartar area, each differing in language, dress, faith and customs. Then on across the frozen steppe, till they came to Perm, in the foothills of the Urals, where she was struck by the neatness and prosperity of the upland cottages. Miners' cottages, some owned by nobles, some by the Crown. Here the people loved pictures, crude daubs of the saints, but with landscapes behind made in mosaic of topaz and amethyst, emerald, aquamarine and sard . . . her eye is caught by the beauty of these jewelled landscapes. There was art here . . . but no theatre. The human soul, even in prosperity, finds beauty in the earth, but not in itself. We have only to read the stories of Pavel Bazhov to know that in those days official fists throttled even the art of stone, and this in itself was a reason for mankind turning away from mankind in painful contemplation.*

No theatre at Yekaterinburg (now Sverdlovsk), but masses of malachite turned in ornaments and furniture. No theatre at Tyumen, but bells being cast. No theatre even at Tobolsk, capital of Western Siberia, where our exile met friends also in exile and learned that she was to be sent 1,700 versts further away, to Berezov. But meanwhile she had to wait, and spring broke with the birds singing, and Tobolsk became tolerable to them all, till she left by river.

They steamed north down the Irtysh. Agriculture ceased ; and

---

* Pavel Petrovich Bazhov, now an old man with a white beard, has devoted all his life to writing one immense book of short stories about his native Urals. It is called *The Malachite Casket*. Preserving and establishing as a literary medium the Urals dialect, it also preserves and makes literature of folk-lore and historical tales.

immense virgin forests of conifers loomed on both banks, grandeur, but pitilessness, and above all, loneliness. Thousands and thousands of miles of solitude, with native Ostiaks still worshipping pagan gods. Once, when this Polish lady had settled into her remote home, she got lost in the forest, and found a group of these performing a ceremony to a larch tree. This impressed her in several ways ; for not only did she fear death for having intruded, but also the larch was the emblem of Siberia and of exile. Easy it was, too, to get lost in the forest, and no rescue. Going for a walk was dangerous for that reason. Neither was it pleasant. In summer, stifling heat and mosquitoes ; in winter, bitter cold and wind ; and mud between the seasons . . . an exile had to stay indoors. That was part of her torture. The exile had nothing to do but try to plant cabbages. And even that was viewed with suspicion by the native people.

In those thousands of lonely miles there were thousands of lonely exiles. Their kind of enforced leisure, their kind of hopeless spiritual state, does not inspire so lively an interest in life as to want a theatre ; and no professional or slave theatre would venture so far. But might they not, to escape the misery of their days, impersonate happier, gayer, more cultured, more social lives themselves ? If they did, there is no record, at least in the early years of the century. And nothing, evidently, came of it. No genius wrote their dreams for them. No little group in any settlement (for we cannot call them towns) developed skill that made them famous.

As we traverse these monotonous miles, we find nothing like a theatrical performance till we come to Irkutsk, a garrison town in Eastern Siberia, founded in the seventeenth century to keep in subjection the newly conquered tribes, and display the power of the Tsar to the Chinese and Mongolian merchants whose caravan routs to the west lay through it. They, and the inhabitants, were continually moving, the latter as nomads in their *kibitkas*, their tent-carts. Only the garrison is static. Static, and since nobody is interested in the local country or people, dreary.

At the end of the eighteenth century in Irkutsk, the wife of His Excellency Vasily Alexeyevich Troyepolsky, President of the Second Department of the Upper External Tribunal, is fond of plays. She organises, produces, and plays the lead in an amateur performance of a Russian tragedy. As usual, she builds a theatre for the purpose. The fashion catches . . . for the garrison only, of course.

In 1803 a permanent theatre is founded, for the whole public in the growing city, by a merchant's son. He used an empty one-storied house, formerly a government office. The audience sat on benches, rising in tiers ; and the musicians played in the wings. The actors were all Russian settlers, who had been theatre-goers in Russia. The first productions were operas, Russian works (by Russian composers, that is ; but there was nothing that could be called a Russian opera yet). Performances were given on Saints' Days, when all were free.

Two years later a better theatre was built, with boxes and a gallery and an orchestra pit. A garrison officer owned this. Junior officers joined the company ; and military bandsmen made the orchestra. Among the plays given were some by Kotzebue. The great days of the Irkutsk Theatre began.

They were punctuated with laughable mishaps. Ambitious scenery, then the rage, led to disaster. For example, an angel was lowered on canvas clouds stuffed with shavings and hung on a cord. On the first night the cloud burst, the shavings showered on the stage floor, and the angel, though apparently a disembodied being, hit the ground with a loud bump and broke a wing. After his aria he was supposed to fly off in the clouds, but he forgot that his transport had ceased to exist. " Farewell ", he sang, and " Farewell ! " and looked upward. But instead of a cloud, lo ! there fell from Heaven a pair of military gauntlets. The disconcerted angel fled to terrestrial shelter on his feet.

Besides the classics, they did home-made vaudevilles with music by the regimental band-master. Enthusiasm increased. Another theatre was opened by a non-commissioned officer and a local citizen. This was intended for civilians visiting the Bazaar. Its company was of clerks and Cossacks.* The fare was mostly popular operas. This theatre also opened only on holidays.

A bigger theatre was started in 1809, and it looked as if Irkutsk was going to become a fine theatrical centre, when a new commanding officer arrived, who could not reconcile theatrical activities with the Tsar's military service, and all theatres were closed. And that was the end of the semi-permanent theatre in Eastern Siberia.[14]

Our parallel here is the English theatre in Calcutta in the eighteenth century, whose manager sent to London for a set of eight scenes by the best designers of the day (these would be used for all productions, as required by the character of the act) ; or with Lady Campbell's private theatre in Madras, where this Governor's wife entertained her guests with the latest trifles from London.[15] Such houses had no connection with India, beyond the fact that they stood in that country. The audience were pure British, except for an occasional Collaborationist merchant who had made enough money to qualify as a friend of the occupying race.

Now, all these provincial towns and little communities have one thing in common : a bored audience that wants to be amused. Any advance

* Not all Cossacks were fire-eaters. Our Polish lady noted of those in Berezov : " I saw young men of twenty years cry like babies when they happened not to get their tea at the usual hour ".

toward truth must come slowly. The actors cannot do it as long as they are slaves. We must look to the free men, and to such free men as can themselves organise a company of free men. This cannot be a stationary thing ; for there will not be enough audience in any one locality, nor actors either. There will not be any great advance till there are many actors " on the road ". And this, as things are, implies a period of relaxed regulations, freer movement, unrestricted competition . . . and broken fortunes, and poverty.

By need compelled to proſtitute his art
The varied actor flies from part to part
  —CHARLES CHURCHILL, The Apology

Part Two

OLD WORLD : LATER NINETEENTH CENTURY

CHAPTER III

THE COMING OF THE PROFESSIONAL MANAGER

EARLY MANAGERS

Many of the first managers to make a living in the theatre were men like Savin, a former Naval officer who left the Service as the result of a scandal ; or like Valyano, an ex-hussar officer who ran an opera-theatre at Rostov-on-Don, and being a linguist translated foreign librettos into Russian.[1] There was just a lingering of gentility still in running a theatre, but it had grown shabby and was soon to become completely commercial. Such men simply hired a local theatre, engaged free actors because they had no money to buy slaves, paid them as little as possible, put on any plays they heard about, and pocketed the receipts. Their only idea of progress was a bigger company at a cheaper rate. And for many, many years such formed the bulk of provincial managers.

This was a vicious circle with which we in our own countries are still familiar. Managers who are in the " business " (and the Russian equivalent of that word was used in stage circles with the same degrading callousness as in ours to-day) for the sake of profit only, are bound to be conservative. They are afraid to put on anything that they do not feel sure will attract. So they continue to supply either what has already appealed to audiences in their own theatres or others like them, or else imitations of past successes. Such men batten on a backward and unhappy society, because they provide not a comment on life, but a fantasy to escape from it ; and it is one of the allures of fantasy that each time it seems to be new, though is really a disguised repetition of an old desire.

Sometimes, it must be admitted, there were conditions in which no theatre could appeal at all. As in Zhitomir, where the population consisted of Poles who boycotted a Russian theatre, poverty-line Jews, low-grade Russian civil servants, and troops. Biyazi made his living here by little less than a miracle.

As soon, however, as there is a move among the actors, a dissatisfaction

with old ways, a more serious attitude to the art of acting, such employment becomes disagreeable. But admission to the Imperial service is
difficult. Even the good actor remains in the provinces. Not quite as in
Britain, with the public-schoolboy Macready in his father's theatre at New-
castle, Daniel Terry at Liverpool, Kean at Exeter, but all with an eye on
ultimate success in London. Some stars in Russia would reach the Maly,
or even the Alexandrinsky stages. But few. The lot of most was to spend
their lives far from the metropolitans, and they knew it.

Good actors, therefore, having made certain savings from their meagre
earnings, themselves become managers. The standard under them improves.
Not much, but a little. There are Medvedyev at Kazan, Dyukov at Harkov,
Miloslavsky at Odessa, all University towns. Here there is more enlightenment, more eagerness, more hope, more freedom of thought.
Shakespeare, Schiller, Gogol, Griboyedov, and later Ostrovsky are performed here. Miloslavsky, the last of the noble patrons, spared no expense
in his productions of *King Lear*, *Hamlet*, *The Merchant of Venice*. He was
himself a good actor, and had ideas about the staging of plays founded on
professional knowledge.

The better the manager now, the better actors he will want in his company. Credit for being among the first to organise a well-balanced
company goes to Rasskazov. Medvedyev (1837-1906) realised the
importance of the actor as a human being, an individual. " For young
actors ", one of his favourite sayings ran, " there can be no line of business ".
Meaning by that, that specialisation could come only late in life as the
result of narrowing down and choosing from wide general experience.
Here we find something important in the provincial theatre. Such a man
will choose his company wisely. Indeed he chose too well : Savina,
Davydov, Varlamov, Strelsky, Maximov, all in their youth came out of
Medvedyev's company. Kazan was delighted with their work for years,
and in time all these young people became metropolitan stars, rich and
famous. But Medvedyev died in poverty, having given the theatre far
more than he had taken from it.[2]

There is a charming story told by the great actress Savina about the
way she joined Medvedyev's company when she was a very, very young
beginner. She was learning, and playing small parts in a company at the
Nizhny-Novgorod Fair, when one evening all the talk in the dressing-rooms
was that Medvedyev was in front, intending, if he approved of the leading
lady's work, to invite her to his theatre. The show did not start till 9
o'clock at night, and as it consisted of Schiller's *The Robbers*, and Savina
did not come on till the vaudeville which followed that, about 2 o'clock
in the morning, she was practically asleep, being only 16 years old, when
the time came for her entrance. The A.S.M. pushed her on stage, and

rubbing her eyes, she delivered her lines with unusually sincere conviction. They referred to the fact she was overcome with sleep and wanted to go to bed. Medvedyev was so taken with her personality that it was she whom he invited to join his company, and not the leading lady ; and so one of the plums of the provincial theatre world fell into her lap when she was little more than a child.[3]

The truth is that there can be no finer training than a provincial repertory for a young beginner, as long as there are no permanent art-theatres (in the best and original sense of that term) with their own schools in the metropolis. And even then, perhaps, a provincial repertory properly run has advantages over such. The young actor grows more interested in the community he or she is serving, and can study the audience better ; and he can also take a share, under enlightened management, in policy and choice of plays.

This happened, though exceptionally, at Voronezh in 1886.[4] The theatre belonged to Dyukov, who was getting old. His right-handman was Borodaï, a man without any education but of strong personality, who in the course of his career had risen to prominent positions in every theatre he worked in, Harkov, Saratov, Kazan. The summer season was opening, but it kept pouring with rain, and nobody came out in the evening. For a fortnight they played " serious " plays to empty houses. The company was called together, and a discussion started, whether they should wait for the weather to change, or exchange the " serious " bill for something lighter. The latter vote won. Borodaï had spoken.

From this it appears that the character of the company is altering. It has journeyed far from the nobles' household slaves, and is in process of becoming a *tovarishchestvo*, a word much used in memoirs of the time, meaning a Commonwealth, a band of good comrades on a common endeavour.

MANAGER AND PRODUCER

Once it becomes the custom for a manager to have been an actor, it soon becomes the custom for him to devote himself to improving the standard of the performance. The company may still " belong " to him, in the sense that he engages and can dismiss the members of it, but at the same time, it is a thing that exists independently of him. A " theatre " in the Russian sense of the word is thus created.

Borodaï was such a man. Having been a Box Office attendant in his time, he was a good business man, and left his company, when he finally got one, to act while he did the front-of-house managing. Nor did he ever let his actors down financially, not even over the Christmas bonus. He had been through it himself, and he knew.[5]

But what was more important, the professional actor turned manager was free to stand outside the acting and direct this independent entity, his company. To " produce ", in fact. And this is what happened frequently. Solovtsov at Kiev (1857-1902) was first and foremost a good producer. He engaged his company for several years at a time, setting up a strong ensemble, and discovering the principle that leads were played best if they were not played by the same artists in show after show. As a result, he could extend the range of his plays : Shakespeare, Victor Hugo, Sophocles, and even, at the end of his life, Chehov. Chehov had a great admiration for Solovtsov and was distressed to hear of his death.[6]

In those days Kiev was not only a University town ; nor only an ancient centre of reverence. It was neither St. Andrews nor York. In those days two hundred and fifty sugar refineries were supplying from Kiev the whole of the Russian empire with sugar, supported by a heavy tax on all foreign sugar, which kept the price too high for the majority of peasants to pay. Pedlars became manufacturers, and manufacturers millionaires. They built themselves stone palaces. They affected the administration of Kiev, and its public buildings were built of stone too. There was an ostentatious Imperial palace constructed on the outskirts, to which the Tsár never came. But these local rogues and worthies were not interested in thought, which might have questioned the moral value of their fortunes. It was seldom the rich who appreciated, or even noticed, Solovtsov's ideas.

The coming of the producer, which began in the 'sixties or even earlier, according to Davydov,[7] was limited at first to the University towns, it would seem. In purely commercial theatres, like that of Smirnov in Yaroslavl, the word *régisseur* was still applied to a personage whose real function was that of *scenarius*, a kind of assistant stage manager. In general, stage managers themselves tended to be barely literate. The standard of rehearsing was so low that education was hardly needed. Plays, Davydov says, seemed to get put on by themselves, with two rehearsals (or runs-through) as the rule, and three as the maximum.

Costumes were crude. A lady of Louis XIV's Court would be apparelled in a nineteenth-century dress with a white wig and one or two patches on her cheeks. Men's costumes for the same period would be a white powdered wig, a black frock-coat with a sort of cape sewn on, gaiters with wide bell-tops, and footman's boots. That was a marquis !

On the other hand, scenery was comparatively simple. The provincial audiences did not expect any highly elaborate stage effects with transformation scenes and all. They came " to the theatre for theatre " as Davydov says. And the actors not having, as British actors had, to compete with burning cities and shipwrecks, did not need to stylise themselves into types or singing machines.

That is not to say, though, that there were no bad actors. In the course of fifty years there were thousands. For if it takes less talent to play a type, it also takes less intelligence. And there were many, very many, who spoke a stage diction of their own invention. Ivanov-Kozelsky, for example, was very indignant when it was suggested to him at Harkov, where he reigned in the 'seventies, that he might stop " singing " his lines and give Russian speech a Russian inflection according to its meaning. " Do you wish me to speak on the stage ", demanded Ivanov-Kozelsky, " like a peasant from Pskov ? " And he explained that he wasn't speaking Russian anyway, he was speaking poetry. At the time he was in his thirties.

Such an attitude is hard to uproot, and indeed it is noticeable even among naturalistic actors in our own generation, who take on a " holy " tone when speaking metrically.

Neither was Harkov at this time only a University town. Next to Nizhny-Novgorod, says George Hume,[8] a British business man who lived and worked there during its enormous expansion from a town of seventy-five thousand to one of over two hundred thousand, it was the largest commercial centre in Russia. It had four great Fairs in the year, each lasting a month. The greatest of these was the Wool Fair in June, to which came merchants from all over Europe, and for which the fields in front of Hume's house were stacked with bales in their thousands, like houses in streets and blocks. Ready money for an evening's entertainment was therefore more easily spent than in Nizhny, and also more evenly through the year. But the standard, that of the uneducated merchant and of the language-less foreign visitor, on the one hand, and that of the resident intelligentsia on the other, would vary according to the month. I don't doubt, from my own experience in Cambridge, that the two audiences would mix only to the call of a big name in the theatre world, about which both classes could be snobbish.

But in Russia prosperity could not be counted on. In 1874 a terrible epidemic of cholera broke out here. Death came so frequently that the ringing of church bells was prohibited. The burials were carried out by night. In a plague-stricken town, with hundreds of deaths a day, even Davydov (who was the man who had had the temerity to make the suggestion above to Ivanov-Kozelsky) could not draw. Deep gloom settled on the city.[9]

THE PULL OF THE ACTOR

In discussing the public appeal of the actor we must not forget that most of the older ones had been serfs or the sons of serfs. Even the realistic dramas of Ostrovsky about the middle class, when they finally began to reach the provinces, described a society the provincial actors did not know from the inside. The influence of Shchepkin and Sadovsky toward realism was an encouragement to them ; but the obstacles against a sincere portrayal of depth and roundness in a character were many. Indeed, few of them were aware of any need for such characterisation. As long as they could establish the convention that they were the person the author had created, and carry the imagination of an uncritical audience with them, that was enough. If the audience had been wanting pure drama, it might have been more obvious to them that depth would improve their performance. But the audience's tastes were wide : drama, comedy, operetta, vaudeville, the audience wanted all, and the same actors had to supply them. In this respect the Russian audience was like the British audience of the time ; and the companies had to be as versatile as those at Brighton and Worthing.

Yet a single inspired artist could make people flock to the theatre. Such a man was N. K. Miloslavsky. " Fate sent him to the rescue of the poor slave-actor," said Medvedyev.[10] " On his countenance was visible a lively protest at a society which behaved so contemptuously toward a stage worker." Hence Miloslavsky's own power in satire. Hence too his value, historically, for the stage. Harkov was his pitch : and in Harkov there is, or was till the Germans got there, an actor's corner in the graveyard. Provincial society is exclusive about its burial places. This was a sign that the actor was to be recognised as a decent person.

But besides this social action of Miloslavsky, there was his artistic action. Before he came to Harkov the company had been half-hearted, running on technique, apathetic. He galvanised them into life ; and the results were instantaneous. The public woke up. Subscriptions mounted from 600 to 2,000.

A similar person, Orlenov, went to Yekaterinoslav on the Dnieper, where the South Russian mining industry was just beginning. He was late among old-fashioned actors and early among new. By the intensity of his feeling, he revivified the old-fashioned monologue ; he seemed to be really thinking, they said. So violent was his realism in the death scene in *The Brothers Karamazov* (Dostoyevsky's novels had reached the provinces) that some of the audience screamed. Which was not only a step toward outer realism, but also good for business.

Some of these actors attained a very high standard. Of Roshchin-Insarov, for instance, Velisariy, who was herself an actress and no easy critic, said that he studied his part in *Woe from Wit* so intelligently that he was superior as Chatsky to any Imperial actor she had seen.

But second-hand or third-hand talk about past performances is unfruitful. And there is an aspect of the provincial theatre during this period which is more important. That is the treatment of the national culture of conquered countries.

It will be noticed that the best theatres were not only in University towns, they were also in Ukrainian towns. But they were Russian theatres. Ukrainian is a dialect of Russian so different as almost to be another language. It is like Lallans in relation to southern or to Oxford English.

Now although the backward nations, or the exotic nations, outside the rampart of the Volga were utterly trampled upon by their Russian Imperial conquerors in every way, including their cultures, it was not necessary for the fat Imperial generals to cross the Volga in order to oppress a conquered race. They did it in Georgia, Armenia, and over the Tartars. They also did it in the Ukraine. The seventeenth and eighteenth and most of all the nineteenth centuries brought cultural after administrative after military mortmain on this much conquered but abundant land. And of all the subject people the Ukrainians were in many ways the sturdiest at keeping their traditions and language alive despite the Tsars.

To get this matter into its right perspective, we must consider another European country under much the same treatment ; and my next sub-chapter will be addressed primarily to my Scottish compatriots.

WHY NO SCOTTISH THEATRE ?

At the Renaissance we had all the promise of a full-fruiting Scottish theatre. There were the mystery plays as popular stock ; there were educated poets like Dunbar, Lyndsay, James Wedderburn of Dundee, ready and able to graft thereupon the comment of great spirits. Life in Scotland was very full in those days, and human curiosity was keen. Wedderburn fled the country, it is true, to escape the ecclesiastical consequences of his pen ; but so did Aeschylus. That in itself would not explain the death of the young tree.

And the people were theatre-ready. One of their favourite amusements was " making a Robin Hood " as for example on the Greenside in Edinburgh.[11]

Long, long before the Union, before even Mary Stewart landed at Leith in 1561, the pussy-foot magistrates of Edinburgh passed laws forbidding this embryo theatre. Nor can it be made part of a religious wrangle. For Lyndsay's *Three Estates*, the most notable example of a purely Scottish court play, presented before the Crown in 1539, was anti-Catholic, or at least anti-Priest. Religion herself was impersonated in a civic Masque of Welcome when James the Sixth rode to open Parliament in 1579. And Mary had been greeted by actors representing Korah, Dathan and Abiram during the first year of her reign.

Perhaps the Burghers as a class were motivated like their equivalents in the London of Queen Elizabeth, but were more powerful than they.[12] In London, if plays were given on working days, they were held to be a

temptation to apprentices ; if on Sundays, they tended to outdo Church as
an attraction. And then again, plays that are really dramatic, make both
evil and good more vivid ; and the lower classes must not have Tamerlanes
in their imaginations. Besides which there were conditions of public
health, and also public morality, which could be urged against all public
assemblies that were not strictly necessary. Something of this may have
been true also of our Scottish cities. For the opponents of the stage relied
on no Scriptural authority. None of the Puritan documents quoted in
E. K. Chambers' *Elizabethan Stage* * cites any more cogent name than
Tertullian, except for the " law " forbidding men to appear in women's
apparel. The widespread objection by the Puritans seems to have been
to a rival draw on the Lord's Day.

With the passing of the King to England, such forces became stronger
till there was no longer any possibility of a theatre Scottish, Classical or
English. In the eighteenth century, when Puritanism had settled down
into a glum and possessive negativism, attempts were made to brighten
Society, which was not so Puritanical, by founding theatres in Edinburgh,
Glasgow, Aberdeen, Dundee, Arbroath, and Perth : but for the most part
these gave mere provincial dates to London actors. Even the venture of
the poet and connoisseur Allan Ramsay was mostly dependent on English
books and performers. Edinburgh had settled down comfortably as a
distribution centre for English notions and as a training ground for more
talented Scots to seek their fortune in the South.

True, there was the Reverend John Home, minister at Athelstaneford,
whose drama, *Douglas*, ultimately made good on Garrick's stage. And
dramatic versions of Scott novels, especially *Rob Roy*, together with the
moralistic tragedies of Joanna Baillie, varied London melodrama and blank-
verse tragedy with " Scotch " scenery. But the metropolitan tyranny
held sway in both countries, and would-be fashionable provincial society
was as anxious then for art news from London as was that in Kuala Lumpur
before the present war.

Perth, a community to itself in the uncertain Highlands, or within
reach of them, and the Dundee district with its still direct connection to
the Continent, were much less English in their character ; but even these
did not create a true, durable " Perth " or " Dundee " theatre in the fullest
sense. Ryder's stock company at Perth was mainly composed of Scottish
artists, Mackay, Henry Johnston and others ; and historical Scottish plays
bore titles like *The Gowrie Conspiracy*, *Cramond Brig*, and so on. But these
were really English plays with a smattering of Lallans for local colour.
No playwright founded a Perth school of playwriting. The repertory
was mainly Shakespeare and Scott. Companies came and went. And

* Vol. IV, Appendix C.

it was not long before Ryder was booking Terry and Young and Kean for appearances on tour from London ; and the metropolis had triumphed again.

The explanation lies, as always, in the audience. De-nationalised by the loss of their King's presence in a still monarchical society, and exploited by the dastardly Union, the Scots lost not only their national outlook, but also their desire to have one. Although they continued in their homes to speak Lallans, it was with a sneaking sense that this was not genteel ; and their English became more and more Southern in consequence. The value of Scott and the Edinburgh cronies of this time cannot be overestimated. Scots was even used at public meetings, sometimes, even on big occasions.

But the power of English example, the continual and increasing selling-out by the upper class for English titles and London connections, were too great even for the Wizard of the North. What the Anglo-Scottish dukes did for the Highlands by their clearances, the Anglo-Scottish and often the purely Scottish business man did for the Lowlands and the cities. Calvin did not have to be called in. Fashion, and its wife and daughter were enough. The public did not want a Scottish theatre.

WHY, THEN, A UKRAINIAN THEATRE ?

The purpose of this digression lies in the resemblance between the Lowland Scots and the Ukrainians ; and also in their differences.

The first known Ukrainian plays were Interludes by Yakub Gavatovich, performed in a village near Lvov in 1619. But their principal nursery was the Uniat church schools. The Church recognised the value of theatrical performance and developed it itself. When the Russian Tsars conquered the Ukraine, Ukases forbade all printing in the Ukrainian language. This did not kill the theatre, weak and tender though its youth still was. It simply deprived it of literary stimulus. The theatre became a mass, or folk, theatre, retained in the mind and transmitted from generation to generation, without being written down.

In time the oppressive methods of Tsarist government were slightly relaxed ; and at once the first theatre building is mentioned : at Kiev in 1803. Later, other towns followed this example, notably Poltava, where nine years later the first permanent Ukrainian company was formed by Kvitka-Osnovyanenko, an author of comedies in the eighteenth-century European style. But the writer who really founded the Ukrainian drama was Ivan Kotlyarevsky, whose work included the still popular *Natalka of Poltava*. Little by little both drama and theatre were consolidated by authors, actors and teachers. But in 1876 the Tsarist boot descended again, and the theatre was included in a general ban on Ukrainian literature and culture.

Five years this remained absolute. Then a way of getting round it was worked out. Plays were given in the forbidden Ukrainian language ; but they were called " Little Russian " plays, and as long as the number of acts in a Little-Russian play did not exceed the number of acts in a Great-Russian play given with it in the same programme, the performance would not be interfered with.

The Ukrainians stuck to their aims, quietly, and therefore with success. After 1905 the Tsarist policy changed again. In 1907 a real Ukrainian theatre was permitted. F. N. Sadovsky opened it in Kiev. In 1916 a studio of young actors was opened. In the forming of this, and in its work, young Gnat Yura had a big influence. He is to-day one of the great names in Ukrainian theatre circles. In 1919 this young studio became the State Dramatic Theatre, named for Shevchenko, the people's poet and patriot, who had also written plays. It worked at first among units of the Red Army. The following year Yura organised the " Ivan Franko " Theatre, and Tereshchenko the Kiev Central Studio, which became a full theatre and lasted till 1925.

Founded in March 1922 the Berezil Theatre (" Berezil " is apparently Ukrainian for March) became a big institution with studios and club premises in various towns, and a mobile theatre for the countryside, thus spreading and consolidating theatre sense in the nation. Later years saw the founding of Ukrainian operas at Harkov, Kiev and Odessa, three mobile opera-and-ballet theatres, a Polish proletarian theatre in Kiev, a Bulgarian theatre, and a theatre of the Revolution with a whole battery of young dramatists writing Ukrainian plays.

One of the most interesting and touching figures of Ukrainian drama was the poetess Lesya Ukrainka, the thirtieth anniversary of whose death was celebrated at a " creative evening " in Moscow in July 1943, when Ukrainian authors like Korneichuk, and Margarita Aliger took part, and Pavel Antokolsky read a paper about her, and several prominent Ukrainian actors like Kozlovsky, Giasintova and others recited.

She was born in 1870, her real name being Larisa Kovach-Kvitka. She took the name " Ukrainka " because body and soul she belonged to her native land, fierily, like Lermontov, when it was neither fashionable nor comfortable always to be fierily patriotic. But, as she herself said, it was her wish that her words " should become a weapon in the hands of unknown friends against their executioners ". And that wish history has granted.

Not that her body bore her spirit well. She died at the age of 43, of a long and distressing illness, and all her life had been a struggle against ill-health. This damaged neither her will nor her output. Twelve volumes she wrote, songs, ballads, lyrics, tales, philosophical dialogues, criticism, journalism, and plays short and long.

At 30 she was a poetess, a follower of Shevchenko, a country singer loving the rich Ukrainian earth, traditional in her forms, making sonnets, ballades, terzinas. So even in its simpler literature the Ukraine was in step with the world-fashion of the 'nineties. Then she burst forth.

She was much of an age with Maxim Gorky ; and with him and Lenin she wrote for the journal *Life*. She came, as Gorky did, to a "revolutionary romanticism", and she had the same love for human individuality and the same hatred of tyranny as he and Lenin had.

The human individual shown in the round, in the light of historical comment, that—all the critics agree—was the base of her drama. Don Juan she created in the round, as Molière and Byron and Pushkin had done ; but she hated Don Juanism, because of the suffering it caused. Because it was tyranny to woman. And she hated well and valuably because she understood. So her Don Juan comes to grief because he is just a fantast, a weak man, whose dream is to be a man of property.

And Beatrice, Dante's Beatrice, in her work is no figure of poetic fancy, trailing clouds of Paradise over the rainstorm of Dante's moods. She is a poet's wife, and not happy. A poet's wife who with her husband, says Antokolsky, " baked the bread of exile, lit a fire for him on an alien hearth, and at the end closed his eyes to all eternity ".

Or, in the Catacombs, a slave is brought before the prelates of the Church, precursors of the Spanish Inquisition. His bitter lot has defeated him, and from the new religion he expects immediate truth and happiness. From Ancient Egypt, Mediaeval Scotland, Puritan England that founded a new life in a new world, always in her plays humanity struggles to conquer its tyrants and be free. ·Even in folk-lore, Mavka, playing in the blue smoke of a wood fire, flares into a forest conflagration, burning humanity and its belongings and creations ; yet the human soul asserts itself and triumphs. Always humanity, always the conflict of personality and Nature, man and Art, love and Convention.

Analytical intellect and womanly intuition seem in her to have been uncommonly well matched. And always her feeling was for the common man all down history, as her brain showed her how, and why, he was frustrated.

With such writers, and their successors, Ukrainian drama came to its maturity.[13]

Why, now, were the Ukrainians so tenacious, when the dogged Scots were not ?

The answer must lie in the circumstances under which they were governed at the time of their respective " Unions ". It is not natural for the people of any nation to adopt the manners and language of another nation unless they are given carrots to follow by the men who drive them.

Both Scots and Ukrainians, as a whole, have kept much of their national custom and language ; but both have to some extent also acquired others from their governors. Scott wrote for the most part, as his readers read, in English. Gogol, after toying the idea of creating a (useless) Ukrainian drama, as his father had before him, wrote in Russian. But the Ukrainian people as a whole have never abandoned their own language to quite the same extent as the Scots have.

At the first sell-out to the English, the Scots were in a monarchical condition, and when their monarch went to England, the eyes of those who remained in Scotland followed him there. The Ukrainians had no monarch ; and their respective *hetmans* were wiped out by the Russian Tsars.

At the second sell-out to the English, the Act of Union was rushed through Scotland by a minority of Scottish business folk who stood to increase their business thereby. The Ukrainians had no business folk ; they were an undeveloped, peasant community. Subsequent treatment emphasised and developed that peasant character. Whether their lairds were Ukrainian or foreign made no difference to them. By the time capitalism and business came to the Ukraine, the peasantry had steeled down into a determined Ukraine-ness that no Ukases could disturb.

Russian connections tempted some in the nineteenth century. Russian merchants and princes ran their affairs. Russian was the language of the tea-table. Gogol, perhaps, was quite right to create in Russian. But the masses of the people remained without hope of rising to better positions, whether they intrigued with rich Ukrainians or rich Russians. With the Scots it was not so. English speech meant better jobs. English civilisation meant capital, research, invention, profits, business. The Scottish brain could conquer the English way, provided it accepted it first. Scotland, inevitably, if only for a few centuries, was doomed by the Scots.

When the political and still more the economic barriers were removed in the Ukraine, the social barriers fell of their own accord, and the Ukraine stepped into the comity of nations. It has passed beyond the assertion of its own language and culture ; it can now interpret into its own language and culture the history and the heroes of other lands inside a greater, common culture. Full nationalism implies and includes an international outlook. But a national art that excludes other nations is only a local one. Only, before that can happen, a nation must be united and it must be independent.

Our stage is now set for the provincial theatres of Greater Russia in the second half of the nineteenth century, and up to 1917 ; but we cannot yet speak of the plays done on it, without first returning to the metropolitan stages in the same period. For there is an organic relation between the two, on both sides of the footlights.

CHAPTER IV

STARS, OFFICIALS AND A PEOPLE'S THEATRE

PERFORMANCE UNDER OFFICIALS

Under Tsar Nicholas the First (1825-55) all the Russians were bound up in wires of organisation that were a kind of magnetic coil. It was intended to govern for the protection of the monarchy and all that belonged thereto, but so many fingers had picked at the insulation that it could generate nothing.

When officialdom works from the top downwards, there must be more than a possibility of corruption and a certainty of inaction. The man on the job, the expert, is allowed no say in policy unless he is admitted to an official post, in which case, to protect himself, he must intrigue as ably as his superiors, and the technical needs of which he has knowledge are again subordinated to office politics. The man at the top, who decides policy, knows little of technical needs, being appointed either by birth or by being " the right type " to administer any organisation. Not having the technical knowledge of the man on the job, he will be reluctant to alter the existing set-up, and knowing only administrative answers to criticism from outside, he will favour a policy that avoids controversy of any kind.

Further, in an autocracy run by an amateur, the high official who has power to make certain decisions, may not trust his subordinates. He will therefore be constantly interfering in their spheres where, though they may know little, he will know nothing at all. Nicholas interfered in this way with the running of theatres, in detail, in casting and play-reading, and even prices of admission, where his own faulty taste and shallow knowledge were dominated by quite un-theatrical aims.

Now the arts, and above all the arts of performance, drama and music, depend for their development on the men on the job. Bureaucratic control from the top is bound to result in a stagnant, undeveloping art. But the arts of performance concern an audience, people ; and people do not remain stagnant and undeveloping. If the artist is working in truthful material, he is bound to stir up controversy. Therefore the bureaucrat in control of the art is certain to frown on truthful, that is, realistic, art. And the truthful artist is discouraged. All down the scale there will be men who fear and deceive their superiors, but cannot trust them (so that in the end bureaucracy defeats its own object) ; and on the lowest level of all, where the job is done, performer and creator alike, knowing that their efforts will be judged only by administrative standards, look at each other and ask, " What is the use of trying ? "

Perhaps the only hope of improvement can come from some outside " ginger " group, collaborating and showing the bureaucrats what knots can be untied and what cut in the red tape. The Quakers did something of this kind to the French bureaucracy in the war of 1914-18 over matters of War Relief. But that was not a monarchic bureaucracy, only a class one. On Russian Imperial despotism perhaps even devastating Quaker honesty would not have prevailed.

Russian artists did try, however. That they tried was due partly to their own doggedness and sense of art values, and partly to the peculiar nature of Russian printed literature. Ever since the reign of Catharine the Great (1762-96) thought and sociological writings had been so subjected to the tempers of the monarch, that criticism of any kind had to be limited to literary criticism. Only literary topics were allowed to be discussed in print.[1] This meant that literary criticism became a cover for all new, practical, political ideas. And this in turn had a remarkable influence on Russian literature, linking it closely and organically with Russian life : so that unlike musicians, painters and theatre people, Russian writers of both prose and verse, but especially the former, were from the very beginning far advanced down the road of realism which other national literatures were not to follow for many years. Now, there is always a connection, however thin, between the theatre and the *littérateur;* and this set up a further conflict in the bureaucratised theatre world.

Under Alexander II (1855-81) the clumsy coil of *chinovniki* became quite unmovable and choked. The Crimean War showed up its in-efficiency, its corruption, the self-destruction it contained in its very self-construction. With grudging firmness the Tsar set about reforms, reforms as unwelcome to the landowners as to the serfs they were intended to benefit, both classes having got so accustomed to autocracy that they were bewildered by even partial liberation. The serfs were emancipated. County Councils (*zemstvos*) were invented, a model to the world. Everything seemed ready for a fine new life. Not enough people saw that the *zemstvos* would be sabotaged by the central *chinovniki*, and the emancipation be worked to the greater disadvantage of the serfs, and that under this Tsar's successor Alexander III, a stupid giant who could bend a cold horseshoe in his hands, the little good would be all undone. On the contrary, the educated classes, few though they were, became optimistic. Used to actuality in their literature, they came, as they gained the majority in the audience, to expect actuality on the stage. Indeed they had that very expectancy and curiosity in life which we have suggested as one of the reasons for a healthy drama.

To this, of course, the men on the job in the theatre, whether actors or authors, wished to respond (Ostrovsky).

This chapter shows their attempts to do so, attempts which flourished under the more or less tolerant aloofness of the Tsar Alexander II, but which, when he was assassinated in 1881, his successor suffocated as he did every other progressive thing in his dominions. Thenceforward development became either timid or clandestine, according as those who tried to develop were in official posts (for there were a few) or in the opposition. The latter could do little, though they might be many. It follows, therefore, that the hope of the performed arts rested with the enlightened few. The period of Ostrovsky comes to an end, and there is a gap before Gorky. . . . But this is anticipating.

Shchepkin had shown that it was possible for an actor to be truthful to a character even in an untruthful play, although his " naturalness " was his own, and did not extend to the whole company as much as he would have liked. And even his own " natural " studies were in the convention of the time . . . he never lost his Ukrainian accent whatever the character he played. But plainly there could be little development of this till authors were following the same line. Meanwhile the stars developed truth in their acting. A personal thing, motivated largely by personal rivalry ; and mostly limited to the stars ; but none the less, truth.

The great names are many : we will select in tragedy, Yermolova (1853-1928) ; in comedy, Fyedotova (1846-1925) ; Prov Sadovsky, who died in 1872 ; Savina (1854-1919), Varlamov (1848-1915) ; Davydov (1847-1925) ; and Strepetova (1850-1906).

Yermolova, with the characteristic quaver in her voice and her intense, eloquent silences, not only carried conviction as Emilia Galeotti or Joan of Arc ; she seemed to " be " the woman she was representing. This, to us, is now a commonplace (though perhaps not so common as it might be). To her audience it was new each time to the point of electrification. " From the depths of her soul ", wrote Yuzhin,[2] himself a fine actor, playwright and man of the theatre, " Yermolova brought out what was concealed in her, under the Maria Nikolayevna we knew ; and she gave birth to a great spiritual figure as naturally as the mother of Socrates gave birth to Socrates, or the mother of Brutus to Brutus, or the mother of Peter the Great to Peter. We don't know well what sort of people these mothers were . . . but we know their children." And Stanislavsky said that she was the greatest actress he had ever known, greater than Duse.[3]

This is plainly a development. It is an inner realism, the creation of a round being, and not born into a void. Yermolova was closely in touch with the thought of the 'seventies. One of the many rumours that went round in the talk of the populace, among facts like her using a cab like ordinary people, in quite undistinguished clothes, and not dolled up in a carriage like a "star", was : "She reads only *Russian Gazette* and *Russian Thought*"—which were two liberal papers.[4]   And she chose for her benefit night in March 1876 the revolutionary play of Lope de Vega, *Fuente Ovejuna*, in which to the immense approval of the Moscow students, Laurencia, standing up for the village women dishonoured by the "High Commander", calls on the village assembly to avenge themselves on the tyrant. Yermolova is said to have delivered this speech with more heroic enthusiasm than had been shown in the Maly since the time of Mochalov [5] . . . but with deeper and more actual earnestness !

The disadvantage of genius in one brilliant star is that it shows up the unreal scenery of painted back-cloths against which such humanity seems out of place.   But its advantage is that dramatic authors of the day can create figures of truth in the round, knowing they will be played in the round.

They did this for Yermolova, and for Savina too, who had not perhaps the depth of Yermolova, but whose performance was more supple, could allow of momentary inspirations, necessary in a young realism feeling its way to maturity.   Savina relied on her inspiration.   Which meant that when it flagged, she acted badly.   She could not feel her part in a stage version of Dostoyevsky's *The Idiot*.   She admitted she never "got" Fru Alving in *Ghosts*.[6]   But at the same time the stress was still on her ; Turgenyev, who protested, when she wanted to do *A Month in the Country*, that he hadn't really written this play for the stage, nevertheless came to see it when it passed into the regular repertoire.*   He was surprised to find that she was playing not Natalia Petrovna, the wife, but Verochka, the daughter.   And he was astonished at the character she had built out of what he had regarded as a small part.   It is possible that Savina's performance overweighted the play.   Stars were still, however realistic, virtuosi.   One evening Savina played four different characters in acts from four different plays.   Not playing, so much as displaying.

And the new realism might be limited by the personal character of the performer.   Varlamov, for example, was a simple man.   He made nice clean studies of Dogberry and Bottom the Weaver.   The figures he created were simple graceful creatures like himself, especially in comedy.   One did not look for self-suppressing realism before a Peterburg audience, not even when transplanted for the season to the Caucasian spas.

Davydov, too, another Peterburg actor, was full of lively natural spirits. "Live, live, live ; two hundred thousand times, live !" was his personal slogan and the base of his teaching.   But if his performance was not a direct copy of nature, neither was it founded on any principle.   He, too, was feeling his way.   Not too quickly.   There were dangers in the success

* Turgenyev spent a large part of his life outside Russia.

of innovation.   There were rival actors of the old school, whose jealousy might be roused to potent hostility.   V. V. Samoïlov, to whom the Tsar had awarded a Gold Medal, was as much to be watched and humoured as any *chinovnik*.

Even the audiences were affected by officialdom.   When Savina visited Moscow, the Peterburg speech habits that had endeared her to the upper-class audiences of the Neva antagonised the Maly audience so much that they forgot their manners.   When she took a curtain call with their own favourite Lensky, they yelled " Lensky solo ! Lensky solo ! " and would not have her.

Even in her own Alexandrinsky *milieu*, she had troubles with the *chinovniki*, some of whom were afraid of her, and others hated her.   To avoid the results of such attitudes from powerful officials, most artists must either intrigue, or become a stooge, or retire to the provinces. Savina was strong enough to survive.

For the junior members of the Alexandrinsky, it was far worse.   " The majority ", wrote Glamá-Meshcherskaya, " used to sit round with folded hands, happy if any sort of a part turned up, or if they got the chance to understudy their luckier seniors."   But they were on the strength, just as if they had offices, and drew their pay as punctually on the 20th of every month.

In Moscow, in the 'eighties, so fine an actress as Yablochkina took an engagement at Odessa, because the *chinovniki* gave her at the Maly such dull parts.   So it became a matter of great energy and persistence for any young actor or actress to develop in their art at all.[7]   And type-casting— " Tsar ", " Noble Mother ", " Young Princess ", etc.—lasted till 1882.

Apart from the stars, general conditions at the Maly were crude.   Two rehearsals were considered enough for a comedy.[8]   For the début of young Glamá at the Alexandrinsky in the 'seventies, there were four rehearsals ; but then there was another débutant in the cast besides her.   Many actors relied accordingly in performance on improvisation.   Varlamov made it a habit.   Sometimes he was so carried away that he would give no cues, and once sent off the stage a junior actor, whom he had not allowed to speak, with loudly expressed thanks for information he had not received.[9]

There was no idea of ensemble.   There was only a certain give-and-take between the principals.   This was an improvement, of course, on the old style, as may be seen in our own countries with the few remaining old-style actors such as Tod Slaughter the melodrama king, whose juniors do not attempt to act in character when he is off the stage, and merely feed him when he is on.   Indeed, the idea of juniors remaining in character when not speaking nor being directly addressed, would in the old days have violated the feelings of the principals, as distracting attention from their own performance ; as if a second clarinet were to stand up during a Violin Concerto. In Peterburg, too, the idea of transferring the centre of importance from the mere entertainment of the audience to the "real" living of events on the stage would in Court audience days have meant asserting the social superiority of the actors, if indeed it had not been held an insult to the Tsar himself. And perhaps the attitude had become a habit that lasted long after the audience had changed its content. At all events there is no denying that Peterburg was far more opposed to development than Moscow ; and even after Ostrovsky had established himself with the Moscow public, he had a long battle to win the Peterburg one.

OSTROVSKY WRITES THE TRUTH

The more open-minded Moscow audience was coming to have more unified ideas, because more and more of its members, the naïve and the forthright, were acquiring progressive ones . . . hence their love for Strepetova. But we must not expect too much nor too quickly. Ostrovsky, when he arrived, was no superman. A superman would have been exiled or executed. As it was, Ostrovsky was honest enough to be put under police supervision for five years, and a "collaborating" Maly management refused to stage his plays, although, or perhaps because, the public wanted them. His very first play, The Bankrupt, was banned.[10]

Nor should we, from contempt for the Peterburg audience, idealise the Moscow one. Most people went to the theatre, as Gilyarovsky describes them in the Korsh Theatre, in the mood for any "catching" play : writers, or amateur actors, or sportsmen in town for the races, or middle-class merchants and their wives . . . "all those people who want to laugh or shed a tear.". Applause is continual, with stampings of feet and shoutings of "Encore !" In the intervals the sons of the middle class stand before the mirrors in the cloak-rooms and imitate the gestures of Petipa or Davydov. Mr. Korsh himself, smiling, always smiling, shows himself in the foyer. "Happy Mr. Korsh !" exclaims Gilyarovsky, "happy public ! happy actors !—however a new-comer to the stage acts, he is sure of a welcome."

So it was in the other "private" theatres, the Rodon Operetta, the Nemchinovka, the Sekretarevka, where each amateur group that hired the stage brought its own public into the auditorium, and you could almost tell the nature of the group from the trades represented in front, the fish trade, the meat business, the greengrocers from Ohotny Ryad. In one case a quite talented "Krechinsky" invited the audience to supper after the show, they being all his personal friends ; but the performance had to be abandoned after the second act, because "Krechinsky" had a sudden business call. He was an undertaker.

Sometimes a private theatre would change its public unintentionally. The " Clown " Theatre was intended to be a People's Theatre with seats at 50 kopeks and no more. It was in fact crowded by the well-to-do.

What were these " private " theatres ? That brings us to Ostrovsky.

" Ostrovsky ", said Vladimir Filippov,[11] a Soviet theatre historian, during a memorial evening in April 1943, " drew his words and expressions from his talks with people, when he was hunting, fishing, visiting country taverns, etc." That was the first step. Now there was a bond of reality in speech between people in the audience and those on the stage. Actors were speaking like other people. Other people could therefore accept them as similar to themselves.

Then, because he knew and could understand individual characters, their wants and problems, he drew these in the round. That was a further step ; because people in the audience could recognise real people on the stage, and could feel sympathy or antipathy toward them, as they did in real life.

Now Ostrovsky saw deeply into their lives and motives and sufferings. Deeper in most cases than they saw themselves. And by the way he made the real characters behave to one another, he made the audience think about other things than just personalities. So that going to the theatre, though it was still entertainment, was not just a matter of laughing or crying. It had the extra interest that there is in a company of people when a man of great understanding is talking or thinking aloud. This was the greatest step of all.

For because Ostrovsky has intellect as well as sympathy, he can put example to example like a scientist, making a principle. He can show the ways in which society as it exists is the cause of these sufferings. His plays, that is, have an explanatory side which is sometimes satirical. They leave the audience thinking. This is dangerous ground for both author and audience ; but it is what the audience wants for the understanding of its own lives. Few will be willing to follow him all the way, though he is no political revolutionary, only a man with clear intellectual honesty, sympathy for the individual human soul, and a hatred of oppression. The same might be said of Shakespeare and Molière and Ibsen, and many others.

This does not mean that he wrote dreary sociological tracts. On the contrary he ranged from the storms of Russian history (*Dmitry the Impostor*, etc.), through a fairy play (*Snegurochka*),[12] to farcical comedies like *One's Own People* or *Balzamin's Betrothal*, wherein a foppish and foolish young *chinovnik* tries to find a rich wife and is caught by a widow, not very fair, but more than forty, and a great deal more than fat.

The Storm is his best-known work ; [12] but there are many as just and poignant. *The Ward*, for example, in which a beautiful young serf-girl is brought up by a rich old tyrant of a woman-owner and educated to her liking in her household. ("I don't like people to think for themselves. That's a thing I dislike extremely. I can allow no one to do that.") Then she is to be married off to a young man of the owner-benefactor's choosing. This was quite a fashion at the time, and in this case the *vospitannitsa* is to be given to a dissolute young boor. For months the owner's son has been trying to seduce her, but though she is only 17 and in a position of utter dependence on the family, she resists him. However, when the rich old woman will not give way to her pleading not to be married to certain misery, she yields to her young master, in order to soil herself as a bride. She does not escape. The wicked old woman still insists she shall marry the waster.

Others are direct satires on officialdom. In *A Lucrative Post* (1856) a young official at the time of the Crimean War offends his important uncle, by announcing that in future he is going to "go straight", take no bribes, intrigue with no superiors, even if it means missing promotion. His extravagant fashionable wife, and her "county-family" mother, however, insist that he should provide a home on the scale to which the wife is accustomed. ("My daughters have been properly brought up; they don't even know the way into the kitchen.") So in the end the young husband goes to his uncle to apologise and admit defeat. However, the old man's coarse triumph so revolts him that he adheres to his first resolve.

Ostrovsky was born in 1823, and from the 'fifties on wrote a play a year till he died in 1886. As a British reviewer of his early collected plays in Russian wrote in the *Edinburgh Review* for July 1868, there is not much "plot" in this drama. "They are, in fact, devoid of original contrivances or startling situations." This also was new.

It will be noted that Ibsen was born five years after Ostrovsky, but he did not come to his maturity till the 'seventies or 'eighties. Naturally the two authors have something in common, since they stood at the same moment of European society. But it is a great pity that our stage did not take to Ostrovsky as it took to Ibsen. We would have been the better if the Russian theatre had had in this country its William Archer.

By all these new steps that Ostrovsky made, he had really done as he set out to do : to found a Russian national drama. Quoting again from the *Edinburgh Review*: "The plays are for the most part thoroughly national, founded upon the actual experience of their writers" (the reviewer is referring to other writers as well as Ostrovsky) "and devoted to the illustration of that kind of life which is led at home by the majority of those who come to see them." And he refers to Ostrovsky's heroines as being "driven into dishonour by the harshness and folly of those who surround

ALEXANDER OSTROVSKY, 1823–1886.

[*facing page* 60.

THE BOLSHOY THEATRE, MOSCOW.

Except for the stage curtains the design in red and gold has been unaltered since its foundation. This photograph was taken on the first night after the company's return from evacuation. The opera is Glinka's *Ivan Susanin.*

[*facing page* 61.

them ".[13] One of the great Russian novelists confirmed this, when he wrote to Ostrovsky, " Only since you, can we Russians say that we have a national theatre ". For the root motive of all Ostrovsky's satire was his love for the common people. Nor was he merely local in his drama, for he knew and translated plays by Shakespeare, Plautus, Cervantes and Goldoni.

He also went into action. It was largely on his initiative that the Society of Russian Dramatic Writers and Opera Composers was formed, with the aim of " creating a focus of ethical influence on writers in the interests of the development of the drama ". The reason was that writers had to get together, because they needed a new kind of actor, like those of Gogol in the generation before, and of Chehov in the generation after. Shchepkin had naturalness and knew life " from courtier to lackey ". But Ostrovsky's figures needed simplicity and a knowledge of life " from cornshop to merchant's residence ".[14]

The required actor appeared in Prov Sadovsky, who developed a simple style and could study the merchants. Shchepkin did not altogether like Ostrovsky's plays, and Sadovsky's style was held by the older generation to be a " lack of acting ". But Sadovsky's realism was founded on Shchepkin's as was that of all the Sadovsky family. They didn't " act ", it was perfectly fair to say. They " lived " on the stage, even when drinking tea or vodka (and you could tell which it was from the way they appeared to drink it).

The tie between author and acting family remained. Prov Sadovsky's son Mihail carried on the parts his father had created. Prov Sadovsky's daughter-in-law was absent from only eight out of Ostrovsky's forty-eight plays, and that only because there was no part for her line of business. Prov Sadovsky's grandson, Prov Mihailovich Sadovsky, a very highly honoured artist of the Soviet Union, retained the authentic way, and taught it to his nephew Mihail Mihailovich, who joined the Maly company in 1928. Largely through this continuum Ostrovsky is inseparable from the Maly Theatre, or from the " New " Theatre, which Lensky opened at the end of last century as a Maly Filial.

Nevertheless the Maly was not always identified with Ostrovsky. It was, after all, a Government department.

OSTROVSKY AND THE FREE THEATRES

Ostrovsky did not achieve his national drama with any help from the Government. Indeed before any such truly national drama could be created, the Government monopoly of the theatre had to be broken down. Ostrovsky was enabled to break that down by the intelligent amateur movement.

5

The rigid control of the Imperial theatres was limited in area.   Outside its sphere of influence in Peterburg, for instance, there were several theatre buildings in the suburbs, on the outskirts, or in nearby, accessible residential townlets.   Touring companies often used these premises.   Often too they were taken by amateur groups serially, so that they could give several performances of the same play.   At Pavlovsk-in-the-Woods, at the summer theatre in Oranienbaum, or best of all at Kronstadt.   The audience drove out and back, or went by train, or however they could.   It was supposed to be a " closed " audience, that is, the purchase of tickets was limited by law to members of a club, or persons " recommended " by them.   But gradually the recommendation became a pure formality.

Often these amateur groups were strengthened by inviting young professionals who were " resting ".   Sometimes the theatre would be run as a business speculation by a manager, and he would engage, for instance, young Glamá for a fee of 35 roubles, as Rappoport did, the manager at Kronstadt.   It is easy to see that from such a mixed company of professionals and amateurs, there might and would be created a rival to the Imperial theatres which would have comparative freedom of policy and re-pertoire.[15]

In Moscow there was a similar tendency, but a more deliberate one. With the intention of performing good plays that had been banned by the Tsar's censors, in 1869 the " Artistic Circle " asserted the right of the bourgeoisie to have its own theatre. Ostrovsky was at its head.   In 1871 during the Polytechnic Exhibition, there was a " people's theatre " playing in a house in what is now Nogin Square, where a number of young actors, Nikolay Rybakov, Strepetova, Lensky, and others, were laying the foundation of future stardom.   But this was an *ad hoc*, temporary organisation, and ceased with the Exhibition.[16]   Other and more per-manent private theatres began to open in rich men's houses like that of the amateur N. I. Davydov at Red Gate : hence called the Red Gate Theatre. Ostrovsky used himself to appear in his own plays here ; one of his banned dramas was performed ; and also a number of classics, Shakespeare, Schiller, Molière, and Calderon, which were not in the Maly repertoire.   Another pioneer was Sekretaryev who fitted up a hall in his sumptuous mansion.

But the most daring and successful, historically, was the venture of a young married woman, progressive and fairly well-to-do, who called herself for stage purposes Anna Brenko, from an ancestor of Alexander Nevsky's time, and whose destiny it was to break the Imperial monopoly and her own life in the process.

Her rounded young Russian face shows real character and independence in the eyes ; and she was much more than a mere charmer.   She was a fine, intelligent, steadfast woman.   Her husband was Joseph Levenson, a young barrister and music critic ; and together they faced up to the actuality of the day. One can parallel them with many young couples in Chelsea in the nineteen-thirties : social reformers, with a high and wide ideal of culture and democracy, always ready to help the victims of tyranny, many of whom were in their own circle of friends. Anna Brenko organised concerts and semi-dramatic performances without costume or make-up (to fulfil the law, which in this respect much resembled our Sunday Performance laws), the object of which was to raise money for comforts for exiles in Siberia. The needs of these exiles far exceeded the small sums Anna could supply from her own fortune, and to qualify as a legal object part of the takings were handed over to a respectable charity like The Society for Christian Aid.[17]

For these shows she hired a private theatre in the Solodovnikov Passage, and out of them a definite theatrical unit began to emerge. For twelve out of thirty " performances " she invited the actor Pisaryev.* It was a success. Yermolova herself came to Pisaryev's benefit. Among other plays done was *The Forest*, by Ostrovsky.

In 1881 Anna Brenko took the inevitable next bold step, and opened the first private theatre in Russia for the general public. A merchant Melkiel, who had made a colossal fortune by supplying boots to the Army during the Russo-Turkish War, was spreading himself in the grand manner as only a Russian parvenu could. He bought simultaneously two palaces on Tverskaya. One was the house where the Volkonsky *salon* had flourished, where Pushkin had been an honoured guest sixty years previously, and which Melkiel's ambitious wife Nina hoped to revive. Only nobody much came to their At Homes, except the young artists and barristers of the Levenson circle. The champagne flowed ; but Melkiel was bored with the At Homes, and when Nina went to Paris for a trip (" in a coach of gold ", murmured the young people naughtily) he decided he would build Anna Brenko a real theatre of her own in the other palace across the road.

He engaged a well-known architect, and the result was sumptuous. Marble staircase, bannisters of gilt bronze, Oriental carpets, statues in the foyer. A fine stage ; a luxurious auditorium, white walls shaded blue, with trimmings of silk and velvet. Front tabs of the same blue, and blue lines picked out on seats and doors.[18] † So came into being the " Pushkin " Theatre, named thus because it stood, as the playbills announced, near the Pushkin monument. But all Moscow and soon the provinces called it the Brenko Theatre.

The company was the flower of non-Imperial talent : Pisaryev, Strepetova,

* M. I. Pisaryev. Not to be confused with D. I. Pisaryev, the author and critic.
† At this time the Maly tabs were a drop curtain painted with the view of a castle.[19]

Charsky, Glamá, Andreyev-Burlak (he was chief *régisseur*).   And beginning their careers, younger men like Dalmatov and Yuzhin-Sumbatov,
soon to be the chief spirit to guide the Maly through a World War and a
Proletarian Revolution.   The policy was decided, and the theatre administered by a committee of three : Anna Brenko, Burlak and Pisaryev.[20]

Lavish salaries were paid.   Strepetova received 1,100 roubles a month,
Pisaryev and Burlak each 900.   At this time a provincial lead would be
receiving between 80 and 35 roubles a month, reduced probably by half
on a year's contract.   The minimum salary in the provinces would be
perhaps 15, or for an unskilled actor, 3.   When Savin invited Glamá to
Kiev (1787-80) as a rising Alexandrinsky star, on the other hand, he had
to pay her 500 roubles a month.[21]

Over settings and costumes no expense was spared.   The repertoire
too was outstanding.   Ostrovsky's *Forest*, which had been written for Pisaryev
as the tragedian and Burlak as the comedian, was given its first public
performance.   A comedy called *The Female Savage*, by Ostrovsky and
Solovyov jointly, showed off the brilliance of Glamá as an ingenue.
Strepetova had a furore in Pisemsky's *A Bitter Fate*.   Lermontov's *Masquerade* came into its own, after its dismissal as "unstageworthy" in the
Alexandrinsky production of 1852.   The German Jewish tragedy *Uriel
Akosta*, now a recognised classic of world drama, was first shown in Russia
here.   There were an adaptation of a Saltykov-Shchedrin satire, two or
three plays that ultimately went into the Imperial repertoire, and *Woe from
Wit*, *Othello*, and *Hamlet*.   Another Ostrovsky play appeared, more daring
than the rest : the original uncut version of *The Bankrupt* (which had been
rewritten and produced under a title of a proverbial saying type, usually
rendered in English *Easily Settled among Friends*).   This sold out before
the night, and at the first performance Pisaryev addressed the author from
the stage and presented him with a gilded laurel wreath.

Plenty of time was given for the actors to study their parts.   Rehearsals
usually began a whole fortnight before opening night ! [22]   First the author,
or Burlak, would read the play to the assembled company.   Then there
would be a считка—a reading round a table, but "in full voice".   The
second rehearsal was on the stage with the actors reading from the book.
Exits, entrances and corrections were noted, and the company went away
to study with the whole plan of the play in their minds.   At the third
rehearsal they were expected to do without the book ; and then followed
the "dress rehearsal" which was, however, far from being what we know
by that term.

At that time such care was revolutionary.

The company lived as a commonwealth, all together.   Stars frequently
took small parts, because the centre of gravity aimed at by Brenko and

Burlak was not the individual performance but the ensemble. This also was a tremendous innovation. In fact we see here the beginning, a very tentative and small-scale, but none the less definite beginning of a process that was to end in the Moscow Art Theatre, seventeen years later.

Cordial relations existed between these actors and many of the actors of the Maly, who would always try to be free to attend Pushkin Theatre first nights. Otherwise the audience came chiefly from the intelligentsia. There was no attempt at a mass theatre. But the social policy of the venture was distinct. Ostrovsky saw to that.

On Sundays special matinees were often given for children.

When summer came and the Moscow theatre season ended, Anna Brenko was unwilling to have a break in continuity; she took the theatre in Petrovsky Park, and the whole company lived happily in *dachki* nearby. They decided to do a Molière play with the Maly actor and teacher Fyedotov to direct it.

This " summer filial " was a success, with scarcely ever an empty seat; and it was resolved that the new theatre having established itself was entitled to enlarge the auditorium and the stage too. But alas ! that was not to be.

Different accounts are given of the reasons for the closing of the Pushkin Theatre when it had just registered itself in the public mind. Yuryev, the great Leningrad actor, calls the whole venture Quixotic.[23] Beskin, in his monograph on Yuzhin-Sumbatov, says it failed through the inexperience of Anna Brenko.[24] There seem to have been several contributory causes. One was the high salaries paid. In March 1881 Alexander II had been assassinated, and all places of entertainment were closed. Glamá says that Anna Brenko, with Melkiel behind her, continued to pay salaries in full. This, if true, would soon place a very heavy burden on the theatre's finances, which no amount of full houses could quickly get rid of.

In the ordinary way, no doubt, the Melkiel millions would have stood the charge as quite a minor item. But Melkiel went bankrupt. He seems never to have known just how much money he had, and the final touch that landed him in court was the collapse of a stucco balcony which he had had fixed on the façade of his palace, thereby ruining the architecture. It was in the shape of a huge conch shell, and projected over the street below. Inferior material seem to have been used; and many injuries were caused to passers-by when it fell. The claims so raised, combined with other debts, perhaps through Nina's extravagance, put help from Melkiel out of the question, and the Pushkin Theatre, as such, came to an end.

Anna sacrificed what money she had, and her husband went on with his profession and his contributions to the *Russian Gazette*. But poor Anna's misfortunes did not end there. Her husband died shortly after, leaving her with two small sons. Volodya, the younger, became a working-man's lawyer, and had a hard struggle. He died soon after the Revolution. Zhozya, the elder, was abnormal from birth, and caused his mother much suffering and anxiety. As he grew up his abnormality became violent, and he died during a paroxysm in his mother's arms. Anna Brenko abandoned her brilliant life in Moscow, and went to Kiev. There she continued her theatrical work, organising a school of acting which turned out many well-known artists. But she had too clear a mind and too complete a personality to be a mere fashion. Years before the Revolution she gave Russian theatrical history another turn by starting the first free acting school for working-class amateurs; and in the winter of 1905 she showed on the Moscow stage a production of *The Storm*, in which every part except old Kabaniha, which she played herself, was taken by a factory worker. A year had gone to the preparation of this.

It was a success, and the company toured the Moscow neighbourhood, giving performances in mills and works of different kinds.

When the Revolution came, therefore, the sixty-five-year-old Anna welcomed it as part of what she had always been working for, and with her company of workers she set out on a tour all up the Paveletsky railway from Moscow to Ranenburg. In 1924 her fiftieth year of stage work was celebrated by a special performance of *The Lower Depths*, staged in the Korsh Theatre; and the newspapers were full of her praise. The theatre poet Gilyarovsky, who had played small parts at the Pushkin Theatre, wrote:

> . . . And I remember her in years of trial,
> When though she was so young a woman, yet
> Snowed in her hair the grey streaks of denial,
> Witnesses of strife, and bitterness, and fret;
>
> And recognise her in the workers' places,
> Speaking to them of art in their own tongue—
> What sparkle in their eyes and on her face is!
> And Age's voice comes fluently and young.
>
> She calls a people from their darkened living
> To goodness, beauty, truth, in act and thought.
> Your whole self to the service of the people giving,
> Your dreams are now alive in those you taught.

THE THEATRE GOES DOWN THE VOLGA

It would have been a pity if so fine an enterprise as the Pushkin Theatre had disappeared entirely. It did not. Burlak got the survivors together in a company called the Russian Actors, a *tovarishchestvo* or Commonwealth, to tour the perimeter of the known Russian cultural world down the Volga. He was himself a Volga man. Burlak was not his real name. It means

" Volga Boatman ". And though the son of a landowner, named Andreyev, at Simbirsk (Lenin's birthplace, now called Ulyanovsk) he ran away from home to become a Volga Boatman. In time he rose to be captain of a river steamboat ; but there were so many Andreyevs in the same position that they had the name of their craft stuck on, Highland fashion, Andreyev-*Olga*, Andreyev-*Holy Mount*, Andreyev-*Mississippi*, and Andreyev-*Burlak*.

One evening at a club he was telling his friends stories of his life on the river, and doing it with such gifts of mimicry, that the manager Rasskazov, who happened to be there, got up a show for him to tell his stories in character. So great was his success that Rasskazov recommended a professional career which Andreyev began at Saratov, calling himself Andreyev-Burlak.

This Commonwealth toured all the cities on the Volga from Rybinsk to Astrakhan, and then crossed over to Rostov-on-the-Don. It is to be noted that it would not occur to anyone at that time to go across the Volga. Indeed, if they had done so there would have been nowhere to go to.

Rybinsk was a dirty little commercial town with a summer theatre made from an old wooden show-booth and a winter theatre where these players performed. It had two Circles and good acoustics ; oil lamps, of course ; and dressing rooms that were adequate but uncomfortable. The audience was unaccustomed to shows that started on time, and the stalls did not fill till half-way through the first act ; but the second night was sold out.

Yaroslavl received them with crowds at the station, because there were close business ties between Yaroslavl and Moscow, and many of the locals there knew the Pushkin Theatre and had told their friends. In many Russian towns the railway station was a kind of town club and meeting-place ; and amateurs sometimes gave shows in halls built at the station.

At Nizhny-Novgorod Burlak was greeted with open arms. At Kazan both he and Pisaryev were almost on their native ground. The manager at the Kazan Theatre was soon to be a great Imperial actor, Lensky, who made the first attempt to break applause during a scene and even refused end-of-act curtain calls.[25] The audience here was still not Tartar, of course. It was mostly Russian merchants, loaded with jewellery but barely able to sign their names.

Samara, Saratov, Astrakhan were all good theatre towns. At Astrakhan, however, the audience ate nuts and threw the shells about noisily during performance. At Tsaritsyn, now Stalingrad, the Commonwealth called on the resident company, who were giving a very poor show, not knowing a line of their parts. " The costumes ", records Glamá, " were pitiful, and the sets beggarly." But the management was not beggarly. It was making a fortune, and paying the actors next to nothing.

Novocherkassk they found with a fine theatre, and Rostov with several.

And so Ostrovsky reached the outer edge of Russian culture ; duly and properly so, for in 1856 he had been on a Commission of authors sent at the behest of the Ministry of Marine to study conditions of life and work among the fisherfolk and workers in the Volga shipyards. And he had gathered a lot of material during this trip, which he used in plays like *The Storm*, *The Girl Without a Dowry*, and *The Ward*. And now here were his thoughts coming back in their most expressive and careful form, and the awakening of the provinces had begun.

PRIVATE ENTERPRISE TAKES OVER

Meanwhile in Moscow, thanks to the abolition of the Imperial monopoly in March 1882, private enterprise had got busy. An entrepreneur called Korsh, whom we have already mentioned, had taken theatre premises in a former house of the Rimsky-Korsakov family, and arranged to bring back to Moscow most of the ex-menbers of the Pushkin company. He was calling this the Russian Dramatic Theatre. Nearly all of them joined him in August, though the committee no longer existed, and all were subject to the will of Korsh.

Korsh was a good business man. At first he kept the policy and repertoire much as before, but he wanted to attract the minor officials and master craftsmen of Moscow ; so he put on matinees at reduced prices. This filled the cheaper seats, but in time affected the choice of plays. Burlak and Pisaryev were for continuing and developing the Pushkin Theatre line ; but despite their wishes, a vaudeville was tacked on to the end of a five-act play, as was the custom in the old-fashioned theatre. The stress thereby fell again on the " entertainment " value rather than on the author's view of life. And promptly the standard fell.

Korsh moved to new premises in Boguslovsky Pereulok, and revised his policy entire. He gave piquant light comedies now, with a tendency to farce ; [26] because, as he said, he wanted a theatre for Moscow's merchants. Ostrovsky wrote of him, " With Korsh, actors get ruined ". And his stars began to seek other constellations. Those who escaped joined the Imperial companies, because there was nowhere else to go. The iron hand of private enterprise had not taken long to rust.

Yet to Korsh must go the credit for having done several new and interesting works : the first Chehov plays, for example, *Ivanov*, *The Bear* and *The Proposal*. But at that time Chehov's stories were all the rage, and there was little risky or enterprising in trying out these innocuous works. It was a commercial move, and no loss to him. All his moves were commercial ; and so successful that he remained in business for forty years.

Another private entrepreneur was Lentovsky from the suburbs. He opened his " New Russian Dramatic Theatre " in luxurious premises in the Hermitage. He was his own producer, and far more seriously interested in the theatre than Korsh. He looked for a new unit, with new authors to write plays for it. He encouraged initiative among the actors, and had real artists to design the sets and costumes, of the finest silk and velvet. He borrowed singers from the Imperial theatres, whose productions he quite outshone in magnificence. His orchestra pit held the best musicians in Moscow. To him, too, goes the credit for the first use of electric light on the Moscow stage ; which Korsh made permanent throughout his Bogoslovsky Theatre, thereby precipitating a revolution in make-up. The Maly went on using gas.[27]

Lentovsky also took an intelligent interest in the stage crowd ; and was in many other ways a pioneer. One old melodrama he staged in the style of the oleographs then becoming a collectors' fashion all over Russia. And one of his productions was said to have made much more out of the play than the author had done. So that Lentovsky can be called one of the first modern producers on the Russian stage. But for his ventures into new values he had to pay heavily. Having made a fortune of several hundred thousand roubles, he lost it all, and died in poverty in 1906. The iron hand of private enterprise had already begun to throttle personal enterprise.

OSTROVSKY IN THE IMPERIAL THEATRES

The break-down of the Imperial monopoly was not enough by itself to free the theatre. But it energised the Imperial ones. Innovations, as we have seen, had never been popular at the Maly ; but Ostrovsky's plays got themselves done there. This was largely due to the actors, Prov Sadovsky and Muzil. The majority of his plays were performed only because individual actors and actresses chose them for their benefits, as was the case with many famous plays, *Hernani*, chosen by Goryev, *Uriel Akosta*, chosen by Yermolova, or the first Ibsen to be seen in Russia, *The Warriors of Helgeland*, which Fyedotova chose.[28] And this was true even after Ostrovsky's death, when his work was kept alive only thanks to similar action by Mihail Sadovsky, Olga Sadovsky, Rybakov, and others, till the public got so used to them that they began to like them, and then to demand them. The reason for the popularity of Ostrovsky's plays among these actors may have been that they liked to act in them. Not only the stars, but the second and third line of actors and actresses, who had little " direction " in the foreign classics and were not good enough to " create " parts without direction, found in Ostrovsky something for them to work on that was within their experience of life.

(Not that there were many foreign classics done. But the management became aware of this lack of skill in the lower ranks, and courses were included to improve it.[29] This, though unintentionally so, resulted in the break-down of the isolation of the stars, and so made ensemble more important. It also made the foreign classics more easily available.)

Ostrovsky himself seems to have been quite indifferent as to how his plays were staged in the matter of costume, scenery, make-up.[30] What mattered to him was that the words should get across in their full significance. For he admitted that he heard, rather than saw, his plays while writing them.* This made them easy to speak, and therefore easy to learn, as there was no contradiction between thought and phrasing.[31] In fact, so closely did Ostrovsky listen to the life around him, that almost everyone of his characters, and on this all the Russian critics agree, has a speech habit of his or her own, thus adding a phonetic differentiation of people to the manners differentiation of Griboyedov or Gogol.

This demanded a new attitude from the actor. The prevalent fashion was to regard stage speech as a kind of cursive script, the speaker being recognisable as himself, not in character, by his vocal handwriting, with a rising inflection at a comma, and a fall at a full stop.[32]

But in the Sadovsky family Ostrovsky found actors that could use and express this dramatic material. " It was largely due to the Sadovskys ", writes a biographer of the family, " that there was an Ostrovsky Theatre as well as an Ostrovsky Drama." For in place of the naturalism of Shchepkin these players gave a realism which one writer has found fulfils the definition of Engels : " fidelity in the rendering of typical characters in typical circumstances ", only the types were " reflections of different single representatives ".

That Ostrovsky entered, posthumously, the Maly permanent repertoire was chiefly due to Yuzhin-Sumbatov,[33] who succeeded Lensky as Director of the Maly in 1909. Himself a famous actor and moderately successful dramatist, Yuzhin was brought up, like his schoolfellow Nemirovich-Danchenko, in a liberal Russian colony in Georgia, under the influence of the broad but weak " Back to the Muzhik " school of philosophy. He wrote some fifteen plays, mostly well-made, craftsmanlike, actor's plays, with a nicely rounded and graded part for everybody, but not very much significance for anybody, and with the conservative framework of type-drawing and strong curtain lines. As a director, though, he was important. He expanded the Maly tradition away from romanticism and toward a deeper psychological understanding, though he could never accompany the Moscow Art Theatre in its journey to " inner realism ". On the other

---

* Even to the length of pronouncing them aloud in his study. On a first night he would listen from the passage behind his box, so as to hear without seeing.

hand, he could not put up with symbolism or mysticism and the pathological decadence of Sologub.*

Some sort of realism was also being evolved in the gentlemanly manners of the Alexandrinsky company. For Mamont Dalsky, a very emotional actor, was able to maintain the tension of an audience in the most extraordinary circumstances. When playing Strindberg's *The Father*, for example, in the scene where he decides to leave home, Dalsky turned his back on the audience and communicated his inner anguish and mental condition by shoulders, nape and back, *for five minutes* by the clock, without speaking. After having suffered for participating in the 1905 Revolution, this actor turned anarchist in 1917, but came to a violent and ignominious death the following year, when he was run over by a tram.[34]

In Peterburg, too, private theatres sprang up, the Aquarium from which a Barnaï production had the distinction of being transferred to the Alexandrinsky, or the Paradiz Theatre, where the Italian actor Rossi appeared in 1890. But the fashionable theatre at this end of the century was still as it had been at the beginning of it, the Mihailovsky, French theatre. The best designers and constumiers still worked only for the opera and ballet, which the court still attended.[35] And the Alexandrinsky, though its audience could appreciate a melodrama by Ostrovsky, did not want plays with a comment in them, and got none, except the time-honoured untruth that the life and relations of the classes are fixed for ever, and anyone who tried to get out of the station in which it had pleased God, and the Tsar, and all the Tsar's *chinovniki* not only to place, but to keep, him, was heading for certain ruin.

* Fyodor Sologub, b. 1863, a lesser Baudelaire and more poetic Wedekind. His play, *Loves*, showed a girl faced with the choice between a bridegroom and her own father. But there was a certain force in his neurotic methods.

CHAPTER V

STROLLING AND TOURING PLAYERS

ARTISTS OF THE ROAD

Frustrated at first by Imperial officialdom alone, and later by private commercial enterprise as well, the metropolitan theatres had small hope of improvement. Conditions were adverse. The little band of improvers at the Maly had not made their name through Europe ; indeed, the Russian theatre had fallen behind the rest of the Continent. Duse, on tour, was horrified to hear that Imperial artists had to learn a new part every three weeks at the outside. She, as she told Glamá, learned only one a year. And if that was the case in Moscow, what can the hopelessness of the provincial actors have been, who had to learn five new parts every week ?

Not that private enterprise was wholly bad ; of course it gave scope to men of initiative. N. N. Solovtsev (1857-1902) went to Kiev and Odessa with his wife and a few friends and brought a new effort into the theatre there. N. N. Sinyelnikov (1850-1939), who had done some production as well as acting for Korsh, raised companies in Kiev, Harkov and the cities of the south.[1]

And there was a feeling of freedom, a possibility of freshness, a direct contact with the audience unobstructed by officials, for the provincial rank-and-file. But this freedom, as we will be seeing, contained within it the seed of exploitation and poor conditions.

During the nineteenth century in Russia as in many other countries, the great mass of actors and actresses were looked down upon by respectable people. The men were regarded as affected, conceited, untrustworthy and liable to disappear without paying their debts, and the women as little better than harlots. It may be true that a lifetime of acting sometimes disintegrates the personality in its deeper ranges . . . a strong, definite character finds it difficult to be continually behaving as if it were somebody else. Especially is this true where the behaviour springs not from study and understanding so much as from habit and convention. And certainly it is true that the economic situation of the actress in most countries drags her through temptations which even strong characters find hard to resist. But for all their faults, moral or artistic, the players of the Russian roads were valuable, and in most cases honest, people.

Rejected as a class by society, they joined the Bohemians, living irregularly from hand to mouth, on a low, simple level, here to-day gone to-morrow, light of heart, attractive. It was what many artists were doing at this period all over the world. The word "art" was often on their lips.

A fine picture of them is given by Vladimir Gilyarovsky in his memoirs, *Theatre Folk*, completed in 1935 when he was 82. He had been a small official's son, born in the forest near Vologda where the bears still prowled, and his life reads like a Dickens story . . . or, perhaps better, a Gorky book. Indeed, as in a Gorky book, so it is sometimes difficult in his, to distinguish fact from fiction. Like Burlak, he ran away from home to become a Volga boatman (this would appear to be the little Russian boy's equivalent at that time to the little English boy running away to sea) ; he became a cadet in a military school but found the discipline and low standards intolerable and was expelled with what he calls "a real genuine bitch of a passport". This debarred him from any decent employment, and being a natural gymnast he became a turn in a circus, transferred to various legitimate stage companies he came upon (under a stage name, and often having to leave hurriedly both company and town, to avoid being recognised and having his papers challenged) ; developed a talent for literature, turned journalist, and ended up his long and active life in a position of great respect in the U.S.S.R., a very colourful portrait of him being painted by Gerasimov, sitting in his garden beside a plate of strawberries, an enormous figure in white striped cap and shirt, with a red cummerbund wrapped round a monumental pair of trousers.

He gives us many vivid pictures of these strolling players and provincial repertories ; the little theatres often in flowery gardens, the artists toiling wearily across the steppes, sometimes in tumbledown hired conveyances, sometimes on foot, sometimes even in costume. The experiences of Charlotte Charke, Colley Cibber's eccentric daughter, who spent most of her life dressed like a man to avoid a debtor's prison, is no stranger theatrical figure than some of these Bohemian folk.[2] Society men, it is true, like Prince Imeretinsky, under the stage name of Zvezdochkin, might join them for a while, partly for something amusing to do, partly from real love for the stage. He even became a manager for a time, commercially, on three occasions ; and went bankrupt, and retired to Tambov, where he appeared occasionally.[3] But in the main these were professional middle-class players.

In the second half of the nineteenth century our view of the landscape alters. There is much more movement, though still retained by the rampart of the Volga, over which no one crosses. Not only these strollers, but the peasants, emancipated, and not quite so inexorably tied to the soil they were born on, are given passports * and permitted to move from places in the poverty-stricken interior. They can come south to the fertile

* Every emancipated peasant residing out of his village commune had to renew his passport every year with a poll tax of 3 roubles (George Hume, *op. cit.*, p. 140).

areas and be extra labour at harvest, until, that is, the introduction of harvesting machinery by British agents reduces the chance of a job. And then they come as tramps. But they are much more on the move.

Rich local families, on the other hand, are not. Distance and discomfort of travel tend to isolate them. The womenfolk do not even go to the cities to shop ; fashions come to them in the baggage of milliners, shoe-makers, dressmakers, travelling from estate to estate, and given hospitality at each while they ply their trade ; together with less elevated pedlars, mostly Hungarians, who bring with them all kinds of goods from cheap prints of saints and heroes to superb Oriental fabrics.[4]

These are useful and regular visitors, known to the local families ; stage people are not, though the landed gentry will go in to the theatre as a treat if it is likely to be really entertaining. Stage people get used to this suspicion and contempt ; but there is little hope of stopping it. Selivanov, at a meeting of them in 1886, spoke eloquently about the posi-tion of provincial actors. For this he was refused an engagement at the Maly, in spite of his success there as Chatsky in *Woe from Wit*. " To breed politicians in the Imperial theatres is forbidden ", ran the reason for the refusal. Thenceforward Selivanov stayed in the provinces. The Secret Police saw to it that he never entered Moscow professionally again.

PROGRESSIVES IN THE WILDERNESS

There were many like Selivanov, able, clear-thinking men, who because of their independent thought were kept on the fringes of their profession. Among Gilyarovsky's colleagues in his first company was Izorin.[5] His real name was Nikolay Petrovich Vysheslavtsev, and he had been working as an actor in Paris. A man of a political awareness that did not end in words, he took part in the Commune of 1871. Not a very prominent part ; he is not mentioned in Frank Jellinek's book. But one of the name-less heroes who survived, and were tried. He was not shot, only because he happened to be a Russian citizen of a well-known aristocratic family. He was expelled from France as a criminal ; as a criminal his name was entered in the secret list circulated in official quarters ; and he was forbidden to reside in the capitals or Government centres of the whole Empire.

Consequently he took a stage name and worked only in the provinces, where he was generally known as " The Jacobin ". A picturesque and attractive person, he always wore a cloak by day, which he used as a counter-pane at night. He had acquired a Gallic grace on the stage, which together with his fluent French and knowledge of French manners was a great asset in the performance of French plays ; and these, as we will see, were not few.

His was the central figure in a picture Gilyarovsky draws of a company *en route* from Morshansk to Kirsanov.[6] In that part of the Tanbov district the steppe is partly wooded, and the journey was not as intolerable as many journeys were. The company had a success at Morshansk, especially Izorin, who had been presented on the last night with a silver cigarette-case (costing 10 roubles) inscribed " To the superb N. P. Izorin from Grateful Morshansk ". Through the sunny streets and out into the open country they drove in a *telega*, a kind of cart. In the fresh morning breeze the windmills with which the steppe was dotted whirled their sails. More *telegi* came towards them, laden with grain for these mills. The actors waved to drivers, and the drivers stood up, doffing their peaked caps and waving back. They remained standing, open-mouthed, staring at Izorin in the eighteenth-century wide-brimmed headgear of Schiller's Karl Moor, and at the tall young actor beside him, putting on comic expressions in a glittering red and yellow brocaded shirt and a full-dress hat with a scarlet band and a cockade, such as only a duke or a general would be wearing. This young actor was a tailor's son, who had just run away from home to become an actor. In three years he would be playing Hamlet at Penza.

Izorin had filled his cigarette-case with two tens of " real " cigarettes, bought for the purpose before leaving Morshansk ; but these had soon been consumed, and out in the steppe he managed to get some mahorka, which he rolled in strips of an old part and smoked in his usual manner, humming the Marseillaise.

Another man of independent thought was Andreyev-Korsikov the prompter,* who had been a Narodnik, and for that offence was expelled from the Alexandrinsky Theatre, and from Peterburg.[7] Vasily Vasilyevich Vasilyev, too, whose real name was Shvedevenyev, had been expelled from Peterburg in the round-up after the affair of the " Blind Men's Commune ".[8] Pisaryev rescued him from utter beggary and got him on the stage. He still went about with a copy of the *People's Will*, the organ of the Narodniks, in his pocket.[9] But perhaps the outstanding example was the famous Nikolay Chrisanthovich Rybakov.[10]

Moscow made Rybakov an angry and frustrated man for twenty years. For twenty years he visited the famous " White Hall " in search of a Moscow engagement. This was a cross between an actors' club and a hiring fair, a very large room in a hotel known as Barsov's, standing near where the Moscow Central Children's Theatre now is.[11] Every actor in the provinces gravitated hither sooner or later, to get his summer or his winter season fixed up. Those who had been presented with gold watches and chains by grateful audiences would be continually consulting the time and

* A specialised and honourable calling in those days, though a dusty and unhealthy one. The Russian use of the prompter is the continental one, a continuous undertone. The comedian Goryev at the Alexandrinsky in the 'eighties seldom bothered to learn his part, but merely followed the prompter and his own fancy.

muttering imaginary appointments, so as to display these acquisitions, partly from pride, partly as evidence of their qualifications.

In the 'seventies there had been an alternative place for the hiring, the Shcherbakov restaurant in Kuznetsk Square, famous for its fish-and-rice patties at 50 kopecks a portion, with a bowl of broth thrown in. This closed in 1881, and the actors used to gather at other cheap restaurants. To such places actresses could not with any decency go, and their chances of meeting managers were limited, until in 1882 Lentovsky, having been a provincial actor himself, threw open the foyer of his theatre for the purpose, and here, of course, actresses could be seen with perfect propriety.

Rybakov had at last appeared at the Maly, in *Hamlet* and *Ugolino*.* It was a successful first appearance, but official correspondence about taking him on the staff dragged out for years, and Rybakov went booming his way through the provinces as before, and frequenting the White Hall. When he did return to Moscow it was to the popular theatre, as a friend of Ostrovsky, who wrote *The Forest* not only for him, but also partly about him and his friend the comedian Kazakov.[12]

The pick of those frequenting the White Hall were engaged only season by season, by Medvedyev for Kazan, or Lauhin for Oryol, Novikov for Samara, Smolkov for Nizhny, or for Yaroslavl Smirnov, the ex-stage-lamp-lighter who married his manager's daughter and inherited a theatre. Conditions and terms varied according to the characters of the managers.

CONDITIONS IN THE PROVINCES

Some managers were honest, some were not. Some were in the business for profit, some for pleasure, some for art. Some insisted on contracts, harsh in their terms, others had no contracts at all.

The harsher contracts treated the actors like slaves, as did that of Voronin at Ryazan. It contained 66 clauses, of which the last ran : " The management reserves the right to terminate the efficacy of the contract without further obligation when symptoms of pregnancy are noticeable in any actress ". There were fines for lateness at rehearsals, fines of a month's salary for failure to appear, fines for disobedience, dismissal if the artist " fails to please the public ". Pay was withheld if illness lasted more than three days. And so on. But even the less stringent terms could be, and often were, so worded that the apparent obligations of the management were nullified in fact ; benefit nights guaranteed might be made to yield very little to the beneficiary, because the manager might sandwich in a large profit to himself as part of the expenses, or the cost of providing parts or music would be charged against the actor, although the paper itself

* A drama, by N. A. Polevoy (1796-1846), a Siberian merchant who became a literary critic and pedant. He also wrote novels.

remained the property of the manager.[13]   And even the wording of the
contract in general might be so involved or so ambiguous that the actor
was delivered into the power of the management without protection or
redress.[14]

At the end of a season some of the luckier members of the company
would receive invitations to return for the next season ; the rest would
depart and join any other company within reach.   On the other hand,
the strolling players, who had no contract, tended to be a permanent
nucleus, generally a family connection, with some semi-permanent ac-
quaintances attached.   Father would play leads and be the manager, mother
would be leading lady or Character Woman No. 1, daughters and sons
would play juvenile leads in descending order by age, and so on.   Round
these would gather cronies whom nothing but death would part from the
little unit, tied by gratitude perhaps for some ancient kindness.   And often
the standard, it seems, was quite high.   Long use, modest aims and utter
sincerity in their personal lives wove them into an ensemble which was
lacking in the snobbish Imperial or the more reputed repertory theatres.
On the other hand, this ensemble was easily broken and repaired.   In case
of sickness, there might be no understudies and a complete stranger would
be taken at his own statement that he was an actor, given a part, perhaps a
lead, into which he walked in his own clothes, played it without rehearsal
but with success, and might stay in the company playing other parts, until
the day when he walked out of it and was seen no more.

Grigoryev's company was just like that.   It contained ten regular
members, bound by no written contract, with no " conditions " other
than good feeling and stage custom.   They toured the Fairs and the little
towns in an unpretentious way, taking *Revizor*, *The Robbers* and even
Hamlet, in versions specially cut for ten performers, which demanded
much doubling and many scrambled changes of costume in the wings.
Rehearsal was replaced by continual use and kindness and determination
when, as every now and then, a new-comer had to be worked into the
repertoire.   But Gilyarovsky says that the performances went smoothly,
almost with no need of the prompter.[15]

Sometimes they would receive special invitations.   Once, for example,
they spent a happy Easter in a little township on the Volga called Borisoglyebsk, which formed one-half of what we would call the Borough of
Tutayev.   In those days the big linen mills had not yet been established,
and the inhabitants were famous for making sheepskin coats worn by
peasants, and also as market-gardeners.   A rich cattle-dealer had built a
big house for use as a " guest house " and this contained a hall useable as
a theatre.   He was in Tambov for the horse-races, where his own blood-
stock was competing, when the Grigoryev company were playing there ;

6

and he was greatly taken with them, though somewhat furtively, since he was a young man, and his mother, of whom he was mortally afraid, disapproved of the theatre. The company was in financial difficulties, and he lent them money, which was entered in his accounts, with the connivance of the company's book-keeper, as hunting expenses, to show to his mother, e.g. :—

> Crocodile-offal ointment, for hardening hoofs, from Paris
> and London . . . . R. 300
> Blinkers, so that the horses may not take fright and bolt ;
> for 12 horses, R. 20 each . . . . . . R. 240
> and so on, to the total . . . . . . R. 12,528

What his shrewd old mother thought of hunters in blinkers is not recorded.

Anyhow, at his invitation and expense, the company went to Borisoglyebsk, being put up in luxury at the guest house, and enjoying a pleasant Easter holiday in the fine spring weather. Ivanov, the rich patron, had bribed the Old Believers * and narrow old women who swarmed in the house not to let his mother know what was really going on.

The company gave ten shows in the little theatre, and on the eve of their departure Ivanov threw a party for them, which the local worthies attended.

It was a pleasant life in fine weather. Travel was a long picnic. They all slept out, side by side, in a rough tent, in case it should rain. Dinner and supper were much the same meal ; they lit a fire, boiled tea, cooked potatoes lifted from fields as they passed, as a variant of their staple food, millet and buckwheat. Or sometimes they could buy a special treat, ham, or eggs, or mutton.

Sometimes they journeyed by train, more usually goods train ; especially in winter. Single actors in those days favoured either goods trains, or travelling " deadhead ", that is, slipping under the seat in a passenger train when the guard or the police came round.

And acting was very pleasant in summer too, in garden theatres. The wooden houses of old Russia were so inflammable that a fire once started could engulf a whole town. Theatres, therefore, where fire was always a possibility, had to be built isolated from other buildings. Even to-day in the Soviet Union there are regulations that a new theatre building must be 10 metres away from any adjacent structure.[16] So that most theatres had alleys in which the audience could walk during the intervals, as at Voronezh, where there was also a square in front of the theatre, with a fountain round which ladies could gather to display their party frocks.

In Morshansk the garden was filled with fruit-trees, on which a two-storied building, where the actors lived, looked out. Here married couples

---

* A sort of Wee Frees.

had rooms to themselves on the first floor, and unmarried people by sexes shared rooms on the ground floor in twos or threes. All met for meals in the common dining-room, to which each brought individual plates and eating utensils. The stars had silver spoons—Presentations, no doubt, from grateful audiences ; the more humble members used wooden ones. Madame Grigoryeva and her daughter Nadya managed the catering, and spent their free time making the garden fruit into conserves for the winter. " On Sundays ", Gilyarovsky recalls with a simplicity that is almost descriptive, " there was always Pie."

But often they had to tramp the countryside, and that was not so pleasant, for it implied a bad financial condition, and that implied low spirits, and the weather was not always fine. Yet no amount of hard weather, hard luck or hard living dismayed this little company, nor hundreds of other little companies like it. Nor did neglect ever dim, as Gilyarovsky says, " the unquestioning awareness of theatre folk that they were people apart. And they looked down from the heights of their shadowy greatness upon well-fed citizens as people beneath them."

In one sense, perhaps, they were right.

STANDARDS OF A PROVINCIAL AUDIENCE

Some of the permanent provincial theatres had quite high standards. The three University towns of Harkov, Kiev, and Kazan maintained the demand of their more intelligent audiences through the century. Yermolova and others of the Maly stars toured them, with several plays in their repertoire. Shakespeare was popular here. And Strepetova writes that in the 'seventies the best provincial theatres were eight in number : the three already mentioned, and Odessa, Tiflis (Georgia), Voronezh, Rostov-on-Don and Saratov. But of course even cities like Kiev had variable theatres. Kiev, indeed, had no theatre till 1857 ; then it had two, one for opera and (rarely) plays, the other officially called the общедоступный (or Accessible) but generally known as the Bergonnier from the French circus proprietor who had built it. This latter stood near the University Quarter and was much patronised by students. Its most famous director was Savin, a very " correct " man, who left the actual stage work to his régisseur. Savin was shrewd. He invited Glamá for a season when she was little more than a beginner, and made her play within the same week a part just played by Strepetova . . . a rivalry that was a good Box Office draw. The repertoire was undistinguished, being mainly translations from mediocre French and German plays. But the audience was always keen, and used to strew the stage on first nights with bits of paper " thick as a snowstorm ", on which were written love letters, poems and invitations to the actresses.

Savin also ran a theatre in Zhitomir, which was a very different place.

Zhitomir was a theatrical curiosity. In the 'fifties it had no theatre building ; and the Imperial Government in one of the strange unthinking impulses that it had from time to time to act and organise, little matter how or what, had drawn up a paper scheme for endowing certain provincial centres with entertainment. They built a very fine theatre at Zhitomir, entrusting the running of it to the local authority, with an annual subsidy of three thousand roubles. However, the local authority added to its funds by pocketing this money and leasing out the premises to managers at two thousand roubles a year. Savin was one of these. He asked Glamá to make some appearances there also, in order to replenish the takings, which were in a bad way. When Glamá arrived at the fine building, she found cobwebs festooning the interior and the company in an almost literally starving condition, having pawned their clothes for food. Savin decamped soon after, leaving debts to the amount of forty thousand.[17]

Odessa, though its streets, like those of most provincial cities, were several feet deep in mud in places, was a smart Government centre and something of a holiday resort. Its theatre was open every night. But in the period under discussion it was owned by a character actor called Forcatti, who also ran theatres in Tiflis and the Caucasian spas. The standard improved a good deal when Ivanov-Kozelsky went there from the Korsh Theatre.

The theatre in Tiflis was of course a Russian, not a Georgian one. It had been organised by Yablochkin, father of the senior actress in the Soviet Union to-day. In the 'seventies he greatly improved provincial production both there and at Odessa, his special forte being historical plays, to the preparation of which he gave special care and study, especially in crowd scenes. In this man we see the ideas of the free theatres of Moscow extending, though slowly and without co-ordination, in the provinces.

But it is rather astonishing to find Yermolova stating that she found the audience at Voronezh sensitive. " How far the provinces outstripped Moscow ", she said to Gilyarovsky, when he met her again, then a famous star in Moscow, ten years after they had acted together in Voronezh. Let us examine Voronezh.

A local advocate told Gilyarovsky why it was an important and interesting place. The advocate was a daily patron of the theatre and frequently dropped in for a chat at lunch time. This particular day they were having lunch in the garden, and a sort of *ceilidh* was in progress, one member of the company giving a song, another a story, another doing an improvised study, and so on. " Voronezh ", he said, " is richer than Kiev ; and more interesting. It stands on a cross-roads, on a railway line linking both capitals with the Caucasus, and a whole lot of southern towns, so that all our best artists cannot avoid coming to it on their tours."

He had previously explained its importance as a centre for pilgrims on their way from Moscow to Kiev and back. And of course not all pilgrims were poor men . . . with the way fortunes were made, to the lament of consciences at that time. But the route round two sides of a triangle is an odd one. Still the Baroque cathedral at Voronezh testified to its religious importance, and the fertile black soil around to its prosperity. So there can be no doubt that life, for the upper and middle classes at least, was comfortable there and not too irksome.

Yermolova's judgment must be right ; and the audience had fairly good taste. For a Cathedral town it was even surprisingly broad-minded about actors' morals. When Gilyarovsky was there, the feminine leads were being played by M. I. Svobodina-Barysheva, wife of a well-known actor, and living " in sin " with Dalmatov the male principal. (Dalmatov was also an author ; he wrote a play later on called *Labour and Capital*, the title of which alone was enough to get it banned.) But in spite of their liaison these two were the darlings of the town. Usually to interest the Voronezh public, it appears, you had to have either a big name or some special tricks of your own, on which grounds Voronkov and Matkovsky who had been managers there summer after summer in turn, were held to be great masters.

Some three years previously there was a mediocre actress called Lyubskaya, who chose *Hamlet* for her benefit night and played the Prince herself. She was greeted with hisses and whistling. In Russia whistling is not the sign of excessive joy and friendliness that it is among our working-class audiences. She was a pretty, pert, person, sometimes overstepping the bounds by using uncensored swear-words, and behaving with what our loyal legitimate stage author calls " café-chantant licence ". Dalmatov fell in love with her, and they were rather ostentatiously married.

The emphasis was still on the performer, not the play. The next time *Hamlet* was given in Voronezh was for the benefit of the actor Tamara. Raïcheva, an ex-Maly actress of some provincial renown, was playing at Rostov-on-Don, some three hundred miles away, but it was rumoured that she would be coming to play at Tamara's benefit. In fact, Tamara in the usual frock-coat and the best cab in town, was visiting private houses, shops, hotels and clubs selling tickets and announcing " Money returned, if no Raïcheva ! "

Hamlet was duly performed. Gertrude and Ophelia appeared ; but neither was Raïcheva. Till the fifth act there was no sign of her. The gravedigger scene. Enter Hamlet and Horatio. Business with the skull. Ophelia's funeral. Then suddenly, enter Raïcheva in the bright costume of La Périchole from Offenbach's opera, complete with basket, napkin, and all. Tremendous enthusiasm from the public ; for Raïcheva is a famous

singer of operetta.   After telling her uncle (presumably the First Gravedigger) that she has brought his dinner, she announces her intention to
sing, and does so : Périchole's Letter song, sung well down stage, and
tumultuously encored.

Such intermissions seem not to have been uncommon ; so if Yermolova's
opinion is to be trusted as representative, then we have a guide to the taste
of the provincial audience.   It is the taste for personalities.

But we must not forget that Yermolova had a weakness for student
audiences, and the Voronezh audience was full of students ; some wore
spectacles and had serious ideas about the drama, but the majority were
gay, and only wanted entertainment.   The best entertainment is provided
by an attractive actress in whatever part.   So naturally the part is subordinated to the attractions of the actress.   When Yermolova left Voronezh,
the receipts fell.[18]

It ought perhaps also to be mentioned that it was in Voronezh that in
1879 was held the secret conference of the Narodniks at which the more
active members of this movement formed the organisation called the
" People's Will ", whose act in assassinating the Tsar two years later was
doomed, by the harsh reaction it evoked, to make its own policy impossible
in the end.[19]

Provincial Repertoire

What sort of plays did these provincial companies perform ? Of
the strollers, Grigoryev's seems by all accounts to have been fairly representative.   Every season of his opened with Gogol's *Revizor*, which was
taken by the audience more as an evening's fun than as a serious satire,
much as the middle-class London audience took the early plays of Shaw.
Krechinsky's Wedding, another comedy on the border between fun and
satire, must have been a draw, because Zvezdochkin chose it for his benefit
when managing his theatre in Tambov.   Offenbach's *La Belle Hélène*
is frequently mentioned . . . for these players were singers as well as
actors, and the repertoire regularly included operettas and even operas.
Here are some titles in the repertoire of this or other companies :

Le Gouverneur and *Don César de Bazin* (French).

The Robbers (Schiller).

Don Pedro, or The Spanish Inquisition, a home-made melodrama taken
   by Mosolov from a Spanish novel.

The Great Noble Basenok, by the imperishable and unimpeachable
   Kukolnik.

A Lunatic's Diary (after Gogol), *Arkashka*, and *The Bailiff*, all Russian
   products.

A Bitter Fate, by Pisemsky.

Lucrezia Borgia (possibly Victor Hugo's).

The Idiot, a dramatisation of Dostoyevsky.

The Mystery of Heidelberg Castle, a German melodrama.

Playbills quoted by Gilyarovsky [20] add little to the range :

At Kolomea, *The Jew, or, Honour and Infamy;*

at Oryol, *Thaddeyich the Matchmaker*, or *Robbers in Winter Hiding;*

at Ostorozhe, *The Unbiddable Boy;*

at Oryol again, *Death to the Infidel !*

Most of these blood-and-thunder creations were the work of Russian authors. They usually had high-sounding descriptive captions : thus the last-named is advertised as " A new lyrical tragedy in five epochs, with costumes from the First to the Nineteenth Centuries ". And further bait is dangled, as for our own melodramas, before each scene : " The Queen's Hunt ", " A Scoundrel's Bribe and a Father's Curse ", " The Tale of a Foundling ", " Plague ! " " The Oppression of the Jews, or A Life for a Life ! " *

This is a world of sensation, of cardboard figures in a child's history game. There is no comment on life ; nor did the audience want one. It is a mere romantic sharpening of soft emotion.

Realism in such a case is mere effect. Kazakov relates a story of his provincial days in such stuff. He was playing Don Pedro in the melodrama mentioned above, and in the course of the action had to be broken on the wheel. A huge property wheel discovered in a scene store in Tambov evoked the reminiscence. Such a sensational effect had to be shown on the stage ; so executioners surrounded Kazakov, and while he himself disappeared, by the usual trick, through a stage trap, a dummy was fixed to the wheel, and the torture began. It was in a summer theatre, and the stalls and boxes were filled with landed gentry from the neighbourhood, their servants and muzhiks standing round in great crowds. Among them, sitting in a corner at the back sharing a bench with the families of a theatre attendant and the commissionaire, were Kazakov's mother and sister. When the torturer started to turn the wheel, Kazakov's mother could bear the suspense no longer, and shrieked his pet name, " Sanka-a-a' ". Instantly a kind of " whine " ran round the audience. Ladies even had hysterics in the boxes, and so much commotion and distress was caused that the stage manager, Mosolov, had to fetch Kazakov from his dressing-room, still in costume but with no wig and only one boot on, and produce him safe and sound on the stage. He was greeted with a yell of " Forah ", " like the roar of wild animals ", Kazakov said, " gentlefolk and ordinary people together ". [21]

This was the triumph of hallucination.

---

* Such scene titles were in use on Maly bills in the 'eighties even for Pushkin's *Boris Godunov*.

How they got their Plays

The plays themselves were obtained in two ways. Grigoryev carried a little library with him ; and many a young actor learned the drama as Gilyarovsky did, studying Shakespeare and other classics in bed at night after the show, borrowed from the manager's little store. But more usually, and especially with the majority rubbish indicated above, parts were obtained from a central library in Moscow.

To be accurate, there were two libraries in Moscow.[22] But one was small, and rather recherché, serving mainly the Moscow amateurs and a very few provincial managers. The big one was run by a certain S. F. Rassohin, whose business ranged over all the provinces, including the Russian theatres in the Caucasus and other remote parts. It stocked a small number of classics in printed-book form ; but there was little demand for them. The bulk of his trade was in hand-written or lithographed copies, with separate parts cue-ed in for each player.

The copyists, known as *Pisaki* or Scribes, were mostly men of some education who had come down in the world. They were miserably paid, at the rate of 35 kopecks an act. An act consisted of from seven to ten sheets ; and not more than six or seven sheets could be written in a long day's work. So the scribes seldom earned more than 20 or 30 kopeks a day, even if the acts were short ones. The library on the other hand charged something like ten times the sum they paid their employees, a very profitable business for Mr. Rassohin.

The library had what might be called its pool in the filthy, notorious doss-house called the Rogues' Market . . . soon to become famous to the world as the original from which the Moscow Art Theatre took its setting, and atmosphere, for Gorky's play, *The Lower Depths*. Here in flat no. 6, on the first floor in an outlying wing, was a very large room divided in two by an open screen of planks. One side was inhabited by the down-and-outs, the other by Rassohin's scribes, working sometimes the whole night through in an air foetid with sleep, sweat, tobacco smoke and lamp smuts. Those not working would be lying on benches round the walls, covered with their verminous rags. Conditions next door were rather worse. Many an old player ended his days there, outcast even by his own profession. And one of the most moving incidents in Gilyarovsky's book is where, in the ragged and downfallen but defiant figure of one of the inmates, he recognises the once gallant rebel Izorin. He had no chance, however, to speak with him, for Izorin was asleep (or seemed to be), and when Gilyarovsky returned a month later, he had disappeared again.

Copies and parts so made might be sent out and used over and over. Although there was little in the way of production, each user of the part would mark-in moves or instructions in different coloured pencils ; and because summer audiences like shorter plays than winter ones do, there would be cuts and restorations, by no means identical for each user. And as there were so few rehearsals, it was an advantage to a budding player to memorise as many parts as possible, permanently, so building up his own repertoire to be drawn on at a moment's notice.

This is good training for an actor, and doubtless for this wandering theatre there was much to be said, as self-discipline and experience, not to be found in the long runs of our own West End theatre, nor in the single-play companies that tour our provincial cities on circuit.

But, indeed, from any other angle the standard was horribly low.

PRODUCTION STANDARDS

Scenery, for example, was generally canvas back-cloths, a few strips and borders, and nothing more. Sets stood for almost any scene in any play. Even Hell would be the same in *Death to the Infidel !* as in *Orpheus in the Underworld.*[23] That is a picture of souls being boiled in cauldrons, with devils piling firewood below, and in the midst Beelzebub sitting on a throne among his retinue. There was no " truth " here . . . not even stage truth. But another kind of truth was once revealed to the Governor and his circle in Ryazan, when the front tabs opened, or rather, rose, to display the faces of himself and his underlings portrayed to the life, by a few strokes added at the last moment before the overture began, in the faces of the lords of Hades ! Even the police inspector was recognisable, with his forked beard, sizzling in one cauldron, and the handsome chief of the town in another, while half the local worthies stood round the Governor himself on the throne of Beelzebub.

Lighting continued very late to be by oil lamps. Vilna in 1879 in its converted, fortress-like Town Hall had gas for both stage and auditorium, but that remained a rare exception in the provinces.[24]

Costumes and properties were amateurish. The most important qualification for a " lead " was his or her wardrobe ; * [25] but that was for contemporary plays. Provincial audiences did not expect the " real thing " in period plays. Actors ought to wear a paste-board crown and carry a wooden sword ; and as it was only make-believe anyway, there was no objection to the same dummy being held by robber, prince, Roman or Khan. Many a show, too, was spoilt by the meanness of the management in this respect. Smolkov at Nizhny-Novgorod was staging *Mary Stuart*. As they had no means of representing the execution properly, and Smolkov

---

* Compare in Britain *The Actor's Handbook,* quoted by Allardyce Nicoll (*XIXth Cent. Drama,* 1800-50 (Cambridge, 1930), Vol. I, p. 49). " A good stock of tights, boots, hats, swords, etc., etc., often procures a young man an engagement when he could not obtain one on his merits."

did not wish to spend any money on it, the poor Queen of Scots had to be shot with a pistol !

There was never any time to give care to the staging. Nor was it worth while to do so. New plays were given at Vilna, for instance, four times a week, and seldom for more than one performance.[26] Thus not only was it not worth while to take trouble, but the supply of good plays soon came to an end, too. Hence the majority of rubbish. At Vilna the audience was mostly Russian *chinovniki* and their families and Army people. A few Jews were allowed in, and a few Poles came, because there was nowhere else to go. Polish speech was persecuted in the street and notices in Polish forbidden. The more patriotic Poles boycotted the Russian theatre for this reason. On the other hand, on days of special celebration, like that of Public Thanksgiving for the Tsar's Escape from Assassination, the Governor-General himself attended in state with all his motley crew.

As these provincial places became used to theatre-going, they developed a snobbish " taste ", which responded to the lavishness of the commercial managers in the matter of spectacle. From ecstasy at a fine performance, the audience went over to ecstasy at a fine effect. This had a serious result on the fortunes of the strollers, who could not compete with commercial managers. Their " art " became unprofitable, and finally unliveable. The strollers found rents too high for their reduced means, and had to take any pitch they could find, even in one case an executioner's scaffold.[27]

Gilyarovsky has left another unforgettable picture of a company of whom three members were his old friends.[28] They were arriving in a small town in an ancient carriage covered with dust from the steppes, and possessed of just enough money to buy vodka for the even thirstier journey to Simbirsk. One still carried himself like a man of fashion, with a monocle in his eye ; and all spoke bravely of the " business " they would be doing in that Volga town. But the refrain that echoed in Gilyarovsky's ears as the squeaking axles died away in the evening twilight was what one of them had muttered to himself : " God grant us something to eat ".

So in time the strollers disappeared. Some left the profession. Others joined the commercial racket. Yet others sank lower, to show-booths at Fairs, where amid roulette-tents, houpla, clowns and men with snakes round their necks, they played *Yerusslan and Lyudmilla the Fair* twenty-three times in one day ; and spent their Sunday evenings with drunken old hags, who, from the depths of degradation, could still recall their Ophelias. . . . " What are you laughing at ? I'm Lanskaya, d'ye hear ? I'm an actress myself. I'm an old drunk now, but I'm Lanskaya."

For even in its decay the theatre still calls to its children ; and as the author remarks, half in sympathy, half in derision, " Applause in a show-booth is still applause ".

A Theatre in Ice

The theatre is still Empire-bound west of the Volga. The actors do not yet cross that river. Yet the theatrical impulse is a human thing, and we cannot expect no sign at all beyond the rampart. In the furthest parts of the Empire, as earlier in the century, utter loneliness and unendurable conditions of climate make ordinary Russians exiled for their humanity tremble for the health of their minds. We now find them getting up amateur theatricals in the terrible arctic winter.

I. W. Shklovsky, who spent four years in Yakutia, living in native huts, dressing in furs, eating frozen fish (which was all the Yakuts had to eat in the winter, and even their hip jam was boiled with fish-fat instead of sugar), describes such an entertainment got up by some exiles, most of them Tolstoyans.[29] At Christmas 1890 in Srednye Kolymsk, on the Kolyma, within 200 miles of the Arctic Ocean, someone discovered among the philosophical books they had brought with them from civilisation a play written by, or founded on a story by, Saltykov-Shchedrin ; hence, presumably, satirical. They took a hut somewhat larger than the others in the " town ", which was used as a reception centre for such inhabitants as wanted shelter ; whether the ice-window had fallen out of their own hut, or the roof-aperture had caught fire, or whether they just felt lonely, they could take their deerskin and sleeping-bag and doss down on the floor in this large hut.

The exiles made their curtains of rugs and coloured paper (brought with them into exile). Uniforms were hinted at by soaking paper in red ink and covering buttons on their ordinary clothes with this, and stitching on facings of red calico. Lighting was by ten candles, obtained with difficulty, as the locals used only palaeolithic crusies and fish-oil. Make-up was provided in the most original method on record. One of the exiles actually sacrificed his own splendid black beard, out of which moustachios were shaped.* Tooth-powder was used to grey the head. The bell rang thrice, in the correct professional manner before the curtain opened. It had been borrowed from the harness of a dog-team.

But this was entertainment purely for the other exiles. There was no room for any " natives ". The only thing approaching an indigenous drama took place at midwinter. Nominally the Yakuts were Christian ; that is, they added a few Orthodox saints to the spirits of Fire (a talkative little old man in red fox-skins), of various mountains, of small-pox (imported by the Russian traders with syphilis and the saints) and others of

---

* Perhaps not showing the lack of vanity one would think. Native women (who, Shklovsky says, were not bad looking under their dirt) thought the Russians hideous, having hair on their faces, like dogs ! Arctic peoples are bearded only in extreme old age. A smooth face might thus compensate for disgusting blue eyes.

their own deities ; but their religious ceremony at Christmas was confined to lighting a candle-end (specially kept for the purpose), saying " Christos " rather severely several times, and blowing the candle out. Then they made off to a grand mumming in fancy-dress, visiting each other at home and overhearing the future by listening-in under the body of a horse.

In Yakutsk itself, the chief town, this procession was just beginning to become a kind of impromptu folk-play, with various local officials being impersonated in costume and couplets . . . the policeman, the judge, the exciseman, and others. The Governor's house itself was visited, and re-freshment duly imbibed after the fashion of guisers the world over. Unfortunately the Christmas that Shklovsky was passing through Yakutsk on his way home, the party had been all too well refreshed, a new and bolder verse being added at each stage of the procession till by the time they reached the Governor's residence, one character, the " General ", was parody-ing in no very pure-spoken way the very words used by his original. The Governor was scandalised ; and next day the police sought the offenders. These went into hiding ; but came forward of their own free will to apologise. Instead of being exiled, as they feared, to some terrible shanty down the Kolyma, they were merely put in prison for a few days. The Christian spirit was feeling merciful. But an interesting development of native drama was lost for ever.

MAXIM GORKY

Such then is the Russia we see below us in our bird's-eye view at the end of the nineteenth century. At first, all was static ; and there were slave theatres. Then the localities wake up, with free and expert players gradually winning the people of the neighbourhood to come to the theatre. A freer flow of people, now, from place to place ; but all is still very quiet in the landscape. To quote a letter of George Hume :

"Industry, progress, eduction, all sleep ; and looking out of the carriage windows at the vast expanse of snow, the mind naturally receives the idea that it is the counterpane of a sleeping nation." [30]

In this sleep the theatre provides a place to admire the skill of a performer in ; it is not a place in which to expect, or to find, truth. Even the great performers of Moscow and Peterburg do not seek to render truth, except in their own persons, and through existing conventions. The few ex-ceptions struggle against officialdom and intrigue. Two things must happen before the theatre in the provinces can become true : life in the provinces, on the one hand, must be worth taking an interest in ; and the art of the provinces must become more genuine, more interested in life, breaking the old standards of performance. But this cannot happen till the central theatres, where the best artists go, give the lead.

And now there comes into our landscape a gigantic figure who understood these things, and though he did not write from inside any theatre,
like Gogol or Ostrovsky, was none the less destined to have a tremendous
influence on the Russian, indeed the whole Soviet, theatre. A figure in
world literature whose work is still ludicrously unknown in our countries
. . . Maxim Gorky.

In the 'nineties Gorky was still in his twenties, known to a widening
but small circle for his short stories, and earning a few roubles by pithy
articles in the local press, first at Samara, then at his birthplace Nizhny-
Novgorod, now called Gorky after him. These articles ranged over
nearly all the arts and carry as much sociological comment as local editors
ever dare to print. And from his reviews of the theatre there, during the
winter of 1895-6, we get a picture of a typical local company and of a
typical local audience.[31]

The theatre, he says, is the one diversion in town, and in the monopoly
of a Mrs. Molgacheva, who brooks no rivals. The interests of the locals
he places in the following order : (1) Theatre, (2) The Fair, (3) Cycle-
racing, (4) Puppets, (5) Professional whistlers. The citizens, whom by
a pun he constantly calls " Mustard-pots ", " have an organic hatred of
anything that smacks of culture ". Hence the theatre has to cry down
its best wares. *Don Quixote* is given the sub-title, " Was He Saint or
Simpleton ? " The theatre seems also to charge by length, like a draper.
An epic production of Tolstoy's *Power of Darkness*, which lasted from 8.30
till half-past two in the morning, required benefit-night prices to be paid,
though it was nobody's benefit ; in spite of the fact that both audience and
company got very sleepy, and were half-suffocated by the smell of gas.

Partly the company was to blame if the audience was bored. It was
run by the leading man, Sarmatov, and it often came under Gorky's
scathing Russian sense of humour. One play, *The Prodigal*, by Stebnitsky *
he reviewed as if he had seen a pile of worn-out puppets wake up and try
to throw each other out of the window, Punch-fashion. For even good
plays were ruined. Schiller's *Robbers* was dull, even in old-style acting ;
and the audience laughed in the most dramatic places. Boris Godunov,
he diagnoses, obviously died of constipation ; and the vaudeville that
followed this event was played by a couple that had no gifts whatever for
so skilled a type of show. In Sardou's *Madame Sans-Gêne*, the actress playing the name part was certainly Sans-Gêne, which the audience liked ; but

* In reality, N. S. Lyeskov (1831-95), a reactionary novelist who viciously attacked all progressive movements as leading " Nowhere " (the title of his most
notorious book) ; and relying on a kind of religious mush to get mankind resigned
to the troubles its governors were inflicting on it. The antitype to Gorky, whose
favourite ideological Aunt Sally was this very idea of " the comforter ".

otherwise " on the stage there were a few actors who talked and moved
about a bit ".* Of reality, or of the team-work that made a possible base
for reality, there was not a sign.

Yes, there was one sign ; and it is important in its implications. It
came in Potehin's play, *The Evil of the Day*. A. A. Potehin (1829-1908)
wrote several plays about real life, from a rather naïve protest against serf
law to a study of the real *muzhik* as opposed to the literary idea of him.
His characters were greatly helped by the way Martynov handled them.

The benefit night of a young actress Lodina. She gave a performance
notable in itself ; for so moved was she that the reality of her behaviour
galvanised the rest of the company. That old ham, Sarmatov, Mrs.
Prokofieva, the prima-donna soubrette Petipa, the comedian Hoffmann,
all suddenly came to life. They really played to each other for once in
their lives ; and came off the stage feeling as if they had lived, not acted.
" The performance ", says Gorky restrainedly, " went with an ensemble
far from frequent on our stage." Lodina had a divine spark.

Two years were yet to elapse before a company would be formed that
was to blow mutually on its divine sparks, and was willing to learn that
ensemble as the essence of good acting. That was to be the Moscow Art
Theatre, and young Lodina, then in Nizhny, was to beg Gorky to get her
into it. I do not think she ever got there ; I can find no trace of her in the
years that follow ; but the Moscow Art Theatre was to have a tremendous
effect on such provincial companies as that in Saratov ; and so was Maxim
Gorky. But not until life itself had changed for the majority of men and
women in Saratov and elsewhere.

Gorky, tramping Russia and Siberia, writing books in which the lives
of men and women are so vivid and strong that it is impossible to tell fiction
from memory ; studying, and understanding people of every kind from the
drunken outcast to the millionaire ; and their womenfolk ; and getting
to know the millions of the Russian Empire as personal friends, noting in
his undimming memory exactly how they spoke and walked and suffered ;
the clothes they wore and the hopes they had ; Gorky summing up his
experiences in direct and objective thought ; Gorky the novelist, reporter,
art critic ; the consummation of realist literature after more than a century
. . . this is the man on whom more than any other the future of the
provincial theatre is to depend. As yet he cannot write for it. There is
no audience to hear him ; no theatre to carry his truth, if there were an

---

* This actress was a member of an illustrious stage family descended from a
French dancer of the eighteenth century (Petit Pas = Petipa). The Soviet actor
Radin was an illegitimate scion of the same stock.[32] *Mme Sans-Gêne* had been first
produced in Paris in 1893. Sardou's fortieth produced play, and still ten to come.
Actually a re-hash of a play about a *vivandière* by Emile Moreau.

audience. That audience did not enter the theatre till the workers and peasants entered their own theatres; and they could not enter, till by a paradox of the kind history is so fond of, the Moscow Art Theatre had educated the middle class, and parted from Gorky, and come to its own truth almost despite itself.

The pivot of our story is now this Moscow Art Theatre; and in setting it down, we will find that the sacred emblem bird on its grey tabs is certainly a bird of the sea, but more like Gorky, the Storm Petrel of the new world, than the dead gull of the old world, the seagull Chehov's Treplov shot.

CHAPTER VI

THE SEAGULL AND THE PETREL

WHY THE " GORKY " MOSCOW ART THEATRE ?

In Appendix I of this book will be found a list of Soviet theatres which bear the name of some notability connected with their work or the districts they serve. The list is not complete, but it is indicative of the types of notabilities attached. Two things are at once obvious : the great popularity of Gorky, shown by the frequency of his eponymous appearances ; and the fact that the premier theatre of Russia, the Moscow Art Theatre is named for him. Now many British readers and playgoers may be surprised at the choice of Gorky rather than of Chehov in this position ; for Chehov, most of whose plays are known to them, seems inseparable from the Art Theatre, while Gorky, few if any of whose plays are known to them, seems to have had very little to do with it. One of the aims of this chapter is to show that on the contrary though Chehov did have a close relation with the Art Theatre, Gorky had an even more intimate one, and that further, of the two, Gorky had more importance to the Soviet citizen as a great author responsible for the development of this theatrical unit.

The position cannot be understood without tracing in some detail the first development of it, in which both authors had a share.

The Moscow Art Theatre was the outcome of an eighteen-hour, non-stop, all-night session in a restaurant called " The Slavic Bazaar " in 1897 between Vladimir Ivanovich Nemirovich-Danchenko, a successful play-wright, and Konstantin Sergeyevich Alexeyev, who came from a family of keen amateur actors and had made quite a reputation as a brilliant if untrained amateur actor and producer under the stage name of K. S. Stanislavsky.

NEMIROVICH-DANCHENKO AND THE OLD-WORLD THEATRE

Nemirovich-Danchenko had by that time written six successful plays [1] (he wrote eleven in all) : *The Wild Rose* (1882), *The Dark Forest* (1884), *Ultimate Freedom* (1888), *A New Line of Business* (1890, generally thought his best, and confirming his fame as the successor to Ostrovsky who had died in 1886), *Gold* (1895), and *The Price of Life* (1896), which won the " Griboyedov " Award for the best play of the season. It was an innovation in playwriting, for as Nemirovich himself in later years pointed out, partly in pride and partly in humour, it contained a suicide at the beginning instead of at the end. The people in these plays were nearly all middle class—literary men, lecturers, young officers, and so on ; but he developed one theme which Ostrovsky had overlooked, the conflict between the generations, and the relation of fathers and children.

How successful he had been ! Actors and actresses of the Maly Theatre regarded him like Ostrovsky as their own dramatist, and chose many of his plays for their benefit nights. Muzil chose one for his first benefit after the death of Ostrovsky, whose plays he had always chosen before. And once a Nemirovich play was wanted by two players at the same time, a conflict resolved only by personal appeal to the Director of the Imperial Theatres. (This official at that time was one ready to let anybody at Court interfere with theatre policy, even the Tsar's mistress.) [2]

They were written in the old style ; Nemirovich himself tells us with not much pride and not much humour that in the third act of *Ultimate Freedom*, he had supplied one dramatic exit for Muzil, two for Fyedotova, and three for Nikulina. He had not yet reached the point of approximating stage truth to truth of life.

At the end of the eighteen-nineties, however, on the recommendation of Yuzhin-Sumbatov, he was appointed to teach at the Philharmonic School, the only alternative in Moscow to the Imperial School. He had come to see that if as author he was faced with the problem of putting truth on a stage which was not disposed to have truth on it, at the same time conscientious actors were faced with the same problem in their work ; there were no plays to be truthful in, except those of dead men. At the Philharmonic he found that the younger people were not unwilling to pioneer. Eight years he taught there, producing his pupils in some of the first Ibsen plays to be seen in Moscow. Among them was Olga Knipper, who had left the Imperial School, where she had made little impression and shown little ability to acquire the technique of the conventional style of acting. She seemed doomed to an obscure career in the provinces. In fact she was destined to become Chehov's wife and one of the leading actresses in pre- and in post-revolutionary Russia. Another pupil was Moskvin. He left before the others did, and began a career in a touring company. Roxanova and Meierhold were in the class too, Meierhold already showing gifts as a producer with " ideas ".

Teaching is the best way of learning. In 1891, though Nemirovich was still writing plays that could be acted in the old style, we find him beginning to agitate. He demands dress rehearsals. The first proper dress rehearsal in Russia took place in 1894-5. The play being his own *Gold*. Also he wanted fresh, colourful and theatrically relevant sets. In these and other first steps of the professional reformer, he was supported by Lensky, by now head of the " New " Theatre, that is, the Maly Filial we have already mentioned. Lensky had been lamenting the decay at the Maly of the Shchepkin tradition in life-like acting and the Gogol-Ostrovsky tradition of truthful plays. In 1897 he spoke at the Conference of theatre workers on " The Causes of the Decline of the Theatre " (see chap. III, note 13).

So Nemirovich was not alone. The Meininger company had few good actors, and their ensemble was to them of more importance than deeply truthful individual acting ; but their visit to Russia in 1885 had shown all serious artists of the stage that art could be true to life. That both that art and that life in Russia were false was beginning to be seen by the more liberal-minded of the intelligentsia ; but because of the prevailing conservatism of the *chinovniki* controlling the established theatres, and of the lack of funds among poor professionals to found a private theatre, it was not yet possible to express real life at all. Nemirovich went on hoping and planning and getting his ideas together.

STANISLAVSKY AND THE OLD-WORLD THEATRE

The situation was improved, once again, by help from the amateurs. In 1897 Stanislavsky had reached much the same conclusions as Nemirovich but by a different line of thought. Both men have left autobiographies (before his death Nemirovich had used his vacation in Georgia to write a second volume, not yet published) ; and although Nemirovich pays higher tribute to his colleague than Stanislavsky does, it is not easy to get rid of the impression that for all Stanislavsky's superb showmanship, his magnificent presence, his gifts as actor and producer, his (so rare !) ability to profit by his own mistakes, nevertheless it was the modest little Nemirovich-Danchenko who was the real brain behind the Art Theatre.

Stanislavsky's family was, like Anna Brenko's, well-to-do. In 1888 he had spent a good deal of the money he had inherited while still very young in part-founding and finding premises for the Society of Art and Literature in Moscow, which was to stage amateur and other shows for the delectation of an upper middle class and minor aristocratic audience. This audience had already been organised by Fyedotov and F. P. Komissarzhevsky. The former was father of the Maly actress Fyedotova and himself a well-known theatre figure ; a progressive, too, in some ways, who had tried to improve Maly *décor*. Beltzev, the designer, had done some special sets for the Maly production of the Ostrovsky play about theatre life, *Talents and Admirers;* but that was as far as scenic reform had been taken. Komissarzhevsky was the father of Vera Komissarzhevskaya, and also of Theodore Komissarzhevsky, known to London, Stratford and American theatre-goers as an *émigré* producer and theatre historian.

Stanislavsky started with operatic ambitions, and had always to struggle against a certain operatic tendency in his acting ; Komissarzhevsky had trained his voice, and Fyedotov had helped him in his rather haphazard and unguided study of acting.

THE MOSCOW ART THEATRE IN THE OLD WORLD

When the Society failed and was reconstructed on a subscription basis, Stanislavsky became its producer, though he still worked in the family business. Among the amateurs he produced in his spare time were Samarova, Lilina (his wife), Luzhsky, Artem and Alexandrov, all later to bear famous names. He himself was still learning what good acting ought to be. He had started on the first of his quests, for truth, honesty, freshness, instead of convention, make-believe, and rule of thumb. Seeing that good acting must spring from the life round him, but that this demanded self-discipline, study, and the end of the star system, and that these in their turn demanded a complete reform of stage conditions, he had to see also that piece-meal reform in spare time could achieve nothing. Hence, when Nemirovich approached him [3] with a suggestion that they might together explore the possibility of opening a new theatre entire, he was more than excited.

The money for the new venture was not put up by Stanislavsky, as is sometimes said; he had nothing like enough for the purpose. It was raised, after futile search for a Melkiel, and equally futile application to the Town Council, by subscription. The opening of the subscription list and the fashion to subscribe were largely due to the approval given by the new Governor-General of Moscow, Prince Sergey Alexandrovich, who had been instructed to reconcile the Moscow aristocracy with the merchants, and thought this a good way of doing it. Nemirovich he knew as a responsible playwright, and Stanislavsky he knew from some fashionable amateur theatricals he had been asked to produce as a change from routs and balls.

The history of the Moscow Art Theatre was like that of most minority ventures.[3a] Despite a very favourable start, it got into financial difficulties almost at once, and would have closed down but for the donations of Savva Morozov, a rich merchant, a rough, self-made man, but personally interested in practical details of stage work, lighting, and so on. When his family had gone to the country, Morozov and the two co-producers would try out new ideas in his house. It was he who helped to construct the revolving stage (one of the earliest in Europe) for the new premises in Kamergersky Pereulok, which he assumed the chief financial responsibility for building in 1902. The parallel (and the differences) between Morozov and Melkiel are striking.

The two co-producers had arranged that they were to be equals, sharing production. But Nemirovich-Danchenko as an author was to have the

last word in what concerned " content ", while Stanislavsky, as a more or less experienced actor, was to have the last word in " form ". An excellent arrangement . . . on paper. But sooner or later a clash was bound to come ; for Form and Content are only aspects of the same thing, and cannot be practically nor permanently separated. It was a Chehov play *
which brought this fact to light, and which also reconciled the two men. For who shall say in a Chehov play whether a stage effect like the chirping of a cricket is Form or Content ? Production here becomes authorship also, just as the relationship of the characters is also a matter of stage position.

Both men were reticent and loyal to each other. But differences of opinion did arise, and it is legitimate to guess that Nemirovich yielded courteously as often as he could . . . and got his own way in the end.

He was without doubt the intellectual superior. Stanislavsky was not interested at the outset in new drama. He was interested in new ways of doing what existed. When his new way of naturalism became estab-lished, he grew tired of it and pioneered on other quests, for newer and better ways. Also he developed a rather flabby kind of spirituality, because he wished art to be beautiful and at the same time to spring from life ; but life was not beautiful.

CHEHOV IN THE OLD WORLD

Before we can explain Nemirovich's position, we must consider how Chehov fits into this first phase of the Art Theatre. Chehov described himself as first a physician, then an author, and only thirdly and incidentally a playwright. He wrote for the stage only late-ish in his literary career. He repudiated the idea that he was out to reform the theatre, though he did express a wish that the Russian theatre of his day were more of a literary one, and from his youth had hoped to help to make it so. We should remember that he had made his reputation as a writer of sensitive, reticent, observant, profound, subtle short stories. Casebooks of human souls.

There was no room for dramatised work of such a kind in either the Imperial, the metropolitan private or the provincial theatres. Neverthe-less his first long play, *Ivanov* (the name would be Smith in England or Wilson in South Scotland), though still slightly adhering to the old-fashioned, was an 1887 study of real people, as in those short stories. He realised, as Nemirovich explains, that an old-fashioned actor coming to the word " rogue " in his part would enunciate it in such a way that a round of applause would be certain, thus giving it a theatrical value, whereas Chehov, not being a professional playwright, was not working in theatrical values, but in those of human speech and relationship. So he did not give

* *The Seagull.* As a matter of fact the point at issue was the interpretation of the character Nina.[4]

this play to any Imperial theatre, but to the Korsh Theatre, where Davydov was then working.

It was not a great success; and this, in a private theatre, as in one of our own Repertories, meant it was a failure. Chehov let several years pass before he wrote another play, *The Wood Goblin*, which he gave to a new unit called the Abramova company. This play also made little impression. Several years now went by before he wrote *Uncle Vanya*. He disliked people saying that this contained bits of *The Wood Goblin*. It was first played in the provinces, by a touring company.

The Seagull, on the other hand, received its first performance at one of the Imperial theatres, the Alexandrinsky; though what possessed Chehov to give it to a Peterburg theatre, and to the most old-fashioned of the Imperial ones, I do not know. It was, as Chehov might have known it would be, a dead failure, hissed and dismissed as the crazy product of a literary man's study, who, for all his clever fiction, knew nothing about the stage.

Chehov resolved not to write another play if he lived 700 years. It was Nemirovich who saw what Chehov had intended in *The Seagull*, and persuaded him to let the Art Theatre revive it.

Stanislavsky was not greatly taken with it, as a play; it offered him little in the way of production points and the company few chances to "act".[5] But Nemirovich had mentally earmarked Chehov as one of the writers of the day whose work he wanted to try out, though he admits Chehov's name was not actually mentioned in the first eighteen-hour talk.

At Nemirovich's suggestion, *The Seagull* was the fifth play of the opening season, a risky experiment with fortunes going the way they were. But with world-famous results. The excitement caused by the opening play was revived, a telegram with the audience's congratulations and the theatre's thanks was sent to the absent author, and the financial position of the Art Theatre was for a time restored to health. The directors were emboldened to try another Chehov, and asked for *Uncle Vanya*. Chehov refused. He made excuses. He had already promised it to Lensky and Yuzhin at the Maly. However, the Theatrical and Literary Committee which now controlled that theatre under the Imperial Director for all Russia, required certain changes in the third act. Chehov was not disposed to make them. The Art Theatre could put the play on as he wrote it. He gave it to them. Perhaps he realised that this queer theatre could help his reputation. He changed his attitude. He would not even let the Peterburg actress Yarovskaya have *The Seagull* for her benefit night, on the not quite truthful grounds that it now "belonged" to the Art Theatre. Nor would he let the Alexandrinsky do *Uncle Vanya*.

The expedition of the Art Theatre to perform *inter alia* his two plays

to their author at Yalta had as its secret object, as Stanislavsky tells us,[6]
that Chehov should be persuaded to write some plays specially for it. He
did so. But like *Uncle Vanya* they took some time to establish themselves.
The old reproach that Chehov was no writer for the stage was gaining
ground. Lunacharsky found *The Three Sisters* enervating, because although
there were kind and wise people in it, they seemed to have no wish to take
action against the cause of their misery. As for *The Cherry Orchard*, even
Chehov was dismayed by its treatment. He had at first intended to write
a farcical comedy about a silly old provincial woman who never had any
money, and when she had it, gave it away. Lopahin was to be a rich comic
part for Stanislavsky, now an irresistible comedian. In the first version
this was so ; and many remains of the first intention were brought forward
into the play as we know it to-day . . . disconcerting the unwary producer
in all lands. Chehov forgot this change. Petulantly he wrote to his wife :
" Nemirovich and Stanislavsky see in my play something absolutely
different from what I have written, and I am ready to bet anything you
like that neither of them has once read my play through attentively ".
And he demanded to know why it was advertised as a drama, when he
had described it as a comedy.[7]

We need not take this libel too seriously. The world continues to see
in the play what the two directors saw, and Chehov really did respect the
Art Theatre. At its suggestion he made alterations and emendations in
his scripts. These may be studied in Stanislavsky's Producer's-copy of
The Three Sisters; [8] and changes were similarly made in *The Cherry Orchard*
and *Uncle Vanya*. Coming from Stanislavsky, the suggestions for alterations were mainly scenic. Thus it was inconvenient to have Tuzenbach's
body brought on at the end of *The Three Sisters* without a proper crowd
scene. Such a scene would cause too much disturbance to the quiet ending
by its necessary noise of boots ; and the scenery left no room, anyway.
Chehov agreed to the end as we now have it. For the Art Theatre and
Chehov had fused. The agent was Naturalism. Intense eloquence of
detail was the art method used by both. Stanislavsky relates that in a
moment of depression, with the morale of the company breaking down,
and everyone puzzled by *The Three Sisters* in rehearsal, a mouse scratched
during a silence, and this showed him how to produce this play.

And Chehov had realised that this theatre alone would consider, and
could express, what he wanted to say about life. But he was beginning
to tire. Half in jest, he threatened to write a play in which he could call
attention to the fact that " the action takes place in a country where there
are no gnats, crickets or other insects to prevent people from talking ".

And Stanislavsky's quest for newer ways, his hunt after " inner truth "
was taking him to the point where what a man is thinking and feeling is

less important than the way he expresses this. For unless the content is pointed, unless the position of any character is shown in relation to other people through his and their words and acts, then " inner truth " short-cuts human content and is related only to super-human, mystical, im-aginative " ideas ". These can be shown on the stage only by shapes and objects which the character approaches or recoils from, and so on, till the value becomes formal and not human. So we follow Stanislavsky through the plays of Andreyev, past the studio on Povarsky Street, where he and Meierhold collaborated, to the demand for " sculptural gestures and musical speech ". And lacking an intellectual base, a technical advance becomes a retrogression in meaning.

Stanislavsky, after the return from the first tour abroad, deserted nature. He was interested in the " unreal " theatre. He staged symbolic dramas by foreign mystics like Knut Hamsun and Maeterlinck, and did up Dostoyevsky. With Meierhold he experimented in deliberately stylised productions. He studied Gordon Craig, and invited him to Moscow to direct *Hamlet*. Craig went back to Florence leaving sketches and in-structions for the show, and it was discovered that his designs were impracticable, and so far as they could be realised they would dwarf the meaning out of Shakespeare. Finally, Stanislavsky fell under the spell of Sulerzhitsky.

Sulerzhitsky was an idealist, a follower of the Simple Life doctrines of Tolstoy in Tolstoy's old age. He was small, muscular, vivacious, sym-pathetic and a sufferer from kidney disease. He was painter, musician, literary man, and a kind of hobo. He had gone to Canada with the Duhobortsi * and stayed there with them two years. Now he was living in a railwayman's cabin, desperately poor, and often spending the night on the Moscow streets. The Art Theatre gave him various jobs to do, because it liked him. Everybody liked him ; and soon he was teaching the students, and teaching them so well that when he left to found a com-munity of his own in the Crimea, several of them went with him, abandon-ing their stage careers. In different degrees of simplicity and discomfort they lived, building primitive dwelling places, an object of puzzled interest to the summer visitors who made excursions to see " the wild students of the Moscow Art Theatre ".

In all this instability and crankiness, in all this running away from the real problems of life, Stanislavsky was travelling in a circle. Each new quest showed him that for the actors' sakes alone, whether in naturalistic, formalistic, " unreal " or any other stage surroundings, a greater serious-ness, an " inner truth " was necessary. And with characteristic honesty

* A religious sect which, like the Quakers, refused military service. The name means " Spirit-wrestlers ".

he describes the characteristic application with which he set himself to elaborate this into a " system ". A system of acting, for actors, and limited to the assimilation of the inside life, of which the words and acts supplied by the author were only hints and sketches. In this way Stanislavsky hoped to bind the physical reality of the stage with the spiritual reality of Russian life.

We cannot here trace in detail the way he perfected this system, first of all on himself (it spoilt his acting for the time, till he had perfected it), next trying it on the supers, then with Sulerzhitsky's help on the pupils in the Adashev school, and finally, not without much opposition, on the Art Theatre company. What is important is that Nemirovich-Danchenko had arrived at the same point independently, and for reasons far deeper than the relevance or truthfulness of acting ; reasons, indeed, which go far down into the nature, and far out into the future possibilities of Russian theatrical art. In fact, of Russian society.

Nemirovich was sent to Rome to get authentic detail and " atomsphere " for *Julius Caesar* (1903) ; he wrote in a letter to the critic Efros who attacked that production : " True, Shakespeare made many a mistake from the angle of historical detail, but the spirit of the historical occasion in this case, and of the events going with it, is grasped with an astonishing psychology of human history. In this lies the centre of the tragedy, and not in separate persons." [10]

This is a big step forward toward not inner and subjective, but outer and objective, truth. With Stanislavsky questing after naturalism, however, the content still had to miss its chance. Mosquitoes and the correct width of a toga stripe have to be handled by experienced masters if they are to express the psychology of human history in Shakespeare's head. It is important to bear this attitude in mind, when comparing Chehov with Gorky.

CHEHOV AND GORKY

Chehov was a doctor, but himself a sick man, morbidly sensitive to suffering. So sensitive, that in some of his work he seems to be torturing himself. Compared with his stories, which describe all classes and types, the principal figures in his plays have a limited range. Any company that can perform one of his plays can perform them all. They are drawn on much the same formula, with much the same figures out of middle-class country residences. The same sort of events happen, or fail to happen, to them all. Within this narrow range, he created people whose silences are more poignant than their speech, who live like invalids each in a world of his or her own exaggerated symbols, giving an irrational meaning to everyday sights and sounds and things. So, not unlike Ibsen, when he deserted the particular for the general, he arrived at general symbols, the seagull, the cherry orchard, like the wild duck and the master-builder's tower. For this reason the characters acquired a false spirituality, not unlike that very spirituality which Stanislavsky was to find after Chehov's death in " inner truth ".

Certainly, within this narrow range there are people who can glimpse a better life than the one they are forced to lead, a fairer world to come " when everybody will work ". But the glimpse has no effect upon their lives, except to point their nicer natures and give them a progressive out-look. Hence a misty, wistful impressionism, like some of the Debussy preludes. And for the same reason . . . that both Chehov and Debussy were speaking for the leisured, semi-cultured classes, without larger vision. And just as Debussy is improved by being played as if extempore, so Chehov's plays were improved if treated naturalistically. But the content of neither is enlarged thereby.

Gorky also was an established author when he came to write for the stage, which he did at Chehov's suggestion and out of admiration for the Art Theatre. He also was an invalid, but he had lived tough. His tough life left him with a great pity for suffering, and a great hatred of it and of the causes of it. He was so great a lover of mankind that he could hate well.

He, too, in most of his early plays, which sometimes resemble Chehov's in formula, took the middle classes as his material. But with what a differ-ence ! He had ideals, as Chehov had ; but they were ideals of heroic people in heroic action. As long as heroism was romance to him, he ex-plored folk-lore. When heroism was seeing the truth about society and asserting it against those who evaded it, he showed this happening on the stage. So he shows the middle class robustly in his plays, why they are what they are ; and creates characters who challenge their right and need to be so, and who go into action for a better life and a fairer world. Gorky repeatedly objected to the complication " when the inner world of a man becomes for him and for the writer portraying him the only reality, an end in itself ".[11] His very first play, *Meshchane*,* contains in the young man, Nil, the very first real revolutionary on the modern Russian stage.

Which brings us to the vital difference between the two. Chehov's plays were just speculations, safe, only describing, not threatening anyone. Gorky's plays provoked thought and discussion, threatening the security of some lives because of the insecurity of others ; they disturbed the not disagreeable blindness and languor of middle-class art ; and they got several theatres, including the Moscow Art Theatre, into trouble.

* The title has been rendered *The Middle Class*, *The Smug Citizen*, and *Philistines*, the last being the most usual ; but it is open to the objection that the term can be used without any implied reproach. A character in another of Gorky's plays uses it proudly of himself ; and it was a frequent noun of description. Gorky seems to use it of an ethical condition which was a class symptom, but could be acquired by any class.

This was because they were truthful, outwardly as well as inwardly. They showed men's souls in contact with men's surroundings as well as with the Universe and theories about the Universe. They showed a new kind of heroism.

GORKY IN THE OLD WORLD

Gorky's plays may be seen in three groups : those written before the abortive 1905 Revolution ; those written during that revolution and the dark years after it ; and those written (these are few) when Soviet ways of life had established themselves, but Gorky had other work to do. Nearly all have middle-class matter. The class is treated with great understanding and emotion, although its position and power, and abuse of that power, are never lost sight of. Examples, more or less at random, are a poignant scene in *Dachniki* * where a bewildered young man declares his passion and desperate need of an attractive, but equally bewildered middle-aged woman, who, he believes, can save him from spiritual ruin ; or the no less heart-rending scene in *Barbarians* (1905-6) where a husband informs his devoted wife that he can get along without her very well, and she tries pathetically to find the right words to show him he is making a mistake. But Gorky makes it clear that there is another side than just sympathetic understanding. Other characters (in *Dachniki*, for example, which in some respects is almost a deliberate use of Chehov's formula and incident to correct Chehov's perspective) attack their own class, knowing and showing a way out of their miseries, and taking it themselves. Once these have spoken, the issue is joined. There is no mere debate. In *Dachniki* this is the basis of the action and its climax. In *Enemies* (1906, but not produced in Russia till 1933) class warfare has become specific. The younger generation brings it to the surface among the grown-ups, and reveals it to itself by inviting a worker to a meal in its very respectable home during industrial " unrest ". From now on, Gorky is committed to a line that must actively make the ruling class his own enemies. Understanding them made his indictments more true and more powerful.

The cultural cruising of the Art Theatre was bluntly ended by this declaration of war. True, it had originally opened as a people's theatre, the " Accessible Art Theatre ", like the theatre at Voronezh ; and in early years it gave special performances for workers, limited in number because the authorities limited the number. These *chinovniki*, though it counted

---

* English or American titles : *Villa Residents, A Country House, Summer Folk, People with Country Houses.* Nearer the mark would be *Week-Enders*, since the professional classes in Russia hired villas in the country for their families to spend the whole summer in, while they went to and fro. There were, and still are, whole areas of such " country cottages ".

as a private theatre, used to pay tactful visits, and recommend, in the friendly way used all over the world by middle-class officials to people of their own class, that the directors might " go slow " on this. They did not go slow ; and this was due partly to Nemirovich, and partly, odd though this may sound, to the purely artistic principles which made Chehov recommend Gorky to Stanislavsky. *Chinovniki* might suggest sticking to matters of art, and avoiding politics ; but if you are going to perform a naturalistic play naturalistically, and the play has a sociological, not to say socialistic, content, then your performance must have a sociological content whether you wish it or not, and will only not have a socialistic one if you sacrifice your artistic principles and " cut " it, politically. Gorky's brain, surveying his world sociologically, laid bare the class war.

In those days there was a fourfold censorship : separate censors for publication and for stage performance, the common censor, and a special censor of public entertainment, on the advice of which last the *chinovniki* made their friendly visits. Now Gorky's first play, *Meshchane*, was licensed for publication, but not for performance by the Moscow censors. Its first performance was accordingly given in Peterburg, at the private Panayevsky Theatre, when the Art Theatre was giving a short season there in March 1902.

Peterburg was in an uproar about Gorky. His election to the Academy had been countermanded by the Tsar himself. One Prince had protested against this insult to a distinguished author ; and another, a Minister of State, had joined issue with him. Feeling ran high ; and gendarmes and plain-clothes policemen were stationed inside and outside the building. The first night roused a storm of applause and abuse. Gorky was not able to be present. He had been exiled to a little place called Arzamas, where the play had been written, and read, at least in part, to Nemirovich who had gone there for the purpose, and was greatly taken with it and with its author.

In Moscow where the ban was lifted, so that it could be performed to a subscription audience only, and the play appeared the following autumn, feeling was not so high. Perhaps the Moscow Ostrovsky public was less susceptible to truthful but painful dramas, or perhaps less susceptible to insults at literary prestige. Or perhaps reading the play first in the sixty thousand copies that had been sold, had rubbed off some of the poison. In any case the satire of the middle class though pointed was not deadly. Not even Nemirovich was yet ready for this.

It was performed more as a study in personal relationships among people who had dramatic liveliness and human roundness, but were not necessarily significant of any social movement. A provincial citizen tyrannises over his timid wife, his son, his daughter, and his foster-son. The daughter, a school teacher, is in love with her foster-brother, Nil. She takes poison and nearly dies. Nil renounces a " good match " which his father has approved of, and marries a local seamstress. Peter, his foster-brother, a radical student who has been rusticated from the University, is in revolt against society, as Nil is. He, too, upsets his father's plans by going off with a prison governor's widow who had found convicts preferable as society to the smug middle class. The daughter, left alone in the house, hammers out wild discords on the piano at the final curtain.

Gorky's second play, written at about the same time, was done by the Art Theatre a couple of months later. With *Uncle Vanya* and *The Three Sisters*, it was among the five plays given by the Art Theatre in Germany in 1906. The Russian title means " On the Bottom ", but it is known in Britain and America as *The Lower Depths*, *In the Depths*, or *A Night Shelter*, usually the first.[12] It is a terrifying and gloomy play. The locale ; a slum basement used as a doss-house by riff-raff. A ticket-of-leave man, a drunken ex-actor, a fallen gentleman, a Tartar, a prostitute, a low-class locksmith and his dying wife, etc., are the characters. Gorky had made a name for low-class characters in his stories. He knew his subject at first hand, having grown up with it.

The people are created with profound sympathy, each in his or her own misery ; but not as invalids, as victims. At first the course of the action seems obscure and complex ; but the author's intention is seen by un-winding each character-thread in turn, as would occur on the stage. Nearly all are influenced, either for good or evil, by a pious, but malignant, " consoler " Luka, an elderly humbug, who raises hopes that can never be fulfilled. The atmosphere of crime, dirt and despair is not unlike that of Tolstoy's *Power of Darkness*, published in 1886. And there can be little doubt that the Art Theatre, soon to fall for " Suler ", thought Gorky was just doing for the urban poor what Tolstoy had done for the rural. Nothing could be more mistaken. Gorky had come to see his riff-raff friends as parasites, dangerous parasites, who in time of unrest, such as was about to come, would be capable of siding with any moneyed element, even the police and their natural enemies. It was not them he attacked, however, but the society that made them such. He always felt he had not made it clear that Luka was a false figure, and thought he ought to rewrite the play. But a study of it does not give this impression, and the fault must have lain with the Art Theatre's interpretation. Moskvin played Luka, and after the Revolution altered his rendering of the part to make it closer to Gorky's description of " socially pernicious ".[13]

The performance was naturalistic. Before the play was put in hand, an excursion was made to the Rogues' Market under the guidance of Gilyarovsky, now a successful Moscow journalist. The inmates were interviewed, and notes made of their method of speech, stance, appearance, hopes, dreams and views. Sketches were made of the room for scenic purposes. In general the inmates were intrigued by the idea of being " copy " for a gentlemen's theatre-show and played up well. A weird experience for the aristocratic-looking Stanislavsky. Under the sketch made for a set by Simov, who went on the excursion, he wrote : " I felt like Dante going through all the sections of Purgatory ". But he admitted that the excursion was more useful than any discussion or analysis of the play.

The Lower Depths had an ovation on its first night from a thrilled and stirred middle-class audience. That was in December 1902, and it has never lost its place in the Art Theatre repertoire. Workers' audiences of later years found it still full of meaning for them historically. But interest in Chehov, whom at first the revolutionary workers could not understand, whose characters were so foreign to the Russia they lived in, and whose interests seemed so limited and meaningless, dropped off at the time of the Revolution.

Sobolyev, in his book on the Moscow Art Theatre, says [14] that it was in this play that it first felt the real " social optimism " of Gorky, marking its first turn to realism. Certainly the Art Theatre knew what it was in for, when it produced plays by a writer who had publicly identified himself with the masses of the people. Stanislavsky said that after his contact with the riff-raff he played Satin " with deliberate political knowledge and interest ", although only two years before he had played Dr. Stockmann in An Enemy of the People as merely a just, honourable man, " not realising that he was a powerful speaker at political meetings ".

But much time was to pass yet before Stanislavsky awakened politically ; and even Nemirovich had some way to go, though, as we will be seeing, what he learned from Gorky he never lost sight of.

Meanwhile Gorky leaves the Art Theatre for a time. His next play, Dachniki, was not performed there, but in Peterburg (November 1904) at Vera Komissarzhevskaya's theatre which had just opened. Vera Komissarzhevskaya was a beautiful and talented actress with high ideals and a deep devotion to her art. Having made a great name as an actress at the Imperial Alexandrinsky (I understand she started as a Moscow Art Theatre pupil under the name Komina ; certainly she had been produced by Stanislavsky in the Society of Art and Literature days), she decided to leave the service and form her own theatre. Her motives seem to have been partly that the complex, deep psychological style of acting that was her natural bent clashed with the simplified, classical style required in Imperial Peterburg ; partly that she could stand no more of the chinovniki ; and partly that she simply wanted to put her own ideas into practice. " This

is really my faith ", she wrote in a letter,[15] " that art must express the eternal
—the soul.   Hence only one thing is important : the life of the soul in all
its manifestations."

Gorky, who showed many manifestations of the soul, was therefore
suitable for her purpose ; and his was the first new play she accepted in
her opening season, the other plays being *Uriel Akosta*, *A Doll's House*
and *Uncle Vanya*.   Her producer at this time was I. A. Tihomirov, who
later joined the Moscow Art Theatre.

FALSE DAWN OF A NEW WORLD

Events were gathering swiftly for the abortive revolution of 1905.
Everyone in the country was involved, either for or against.   The very
middle class, among whom this play showed an unbridgeable and eternal
rift, was in real daily life divided sharply against itself at the very time of
performance.   The play's reception was stormy.   The audience was divided
and vociferous.   Cheers were answered by derisive whistles.   The long-
haired Gorky faced his audience, before the curtains, like a rock facing
the sea.   For he knew he had created the middle-class *dachniki* on the stage
in the living image of the middle-class *dachniki* in front ; and perhaps he
knew that neither the right theatre nor yet the right audience had arrived
for his play to be understood as he had written it.   " It is not a question of
awakening the sympathy of the audience for these people ; this is not
possible.   But of not awakening antipathy at first sight, not shrinking
from stressing their humanity, not losing their intrinsic charm ", writes a
Soviet critic.[16]   For although Gorky was leading the pre-revolutionary
theatre away from Chehov, by setting characters in a perspective of time
and place that must necessarily involve a political focus, revealing the class
war, yet he said quite firmly : " A class symptom doesn't have to be
pasted on a man from outside, on his face, as we are doing.   A class-
symptom isn't a wart, it's something inward, neuro-cerebral, biological." [17]

Dachniki was withdrawn after twenty performances.   The excuse was
Komissarzhevskaya's indisposition.   Her understudy also, perhaps, was
indisposed to play so dangerous a part.   For this was indeed a perilous
way for art to express the eternal, and Komissarzhevskaya gave up Gorky
for the time.   Shortly after, she left the little theatre (" The Passage ")
and went touring the provinces, moving on her return to the more famous
Komissarzhevskaya Theatre in Officer Street, where with the help of
Meierhold, Yevreinov, her brother, and other experimental producers,
she passed the inevitable journey through Ibsen symbolism to the mystics
of Maeterlinck.

Bloody Sunday (9 (22) January 1905) came and went, leaving its trail
of tears and horror.   For having written and circulated an account of it,

Gorky was put in the Peter-Paul Fortress. To perform his plays thus became almost an act of sedition. While in prison Gorky wrote another play, *Children of the Sun*. This was produced both by Komissarzhevskaya and at the Art Theatre, which landed itself thereby in further trouble.

We cannot describe these plays in detail ; and as far as I know, few if any, other than *The Lower Depths*, have been translated ; while merely to sketch plots or persons cannot describe plays. *Othello* is not described by saying that a trusting Renaissance coloured soldier is egged on by a Venetian mischief-maker to doubt the fidelity of his wife, till he goes crazy with jealousy and strangles her.

In *Children of the Sun* the central couple are a doctor and his wife. The doctor is deeply concentrating on researches and neglects his wife, who tries to rekindle his interest in her by flirting with an artist. A rich woman in the neighbourhood, desperate for lack of male company, offers to build the doctor a fine laboratory if he will leave his wife for her. But in his own queer way, he is devoted to his wife, and though he makes momentary proof of this in a crisis, cannot change his disposition or his job, so that everybody remains unhappy. There are other unhappy couples and tri-angles, but most are due to the fact that all these people, though occupying a place in the sun, cannot live sunnily because socially and economically each is living in a world of his or her own. Neuroticism, suicide, insanity, result.

Into this sunlit world breaks real life in the shape of a cholera epidemic. Superstitious peasantry blame the black magic of research, encouraged by vested interests which try to ruin the doctor by invoking laws against air-pollution in time of epidemic. The climax, or semi-climax, is the arrival of a crowd of toughs chasing a colleague of the doctor's on stage, before the gates of his house can be closed.

This, at the first performance, had dramatic consequences. On the 24th of October all Moscow was in terror of the Black Hundreds, who were Fascist thugs used by the conservatives after 1905 to suppress anyone who stood up for the ordinary people. It was anticipated that the Art Theatre would be closed down for daring to act a Gorky play. In fact, of course, the Art Theatre was quite non-political, and one of its prominent actresses never set her eyes on a newspaper of any kind. Nemirovich says that they expected a poor attendance. Wars fill theatres, but revolutions empty them, and Moscow was alive with revolution. To their surprise the auditorium was full.

This in itself was disturbing. But rehearsals had been uneasy. That year had seen a strike at the theatre. Public support had dropped. Commonwealth funds were dwindling. There were dissensions in the company and even between the directors. Gorky, called in to settle a dispute, had paid little attention, his mind being elsewhere. The first night had already been postponed, because at the first date the new bogus constitution had been announced, and no one would have turned out to a play. For all Russia was personally involved in the political chances of the time. Liberalism was a matter of life to every person. In a few months it would also become a matter of death to many. And there had been a street demonstration the day before, with some million and a half people on the boulevard and mourners beaten up on their way back from Bauman's funeral.

So if the audience was on edge, so were the company.

In the last act the appearance of a fugitive, hatless figure, not previously seen or referred to, shouting " Hide me !   Forbid them the door ! " startled the audience.   When a plaster-stained face glared round the wings, they took fright.   When the central character began rather feebly to shoo with his handkerchief a crowd of men who pushed their way on to the stage brandishing picks, shovels and lengths of wood, and advanced threateningly toward the actors on the stage, the audience was convinced that the Black Hundreds had certainly arrived by the stage door and were about to break up the theatre.   And when the leading lady appeared on the staircase with a revolver in her hand and a determined look on her face, panic set in.   A woman was heard to scream " Sergey ! Sergey ! " ; another called for water ; a well-known ballerina fainted ; even those who realised it was part of the play stood up and shouted that the management had no right to play on people's nerves like this.   But their shouts went unheard in the general scrimmage.   Seats emptied ; cloak-rooms filled.   The audience had lost itself beyond reasoning ; and one young professor stated afterwards that as the curtain closed he had distinctly seen the rioters aiming at Kachalov with guns in their hands !

Quiet was restored, the play was finished. It had only a few minutes more to run. But the house was half empty.

In 1906 Gorky published *Barbarians*. A study of the demoralisation of middle-class men and women caused by the arrival in a remote town of a party of railway engineers and surveyors to build a railroad. A very sensitive play, which the Art Theatre seems to have considered producing, to judge by a note in Gorky's *Collected Works*.[18]   The production did not in fact take place. Matters were getting worse. There was fighting in the streets, and though the Art Theatre took no part in that, one of the foyers was put to use as a casualty ward. The company had no heart to rehearse. The theatre closed.

But it soon reopened. By order of Admiral-General Dubasov, who had been given the task of restoring order in Moscow. Open theatres were a sign of normality. That was in December.

The bewildered company and management were tired of politics. What they wanted was Art, and to be let alone to create it. And what they needed was money. Help not forthcoming from the subscribers, who were far too scared to risk their money in such investments at such a time, application was made to Yuzhin-Sumbatov as President and Founder of the Literary and Artistic Club. He advanced some money, and the theatre went for a tour in Germany.

Gorky also went abroad. For his health's sake, in both strict and slang senses. To Capri.

Nobody took his place as a dramatist. Naïdenov was tried, and Yushkevich, and Leonid Andreyev, especially the last. Strange paths he led them down. The classics were tried, both Russian and European. The taste for Gorky's contemporary truths faded. " Realism and *byt* [19] have outlived their age ", said the Studio on Povarsky Street. " The time has come for the unreal on the stage." And, it might have added with middle-class cynicism, " in the streets ".

One hundred and ten rehearsals were given to a single Dostoyevsky adaptation in two months. [20]

Gorky from Capri protested against their doing Dostoyevsky. As early as 1896 he had attacked what he called the St. Vitus' Dance in the arts. By that he meant all the theories and isms and crank notions which had been concocted as nostrums to cure decadence by causing new symptoms, instead of restoring a clean habit of art by a surgical operation on the society on which it depended. But the St. Vitus Dance went on. In Yevreinov's theory of a " theatrical instinct " and the " theatricalisation of life in order to express it "; in Komissarzhevsky's amateurish observations and opinions about the theatrical in children's games; in Andreyev's anticipation of surrealism; and all the other art-quaintnesses of Meierhold and Tairov, artistic equivalents of the freak ships that jaded Russian aristocrats had built, circular, turbot-shaped, in a pathological attempt to escape from the ship shape. [21]

GORKY AND THE WAY TO THE NEW WORLD

Gorky was probably not thinking of the Art Theatre when he made a Frenchified character in one of his long novels [22] say, " Very original ! But, you know, it's too serious for a theatre. In fact, it's not a theatre, so much as a Salvation Army." But he did object to the revivalist attitude of the Art Theatre, both on stage and in the wings, during its Dostoyevsky period. Just as he objected to Meierhold's production of *The Lower Depths* at Kherson during the 1903-4 season, because it was too mystical. Notwithstanding the fact that when Meierhold left the Art Theatre and became head of the Association of the New Drama, he produced all the plays Gorky had written up to that time, none the less he and Gorky were direct opposites.

Equally, Gorky respected Chehov. " No one ", he wrote,[23] " understood as clearly and finely as Anton Chehov the tragedy of life's trivialities, no one before him showed men with such merciless truth the terrible and shameful picture of their life in the dim chaos of bourgeois everyday existence." But he added,[24] of the owners of the Cherry Orchard, " They missed the right moment to die. . . . The wretched little student Trofimov speaks eloquently of the necessity to work . . . and does nothing but amuse himself out of sheer boredom, stupidly mocking Vanya who works ceaselessly for the good of idlers." He realised that Chehov had invented a new literary form, the " lyrical play " ; but he found the Art Theatre's treatment of this " drama " too heavy. As early as 1898 he wrote to Chehov : " Other dramas do not draw the attention away from reality to philosophical generalisation. Yours do." And Gorky approved of this, then ; for he was never a naturalist.

Only the philosophy was a personal, bourgeois one. It did not lead to action, nor include the motives of governors. Hence, though he demurred to the results, he praised Chehov for " killing realism ". He praised this out of his own love for realism, his desire to create a new, heroic realism for " the hour had come for heroism to be needed ".

Therefore when Alexander Benoit defended the Art Theatre in Dostoyevsky, Gorky attacked again. " We need action, not self-contemplation. We need a return to the source of energy, to democracy, to the people, to sociality, and to science." [25]

The protests failed. The Art Theatre continued to encourage people to " slumber on in oblivion ". But the seeds cast by Gorky and the implications of what the theatre had gone through, ripened in Nemirovich-Danchenko's thought.

NEMIROVICH AND THE WAY TO THE NEW WORLD

In a letter to the critic Guryevich, which lay in MS. in the Art Theatre Museum unpublished till the critic Freidkin printed it in the article in театр quoted, Nemirovich wrote about the kind of people who formed the audience of his beloved and now famous theatre : about their mean-mindedness, snobbishness, cheap shallow scepticism, absurd love of tittle-tattle and general paltriness " so peculiar to slavishly tuned bourgeois souls ". Words that Gorky might have written ; qualities that Gorky depicted in his plays ; but a new attitude for Nemirovich. This was in 1915. He went on : " When I think of this, my one desire in spite of the theatre's dependence on them, is to stage only the kind of plays that will annoy them ".

And he complained that the Art Theatre, with its " beautiful " shows of Turgenyev and Gogol, was doing the exact opposite. It was a mere relaxation, not for those whose days were filled with honest toil, but for those whose days were filled with the best way of avoiding honest toil. And he continued : " To me it has become clear that ' beauty ' is a stick with two ends. It can rouse and maintain thought, or it can send the conscience to sleep. But if beauty lacks that revolutionary spirit without which it cannot be a great work of art, then in general it is a mere caressing of the conscienceless."

A big advance here : " . . . that revolutionary spirit without which . . .". So Nemirovich was at last ready for the revolution. But when it came, two years later, he had little as a company to work with.

The theatre had degenerated. After the February Revolution, so great was the available public that the Art Theatre, whose auditorium was and is quite small, gave performances each week in the big Solodovnikov Theatre, although they lost intimacy thereby. On the night of the October Revolution they were there playing (is this significant ?) *The Cherry Orchard*. The company was afraid to go on in case they might be chased off the stage by the brutal Bolshies. But the play held its public, all the same, and had a big reception. There was firing in the streets. It was dangerous walking home.

THE MOSCOW ART THEATRE AND ITS NEW WORLD

That night a new public came to the Art Theatre. It came again. It got into the Art Theatre habit. It paid no entrance money. It had to be taught not to smoke, not to crack nuts, not to eat or chatter during the acts ; and to be in its place on time, and to take its hats off. Stanislavsky stood in front of the curtain and taught it. It respected him. Soon it loved the Art Theatre. And in time, like all other theatres worthy to be maintained, the Art Theatre became State supported, with Stanislavsky and Nemirovich-Danchenko jointly in charge.

This meant no more financial worries, just as it meant greater worries in the matter of repertoire ; for the Art Theatre had little to offer the new public in its revolutionary mood. But that is a story I have told elsewhere. In June 1919 the whole concern very nearly came to an end. Part of the double company under Kachalov and Olga Knipper were in Harkov, and got cut off from Moscow by the army of the White general, Denikin. The remainder carried on without them in Moscow as best they could. There were no plays. When, three years later, the Knipper-Kachalov contingent returned, there were still no plays. And the classics were wrong for this audience, or at least their productions of the classics were wrong. The Art Theatre as a whole, feeling out of tune with the times, faced with another crisis, again took the easy way out and went abroad for a long, long tour.

Nemirovich wouldn't go abroad. He stayed. Having no company he turned to musical productions, in which he was only returning to his first love at Tbilisi, the Opera. He tried to apply his new principles to the performance of opera. He founded a studio, called by his name, for the artistic playing, no, the "truthful" playing, of opera, whether light or grand or national. In the finding of adaptations of the librettos used by Lecocq and Offenbach proper for the new revolutionary proletarian audience, he began to get ideas about all theatrical performance for such an audience, and a more dynamic approach to production. Art was now more than an end in itself. Working it out, he fused the stage and the audience. This was what Gorky also had wanted.

When the Art Theatre returned, very likely with some misgivings, in 1924, everything was reorganised. Some of its studios became independent theatres. The parent body, with Stanislavsky having been out of the country so long, took some time to find its way about theatrical Moscow. Nemirovich tried to show them where they stood, by his production in 1925 of Trenyov's *The Pugachov Rebellion* . . . herald of a great body of plays about the revolutionary past. It was by no means a perfect Soviet play ; but it was a beginning.

Stanislavsky tried his hand with an Ostrovsky in the next year, and another historico-revolutionary drama about the Decembrists (these were the only two new productions that year, a fact to note in itself), trying to realise what he was fumbling for, a fusion of inner truth and outer history. He found it in the second year's production, *The Days of the Turbins*, about the Civil Wars. The recent past. But the dawn broke in 1927, when Stanislavsky and Sudakov closed in with Nemirovich's experience and set up the first really new and revolutionary Art Theatre product : *Armoured Train 14-69*. From then on the Art Theatre never had to look back. The principles and aims for which Gorky had stood in the theatre became its own principle and aims, its essential thought. The middle-class temple of beauty became the leader, pioneer and model of the actual proletarian theatre. Well might Stanislavsky himself write : *The chief beginner and creator of the social-political line in our theatre was A. M. Gorky.*

In January 1931 there was a special matinee in memory of the 1905 Revolution.

In May 1931 there was a special matinee in honour of Maxim Gorky.

In 1932 celebrations in honour of Gorky were held all over the Soviet Union. On the 17th of September, by decree of the Presidium of the Communist Party, the Moscow State Art Academic Theatre of the U.S.S.R., as it had been known since the previous December, was declared to be "the Moscow State Art Academic Theatre of the U.S.S.R. by the name of Maxim Gorky". The reason was added : "as a mark of the forty years' artistic and public activity of Gorky".

This reason is interesting. It was an honour for the theatre to be connected with the hero of the day ; and yet so great was the theatre's prestige that it was primarily the honour for Gorky suitable for this occasion. It recalled, surely enough, the perils to which the combination of author and theatre had exposed each in Tsarist times.

On the same occasion the same eponymous honour was bestowed on another theatre, the Grand Dramatic Theatre at Leningrad. Gorky had sat on the Collegium of this since its foundation in 1919. He had advised it on policy ; and made personal contacts with its audience. It was the first theatre to be created from nothing by the Soviet Government, and Gorky was its nurse. He it was who formulated its aim : "To introduce the new audience of workers, peasants, and Red Army men to the classics of their inheritance, and to be a theatre of romantic drama, classic tragedy and high comedy".

It was this theatre which gave the first performance of *Enemies*,[26] so many years after it was written, an example in 1933, which was followed by the M.O.S.P.S., the Maly, the Moscow Art Theatre, and thereafter by dozens of theatres throughout the Soviet Union. It was a play in which the class war came directly to the feelings of the audience through its effect on the members of one family. When the Moscow Art Theatre did it, in 1935, Nemirovich-Danchenko found it brought a "definitely political and revolutionary understanding of what Gorky had been after". "Now this is the theatre of Gorky", he said, on the eve of its fortieth birthday.[27]

It is apt to end with Gorky's remarks in 1919.[28] "It is essential", he wrote, "to teach people to respect what is truly human, and necessary that they come to know how to take pride in themselves. To this end people must be shown on the stage of the contemporary theatre, by means of those who are essentially heroes in the wide, true sense, the ideal thing for which the world has been languishing since days of yore. . . .

"In our time a heroic theatre is essential, a theatre which would set individuality as the aim of its idealisation, would regenerate romanticism, would colour mankind poetically. . . .

"It is essential to show man-the-hero with the self-denial of chivalry, passionately in love with an idea, mankind of upright deeds, of great exploits."

Such aims were, and such words would have been, meaningless sentimentality, as long as they were just hopes. But Gorky was not indulging here in hopes. He was stating what he saw, with realistic eyes, in the new world round him. The heroism of industry, the heroism of pioneering, of exploring, and later the heroism of war . . . these were foreseen by Gorky as an essence in Socialist life. He was the first to prophecy the evil that Fascism would bring upon the world. And he trusted, because he knew and understood, the proletariat of the world's first proletarian state.

The spirit he here describes was the spirit that did at last cross the Volga, to lands of men hailed not as natives but as equals in an advancing civilisation that was an adventure in itself. If in his last working period his unfinished trilogy of plays did not concern itself with the new world but with the old, that was because he had yet to add his last word to that old world, viewed from the new. Had he lived, it is likely he would have written great plays about life in the Soviet Union, and the Soviet Drama would have been richer. But it was not to be.

When the Art Theatre, though, came to do the plays of his maturity, *Yegor Bulychov*, *Dostigayev and Others*, and a *mélange* of incidents from his own autobiography, it found them full of new meaning and richness. Nor was the Art Theatre alone in giving them full expression. For they are the basis of Socialist Realism ; and Socialist Realism was to be the ultimate stage of a logical development, traced by Stanislavsky in a rising circle, by Nemirovich-Danchenko in a widening straight line, from the ideas they first exchanged all night through in the Slavic Bazaar. Gorky knew this ; Chehov never did.

That is one of the reasons why the Moscow Art Theatre is called by the name of Gorky.

Part Three

THE WAR: FIRST ASPECT

CHAPTER VII

EVACUEES

ACTORS CROSS TO THE EAST

For nearly a quarter of a century Russia, with most of the foreign lands her Tsars had conquered now in federation with her as Socialist republics like herself, has grappled with trouble after trouble; civil war, the intervention of most of the great nations of the world, famine, and defence against a new world war. She has won through. She and her Confederates have established the Socialist principle as the method of living that solves her problems; and the fruits of early years of renunciation for that end were beginning to appear. Life was not only free, it was becoming very good. There was a deep curiosity about life, one's own, one's neighbours, and that of other peoples. This was not the prerogative of townees. Science, virgin-mother of truth, mistress-daughter of truth, was served by farm-workers, by remote tribes. Life was an organic experience, developing into the future, exciting in its possibilities. Men and women were nearer to each other in a common adventure, affecting daily acts and events. Even where there was no theatre, conditions were ripe for a theatre.

This was general, all over the Union. The Volga is no more a rampart. It is, as never before, the life-stream of Russia. Actors have crossed it many, many times. Theatres have started in almost every country federated with Russia, in almost every division inside her.

I have tried to show in *The New Soviet Theatre* the part played by the theatres in these lands; how, thanks to the Bolshevik policy since 1913, the problem of national minorities and sub-minorities was solved to a degree no other statecraft in the world has achieved (nearest, maybe, was Czechoslovakia; but her solution failed at the critical hour because it had not the political, social and economic completeness of the Bolsheviks). I have tried to show in that book the immediate response of the theatre profession to the new hope and life of those nations; and how the national traditions of each were preserved and drawn from and built upon in the new Socialist world.

In the next chapter of this book I will try to show how these nations responded to invasion, and how their theatres operated in it. For war is the supreme test of a theatre. It is a test of a theatre's efficiency ; for in proportion as the communal sense of the audience quickens in war-time, so difficulties and obstacles to its smooth working multiply. And it is a test also of depth and understanding ; for both life and death, and therefore motive and character, become more distinct, more defined. Doubly is this true when the war is total war. Triply is it true when the total war contains invasion.

For now the long expected attack has come, and it is the summer of 1941. Monopoly capitalism in its extreme form, Fascism, has turned on the Socialist sixth of the world, as it has all along declared its intention of doing ; blinded by its own theory of racial superiority, it blunders forward against what it has to believe is an artificial society of a decadent group of races. True, it has failed to enlist more than a few reactionary powers among the other monopoly-capitalist states on its side ; and the rest are committed to revenge for its depredations on their possessions. But it has satellites : armed men or armaments or material from Italy, Rumania, Finland, hordes of fanatical steel, sweep into the Soviet Union.

Hovering over the steppes, we see them spreading east : through Byelorussia towards Moscow, through Latvia, Lithuania, Estonia towards Leningrad, through the broad Ukraine towards the Volga.

The Soviet republics are faithful. Forced to retreat, they scorch the earth as they do so. Everything that can be evacuated, human, animal, metal, is evacuated : what cannot be, is burned or blown up. Theatres in frontier states go with the rest. One after another. It is like a man walking into a flock of starlings in a field. The first few in his path rise and wing to the other side of the flock ; then the next few, more ; and suddenly the whole flock is gone to the other end of the field.

As the Fascist hordes neared Kiev and Odessa, as they took these cities and made for others, Moscow, Voronezh, Harkov and Rostov-on-Don ; as they took some of these and made on to Ryazan, Saratov, Stalingrad, and swept over the Black Sea regions to the North Caucasus, occupying or destroying Stavropol, Maikop, Mozdok, all that was of value was withdrawn in front of them—factories, stores, laboratories, scientists, engineers, artists, and theatres too. Of the thousand or so permanent theatres not one has had to close down even though its premises were pillaged or mined.[1]

So now, as we study our theatre map, we see motion, nothing but motion, from west to east. Road, rail, river and steppe are full of evacuees in good order making with their theatres for distant areas where best they can carry on and use their special abilities and resources for " the successful prosecution of the war ". In a Socialist state most institutions, like most individuals, having by nature a special ability or resource, it is the function of society to discover what that is, and help it to develop. And society is, of course, just the other such individuals or institutions.

Let us now descend and view the operation from near-to.

THE WEST

The scientists of the Byelorussian Academy of Sciences, working in peace-time as Byelorussian members of the whole international Soviet community, were still regarded, when war engulfed their country, as members of the whole community. Their discoveries and inventions were just as important as ever they had been ; more so. Therefore they, with their intricate apparatus and records, or as much as was needed and practicable, were transported to Tashkent in Uzbekistan. There they went on working for the good of the Soviet Union and the honour of Byelorussia. With them went many of their compatriots who were not famous scientists. Let a girl instructress in athletics stand for all. Evacuated to the east, she wished a more direct part in the war effort. Finding a factory that had been evacuated from Leningrad, she entered it and was given four months' training. She found the rhythm of her expert bodily habit so useful in her work at the lathe, that she rivalled life-long turners and won a Labour medal within a year.

So was it with the Byelorussian theatres. By 1942 they had all been received in the Urals or in Western Siberia. The First Byelorussian Theatre, run by Glebov, went to Tomsk and Novosibirsk. They had eight plays in their repertoire that season of 1941-2 : one called *Partisans*, Rahmanov's *Unquiet Old Age*, plays by Korneichuk, Simonov and Afinogenov, a Lope de Vega, a Sardou, and *He Who Laughs Last*, by the Byelorussian Stalin prize-winner Krapiva. At Tomsk they gave their new production, *A Fool to Others, Clever to Himself*, by Lope de Vega. Later in their stay they added the play about their own national guerrillas by their own national playwright Romanovich.

The second Byelorussian Theatre arrived at Uralsk with fourteen productions in its repertoire, seven being of contemporary Soviet plays, the rest including Gorky's *Yegor Bulychov*, a Molière, a Sardou, an Ostrovsky. Uralsk is in Kazakhstan, towards the Caspian Sea ; and the Byelorussians proudly interested that Oriental people in Loiter's production of one of their most famous national plays : *Nesterka*, by Volsky, which had won the national prize for the best play of 1941. Other shows within that year were Korneichuk's *The Front*, Leonov's *Invasion*, and *The Man They Wanted*, produced by Loiter, Mitskevich and Anoyeva, respectively. In the summer of 1943, being still in evacuation, Loiter produced an important new Byelorussian play, *Ordeal by Fire*, which Krapiva wrote in collaboration with the theatre collectively.[2]

(Many of the plays mentioned in this chapter but not described in it will be found treated in more detail when we discuss the Soviet war-time drama.)

Meanwhile the State Jewish Theatre of Byelorussia had arrived at Novosibirsk with the heroic Jewish battle play *Bar-Khokhba* (see *New Soviet Theatre*, pp. 81-2), opening in March 1942, and followed by *Tevye the Milkman* and a Musical Comedy. A new play by the Soviet Jewish author Galkin was also given. This theatre had been in existence for sixteen years ; for by Soviet constitution and custom all Jews being entitled to their own culture, religion and art, and unmolested, the Jews of Byelorussia were naturally entitled to theirs, a sub-nationality's. The work of this theatre in evacuation not only broadened the culture of the Byelorussian Jews evacuated to the east, but intrigued the other nationals there, who had had small occasion to see Byelorussian culture, still less that of Byelorussian Jews.[3]

THE UKRAINE STEPS OUT

The same is true of the vaster organisations and larger multitudes of Ukraine. Their Academy of Sciences, for example, was taken to Ufa, capital of the Bashkir Republic, which stands where the foothills of the Southern Urals melt into rolling plains of silver feather-grasses, plains that are mild to man and aromatic to invalids, plains that breed fine mares, whose milk, fermented, is that *kumiss* which turns out strong men and helps to heal tubercular and neurotic ones.

There the Kiev Theatre of Opera and Ballet settled ; but most of the Ukrainian theatres went further on. The Dniepropetrovsk Theatre, named for the Ukrainian Burns, Shevchenko, went first to Kazakhstan and some months later to Uzbekistan. There at the town of Namangan, in the fertile and industrious Fergana valley, it celebrated in 1943 its twenty-fifth birthday. Besides war plays from the Russian, it presented *Othello*, Trenyov's *Lyubov Yarovaya*, Lope de Vega's *Fuente Ovejuna*, Lesya Ukrainka's *Forest Song* (see pages 50-51), and even *Les Cloches de Corneville*.

Not far away from there is Samarkand, older than Alexander the Great, Tamerlane's capital, one of the most famous and romantic cities in the world. The past of Samarkand is very precious to Soviet citizens. Tamerlane's tomb was opened in 1942 by Zarifov at the head of a party of archæologists. Fabrics and relics were examined ; and one or two facts were proved, as that Tamerlane's limp was caused by tuberculosis of the right knee-cap, and that his grandson Ulugbek, statesman, humanist, astronomer and mathematician, was certainly murdered. Hither came the Harkov

Jewish Theatre, also playing *Fuente Ovejuna*, and opening a new season in 1943 with Sholom Aleikhem's *200,000*.[4]

The oldest and best known of the Ukrainian theatres, the "Ivan Franko" Theatre of Kiev, also travelled a good deal. Evacuated first to Tambov (S.E. of Moscow), then to Semipalatinsk, a Kazakh market town where the Tirk-Sib railway crosses the River Ob, they proceeded on the first of July 1943 to Tashkent, the Uzbek capital. With two Soviet war plays, they also showed Schiller's *William Tell*, *Much Ado About Nothing*, and many comedies or historical plays by Ukrainians, including one by Franko himself : *Tentie Fortune*. This had a success with the local population, and the theatre prospered so well that by September 1943 it had raised almost 100,000 roubles for the Defence Fund.[5]

To Kazakhstan also came the "Artem" Theatre, to Kzyl-Orda, the former capital, standing in a poor climate on the Syr Darya near the Aral Sea. In Jamboul (formerly Aulie-Ata on the Turk-Sib railway near the Kirghiz border), so named nowadays for the Bard of the Steppes,* the Kiev Jewish Theatre opened the 1942 season in June with five Jewish classics and a translation from Korneichuk.

At Karaganda, which is also in Kazakhstan, the new city of coal, worked for a time another Kiev theatre, bearing the name of Lesya Ukrainka, which none the less plays in Russian. The pitmen there were given Pogodin's *Kremlin Chimes* among other plays, before it moved back to Chechen-Ingutia, at the invitation of that Government. Chechen-Ingutia lies between the Caspian Sea and the line of the Fascists' furthest southward advance. The chief town is Grozny, where the theatre settled. In the summer of 1943 they were doing two Soviet war plays, Gorky's *Children of the Sun*, *General Brusilov* (about the last war), *Krechinsky's Wedding* (a nineteenth-century classic), and Bernard Shaw's *Pygmalion*.[6]

Over in Kirghizia we see the Odessa Theatre of the Revolution touring about for a time. In March 1942 it was at Tokmak, north of the Sea of Azov, where it showed translations of the pre-war Russian plays, *A Fellow of Our Town*, *Platon Krechet*, and *In the Steppes of Ukraine*, together with Schiller's *Intrigue and Love*, and Ukrainian plays with titles like *Aza the Gipsy Lass*, *Natalka of Poltava*, and one which might best be rendered : *Och, dinna be rinnin' awa', mon; Bide ben wi' me here i' the gloamen*. And from there it wandered elsewhere. The "Gorky" Theatre from Dniepropetrovsk, on the other hand, went straight to Barnaul, in Western Siberia,

---

* See *N.S.T.*, p. 51. When they brought him news that his son had been honoured for an exploit in the Red Army at the front, this magnificent old poet, then 97 years old, stood up and recited a new impromptu song on the occasion, which has passed into the folk-music of Kazakhstan. A film was made in 1943 about the life of this famous *akyn*. He has since died, after greeting with a lament the news of his son's death in action.

and after nine months' work there had by June 1942 shown eleven plays. Barnaul is south of Novosibirsk, within a day's journey of the Altai mountains ; an eighteenth-century settlement which had grown to a city the size of Bath. Among the eleven plays were two by Korneichuk, *Long, Long Ago,* and a historical play by Ostrovsky with the unwieldy title, *Kozma Zaharich Minin-Suhoruk.*

The Zhitomir Theatre, named for Shchors, one of the guerrilla leaders of the Civil Wars, was among the first to leave the Ukraine ; but, as its director, Magar, proudly claimed after its return to the liberated parts of its own country in 1943, it had hardly forsaken the Red Army at all, as it had been working in the immediate rear in Northern Ossetia through the fearful winter of 1942. But of this kind of war work we will be talking more closely in Chapter 9. Its repertoire was much the same as that of the last-named theatre.

The Dniepropetrovsk Opera Theatre settled further east, at Krasnoyarsk in Siberia. The Zaporozhe " Zankovetskaya " Theatre travelled to the Tobolsk forest area, not so far east, round the River Irtysh. (What a change from a century back ; and how our Polish lady would have enjoyed a reminder of lost civilisation and company even in an unintelligible language !) Still further back toward the Volga, we find at Buguruslan the " Shchepkin " Theatre from Sumy ; and at Tolmak the Odessa Theatre of the Revolution. In all, there were sixty-one Ukrainian theatres playing their usual repertory, expanded of course for war audiences, in what they call so justly their " brother " republics.

Further yet, the Harkov Russian Theatre, interpreting to the Siberians of Barnaul and the Buryat-Mongolians and the Russian settlers and evacuees there, *Kremlin Chimes, Mashenka, The Smoke of the Fatherland* (a Russian play about the occupied Ukraine), with reminder of former wars for freedom in *A Fellow of Our Town* and *The Optimistic Tragedy,* and of the services of the great brains in *Unquiet Old Age.* Week after week it had full houses.

The Ukrainian theatre from Stalino in the Don Bas was reported from Jelalabad (not, of course, the Afghan town of that name, but another in the Fergana Valley). It was playing *A Soldier Leaves for the Front, Natalka,* and a less well-known Ukrainian play, *The Luckless Lassie.*[7]

MOLDAVIA

Kishinev in Moldavia had a Russian theatre as well as a Moldavian one. The former was run by Aksyonov, who had been in the Moscow Art Theatre for nearly fifteen years. The Fascist advance meant an early evacuation for both ; and in January 1942 they amalgamated, with Aksyonov as head of the combine. The Moldavian section continued to perform in that language, reviving a pre-war success in a historical play, *Haiduki,* a kind of seventeenth-century *Fuente Ovejuna*, with the people resisting the Turks. As an example of Soviet solidarity, it is interesting to note that this play was seen when the theatre was evacuated to Turkmenia, a Mohammedan country with a Turkish language. In 1943 the Russian section toured some of the outlying cities of their hosts' arid region. It must have been a sore change from the orchards and vineyards of luxuriant Moldavia to Krasnovodsk, where, in spite of etymology, all water has to be boiled from the un-beautiful Caspian, and in the city parks only a few stunted bays will grow. But the Soviet war plays they brought were interesting to the Turkmenians, as was Lope de Vega's *Dog in the Manger*.[8]

The Baltic States

Estonia, Latvia and Lithuania seem to have fared less happily ; and so did the Karelo-Finnish Republic. The first three were in the Soviet Union only about a year before the Fascists occupied them. They had barely organised themselves to their new way of life. And yet, despite the propaganda we hear from *émigré* Poles in England, and more so in Scotland, the industrial efficiency which they themselves chose to adopt had increased, in Estonia, for example, by 50 per cent. in that time.[9] And in the Soviet way of life a 50 per cent. increase in industrial efficiency means, apart from a proportion allocated necessarily for defence (itself a form of prosperity, though a negative one), a 50 per cent. increase in prosperity for everyone.

But the Fascist advance in tanks and Panzer divisions was rapid. It would seem that not all the theatres in these unfortunate countries could get away. At least I find few traces of any permanent Baltic State theatre of drama travelling through or to the reception areas. The Estonian references concern Opera, with the composer Eugene Kapp, who had written incidental music to Goldoni and Shakespeare, and an ensemble of well-known Estonian players, together with some junior ones, formed in Yaroslavl and travelling to the Tatar Republic in July 1942.

The Department of National Theatres of the V.T.O. appointed a commission to consider the position of the Baltic State theatres in July 1943. It included an Estonian actor, the director of the Workers' Theatre at Tallinn (Estonia), the artistic director of the Vanemuyne Theatre at Tartu (Estonia), a Latvian actress, three theatre administrators from Latvia and from the Karelo-Finnish Republic, and a Latvian author. But the only concrete fact I have come across so far about the matter is that a Finnish theatre collective was at that time preparing a play by the national author M. Lassil, called *The Miller*, in the same repertory as Ibsen's *Doll's House*. Finnish writers, however, have written several war plays, notably *In the Tracks of the Wolves*, by V. Ervasti. This Finnish theatre settled in Kem, a town on the river of that name, at the beginning of the tract known as the " Seaside " on the shores of the Gulf of Onega. At first the native Karelians did not take very kindly to the idea. They had not asked for a theatre, and did not quite understand it. But the collective persevered, and by August 1942 they had become popular in the neighbourhood with their open-air amphitheatre of " green leaves and faces ". The repertoire included translations of Russian plays also, both classics : *The Girl Without a Dowry* (Ostrovsky), *Vanyushkin's Children;* and Soviet plays : *A Fellow from Our Town, Gardens in Bloom* (see N.S.T.) and *Russian People.* In February 1944 this Karelo-Finnish theatre opened as a permanent re-established State Theatre at Byelomorsk, under the direction of N. Demidov, a serious artist who had studied under Stanislavsky and brought Moscow Art Theatre methods and standards to this northern people. The opening play, *A Doll's House*, was made the occasion of a national fête.[10]

The reason for Simonov's first play being so popular with these units and in these countries was that at the time, although it dealt with an incident on the Soviet-Japanese frontier, it was as yet the only available Soviet play kindling and kindled from the spirit of patriotic war.

Such initial apathy is rare in the Soviet theatre, but the British writer and theatre man cannot help a certain sneaking sense of comfort that it exists at all ; for it is a definite factor to be assessed in all new theatrical ventures in our countries, and an entire lack of it would make the Soviet theatre seem unreal, inhuman, to us !

How they Travelled out of Russia

The other scores of theatres on the road, or rather on the rails, cannot be called " refugee " theatres. They were evacuees. Their going was as orderly as that of the factory plants and the civil population itself. Cyrus L. Sulzberger, correspondent of the *New York Times*, has written : *

> Among the factories shuttled eastward lock-stock-and-barrel were the Dnyepropetrovsk steel works, the Zaporozhe aluminium and magnesium plants, the Kiev machinery factories, the Harkov turbine and electrical equipment plants, the Zaporozhe Harvester Combine factory. Much of the equipment of the Dnyeprostroy power station was dismantled and removed before the destruction of the dam. . . . An idea of the extent of the movement can only be given by stating that to transport the equipment of one single Dnyepropetrovsk plant required 1,400 freight cars.

All had been pre-arranged. All was carried out smoothly and calmly, despite the inevitable complications. Larry Lesueur in his book, *Twelve Months That Changed the World*,† describes with all the innocent freshness

* *N.Y.T. Magazine*, 10 May 1942 ; quoted by Davies and Steiger ; *Soviet Asia* (London, 1943), p. 36.   † English edition, 1944.

of a North American reporter's heart, the fine fettle of these people, as they travelled in uncomfortable trains, lighting railway-side fires of wood brought from the forest where the train stopped, and cooking good food in an almost picnic spirit. They were leaving their homes, it was true ; but they were taking them with them, also ; and also going to them. They were taking their livelihood with them as well, in the colossal freight-cars. Of course they were anxious, and many had lost their dear ones. But they were not in want ; they were not fleeing ; they were executing their own industrial manœuvre.

So were their theatres. That was the reward of State planning, even in the arts. It is almost disappointing not to find any record of shows given to them by the theatres on the trains at these wayside halts. Big must the temptation have been ! But for this there would be no time. It would certainly have caused disorganisation ; and disorganisation was neither wanted, possible, nor permissible. The Soviet Government had not been taken by surprise. They had studied *Mein Kampf.* They had all their plans ready. The local Soviets in the reception areas, having so long been accustomed to putting local ideas into a national plan, and vice versa, and being linked so organically, despite their independence, with the central executive through the Soviet " system ", lost no time in devising their own plans and putting them into effect. But this they could not have done without the years of local development, ensured by the Five-Year Plans . . . themselves the product of joint local and central planning.

The theatres therefore owed their survival to the whole Soviet system, of which they were a part. It would be strange if they did not reflect this unique combination of regional and central purpose.

As the approaching Fascists cut into Russia itself the Russian small town theatres followed the Ukrainians. We cannot trace all their histories, there are too many small town theatres in Russia, as in the Ukraine, each with its company and staff, and its individual right to protection and work. But to mention a few, the theatres from Oryol and Voronezh arrived in the South Urals, the former to Zlatoust, where high-grade steel furnaces were lighting up, without need of black-out, the lake in the gorge . . . an eighteenth-century town long famous for its militant workers, from Pugachov's day to 1919. The latter went to Kopeisk.

Thousands of Russian workers had been evacuated with their plants to the Urals, the second line of industrial defence ; they welcomed their theatres as a breath from home. And as a sample of work done, we may cite the Oryol theatre's young company in Calderon's *The Invisible Lady* less as a *capa y espada* adventure story than as a lyric of human feeling, and in *Oleko Dundich* (about Serbia in the last world war), *The Immortal* (about young people who join the guerrillas near Moscow), *Russian People*

(Simonov's famous war play which was filled with songs), and a stage version of *Born of the Storm*, by the Soviet novelist Nikolay Ostrovsky.[11]

The "Gorky" Regional Theatre of Rostov-on-Don left for the East in October 1941. It went to Kokand in the Fergana Valley, a fourteenth-century town ; and thence to Kovrov in the Ivanovo region, not far from its namesake Rostov-the-Great (one of the gem cities of Russia proper). E. Brill was at its head, a well-known producer ; it performed three Soviet war plays, with *Anna Karenina*, *Field-Marshal Kutuzov*, *A Dog in the Manger*, *La Locandiera* (Goldoni), and a historical, rather romantic, play about Till Eulenspiegel called *The Siege of Leyden*. The Rostov Musical Comedy Theatre went to Penza in the Middle Volga region ; and the Rostov City Theatre, leaving its fine new premises to be sacked by the Huns, made for Dagestan and Uzbekistan.[12]

The incoming tide swept on to the approaches to Moscow. Air-raids made theatre shows difficult ; for Soviet precautions were more stringent than ours and civilians were compelled to take cover. That comparatively few machines got through was irrelevant to the organisation of A.R.P. There were too many theatres ; and too few people. Some went ; others stayed. The Art Theatre, for example, went.

The Moscow Art Theatre Goes

As a matter of fact on the day that Hitler attacked, the Moscow Art Theatre had started a tour of Byelorussia and Lithuania. One group, with all its sets, props and costumes, was playing *The School for Scandal* at Minsk, uncomfortably near the frontier by Blitzkrieg measure. The first air-raid took place during a performance. As the crackle and crump of falling bombs broke into the show, Yanshin (Sir Peter Teazle) would break off and gag at the Luftwaffe. But the position deteriorated, and the company, with Moskvin in charge, left the city in flames ; at first going on foot, later by car and train, they managed to regain Moscow. But they could not stay there.

They started their long absence at Saratov, chief town of the Lower Volga Region, some 200 miles above, but not far to the east of Stalingrad, and a place which in the early 'thirties was about the size of Nottingham. This patriarchal exodus, no mean feat, was a great tribute to the organising powers of the management. For the entire theatre left Moscow, company, musicians, designers, stage-staff, pupils, together with sets, costumes, properties and as much of the equipment as was transportable. Nemirovich-Danchenko, in an interview with the Press, said that the number of persons involved was over a thousand . . . (" Our theatre has grown very rapidly during the last few years ", he explained modestly). And when it is re-membered what " properties " include, the magnitude of preparation for a sudden and long war-time journey can be imagined : for in *Woe from Wit* (Griboyedov), as they did it at this theatre, no small effect was given by real antique china cups which the widower Famusov handled with clumsy care, there being no mistress in the house.

The theatre had some time in hand before settling to its long-term task. This was spent in organising tours of nearby hospitals, and in giving "benefit" concerts. The words no longer implied rewards for stars, nor their preliminary canvassing in the best carriage in town. Now it meant entertainments, vocal or dramatic, without scenery, helping the town's drive to raise enough money for a whole tank column to go to the Front, or on other occasions, to swell funds for comforts and warm clothes for the men already there.

The company and staff occupied chiefly the old Europe hotel, and performed at first in the local Young Spectators' Theatre, fitting up the famous Seagull curtains there to show that distance and locality made no difference to the aims and standards of the Art Theatre. This was a small building, with a capacity of only 500, that is, a wee bit bigger than the Birmingham Repertory Theatre ; so concurrent shows were given soon in the Opera Theatre, as well as in Engels, the sister town across the river.

The first plays were *The School for Scandal*, *Anna Karenina*, *The Three Sisters*, and *The Lower Depths*. Put *Uncle Vanya* for Tolstoy's play, *Tsar Fyodor* for Sheridan's, and add *An Enemy of the People*, and you have the repertoire of the Art Theatre on its first tour out of Russia in 1906 : but, of course, the Chehov was now in Nemirovich's revised production. All these were in the current repertoire, but early in 1942 came a new one, Pogodin's *Kremlin Chimes*, the final version, with Moskvin, Hmelyov and Tarasova playing the leads. This was rather a special show, partly because the Art Theatre's technique was giving a popular work its deepest and most thorough interpretation, partly also because of its special application to the Saratov audience of workers and Red Army men. Still better did it apply to that of Sverdlovsk, in the Urals, where the Art Theatre toured during the following winter.

When we consider the vital importance to places like these of the regional development of the Soviet Union, and the immense importance to the whole war effort of the electrification scheme on which it was founded, and recall that it was all the product of " Lenin's Dream ",[*] then we can imagine the effect on such regional audiences when that idea is born in Lenin's mind before their very eyes amid circumstances of historical and biographical truth. One scene in particular stood out from the fervent remainder : Grigory Rostov has described it in an article in *Trud* [†] :—

[*] In many parts electric light bulbs are known as " Lenin's Lamps ".
[†] 19. ix. 1942.

9

" The President of the Sovnarkom is alone in his office. He has just had a long and earnest talk about the Soviet Russia of the future, about electrification, about Communism. Lenin paces from corner to corner with quick, short steps. Now he sits down at his writing table and thumbs the pages of a book. The lamp lights up his high forehead, his thinker's head. Lenin writes, quickly. In the auditorium there is a brooding silence. Lenin throws up his head, tilting it slightly to the right, and, screwing up his eyes, gazes searchingly into the distance. He says not a word, but goes on gazing searchingly. And we see Lenin's tremendous idea being born. There is not a stir in the auditorium. Slowly the curtain comes to. Quietly. Lenin is thinking."

This production was by Nemirovich-Danchenko, Leonidov and Knyebel jointly. It was also remarkable for containing a guest artist, the Georgian film star Gelovani, playing Stalin, who appears in the play. And this artist's appearance was also remarkable, as being his first on the legitimate stage. As a rule in the Soviet Union there is no division between screen and stage.

In the course of its stay at Sverdlovsk the Moscow Art Theatre more or less adopted the Urals Machine-Building Plant, which they used to visit at least twice a week, giving scenes and recitations in the shops during the dinner break. The theatre itself was always full, but this factory was given priority and could book the entire house for any performance. Further, the theatre's producers helped the factory's amateur dramatic clubs (so large a concern would naturally have more than one), whenever they were asked. But Sverdlovsk was full of Red Army men too ; and a similar liaison was set up with them, just as it had been with the Army units, and hospitals, in Saratov. In return, political workers would visit the theatre and give the company and staff, in lectures which were very popular, their analysis of the political and war situations ; and would explain with scientific authority what was happening in the industrial world.

A section of the Moscow Art Theatre went to Georgia, combining with a few players from the Maly Theatre of Moscow. They toured other places beyond and in the Caucasus. This section included Kachalov, Tarhanov, Ryzhov, and the septuagenarian Olga Knipper, Chehov's widow, who was really on sick leave. Nemirovich himself, then 83, also had been given a year's sick leave, which he spent for the most part in Tbilisi, his birthplace. While there he wrote a second volume of reminiscences, chiefly about, it is said, the years between 1905 and 1914.

The full company returned to Moscow in the late autumn of 1942, using, as of old, both their principal stage and that of the Moscow Art Theatre Filial ; and in their next three productions, their experience of living people's reactions in other parts of the Soviet Union gained by their travels, was clear to be seen in the actuality displayed with Simonov's *Russian People*, Kron's *Depth Prospecting* (September 1943), and Korneichuk's *The Front*.

The second of these plays I have briefly described in *The New Soviet Theatre*. In 1943 it was no longer a new play, but for the Art Theatre's production, I understand, its peace-time location was altered, and references to the war introduced, chiefly, it is to be supposed, in the dialogue. At least it was held to be a good enough play to bring strictly up to date . . . treatment that does not violate its theme in any way, but rather improves its urgency. Nevertheless it has by no means always found favour with Soviet critics. The depth prospecting bores deeply into psychology, especially abnormal psychology. Soviet critics do not object, on the contrary they pay respect, to sound psychology ; but they are on the lookout for anything that smacks of the academic or the mechanistic. And the trouble with bringing sub-conscious factors on the stage and naming them is, that an author who succeeds in avoiding the academic is in peril of merely establishing symbols ; while symbols on the stage have a faculty for taking charge and diverting the attention from man to mysticism. This not only leads to the denial of the importance of the individual man in his differences from his neighbour, it also, in a realistic theatre, has a bearing on life. And symbolism in life leads to Fascism, the warping of human values into abstract ones. The Fascist admits character only as a deviation from an impersonal principle. In drama, this creates types. The Marxist, on the other hand, values the individual, whether person or event, as unique, but correlates this scientifically with the whole body of the community or of history. In drama this avoids types and conventions of plot. So abstract psychology is out, on both social and theatrical counts. Kedrov, who produced this play for the Moscow Art Theatre's production, seems to have avoided treatment of features in the play which, if exaggerated, might have led that way.

The former play, *Russian People*, needs to be considered more closely ; and though it might more consistently be so considered in Chapter XI, a word or two will be in point here, to show the Moscow Art Theatre in war. For this play is known to London playgoers more as a play of action, like *Inside the Lines*, than as a drama of war mood and *byt*. The London production of 1943 under the title *The Russians* did not reveal the characters of Russian people. It did not even move in Russian characters. This may have been partly due to the adaptation, which transferred the straight, forthright idiom of the Russian fighter and civilian to some of the speech habits of Mayfair and of the British public schools. When these figures were light, they seemed superficial ; and when serious, sentimental. The originals in Russian were neither of these. Kalashnikov describes the play as the " movement of minds and hearts ".

The Moscow Art Theatre production was not the first by any means. But the play benefited there by long meditation and care for detail. Thus

the "atmosphere" was set from the beginning by an introductory syn-
thesis, of searchlight beams in the sky lighting up onion-spires and rows of
low houses, the drone of planes, fall of bombs, breaking of glass, shouting
and orders in German.   None of this was explicit in Simonov's text, but
all was implicit.   And inside this frame of the war and of the occupation,
personal events had a new perspective.   Valya * linked up with other young
women known to the audience, and so achieved a greater significance.
Safonov and Globa, without becoming in any way symbolical, are by their
very concreteness and "roundness" convincing as human beings, and so
link up with actual people known to the audience.   When this happens
to soldiers like these two, the result is a great patriotic urge, far different
from the abstract falsely patriotic sentimentality that would be aroused by
a dummy figure working in verbal or emotional *clichés*.   When it is done
to figures detested by the audience, like Haritonov the Quisling doctor
whom the Nazis make their mayor, it has a curious result, which Kalashnikov criticises, but which to me is an assertion of the deep and progressive
humanism of the Moscow Art Theatre.   Haritonov, played in the round,
you loathe and despise, but you understand how his mind works.   This
understanding leads to a desire for action to combat him, just as a complete
understanding of the ways of the tsetse fly leads a scientist to combat tropical
disease.   Insight gained into a traitor's mind (an apparently real traitor,
and not just a player impersonating one in order to make the action more
exciting) helps you to be on your guard against real traitors.   You have
gained something, a little more knowledge into evil, even into the hearts
of your enemies.   That is one difference between drama and melodrama ;
but its effect here in war is a new function for drama.

On the 25th of April 1943, in his 84th year † died Nemirovich-
Danchenko.   All the premises of the Art Theatre were draped in mourning,
and something like the number of four hundred thousand people came to
pay him their last homage.   Four months later Lilina, Stanislavsky's actress-
widow, died too ; and as Vishnevsky, the theatre's oldest living actor, had
died in March, and Teleshyova, actress, producer and teacher, was to follow
in July, it was a year of sad departures for the Moscow Art Theatre.   But
the general direction continued as the two founders had planned.   Indeed
much of what it was to produce in subsequent years was still Nemirovich's

---

* Played by Anna Komolova.   I was specially interested to note this, having
been much impressed by her performance as Anya in *The Cherry Orchard*, seen at
the M.X.A.T. in 1937.   There was the same жизнерадостность (joy of life) as
Kalashnikov observes in her Valya, and *extended* in the same way, so that while fully
accepting her as Anya, one could not but think of the Russia to be, which she would
one day build.   Particularly in her last exit with Trofimov.   She was then quite a
junior member of the company.

† An article in the London Press of the next day gave his age incorrectly as 85.

handiwork. Since 1940 he had been preparing *Hamlet*. The evacuation, and his own stay in Georgia, interrupted this ; but Sahnovsky knew what he was meditating and had worked on the preparation with him. Under Sahnovsky's hands the production went forward. The meaning of the play was to be very different from that put upon it by Gordon Craig in 1911-12, when the stage was covered in gold and grey to symbolise on the one hand the power and the glory, and on the other the futile emptiness of life, with Hamlet in traditional black as traditionally belonging to neither. Livanov, playing Hamlet as a live, real person, is a tall, handsome man, who joined the Art Theatre in 1923 when he was 20. He has a powerful voice and uses few gestures.*

On internal evidence the period of the play was judged to be that of the Middle Ages. Hamlet was to be gifted with greater foresight than his fellow-men, and hence misunderstood by them, and compelled to fight for his ideals against his mother, against the girl he loves, these being part of the way of things in his time, countering all he believes in. British readers will observe that this shares something with Masefield's conception of Hamlet as a man of intellect, but it is defined with greater precision by the historical approach from the Socialist angle. Boris Pasternak's translation was used, and special music written by Shebalin.

Nemirovich had also discussed with Nikolay Volkov, the playwright who made the Moscow Art Theatre's adaptation of *Anna Karenina*, the lines that ought to be taken in a similar adaptation of *War and Peace*. He had been working on *Antony and Cleopatra*, too, and Ostrovsky's *The Last Sacrifice*, of which the main theme is the corrupting influence of money upon the bourgeois society of Ostrovsky's time. Nothing is reported as yet about the production of this, which was undertaken under Nemirovich's master-ideas by Hmelyov, the actor whose interpretation of Karenin in 1936 crowned a career of subtle study. Hmelyov's first Art Theatre appearance dated back to 1919, and since then he had appeared in twenty-five parts, including Firs (*Cherry Orchard*) and Tusenbach (*Three Sisters*). As a producer he had done outside work like *As You Like It* for the Moscow "Yermolova" Theatre of which he was artistic director.

He now became artistic director of the Moscow Art Theatre, with Moskvin as Director, positions they had occupied during Nemirovich's stay in Georgia. Below them was a panel of producers, Sahnovsky, Stanitsyn, Prudkin and Kedrov, all tried servants of the theatre, and future trainers of the young recruits. The immediate work of the new directorate was to be new productions of Maeterlinck's *Blue Bird*, *The Pickwick Club*,

---

* Markov, author and actor of the M.X.A.T., says that Livanov has a great respect for John Gielgud's Hamlet, which he was studying in 1943. See *Soviet War News*, 23.x.43.

The Armoured Train, *A Burning Heart* (Ostrovsky) and even *Tsar Fyodor*, *The Seagull* and *The Forest*. But even these would bear the print of Nemirovich's hand, for it was he advised the frequent stripping of old agglutinations and barnacles from shows however successful . . . a process he once dubbed " face-lifting ".

New plays were to be Marshak's *Twelve Months*, a new historical play on Ivan the Dread by Alexey Tolstoy, and Korneichuk's *The Front*. The historical play was to be produced at Nemirovich's invitation by Alexey Popov, of the Red Army Central Theatre, " who ", said Hmelyov, " in his creative views is close to our theatre ".

With both its founders gone, the Moscow Art Theatre still had several original members very much alive ; and the tradition of the founders, which had developed organically, not without several fallow years, as is good for any organism, but also had spread as an influence over a large proportion of the theatrical earth, directly or indirectly, was now too solid to decay. It was also in its very nature too supple to become a convention. Dispelling any doubts about the contribution the Moscow Art Theatre can continue to make, the Committee for Art Affairs asked it in 1942 to set up an experimental laboratory where problems of materials, lighting, and other technical production matters could be explored for the good of the Front Line theatres. In the keen competition of the Soviet theatre not even the finest units can rest on their laurels. If there were any danger of the Moscow Art Theatre spirit drying up into the glorious past, its audience alone would be enough to prevent this. And the fate of the Art Theatre is important ; not only for itself ; not only for all the Soviet theatres ; but also for us.[13]

THE MOSCOW MALY IN THE URALS

The Maly Theatre left Moscow in October 1941 and was absent for ten months only, in Chelyabinsk, within a hundred miles of the Ural River. From a small eighteenth-century town Chelyabinsk had become a city of 100,000 inhabitants, with the largest grain elevator in the Union, a huge refrigerating plant and a big share of the Urals munitions industry. An influx of evacuees doubled its energies. New bakeries were built. Schools adopted the shift system. A new tram-line was planned and trolley-buses introduced. Already the residents were dutifully cultivating vegetables in their gardens and allotments, to ease the food problem. These permanent residents and their evacuee guests were provided by the Maly with thirteen current productions and three new ones, the chief of the latter being a stage version, in two parts, planned to last two evenings, of Tolstoy's *War and Peace*. To show that this transcription did not claim to reproduce the whole novel, the second part was called, when it at last got on the stage,

The Patriotic War of 1812. Nevertheless a number of Soviet critics complained that it was impossible to stage such a work and wrong to try.

The aim in fact was to make theatrical use of a comment on one of the greatest wars in history by one of the world's greatest masters of fiction. Necessarily it was crowded with incident and action, and in this part the stress fell more on the war scenes than on family interactions. But this did not mean that the character drawing lacked depth ; the dialogue saw to that. On the other hand, there were no complex battle scenes. The atmosphere and nature of the war were painted in cameos, a night scene in Napoleon's tent, the incident in the battery when Andrey receives his wound. Kutuzov and Napoleon thus became the important dramatic foci.

Work had begun on both parts in the spring of 1941. For years Soviet drama had been concerned with war, and this proposed epic was intended to add weight and authority to the contemporary comments. But the outbreak of a real war led to the decision to concentrate on the second part only. It also resulted in certain incidents receiving a new, more exciting, more profound significance, for example, the volunteer army in white, saluting the Smolensk Madonna (scene 2), Napoleon at Borodino with a bad chill (scene 3), Kutuzov giving the confident order to attack and beat the enemy off the soil of Russia (scene 4). This version was made jointly by Sudakov, who produced the show, N. M. Gorchakov, and N. N. Kruzhkov. The critic Durylin in a review in *Pravda* called it " not a stage version of a novel, but a stage story of the Patriotic War as the heroic feat of a people ". The episodes were linked by a narrator in the person of Ostuzhev, and the sets were by Peter Williams.

Other new plays were Korneichuk's *Partisans in the Steppes of the Ukraine*, a sequel to an earlier play, with the same characters on a collective farm now involved in the war ; and *Russian People*. These were followed on the twenty-fifth anniversary of the Revolution with Korneichuk's other new play, *The Front*. But that was after the Maly had gone home again. It left Chelyabinsk on the 10th of September 1942 and arrived home on the 16th. Thus it was one of the first theatres to return to Moscow, and despite the ovations they had received at Chelyabinsk, everyone was glad to be back. It reopened with the Tolstoy, but apparently its own premises were not available, since the opening night at the beginning of October was advertised to take place in the Central Theatre for Children, which was dark at the time ; and among productions shown in the course of 1943 were three Ostrovsky plays, *The Forest*, " *Truth is Good . . .*" and " *A Bit of a Fool . . .* " ; a revival of *Eugenie Grandet*, after Balzac, a revival of Sadovsky's 1938 production of *Woe from Wit* in Lanser's settings, which had celebrated the 150th anniversary of Shchepkin's birth ; Leonov's *Invasion*, *Revizor*, *Rasteryayeva Street* (after Gleb Uspensky), Gorky's

Barbarians, and a new play by V. Kaverin called *Great Hopes*, about a youthful battalion in Leningrad.   An imposing list, and an enterprising one ; especially if the mention of Shchepkin leads us to look back for a moment to Part I of this book.   That grand little man, so thwarted by the conditions of his time, and yet so in touch with his time, would have found in this exodus to the working East all the material he longed for ; and the foundation of dignified realism that he laid, built upon, as we have seen, by the straightforwardness of the Sadovskies, would have been perfectly suited to carry the heroic theme of Tolstoy.   Yet is it not possible to guess that without that journey to the East, even Maly realism would not have approached so closely to the real life of the audience of to-day ?   Moscow would have been heroic material to work in and for ; but the Urals, with their influx of evacuees, were that too, and more vividly, more urgently, more widely.   The whole Soviet Union was present in that audience, as it could have been in Moscow only in imagination.

The Maly company had returned to its premises by 30 September, 1942, when *Eugenie Grandet* was advertised there.   The empty Kamerny Theatre, repaired by the end of December, was used as a ' Filial ', where a ' No. 2 Company ' (so to speak) opened with *Woe from Wit* (presumably the revival mentioned above) and went on to give Korneichuk's *Partisan* play (produced by Tsyganov with sets by Knoblok), *The Attack on the Mill* (founded on a short story by Zola), Shaw's *Pygmalion*, Molière's *Don Juan*, *The Precipice* (on a Goncharov novel), *Fuente Ovejuna*, *Guilty Though Guiltless* (Ostrovsky), and Scribe's *Une Verre d'Eau*.

This again is another imposing list, and shows the remarkable catholicity of a representative Soviet theatre's choice in plays.   Zola, on the rare occasions on which any of his work appears in Britain, does not seem to hold an audience very deeply.   Scribe we regard as a purveyor of plots for Duse ; and even as early as 1893 William Archer suggested that his most famous play, *Adrienne Lecouvreur*, ought to be kept under a glass case in a historical museum.   But that, perhaps, is because our producers approach such plays from another angle than Soviet producers.   Socialist realism could extract from a Victorian melodrama something more than novelette characters and violent plot.

The Filial is not a junior branch of the Maly, but merely what might be called the " Small Stage ".   It was founded in 1922.   It seats 620, compared with the main theatre's 1080, and has only one Circle.   But one of the productions, *The Immortal*, was to be the preserve of the younger members of the Maly company only ; nearly all the characters being young, and the whole a special inspiration to audiences at or near student age.   This had its *première* for the Red Army's twenty-fifth anniversary ; and this, too, was fitting to its theme.   Sometimes whole plays are transferred to the Filial stage, as *The Forest* was to be in the 1943-4 season ; sometimes separate players go from one to the other, as did Zubov and Turchaninova, the Napoleon and the Countess Rostova in the main stage's *Patriotic War,* who played the leads in *Pygmalion* at the Filial.

Forthcoming plays in the 1943-4 season were to be *Romeo and Juliet, Antony and Cleopatra, Twelfth Night*, and two Ostrovskies, *The Last Sacrifice* and *Wolves and Sheep*. With these were to come the newest Leonov play, *Lyonushka*, and the Alexey Tolstoy drama of Ivan the Dread. Alexey Tolstoy had become literary adviser to the Maly and taken charge of its literary department.

The administrative head of the Maly was Shapovalov and the artistic head Sudakov. It had a panel of producers similar to that of the Moscow Art Theatre, B. Vershilov, Zubov, Yablochkina and others, but guest producers were invited for special shows, such as Diky and Reuben Simonov. Ostrovsky plays were generally produced by Maly veterans like Prov Sadovsky or Vera Pashennaya. Sets for these were usually done by K. Yuon, but the 1944 revival of *The Forest* was to be set by A. Gerasimov.

Many were the authors in touch with this theatre nowadays : Trenyov, Romashov, Fedin, Kozakov and Paustovsky, all well established, were writing plays for it. But it did not abandon the classics, as will be seen. Indeed, for revivals of old plays, especially Ostrovsky, a kind of Senate or Second Chamber had been established, called the " Institute of Trustee Producers " (режиссеров-кураторов), whose function was to watch supplementary rehearsals of old productions, and if necessary introduce new performers into any parts that were not being satisfactorily carried by their traditional guardians. In this way tradition was kept from getting stale and the temptations to rest on laurels, whether personal or those of the whole theatre, were avoided. Complacency was no more a fault of a Maly actor than it was of a Red Army General.

The theatre had also introduced a system of débuts by which pupils of the " Shchepkin " School attached to the institution could be worked into current repertory. One gathers from the success claimed for it that to this there had been perhaps a little opposition. But the performances of " Shchepkin " pupils in *The Front* and *Invasion* seem to have silenced the objectors if there were any. In this way the conditions that Glamá complained of had been removed. Conservatism of personnel was no more a fault of the Maly management than it was of a Soviet factory.[14]

The Moscow Central Theatre of the Red Army

The intimate tie between the Red Army and the Central Theatre of the Red Army had never been broken, although in peace-time, as far as audiences go, it was much like that between the Red Army and any other theatre. But with the coming of war, plainly this theatre would have a new function altogether. An old function, too, in some ways, its original one ; but reborn, revivified, for a People's Army now professional, ranking with, rivalling, and perhaps to excel any other army in history. Plainly, also, a conscientious director could assume nothing about such an army ; for nothing like it had been known before. Expression, service, meant direct and first-hand knowledge of it.

So Alexey Popov, who was rapidly becoming one of the most interesting figures of the Soviet theatre, set out at once to see for himself what the war and the front and the Red Army at the front and behind the lines were like. " If you genuinely know army life ", he explained, " that will save you from any false heroicisation, in which there might be plenty of pathos but little of the truth of life ; and also from any dim documentation, which, though it might create an illusion of actuality and living figures, might murder the inner heroism in them."

His war theatre, therefore, was founded on fact, observed and felt on the spot, but it was built with both the prosaic and the heroic, with both the actual and the theatrical ; and in a war such as the Red Army was waging, as a portion of the Soviet peoples, the prosaic and the heroic, the actual and the theatrical, may often be one and the same. The expression of this is Socialist realism, as I have described it elsewhere, always, by the very suppleness of its structure, able to find truth in each new turn of human history.

But as a performing unit, the T.S.D.K.A.* was under the same responsibility, and the same liability to evacuate as any other theatre. It had indeed a special job to do outside Moscow. In the Urals not only were new factories and new populations springing up, but also there were new units of the Red Army being trained. Here was a special need for a theatre that would display the tradition of that Army to those recently joining it, and the place of the Soviet peoples in war to those who would have the most active and essential part in its defence.

So away to Sverdlovsk went the main body of the Red Army Theatre, arrived there on the 29th of November 1941, and twenty days later opened in the District Red Army House with a play called *The Winged Tribe*, by Perventsev. This was not directly about the Red Army, but it was new and topical. It was about Soviet pilots and their part in the war. Perhaps not a very distinguished play, a little too hot from the oven, the ingredients too hurriedly mixed. But the war had only been in existence half a year, and author and theatre were as yet feeling their way. They could not force a way by preconceived theories, but by following the course of the war as it twisted and turned in the theatre's beam. The light of that beam

* The initials stand in Russian for Central House of the Red Army.

was the militant past, further back even than the founding of the Red Army. So the second show of the season was a revival of *General Suvorov* (see *N.S.T.*) ; after that, Gorky's *Meshchane* in the general survey of the previous régime, whose ills had been felt in the Urals exactly as in Moscow ; and, in the general cultural heritage, *The Taming of the Shrew*, one of Popov's most celebrated productions. In January 1942 followed *She Stoops to Conquer* and Ostrovsky's " *A Bit of a Fool* . . .", reminders, maybe, that life is good when it is buoyant and honest, and those men win in old peace-time love affairs, who are adult, full-living, self-reliant, but not self-absorbed.

Then better plays became available about the war, and the horizon of the present could be enlarged. *The Smoke of the Fatherland* was still rather a raw play, but it did show the Fascists in the Ukraine, real Fascists, raping, murdering, plundering ; and it showed the Old Order for a while returning to the Ukraine. The son of a previous landowner, hand in glove with the occupying Fascists, was a reflection on the stage of a member of the Mirsky family who did the same thing in actuality ; and, by a further throw, there was not so much difference socially between the S.S., shoring up with studied brutality a cracked and illogical capitalism and the Black Hundreds similarly preserving, and with much the same sub-human standards, a cracked and illogical Tsarism. A few malcontents may welcome such a restoration ; but only for a while. Then even the relics, the ex-bailiffs, the old servants can bear it no longer, and turn against the invader-lord. Another step in this theatre's development.

A much better play opened the international horizon. *Oleko Dundich*, Serb patriot of the last war, who though a Monarchist Colonel, found himself by fighting for the people on the side of the new Russia. Another step.

But Socialist realism is unpredictable. It can be assessed, perhaps recognised, only by the result. In the hands of men like Popov that result takes unexpected forms. Who would have thought that the next achievement would be a graceful heroic costume comedy, written in verse ?

The author was Alexander Gladkov . . . not to be confused with Fyodor Gladkov, author of *Cement*, whose 60th birthday was celebrated by literary circles and the Press in June 1943. Alexander Gladkov was a younger man, and his verse in this play was light and pointed, nicely rhymed, with lines irregular in length spanning the thought as in Lermontov's *Masquerade*. *Long, Long Ago* showed a girl in a well-to-do country family of the time of the Napoleonic wars. She is a bit of a tomboy, but with the heart of a man. She cannot bear being a woman, as women in her time have to be inactive, permanently civilian. She dresses in a Cornet's uniform and rides to the Army. The idea comes quite naturally, when she dresses so for a fancy-dress ball, and finds she can deceive a rather insufferable young officer, who tells her he intends to marry (for her fortune) the very girl he doesn't know she is.   Much theatrical fun is got from her dexterous changes of costume in this scene, while he is off stage, from her real self to the Cornet, and back again.

Shura is a real girl.   Her soliloquy at night, waiting for the old servant to saddle her horse, is a very truthful, human and moving passage.   There are no false heroics about her.   And yet she is heroic.   So heroic in fact that her conduct at the front earns her the commendation of her superior officers (having been brought up in a strictly military household, she is already at home in the detail of Army affairs, especially as relaxed in the field) ;   and so she qualifies for a decoration.   Kutuzov is informed, however, confidentially, that she is suspected of being a woman.   There is an amusing scene between the scandalised but admiring Field-Marshal-Prince and the feminine and very determined Shura, who compels him to deny her " secret " as just a joke and let her remain in the Service.   This completely bewilders the young officer.

He has been discovering in himself feelings toward the young " Cornet " which he ought not to be feeling for a brother officer ;   and this, incidentally, makes him a good deal less insufferable both in Shura's eyes and in our own.

Their growing interest in each other proceeds through scenes of deep patriotism, tragedy, suffering, and military action, homes wrecked, relatives murdered, like any true story of to-day ;   but threaded by the soldiers' song, " Long, Long Ago ", which runs all through, and the music of Tihon Hrennikov * which frames it.   Dobrzhanskaya, who played Shura, was the captivating and feminine Katharine of *The Taming of the Shrew* in Popov's production, and she is said to have given a quite enchanting performance in this part.   The production, according to the critic Gerasimov, was far the best of all, though many theatres did this play.   He says that the verse sounded in the mouths of the performers " with such noble genuineness as alone has the ability to provide artistic fiction in a context of historical truth ".

For the curious thing about his romance is that it was true.   It was true not only in the tale—for there was such a person as Shura ;   only her name was Nadezhda Durova, and it was not Kutuzov who knew her secret, but the Tsar Nikolay himself, who sent for her, and allowed her to remain a soldier.   But it was true also of Russian women.   To-day there are thousands of girls like Shura.   Their war service is as heroic as hers, if less secret ;   their hearts are as passionately patriotic as hers ;   and they win awards for their courage and admiration for their skill as she did, without

---

* Hrennikov is one of the younger Soviet musicians.   At the age of 29 he had written two symphonies, a piano concerto, an Opera, *Into the Storm*, and a great deal of incidental music for screen and stage.   His haunting tunes for the Vahtangov Theatre's *Much Ado About Nothing*, though an early work, have always been popular.

losing their feminine sensibility or charm. Let Lyudmila Pavlichenko
stand as evidence for that.

Here the Red Army Theatre reached out beyond the Red Army and
showed the audience its own womenfolk. It could afford to do so; for
Army and audience were one. The self-discipline of the former depended
on and proceeded from that of the latter, and vice versa. There was no
barrier of politicians or officers' schools or manufacturers between them.
For the same reason it could also with perfect effectiveness show that audience
the guerrillas, in a sense their rivals for glory. This it did in the next production . . . glory, be it added, that started from not altogether promising
human material.

This was in a prose play by Gladkov written with Alexey Arbuzov,
an older dramatist, two of whose plays, for example, *Half a Dozen Favourites*
and *The Long Road* were new productions in 1935 and 1936 at the Moscow
Workers' Art Theatre and the Moscow Contemporary Theatre, respectively.* It was called *The Immortal*.

A group of Moscow students is out in the country near Oryol between
Moscow and the advancing German lines. They are helping to lift
potatoes. With them is an American journalist on the look out for a good
story which will serve for a really unusual book to make his name. (His
name, incidentally, is Jack Warner!) In the party are a Foreign Language
Faculty freshman, a Literature senior student, a History student, a fencing
champion, and a young gourmet. Jack Warner, pretending to be asleep,
writes notes of their talk, their love affairs, their feuds and jealousies.

But it is learned that the Fascist tide has surrounded them. They are
cut off. Tank-borne troops break through. They face up to the situation and
form a guerrilla unit, taking the name of one that has been wiped out, except
for one old peasant who survives, and who joins their unit: "The Immortal",
it was called. A girl tractor driver from a nearby collective farm joins
them, and a wounded Red Army sergeant. Their leader is a young professional pianist, who is killed in battle. Many of them are killed. But
their characters, and those of the survivors, develop and toughen in the
fight, even that of the young flapper who had been rather a butterfly. The
Germans hang her for refusing to give her fellow-partisans away. And
even the " exquisite " sacrifices himself for the sake of the others. Only
the fencing champion (by that surprising honesty which characterises Soviet
drama, and is so unexpectedly dramatic) is found wanting in spirit. But

---

* The former was founded in 1929 from a group of players of the First and Second
Art Theatres. It toured the DonBas miners, the Urals and Ukrainian factory workers,
for two and a half years, settling in Moscow in 1932, because perpetual touring
made creative depth impossible. The latter also was peripatetic, originally called
the First Moscow Mobile Workers' Theatre, U.M.Z.P., and organised in 1925 to
bring the theatre to workers in all quarters of the city. It performed in clubs.

the transformation of mere mortals (and no Soviet dramatist would be thought a realist if he dealt only in people that were entirely good) into The Immortal comes gradually. Some are quite as frightened as they are heroic ; and there is always a slap-dash undergraduate quality even in their discipline. But the psychology deepens. Love develops ; and a collective sense so strong and direct that even Jack Warner, who in 1941 could have got away on the plea of non-belligerency, and written his book, and become famous in two continents, joins in and fights and loses his life.

Heroism without heroics is achieved on the stage by three means. First, authors must have drawn the people as individuals, inconsistent if need be, but not as types. Second, actors must know these inside out even in the first act. Thirdly, the whole company must have a high degree of ensemble, in which the powers of the producer will be tested. Otherwise there will be no sense of community, and to " die for it " will be a mere sentimental abstraction. People do not die for such an abstraction. The ideals they die for are concrete ones.

Gerasimov says of this production, that the actors knew ".the very budget of the characters, and their likes and dislikes, and their dreams ". But for the ensemble much of the credit must go to Popov, since except for Honoured Artist Hohlov, who played Jack Warner, most of them were juniors.

Long, Long Ago was produced on the 2nd of December 1942, *The Immortal* the following March. In June 1943 the theatre returned to Moscow after an absence of seventeen months at Sverdlovsk, during which it had given 555 performances and presented seven new shows.

In addition to its own fine premises in the Park of the Central House of the Red Army, it was using also the Moscow Art Filial stage. Not only the plays they had created in the Urals were shown, but also Schiller's *Intrigue and Love*, wherein the Fascist-like methods of the grim, corrupt German officialdom of the eighteenth century took on a new shade ; and new plays, *The Front, Invasion*. Later plans were for a new play by Gladkov, to be called *A Cruel Romance*, the action of which was to take place one New Year's Eve in war-time Moscow ; a play by Gerasimov, *Big Country*, on the terrific industrial effort of the Urals (directly aligned to the theatre's war-time experience) ; a comedy on a defence theme, by Dyhovichny and Slobodskoy ; a Gogol ; a Chehov. In addition, the following writers had attached themselves to this theatre : Lev Kassil, Romashov, Slavin, Golubov, Sergeyev-Tsensky, Kozhevnikov, Perventsev.* The next European classic to be done was Calderon's *Lady of the Heart*, in a translation by Shchepkina-Kupernik.

* Kassil has written for Children's Theatres ; Slavin wrote *Intervention ;* for Romashov and Tsensky, see pp. 243 and 247. The rest are newer writers.

But by far the most interesting of all was a new plan of Popov's. The theme for the principal undertaking of 1943-4 was decided upon in the superb stand made by the Red Army at Stalingrad. Only there were no plays ; and, as far as could be seen, no playwrights with the necessary personal experience to make the work authentic. One day there arrived in Popov's office a young Captain called Yuri Chepurin, who wanted to write a play about Stalingrad, because he himself had been there and fought there. He and the theatre committee held long and deep consultations, which ended in September, and immediately the scene-designer Shifrin and the producer Afonin set off for Stalingrad.

This is a different kind of expedition from that undertaken by Nemirovich to Rome. Different even from the expedition to the Rogues' Market. Indeed, the whole proposal is something quite new in theatre history. The living newspaper here is brought to its completion. Themistocles, instead of commissioning Phrynichus to write *The Phœnissæ*, gets a poet who had been at Salamis, an Æschylus, to put into stage-worthy shape the story of that superb sea-fight. Or Garrick sends Lutherbourg and a native Indian dramatist to sketch and write a play about The Black Hole of Calcutta ! A living newspaper rushed from the tape-machines, but discussed with Marxian thoroughness, and pondered with human feeling, with the care of Flaubert, before it goes to press.

John Gibbons, Moscow correspondent for the *Daily Worker*, described the result, which he saw in May 1944, as :—

> By far the most popular show in the city. " The curtain ", he says, " rises to show a magnificent scene of Stalingrad as it was before the battle. The morning mist rising over the silent Volga, and the factory chimneys emitting smoke."

This opening recalls that of Popov's production of *A Midsummer Night's Dream*, but it is an extension therefrom. The view of the destined city is not a scenic trick. It states the theme dramatically, visually. The people the audience is to see will be real people, individuals ; but the theme is Stalingrad as a whole, all these real individuals fused into a historical thing, which is what the world thinks of now when it says " Stalingrad ", but which, before the play begins, though it had not yet been called into being, existed, nevertheless, in the way those individuals were already living.

Gibbons goes on to say that some scenes depicted mass air-raids, the city in flames, the stream of refugees, Siberian soldiers marching into an inferno of fire. " The scenes of house-to-house fighting are magnificent. The setting is superb, and the acting such that you forget you are in a theatre, and feel as if you are really in an embattled city."

So perhaps you might have done in those luscious melodramas at Oryol or Ostorozhe in the 'eighties. But there is a world of difference. And the difference is caused by the dramatic purpose. In the old melodramas the purpose was sensation and nothing beyond. The sensation of being present. In this production the purpose was certainly the *sensation* of being present, but at a defined historical point, which has been given a deep and important meaning in the personal lives of the audience. Not only did the citizen of Moscow become for the time being a member of the Red Army, or a citizen of Stalingrad, he or she realised (in the fullest sense of that word) what that army and what those people did and endured for the citizens of Moscow and of the Soviet Union and of all the world.

This, in short, is Socialist realism. Further, it could have been achieved in no other way. The fate of "representative" Stalingrad people, shown on the stage without these scenic effects, would not have achieved the same result. Formalist abstractness, however clad in glorious verse, would not have achieved it either. Verse might deepen the human feeling ; but it would have to spring from real figures ; and if these figures were individuals, then the scenic unity was required. Either of the other methods would have put the whole out of focus, or the individual out of focus. And it was the individual that made Stalingrad, fused as they were together. Only by showing the individual in the city could the Socialist-realist result have been achieved ; and to get it in this case the scenic effect was not a decoration but a necessity.[15]

The LenKom among the Moslems

The "Leninist Komsomol" Theatre of Moscow during the war continued the development I have described in my former book. Apart from its director Bersenyev, it is particularly strong in its women. This must have made it of special interest to the citizens of Uzbekistan, who so few years back had been under the feudal spell, the patriarchal dictatorship of the prophet Mahomet. For sixteen months this theatre dwelt among the Moslems, based in the Fergana Valley, but visiting Tashkent for the summer of 1942, and Samarkand, Namangan, Kokand and Margelan, places that had turned themselves into supply bases for the Red Army. Ten first nights they had, which included revivals of *The Doll's House* and *The Widow from Valencia* (by Lope de Vega), both of which had brilliant meaning for the newly delivered wife-slaves of the Uzbeks ; and Simonov's *A Fellow from Our Town*, which had an encouraging emulation for the youth of the region, even though its Far Eastern fighting had been superseded by graver and nearer battle.

Bersenyev himself is outstanding both as actor and as producer. Serafima Birman, his leading lady, who captured her new audience as Vasya Zhelyoznova in Gorky's play of that name, had also done fine productions, one of the best being Tolstoy's *Living Corpse*. The main

STALINGRAD ON THE STAGE.

A scene from Chepurin's *People of Stalingrad* in Popov's production at the Central Theatre of the Red Army.

[*facing page* 140.

Vera Maretskaya as the Napoleonic war heroine in the Mossoviet production of *Nadyezhda Durova*. This actress gave a deeply moving performance as the heroine of the Soviet war film *No Greater Love*

theme of this six-act tragedy is the apparent suicide of a husband, who disappears to get away from his wife, but is discovered and, after trial, does in fact commit suicide. In general, though, it does for the nineteenth-century nobility what Chehov did for the middle class in the provinces, even if it is planned more like a novel than a play.

Serafima Birman also produced Rostand's *Cyrano de Bergerac* in the translation by Vladimir Solovyov, with Bersenyev as Cyrano and Roxana played by a new discovery of the evacuation period, the young actress Okunyevskaya. Cyrano was seen not as a flamboyant figure in a romantic age, but rather as a Frenchman, self-reliant, rapier-like, subtle and staunch, the kind of Frenchman who makes life intolerable for the Nazis apparently in control of him, by acts of defiance that are ruthless, logical, skilled and often witty. Bersenyev, with his feeling for verse and expressive gesture, made this a warm, living, important person ; but the reality of the whole, the contemporary feel of this French world to-day, preserving the best in its traditions and so remaining strong and genuine, this was due to the qualities of Serafima Birman as producer.

She has analysed these qualities herself in her booklet on the art of the actor : Труд актера (Искусство, 1939). This is a kind of Encheiridion for actors, written from her own experience since graduation as a pupil of Stanislavsky to the position she now holds as a great actress. Some of the searching remarks made in the course of this handbook reveal her mind : about Shakespeare's " mirror to nature ", for example, she says : " It must not be a crooked one, but it is possible to hold it at different angles, hence the reflection of actuality will be altered. A mirror can be nearer or further away, higher or lower, facing left or facing right. In a mirror the prin-cipal reflection can be one very near object, while only at some distance can a mirror reflect the general plan."

" Realism ", she writes, " reflects life. Socialist realism re-makes life."

Or again : " A spectator comes to the theatre not only to hear the author's text, but also to see into the depths of the hearts of the figures on the stage."

From these random fragments it is not surprising that Bersenyev ranks the production of *Cyrano* as an important stage in the theatre's development.

Another important production during evacuation was Alexandra Brushtein's *Day of the Living*. This celebrated children's playwright abandoned young girlhood as her theme for this play, and considered Czechoslovakia during the Nazi occupation. There is a local legend in a Czech village that in the hour of need a curly-headed tailor, who gave his life to protect his fellows from a previous threat of German thraldom, will return to save them again. The scene of action is that same village to-day, oppressed by Nazi brutality. Jan, who is a tailor, and has curly

10

hair, rallies the inhabitants against the invaders at the time of the German ultimatum to Czechoslovakia. He inspires old Kasparek, a retired opera singer ; Kasparek as head of the village is forced to read a German pro-clamation at the microphone. Although a storm-trooper is at his side with a revolver, he bears Jan's words in his heart, and denounces what he has read. He is shot in hearing of the whole country, thereby stiffening the resistance of thousands. Another to follow Jan's example is an old professor, who in his ivory tower is moved to write a passionate appeal to the people. As the culminating incident, Jan sabotages a German muni-tions train, driving it himself to destruction. Throughout, though hatred for the Fascists is never expressed in violent language or bombastic behaviour, the spirit of Czechoslovakia triumphs.

Solovyov plays Jan as a happy, quiet man, cool-headed and confident. This is another way of expressing heroicism without heroics ; and, of course, there is no hint or suspicion that Jan is the legendary figure returned from the dead. On the contrary, he himself is inspired by the old wives' tales, and uses them deliberately. The spirit of the original tailor, the real one, is thus re-born in our time.

The theatre company was small by Soviet standards, numbering only thirty. But it worked very intensely with a marked effect on the juniors reported in spring 1942. When it returned to Moscow a year later than that, it was preparing *The Winter's Tale*, an Uzbek play, *The Eagle's Flight*, Kaverin's *Great Hopes*, and the first part of a big work by Boris Gorbatov, which he had given to it, called *The Youth of our Fathers*. The complete work would be a dramatic history of the Komsomol ; and this portion was to deal with the years from 1918 to 1920, ending with the appearance of Lenin on October the second at the Third Congress of the R.K.S.M. in the foyer of the " Sverdlov " Communist University in Little Dmitrovka, where the LenKom Theatre's premises now are. Solovyov's production of this celebrated the twenty-fifth anniversary of the Lenin-Stalin Komsomol, and was very suitably noted for the activities of the junior players in it.

Another new play of even more burning public interest was being written by the poetess Margarita Aliger. It was about " Tanya " (Zoya Kosmodemyanskaya), the heroine of the Fascist Occupation, tortured and hanged under particularly terrible conditions by the Nazis. Doubtless there were many such superb girls ; but Zoya Kosmodemyanskaya, when the truth of her death became known, somehow took hold of the Russian mind, partly perhaps because she had such charm and because her beauty, like her faith, endured after death. The photographs of her body are in-finitely moving, even to us in Britain, whose sisters and daughters were not savaged as she was. To the Russians her story has been told and retold in literature, painting, opera, play and ballet.[16]

The most notable thing about the LenKom Theatre then is its fusion of actor and producer. This is not confined to this theatre, though it is specially marked in it. It shows the tendency of the time. As realism gets established in the Socialist community, the producer, who in the early days of the Revolution was all-important to shape the unco-ordinated interpretations of the actors into the form that would best carry the revolutionary feel of the time (of which most of them would be unaware, or if aware, uncertain how to express it), now finds himself in charge of aware and deeply studied individuals. It becomes their job to understand as profoundly and to impersonate as faithfully as their minds and skill allow them the people created by the author. It becomes the producer's job, though without lessening the demands on his knowledge and character, to co-ordinate, not to dictate. His material is easier to work ; and his responsibility is therefore the greater. But the emphasis has shifted from him to the players, who are more directly in touch with the Socialist audience, and have greater call upon their personal skill as players.

The special fusion of player and producer in the LenKom Theatre is one of the reasons why this is a unit to watch. And the invitation to Konstantin Simonov to act as consultant, reported in March 1944, indicates a safeguard that the fusion will not be wasted on meaningless plays.

THE MOSSOVIET AND BROADER HORIZONS

Since 1940 the Theatre of the Moscow Soviet had been under the control of the much honoured People's Artist Yuri Zavadsky. It had made what is known in sporting circles as a " come back ".* Evacuation took it to Chimkent in Kazakhstan, some hundred miles from Tashkent and from the Uzbek boundary ; and thereafter to Alma-Ata, the Kazakh capital, lying in a plain rich in cattle and apple-trees below the snow-capped Kirghizian mountains.

In the course of a year it gave more than 320 performances, of Afinogenov's On the Eve and his Mashenka, of Russian People and The Front, of Oleko Dundich and of Nadyezhda Durova, another and more strictly biographical play about the heroine of Long, Long Ago. This last was the joint work of two playwrights, Lipskerov and Kochetkov.

Perhaps the broad horizon of the apple plains gave this theatre a wider outlook ! Zavadsky found a new way of developing theatre policy. He planned cycles of plays. A cycle of Goldoni (La Locandiera, The Liar, An Amusing Situation) ; a cycle of Ostrovsky (the Balzaminov series) ;

* Professor Morozov in a personal letter describes Zavadsky as " one of our most brilliant régisseurs ". Incidentally, I must confess to several mistakes made in my description of this theatre's work in N.S.T., to which he calls my attention. These have been rectified in recent impressions of that book.

a cycle of Shakespeare. The idea may not have been due to residence in
Kazakhstan, of course. The first two Goldoni plays were already in the
repertoire before they left Moscow. But the power to extend it came.
Each cycle was to be designed as a unit by the theatre's special artist Meletiy
Vinogradov, only objects and details being changed for each play in the
cycle. For Zavadsky was continually in search of the " theatre theatrical ".
He eschewed naturalism and any tendency thereto. Hence music was
important to his productions, music that would be a kind of light bathing
the theme in atmosphere and the actors in mood. Zavadsky was no
formalist. Man was his theme ; changing, growing, man. That meant
actors and actresses in full charge of themselves as artists. And for that
reason he opposed stages that were too big. And likewise stages that were
too fully equipped. He was aware of the dangers of exuberant realism.
In his own production of *Othello*, still in preparation when the theatre
returned to Moscow, he was trying to simplify the production of Shakespeare
toward something approaching the stage conditions for which he wrote.
A very different production from his *Othello* at Rostov-on-Don.

In any other producer's head such ideas, such tillings of thorny ground,
might soon become retrogressive. With Zavadsky this was unlikely ;
and even if he was mistaken in his views, his shows would be
saved by his players, especially Mordvinov, his male lead, and Vera
Maretskaya, his female lead, who was made a People's Artist in 1943,
and like Mordvinov received a Stalin award. But in fact it is in the
interests of greater actuality that Zavadsky seeks the simple, to judge from
his intentions in *Othello*, which he said was to be " a war theme ", with
Desdemona less anæmic than she is usually made and Iago brought on an
equal plane of importance to Othello. In the Soviet Union, especially
in the eastern countries, the emphasis hitherto had tended to fall on Othello
alone, as a coloured but honourable man in a white but dishonourable trap.
Zavadsky sought to restore the balance, and so augment the battle.

Forthcoming productions were an anti-Fascist play called *The Cannibals*,
of which I think the author was Kaplev, a new Paustovsky, *Knights of the
Starry Sky*, and *A Quiet Little Town*, by Bela Ballash, a Hungarian writer.
Kaverin's *Great Hopes* was their last *première* in Central Asia before returning
to Moscow in October 1943, and reopening the following month. The
company had been strengthened by two Honoured Artists who had
transferred from the Theatre of the Revolution, Astangov and Olga Pyzhova.
And the younger generation established itself in the person of Nazvanov,
making his début at the Mossoviet in *Oleko Dundich*. A characteristic
production, this ; for Zavadsky likes colour and gusto and alternating moods.
And here was opportunity to show what a small stage could do. Battle-
scenes, ball-rooms, the war songs of advancing cavalry squadrons, staff

headquarters, uniforms, disguises, wit and passion and incalculable Woman, all were given that directness which is Zavadsky's special contribution to the Soviet theatre. Nor did the significance of this Serbian patriot suffer by his treatment.[17]

THE VAHTANGOV THEATRE IN SIBERIA

A similarly laconic production was given to this play by Diky at the Vahtangov Theatre, which spent two years at Omsk, a Western Siberian city containing over 125,000 people in the nineteen-thirties. Originally a Cossack settlement, it became a prison town (Dostoyevsky serving his sentence here), and during the Civil War was Kolchak's headquarters. So in tradition it was found to be half-Siberian and half-European when the evacuees got there. Camels grin at buses in the streets.

What a change had come over the grim convict town! Now it is able to be called the administrative and *cultural* centre of Western Siberia. And what a joy it would have been for our Polish lady to take steamer up the Irtysh and visit the Vahtangov Theatre, she who pined so for the civilisation she had been parted from! And what a variety of lands and periods she would have entered with the Vahtangov actors: those of *Yegor Bulychov*, *Much Ado About Nothing*, *Field-Marshal Kutuzov*, *A Servant of Two Masters*, *Le Chapeau de Paille* (Labiche), *Russian People*, *Cyrano de Bergerac*. The range is so great that one is tempted to find a lack of policy. Yet if any fault is to be found, it would lie less in this than in the unco-ordinated contrasts of the theatre's three producers.

Diky's style was swift, economical, well suited to the rapid tempo of *Oleko Dundich*. Reuben Simonov, on the other hand, was an experimenter. In the second act of *Mademoiselle Nitouche*, a musical comedy by Hervé, the play in which the heroine is supposed to be acting takes place off stage; but Simonov decided he would like to see it taking place, so the company proceeded to improvise one. Simonov also evolved the theory that a musical comedy requires a special communion (общение) between actors and audience, more than a comedy without music, or any other sort of show; so he extended the stage into the auditorium, justifying this by the usage of Davydov, Varlamov, and such old style actors, and the approval of Stanislavsky in his early years.

Simonov himself is a fine graceful actor. His Benedict, like Mansureva's Beatrice, in *Much Ado About Nothing* was more like a ballet-dance than an impersonation when I saw it in 1937. To the music of Tihon Hrennikov, in startlingly lovely earth-pigment stylised sets of Ryndin, the lifting of a finger became the sweep of an arm, drawing the whole body of the actor across the stage so that everything had the extended, or distended, quality of action in a dream.

Something of this dream quality was found by the critics in *Cyrano*, with the same pair of leads as Cyrano and Roxana, when Ohlopkov produced it for the Vahtangov Theatre. Ryndin did the sets, which consisted largely of an enormous puppet or lay-figure as permanent background, with different aspects for each scene. In Act III for instance it was the figure of a woman holding a guitar in her hands, the hole in the guitar being the balcony for the Roxana-Christian-Cyrano serenade.

Such formalist treatment, subjecting mankind to an idea, and typical of Ohlopkov, the third contrast in producers, roused a storm of discussion, especially in the pages of Литература и искусство.* Kalashnikov attacked the lavishness of colour as defeating its own object . . ." Where Diky selects the one correct adjective from ten possibles, *Ohlopkov uses all* ten and an extra one if he can think of any." To this Vasilyev retorted that at least that is better than dullness and visual poverty. It makes Cyrano's unrequited love tragedy all the more moving ; and to take exception to it would imply rejecting all " theatricality ". This raised an old controversy, about which more critical breath is expended in the Soviet Union than about any other theatrical theme, and next month Boyadzhiev asked, " What is this ' theatricality' anyway ? Genuine theatricality consists of selection, not of all-inclusion " ; to which Vasily Sahnovsky, with the weight of Moscow Art Theatre theory and practice behind him, soberly suggested that true theatricality lies in the actor really experiencing what is going on inside the characters he is representing. If he feels intensely, the things on the stage round him will conform.

Which reply is, of course, perfectly true ; and perhaps it is idle to discuss the merits of the Ohlopkov *Cyrano* without having seen it. But there is just as much danger in deluging a play with the opulent fancy of the present-day designer, abstract or symbolic, as there was in deluging it with that of the nineteenth-century painter in the Théâtre Antoine. It might well be a distraction from the essential French tragedy, which Marxism finds in Rostand. Cyrano may be flamboyant ; but Rostand is not.

Nevertheless Ohlopkov is respected as an original artist, entitled to work out his own ideas. How much he was respected may be seen in that he was one of the personalities invited to contribute Victory messages to the towns of Oryol and Byelgorod on the front page of Литература и искусство in August 1943. He is a People's Artist of the Republic, and has received a Stalin award. So did Simonov for his work on *Oleko Dundich*, and Cyrano, as an actor. In January 1943 Ohlopkov was reported to be re-

* Ю. Калашников: „ Спектакли и режиссеры ", 30.i.1943.
Ф. Васильев: „ В зашиту театральиости " 13.ii.1943.
Г. Богджиев: „ Что такое театральиость ? " 13.iii.1943.
В. Сахиовский: „ О театральности подлинной и мнвмой ", 8.v.1943.

hearsing for a stage appearance as Hamlet. He was a fine actor, and may have been noticed by London readers as the young man who put Lenin up for the night on his arrival at Petrograd at the beginning of the film, *Lenin in October*, and again in *Alexander Nevsky*. But in June of the same year he left the Vahtangov Theatre and was appointed to the Art Directorship of the Moscow Theatre of the Revolution.

The Vahtangov Theatre continued its tasks. Konstantin Simonov's *Wait for Me*, Ostrovsky's *The Abyss*, Korneichuk's *The Front*, were among the shows they brought back to Moscow when they returned in November 1943 ; and for *Russian People* they had a set decorated with battle standards borne by soldiers of Alexander of the Neva, Dmitry of the Don, Suvorov of the Danube . . . remote from, yet greatly akin to, the characters of Simonov's play. They played at first in the Moscow Art Theatre Filial for ten days, before moving to the premises of the Central Tyuz.

Forthcoming productions were to be Zahava's treatment of *The Storm*, Diky's of a folk-play, *Frol Skabeyev*, by Averkiev, and a play by Jean-Richard Bloch concerning the French Fleet at Toulon, translated by Pavel Antokolsky. The folk-play was to have rich Russian colour, plenty of crowd scenes, and the advice of Gorlov, a connoisseur of folk art from the State Porcelain Factory.

After Ohlopkov left, Reuben Simonov became artistic director of the theatre, and planned to do *The Great Sovereign*, by Solovyov, *The Blue Scarf*, by Katayev, and a play by Yuri Herman called *Here's to those Under Way*. This last was about a British-Russian convoy. Simonov's theories about musical comedy are serious. He regards it as having origins in street tunes. From the tunes came the plot, and with the plot came a freedom in comment which admitted jests at vices and foibles of the day. The musical comedy, in fact, should have a certain spontaneous " folk " quality. His production of *Mamzelle Nitouche* tried to elevate this not very distinguished work to a higher plane than it reaches in Western European esteem.

The position of the Vahtangov in the comity of theatres may be summed up by the words of Simonov : " In the twenty odd years that have elapsed since the founding of the Vahtangov Theatre, its actors have been indefatigably perfecting their art. They study voice-placing, rhythm, motion and dancing." For this reason, perhaps, it did not contribute anything of very striking value in the war years. For this reason, perhaps, it has failed to maintain the lead it took in the early years of the Revolution. Other units with a more urgent art philosophy have outrun it, at any rate on this lap.[18]

THE MOSCOW THEATRE OF THE REVOLUTION AND HIGH THEATRICALITY

Before Ohlopkov joined the Moscow Theatre of the Revolution, it had had a series of gifted directors and the services of Babanova, one of the most popular actresses in the Soviet Union. He was taking over a well-tempered instrument which might have suffered in the past from poor execution, but was none the less capable of great expressiveness. Its evacuation centre had been Tashkent. There it celebrated its 500th performance of Lope de Vega's *Dog in the Manger* on 31st July 1943. The producer of this was Vlasov, who had joined the staff in 1936, followed by Babanova, Glizer, Orlov and others as co-producers the next year. After twenty-three months in Tashkent, they proceeded to Samarkand and to Termez down on the Afghan frontier. For the twenty-fifth anniversary of the October Revolution they prepared a new play by Pogodin called *Moscow Nights*. Pogodin had been a protégé of the Theatre of the Revolution since Popov's day there.

There is not a great deal of detailed information about their doings, before Ohlopkov joined them, in evacuation. But with him installed they returned to Moscow in October 1943 and opened in November with the Lope de Vega. New productions billed were : *Wait for Me, Russian People, The Front* (these plays occur so often in the evacuated theatres that we might almost adopt a phrase to describe them, or some of them), *Spring in Moscow*, and Gusyev's *A Moscow Girl*. They were also studying the newest Pogodin play, *The Ferryboat Girl*, which had been completed only at the end of August. The ferryboat girl is one of the gallant people who worked across the Volga at Stalingrad, night after night and hour after hour, taking refugees to the eastern bank and goods and materials and soldiers to the western. They were also meditating the production of the newest Gusyev : *Sons of Three Rivers*, an almost symbolical propaganda study of mothers from the Volga, the Seine and the Elbe, with their three separate problems and philosophies. The music to this was being written by Hachaturyan.

Vlasov continued as producer. He was reported in 1943 to be preparing a play about Occupied France, called *Madeleine Mine*, the author of which was Rzheshevsky. Some of the company, meanwhile, had left and gone to the Vahtangov, as we have seen.

On the other hand Ohlopkov brought with him the services of the designer Ryndin and the composer Golubentsev, who had worked with him both at the Vahtangov and earlier at his own Realistic or Krasnaya Pressnya Theatre. These made a strong partnership bound by the common aim of " expressing the theme and atmosphere of a play psychologically as well as theatrically ". Besides these, others with whom Ohlopkov worked and who were ready to do so again, were the designers Akimov, Peter Williams, Yutkevich, and Kozintsev, and the internationally famous composer Shostakovich. Nor were his connections limited to designers and musicians ; for he invited Tutyshkin from the Vahtangov Theatre to produce *Le Bourgeois Gentilhomme*.

Putting all these transfers together, we can trace, without fear of being entirely mistaken, a division of feelings or convictions. In the absence of any specific reason for his abandonment of Hamlet, we may legitimately call his a hurried departure from the Vahtangov Theatre staff. With him come several, one might almost say, many colleagues ; for it is unusual for actors to transfer in this way in the Soviet theatre. And many of those who have worked with him in preparation of plays, remain available to him. On the other hand, some of the Theatre of the Revolution staff leave when he comes.

The conclusion is tempting : Ohlopkov causes debate, because he is a man of ideas and personality. When I met him, I was impressed by him as modest but very firm, and extremely enthusiastic about his art. He seems to be much the same at the time of writing. At any rate he was very outspoken and uncompromising in an interview with the Press about his intentions at his new theatre. He intended to unite all the factors of production into a " high theatricality, that richness of artistic invention and imagination without which ", he said, " the truth about life and man remain *wingless* " ; to make the theatre " an echo of our times, responding to the most essential of their problems " ; to show on the stage " taut struggles of ideas, the bubbling of passions that scald the soul, deep characters of humanity ". Under this interpretation of the function of the theatre, and as a pupil of Meierhold, he saw the new Pogodin play about Stalingrad not as the story of Shura the ferryboat girl, but as the story of all Volga people, all Soviet people, at war. Indeed it had been his suggestion that the piece be called *Grapes of Gladness*, . . . " the gladness of the struggle for the happiness of a people, the gladness of an assertion, truly the assertion of mankind, even in the quite preposterous and cruel circumstances of War ".

This emotional impressionism is diametrically opposed to the concrete, inductive methods of Popov on the same subject. It will be exciting to see which is the more successful. But Ohlopkov's methods are founded on a realism of a kind, although he despises a " photographic, passive, ' observed ' realism ". He is a good Socialist, and has his mind turned toward his audience. His is a kind of Socialist realism. We might call it a deductive kind. But induction or deduction, both he and Popov are masters of their art ; and there is room for both in Soviet theatre logic.[19]

AMALGAMATION

The Theatre of the Revolution went into co-partnership that year with the Moscow Theatre of Drama. This is not to be confused with the old Moscow State Dramatic Theatre, run by Smyshalayev till 1935 and founded on his previous " Sempirante " Theatre of Improvisation ; nor yet with the Moscow Dramatic Theatre which succeeded that in 1937. This Theatre of Drama is a new creation of 1941. Honoured Artist Nikolay Gorchakov, who had been an administrator of the art section in the Moscow Theatre of Satire, was put in charge; and it remained in Moscow without evacuating anywhere. Conditions were cold and dangerous. Stage gunfire in *Long, Long Ago* was often drowned by the Ack-Ack guns outside. Olga Zvereva, the leading lady, had to rehearse her minuet in thick felt boots, because there was no heating. But, as Honoured Artist Dmitry Orlov, one of the company, said : " Life itself helped the actor to play ".[20]

With the return of the bigger theatres to Moscow the work of this smaller unit, though it had been splendid and vital, became redundant. And that, as far as I am aware, is the only reason for its merger. It is certainly reason enough in the Soviet way of management.

THE MOSCOW THEATRE OF SATIRE

Gorchakov, leaving the shell of the theatre just mentioned, was made Artistic Director of the Theatre of Satire in November 1943. This was first formed in 1925. It was formed something on the model of Baliev's *Chauve-Souris*. But whereas Baliev, despite his Moscow Art Theatre training, was rather irresponsible in his fun, and talked nonsense most of the time whether he hit the mark or not, the Theatre of Satire had a social purpose, and hit the mark whether or not it was at the same time amusing. The difference is that of the *Daily Express* humorous column, which is just funny, but sometimes has a point, and " Yaffle " in *Reynolds' News*, which contains wry sense, even though this does not always raise a smile. The first productions of the Theatre of Satire were sketches, songs and dances, and production numbers, all of a political or satirical nature. Before long it wanted to develop more solidly, and took on full-length plays like *Squaring the Circle* and *The Path of Flowers*, by Katayev, or the work of Shkvarkin, Kirshon, Finn, Faiko. But there was a lack of good peace-time satire, and the excursion into comedy was extended. And so when this theatre was evacuated to Magnitogorsk, Chelyabinsk, Irkutsk and the Far East, it had in preparation or on hand, *Nadyezhda Durova, A Moscow Girl* and Shkvarkin's *Somebody Else's Child*. At the same time it included satirical works from abroad, which did not necessarily have a bearing on objects of ridicule at home, such as *Pygmalion*, or *The New Adventures of the Brave*

Soldier Schweik. This latter was an adaptation to conditions of Hitler's time by Slobodskoy of Haček's Czech comic of the last war. Schweik is thirty years older, and now editor of a local newspaper published by the invading Germans. He is also traffic regulator during the German retreat.

But it did also give programmes of short satire, especially when the war had begun. Alexander Werth went to it before it was evacuated, in the late summer of 1941, when it was playing in one of the four theatres in the Hermitage Garden. He describes one or two of the sketches he saw : how a village girl meets a German parachutist and unmasks him when he asks foolish questions that reveal an ignorance of Soviet local improvements ; how two German Generals are afraid of a stampede if they announce, as a trick, the arrival of certain food supplies ; and so on.

On the other hand, by the time it got to Magnitogorsk in May 1943, it was giving the first performance of a new comedy by Faiko (founded on a film scenario) called *The Actress*. This, by all accounts, was rather an unworthy piece.

The Theatre of Satire was one of the few war casualties in the Soviet theatre. At the outbreak it had been on tour in Kiev, and lost much of its possessions when that city was bombed. When it returned to Moscow at the end of September 1943, it opened with *Twelfth Night*, as a permanent and deliberate extension of its repertoire to classical comedy. Its productions were either by Shlepyanov, a former actor at the Theatre of the Revolution and partly in charge till Gorchakov came, or by Pol, who had been an actor at this theatre for years. Future plans included plays called *Sasha*, *The Uneven Marriage*, *Wonder Child* and *The Man They Wanted*.[21]

TAIROV AND HEROES

The stature of the Kamerny Theatre since Tairov's acceptance of the principle of Socialist realism, may be said to have grown with that of his wife, Alice Koonen. Not that he is in any way dominated by her in his work. But we have seen that Socialist realism means more scope for the player ; and the more understanding the player can show, the better will be the production. Now when this theatre was evacuated to Barnaul, in Western Siberia, and later to Balkash, where it performed in the club premises of the big copper works, it had not for several years been the playboy theatre which had earned such a name among " advanced " theatre circles abroad. Nevertheless, like so many of the theatres whose fortunes we have already traced, its war experiences quickened and deepened its sense of reality. Reality on which Tairov did not cease to experiment ; for he thought out a system of scene changing by change of light : but reality in a sense new to Tairov as Seeker of Heroism. Two plays in particular show this.

Litovsky, in a little book on the Kamerny published in 1934, said of its most famous production up to that date, *The Optimistic Tragedy*, " As yet there was no organic conjunction between the new, fully realistic, social sense and the methods of scenic expression specific to the Kamerny Theatre ". That was nine years ago ; and both Tairov and his assistant producer Bogatyrev in the meanwhile bent in both ends of that dilemma. They acquired a deeper social sense ; and they adapted the Kamerny scenic method till both could meet and be of use to each other.

The Optimistic Tragedy of the present war was *Wide Spreads the Sea*, by Vishnevsky, Kron and Azarov. A sharper, more concrete, more comprehensive one. The three authors wrote it during the Siege of Leningrad, and it concerns the people who lived, fought, suffered and sang on the shores of the Baltic : a Baltic Fleet lieutenant, an engineer poet, a boatswain ; and, on the other side, the enemy, a hairdresser, a spy, a German captain : and both sides portrayed faithfully and with care. There were songs and music by Sviridov, a pupil of Shostakovich, and colourful crowd scenes handled with feeling for people. All these, in spite of the tragic background implicit and behind, made a contribution to the deeper side of the Russian musical comedy world. Laughter is a grand antidote to false heroism ; and by its faculty for laughter this theatre made the tragedy of the Fascist advance truly and realistically optimistic.

Optimism may be defined as the conviction that despite its cruelty and disillusions life is worth living. Lower forms of optimism deny the cruelty and dismiss the disillusion (" As long as you keep your sense of humour . . .".) A higher form embraces these things, and still asserts the worthwhileness of life. A still higher form is passionately interested in life, and therefore in the evil, how it comes to be, how it affects its victims, and what affect its victims have on others ; and, putting these studies stone on stone, builds something that is so fine in its reasoned assertion of life that the world will not willingly let it die. Could the Kamerny rise to this height ?

The opinion of Simon Dreiden was that it could if it had a playwright worthy of it. Perhaps it very nearly did in the war tragedy, *While the Heart does not Stop*. This was specially written for the Kamerny by Konstantin Paustovsky, whose plays, Dreiden says, had previously been overweighted by their " literary " quality. By this we are to understand, not that plays written with literary " style " are to be condemned ; for that would be contrary to the prevalent tendency among Soviet critics, as we will be seeing in a later chapter ; but that Paustovsky is inclined to abandon a natural phrase, however dramatically true, and snatch at one that merely sounds more imposing. After all, he was writing for a theatre which liked the abstract.

That did not stop Alice Koonen from being humanly and dramatically true. Deeply true.

She was a present-day Adrienne Lecouvreur, a part which she had played in Scribe's "comédie-drame" of that name. And Paustovsky's play seems to have had something in common with that one. The Russians have little theatrical prejudice, and find good in plays whose failings preoccupy us. *Adrienne Lecouvreur* is perhaps the best of Scribe's multitudinous supplies. It suffers from having a tragic end imposed by means of a detective-story poison-powder on a comedy of misunderstanding which theatrical logic ought to have led to a happy ending. But it is not altogether a bad play. The fact that the Count of Saxony is frustrated in his attempt to raise funds and troops for the liberation of his country by the personal desires and jealousies of High Society in Paris gives it a certain historical meaning and perspective, which the Soviet theatre values and the Kamerny Theatre brought out.

But Paustovsky's actress does not divorce personal feelings from the perspective of her day. On the contrary, they are identified with and intensified by it. Her son has been killed by the Nazis, her husband is risking his life against them, and her anger is that of a Russian woman as well as of a Russian actress. War is almost depriving her of a belief in mankind and his culture. There are some terrible scenes. She wanders through the town with the dead body of her son in her arms. She reads a letter telling of the death of her husband (a monologue, this, breaking naturalistic canons). But being the actress she is, she can deceive even the Gestapo. And being the woman she is, in the last scene she cries to the people, over the heads of her executioners, to resist to the end.

Weak though the play may be, and written in some degree to a pattern, nevertheless the effect Alice Koonen achieved shows how far the theatre had progressed as an executant. And what like that effect was is shown by the invariably full houses at Barnaul for three months. This, in its formalist period, had not been so invariable an experience for the Kamerny.

Balkash is quite a new town on the great lake in the Karaganda steppe. There was no theatre building when the Kamerny arrived, and Tairov had much to say about the difficulties under which they had to work. They used the club of the Medzavod, the roof of which was only $3\frac{1}{2}$ metres from the floor. Little room for visual nobility. There were no props, scenery or costumes ; no workshop to make them in. Small comfort that the Club at Kounrad, 19 kilometres away, was much better appointed, with two Dress Circles to its theatre. Still, everyone worked ; they made all they needed from what they could get. So well did they work that they could open within a fortnight of their arrival. " Roughing it " under compulsion is not the only way of putting new spirit into a group of people ;

but it is an effective one. Community, after all, if it is only a matter of feeling, soon becomes a sentiment; and from there it degenerates into a convention, the prey of humbug and exploitation. But by joint action a community remains itself.

The audience, which had not had a theatre before, seems to have been a little reluctant, at first. Each production could be given only three or four times; which meant hard work, self-discipline, and the resuscitation of old shows. But it also meant improved work. And the audience responded to that.

Among the plays given at Balkash were the show in which Tairov first experimented in the non-experimental, *Stronger than Death; Observation Post*, a new play by the authors of *Smoke of the Fatherland; The Battalion Goes West;* Griboyedov's *The Family;* and the classic Kamerny production, *Desire Under the Elms.*

On 22nd July the Kamerny came out with a new Georgian play, *Moscow Skies*, by Mdivani, about which we will be writing later; Tairov commented that it was " shock-brigade " work. It was with this, and the new Vishnevsky play, *At the Walls of Leningrad*, that it opened its return season in Moscow in the autumn of 1943. Immediately to come were *L'Avare;* a study in Nazi psychology translated from the German of A. Scharrer, with a title something like *A Ploughed Field on the Black Sea; The Incursion*, by Slepyan; *The Front; The Duenna;* and, curiously patriotic and patriotically curious, a revival of our old Aunt Sally Ozerov's *Dmitri of the Don.* This must have contrasted oddly with Clifford Odet's *Golden Boy*, which they had been preparing before they left Moscow.

Meanwhile Tairov invited playwrights to work for his theatre. Shtorm came and lived with the company, writing his first play, *General Ivan.* Paustovsky started on a new work to be called *The Silver Fish.* S. Vasilyev promised a play. Zoshchenko, the humorous writer, got busy on *Make no Mistake!* But how far the " abstractness " of Tairov differs from that of Ohlopkov is seen in the play announced in November 1942 as being written for the Kamerny. Its title was *Missing.* Its author, the young playwright, Peter Zhalkin, had himself at one time been reported missing. Like the hero of his own play, he had been for ten months living and fighting with the guerrillas behind the enemy lines. If a man can write an " abstract " play under these conditions, and the Kamerny can give it appropriate production with success, then the Kamerny method will be vindicated indeed.

The Altai region was pleased to have this theatre as a guest for seventeen months. It gave a public farewell party to the company. The hosts included Red Army commanders and the intelligentsia of Barnaul. Presentations took place.

A good deal of new blood joined the Kamerny in evacuation. Tairov, in an interview with the Press after his return, spoke very highly of Fonina, a graduate of his school, who played the Duenna. Ganshin, besides playing Harpagon, also produced *L'Avare*. And, at the other end of the scale, among new-comers to the staff was the septuagenarian Gaibedurov, of whom we will be writing later. Age cannot wither the Kamerny nor its laurels.[22]

JEWS AND UZBEKS

Of the Moscow State Jewish Theatre in evacuation and its full significance, we will have more to say in the chapter that follows. It went to Tashkent and entered into very close relationship not only with Russian Jews and Gentiles living there, but also with the Uzbeks, and Uzbek theatre people, themselves. The season opened with *An Eye for an Eye*, by the Soviet Yiddish author Perets-Markish, an anti-Fascist play with a locale that showed the joint struggle of Poles and Jews in Warsaw during the occupation of Poland. Needless to say, the Poles that co-operated with the Jews were the poor and progressive ones, not the rich and reactionary.

The theatre's full repertoire was displayed, but also new plays were added, which included Uzbek themes. Mihoels, the finest actor and producer of the Yiddish-speaking, and indeed of all the Jewish, world, studied the Uzbek language, and was thus able to give an authentic interpretation in Yanshen's *Hamza*, a biographical study of the Uzbek poet and hero, helped by the author himself and the Uzbek producer Uigur. The production was by E. Loiter, the music by Yampolsky, and the dances arranged by the Uzbek's People's Artist Turgunbayeva.

Next came *Freilex*, a play on folk-lore themes by Shneyer-Okun, produced by People's Artist Zuskin, with music by Leo Pulver. Before their return in September 1943 they prepared an operetta on a story by Goldfaden, *The Wayward Bride*, for which Pulver again wrote the music, Loiter again did the production, and Tyshler designed the sets. A play on a wartime theme by Dobrushin showed the militant war work of Soviet Jews. These were all given first showing at the opening of the twenty-fifth season of the theatre in Moscow in November 1943. *Richard III* was being considered for future production, and a stage version of Sholom Aleikhem's tale of the early Jewish strolling players, *Shooting Stars*, which Mihoels was to produce.[23]

The inter-relation of the Jews and the Uzbeks is thus seen from one side, the benefit derived by the Moscow theatre from studying and understanding its hosts' language, literature and cultural background. The other side, which is in a sense the more important, will be seen later.

GIPSIES IN WAR

The Moscow Gipsy Theatre, which calls itself so picturesquely the "Romany" Theatre, though centred on its own little theatre in the capital, had always been very mobile. That was in character with the only Gipsy theatre in the world. True to its race, it wandered further afield than any other metropolitan company when its time came for evacuation. To Habarovsk, the river port on the Amur, in the Maritime Province of the Far East, where Soviet territory curls round Manchuria toward Korea ; to Komsomolsk, the new city raised by volunteers out of virgin forest ; to Voroshilovsk and Vladivostok, the precious Ultima Thule of the Socialist world, journeyed this little enterprise, with its richly coloured costumes, its passionate music, its sensuous but sophisticated use of lighting.

And the themes of its shows ? Gipsy life, naturally ; but gipsy life in war. *Dramatis Personæ* showed the feats of gipsy members of the Red Army. *On Dniester's Banks* showed them among the partisans behind the German lines . . . one is almost sorry for an unguarded Hun in fear of a partisan who is also a gipsy ! And in the half year it spent in these distant regions it gave 200 shows to workers of all kinds and members of the fighting forces. But they were not limited to the gipsies' war effort as their theme. The best of the gipsy cultural tradition was given : *A Wedding in the Camp*, Pushkin's *Gipsies*, a revival of Garcia Lorca's *The Bloody Wedding*, *The Gipsy Girl* (founded on a story by Cervantes), and even Afinogenov's *All About You*. The tour finished in August 1943, and they returned to Moscow in October.[24]

RAILWAYMEN

Even more strictly mobile was the Moscow Central Railwaymen's Theatre. This was organised in 1938 to produce plays in Moscow which could be easily transported by rail to places where there were primarily railway-worker audiences. In charge of it from the beginning was Merited Arts Worker Nikolay Petrov, formerly Artistic Director of the Leningrad "Pushkin" Theatre, where in the 'twenties and 'thirties he had been associated in several productions with Akimov and Solovyov, and had produced plays himself, notably *Fear*, by his own close friend Afinogenov. So he was a man of some considerable standing in the theatre world, and the appointment to the Railway Theatre shows that great things were expected of this unit.

The expectation was fulfilled. In the spring of 1941 it was on the road, or rather on the rails. The outbreak of war and the evacuation sent it further afield, and for a longer time than had been anticipated. It was cut off from its workshops and rehearsal rooms. But that did not deter it from producing five new plays, Soviet ones. Rehearsals were held in Petrov's compartment. One actor took over the making of scenery and turned his compartment into an *atelier*; another turned *perruquier* and others became seamstresses for the making of costumes. In this way the Theatre on Wheels was able to support itself for two years away from its base.

Performances were given on all manner of stages, from those in vast Palaces of Culture to trucks in sidings. Audiences varied from a crowd of 7,000 in the open steppe to seven lonely linesmen at a wayside halt. Fifteen thousand miles this theatre covered, in the Urals, in Siberia, and in the Far East. It was even the only permanent Soviet theatre to go abroad in war-time ; for it visited, by invitation on the strength of the fame it had won in the East, the Mongolian People's Republic, where it received a terrific welcome. From this trip abroad it returned with an illuminated address by the Council of Ministers, a flag from the Mongolian art workers, and a letter of thanks from the Prime Minister, Choibolsan, who had attended the first performance. This had been held in the open air, with thousands of horsemen gathered to celebrate the twenty-first anniversary of the founding of the Mongolian People's Republic.

Relations between that country and the Soviet Union had always been cordial, and Soviet and Mongolian film studios had even collaborated in making a film. But this theatrical excursion was almost a State occasion ! The language difficulty was overcome by a short synopsis of each act being given from the stage in Mongolian beforehand. The audience was reported to have followed attentively and even not to have missed many of the nuances. This, if it is true, and I see no reason to doubt it, is evidence of the theatrical ability of the young railway theatre.

Unfortunately I have not been able to discover what play was performed on this occasion. The repertoire of the tour included : *On the Eve, Smoke of the Fatherland*, Romashov's *It Can Happen to Anyone;* it might have been any of these. But they also took a basic stock of classics like *Guilty Though Guiltless* and *Krechinsky's Wedding;* and they also gave several home-made entertainments, whose contents are indicated by their titles : *Hatred*, and *Beat, Beating, and About to Beat*.[25]

Truly the actors that cross the Volga had come into their own !

Dwarf Theatre

One of the smallest theatres in Moscow was the " Yermolova ". It was evacuated to the Cheremkhov coal-basin, and to Solikamsk in the Urals, which takes its name from huge deposits of potassium salts there. This theatre was founded as a studio in 1930 without premises, but received a permanent home in 1933. It was named for the celebrated actress, but had much of its success and methods drawn from Stanislavsky's ideas, and it specialised chiefly in psychological studies of youth and adolescence. Early attempts at " rhythm " showed that its members were aware of Meierhold, especially its director Shumilin. In 1937, however, Hmelyov of the Moscow Art Theatre became its head and greatly strengthened and actualised it. To the growing number of interesting Soviet war plays it added the first performance of *Our Correspondent*. This was after its return to Moscow from the East, and showed how, as in life, so in the theatre, the war and the problems the war brought flooded over the problems that loom so large to peace-time youth.

Another impressive war-time production was *He Who Laughs Last*, and the repertoire also included *As You Like It*, *Children of the Sun*, Ostrovsky's *Poor Bride*, *Twenty Years After* (not the Dumas story, but a patriotic play by Svetlov on a not dissimilar theme), and less well-known work with titles *The Stepmother*, *The Lodger* (or " The Parasite ", for the Russian word means either) and the biographical *Pirogov the Surgeon*. In 1943 their forthcoming work was *A Fellow from our Town*, *Unquiet Old Age*, *She Stoops to Conquer*, *Nadyezhda Durova*, and *Russian People* and *The House on the Hill* to follow. By that time the little band had gone to Dagestan.[26]

" Little band " is perhaps a misnomer, by our standards. Although their theatre seated only 390, the company numbered sixty.

THE ALEXANDRINSKY-PUSHKIN CROSSES THE VOLGA

Leningrad theatres were sent east as smoothly and successfully as Moscow ones. But, for obvious reasons, earlier. The " Pushkin " Theatre, leaving the old Alexandrinsky building, was in Novosibirsk by August 1941. Like the others we have considered, it also reflected the spirit of the Soviet peoples, but not only in the present. In the last few years it had become much more history conscious. Thus Merited Arts Worker Leonid Vivien, its artistic director, said in an interview that when he was proposing to stage Scribe's comedy, *Une Verre d'Eau*, he studied the original scripts and found that traditional cuts had converted into a mere love story what had been written as a comedy of political intrigue. As strict history, perhaps, the play was romantic and false ; but the struggle between Bolingbroke and the Duke of Marlborough, and what each was standing for, was certainly the real theme of the play.

Similarly with Ostrovsky's *Burning Heart*. This was usually played as the portrait of a *samodur*, meaning a person who is so convinced that he is right in all he does that he will even do a thing wrong to show he is right. Vladimir Kozhich, however, to bring out the social conditions of the time and Ostrovsky's comment upon them, made this character much more sympathetic . . . as a talented if temperamental man, ruined by those very social conditions.

In producing *Russian People*, Vivien again put history before convention. He was struck by the poetic qualities of it (Simonov was a well-known
poet) and laid stress on them, thus avoiding any naturalistic depiction of
resistance to Hitlerism.

The reception area in this case, Novosibirsk, was a place first settled in
1893, but in the nineteen-thirties already contained more than 150,000
people. The Red Torch Theatre building (see next chapter), where the
" Pushkin " Theatre played, had a capacity of 1,100 . . . metropolitan
dimensions. The total attendance in half a year was 150,000, showing a
very remarkable popularity. The plays to be seen then or shortly after,
were : *My Son, Prince Mstislav Udaloy, Day of the Living, On the Eve, The
Burning Heart, Yegor Bulychov*, and, rather unexpectedly, the *Œdipus
Tyrannus* of Sophocles, under the dictum of Marx that " only an idiot
does not understand the significance of antique literature for the proletariat ".
Yuryev played Œdipus.

While in Novosibirsk the theatre became " patron " to the Stalin
Metallurgical Combine of the Kuzbas. By the " creative friendship "
so established it helped with propaganda brigades and amateur efforts, and
sustained the morale of the workers, keeping them keen to produce the
stream of armaments they wanted to see departing for the Fronts. There
is no doubt that any enlightened Government, in Socialist conditions, would
understand the connection between Sophocles and an increased war-output.
It is from self-respect and a knowledge of life and of the things worth
living for that a man works double time and double speed. When fumes
of mere extra pay wear off, cynicism has a hang-over.

During 1943 the Pushkin Theatre prepared several productions of a
high order, with invited artists. *Othello*, with Yuryev in the name part,
was produced by Kozintsev, the sets were by Peter Williams, the music
was by Shostakovich. Kozintsev also produced the stage version of *Don
Quixote* which Bulgakov had made, and the sets for this were by Dmitriyev.
In this the magnificent " Pushkin " actor Cherkasov played the title part.

On the 7th of November came its first performance of *Kremlin Chimes*,
produced by Vivien himself, with sets by Grigoryev, and Skorobogatov
playing Lenin. More contemporary plays were *On the Eve, In the Steppes
of the Ukraine*, and *Invasion*. But in the main the 1943-4 season was regarded
as rehabilitating the classics in a new and more historically conscious form.[27]

GORKY'S LENINGRAD SEAGULL

Leningrad during its siege suffered infinitely more damage than Moscow
by bomb and shell, especially the latter. It was much like London during
the first blitz or the bumble bomb period. Notices were put up in nearly
every street saying which was the more dangerous side when shells were

coming over. But the inhabitants got used to dodging them, as Londoners did bumbles. Only this lasted, without cessation, for two years.

The Leningrad Grand "Gorky" Theatre returned to its repaired premises in March 1943. It had been in Kirov since August 1941.* Kirov is the name given to what used to be Vyatka, between Kazan and the Urals, the district whose inhabitants were described, probably quite justly, by our Polish exiled lady as "a barbarous population, remnants of different nations and races". What would any Peterburg theatre, if it had had the courage to cross the Volga, have meant to such people? But now this one had a brand new up-to-date theatre building to act in, though they spent much of their time also in performing to hospitals and camps. They had left Leningrad in a hurry, and could not take all their chattels with them; but with local help they managed to open, only two weeks after their arrival, with their normal repertoire, *The Servant of Two Masters*, *A Fellow from Our Town*, *Kremlin Chimes*, *Une Verre d'Eau*.

But soon they set to work on new shows, achieving ten during their stay. Two historical plays about the Napoleonic Wars, *Field-Marshal Kutuzov* and *General Suvorov*, were established modern classics followed by the new war play, *The Winged Tribe*, *The Reckoning*, by O. Litovsky, *The House on the Hill*, and *Russian People* produced by Rykov.

Rudnik is their chief. He produced *The Front*, in sets by Lebedyev, and *The Road to New York*, after the American film, with sets by Medovshchikov. The same designer worked for Veisber's production of *Long, Long Ago*, for the twenty-fifth anniversary of the Revolution. Michurin, one of the acting strength, was producer for *Krechinsky's Wedding*, in sets by Zhukovsky.

The "Gorky" Theatre has been called the "greatest theatre of frontline Leningrad" and its return in the spring meant a very great deal to the starved and nerve-jagged population of this heroic city. It is interesting to note the plays to be given after the return : *Peter Krymov*, a romance about the evacuation of a factory to the rear ; a play about Darwin specially written by Leonid Rahmanov, who had written the play *Unquiet Old Age* and the film *Baltic Deputy* about Timiryazev ; a new translation of Lesya Ukrainka's *Forest Song;* and, for the anniversary of Gorky's death, *Meshchane*. It also gave a literary matinee, at which members of the company read *Yakov Bogomilov*, an unknown Gorky play discovered in the archives recently.

But the event of the "Gorky" year, and indeed of the Leningrad theatrical year, was the revival of *King Lear*, which had only had a few performances before the outbreak of war. Kozintsev as producer ; Nathan Altman, the Jewish designer, one of the most gifted in the Union ; Shosta-

* Kirov was the Leningrad Bolshevik leader, murdered in the nineteen-thirties.

kovich as composer.   The lead would be played by Michurin and Sofronov alternately.[28]

The " Gorky " Theatre had always been, since its deliberate foundation for the purpose, nearer to the workers of the Union than many other theatres ; and perhaps it had less to learn from evacuation.   Perhaps it would have missed something by not being in the front line with its own audience throughout the siege of their home city.   Nevertheless many of the citizens of Leningrad went east with their work ; and the process of eastward transposition was one which so completely and so deeply affected the general life of the Soviet peoples that, in the long run, they would perhaps prove to have missed more, had they stayed.   They were very pleased at the comparison, made at a conference, of the re-opening of the theatre to the re-starting of the Leningrad trams in Spring 1942.   This made them feel their utility to the people of the city.

LENINGRAD COMEDY

The Leningrad Comedy Theatre, famous for the brightness of its shows and the high quality of its repertoire, got to Stalinabad in June 1942. Stalinabad is the capital of Tajikstan, formerly called Dyushambeh. It lies in a fertile valley which grows Egyptian cotton.   But the region had been known as a primitive country with no large towns.   Even Stalinabad was not gigantic.   At first sight it seems a curious spot to choose for so sophisticated and gay and Russian a theatre as Akimov's.   It is true that the Tajiks had created their own native theatre and their own native drama, and had been doing Shakespeare with great success.   And no doubt there was an influx of Russian workers, perhaps many from Leningrad.   There was already a Russian theatre there, called after Mayakovsky.   At all events the Comedy Theatre played its usual repertoire, opening with *Pygmalion*, then Akimov's famous *Twelfth Night* production, and *The Importance of Being Earnest*.   (Wilde's pun is kept in the Russian by equating " Seryozny " with Seryozha.)   They also played, for the first time in the Soviet Union, Dyhovichny's *Little Brother*, and a dramatic version of *They Ride by Night*, the American film by the author of *The Road to New York*.   In addition they prepared *Krechinsky's Wedding* and an Akimov production of *A Midsummer Night's Dream*.   Akimov varied between work as producer and work as designer.   Suhanov produced *Little Brother* in designs by Akimov. But Akimov, as director, is the leading spirit.   It will be noticed that none of the great Soviet war plays was done.   That would not be the function of the Comedy Theatre as Akimov understood it.   And perhaps it was in a way a confession that evacuation had nothing to teach him, that his rich imagination and impish humour remained unaffected by the stern reality of war.   It was not due to the locality.   For the Comedy Theatre did not stay only in the cotton fields. It went to Yerevàn, to Sochi, to the Caucasian spas.[29] It then prepared that delicious sentimental romance, *The Candle-holder*, by Alfred de Musset.

MINOR LENINGRAD THEATRES

Two more Leningrad theatres, and we have done. The New Theatre was sent to the Urals and later to Komsomolsk, where in July 1943 it gave *Woe from Wit* in a production by Honoured Artist N. Bromly. And to Serov in the Urals in October 1943 came the Leningrad LenKom Theatre, of which little is on record. It had, though, the new war play by Arbuzov, called *A Cottage in Cherkizov*, the action of which takes place in October 1941 among some of Moscow's young Communists. In July of the previous year it had been in Archangel, where the two dramatists, Leonid Radishev and Osip Kucherov, were writing for it a play about beleaguered Leningrad under the title *Blockade*. So it became a kind of ambassador to the east bearing authentic messages from the most bombarded city of Russia.[30]

SUMMARY

Information, as will have been noticed, is more plentiful about Moscow theatres in evacuation than about Leningrad ones ; and this is natural, since Moscow has always been much the more theatre-minded ; and the Moscow theatres are both more numerous and perhaps of a higher general standard than the others.

By October 1943 twenty Moscow theatres which had been evacuated had returned.[31] There is no doubt from the reports of their directors, that they had, one and all, benefited in a quite unexpected degree from their sojourn in so many and so far-away places, places where they might have expected to meet not hostility certainly, but perhaps apathy and the barriers of language or overwork.

The benefit was of two kinds. The companies being compact and facing huge demands, had to concentrate their work. Without in any way abandoning their standards raised in peace-time, every artist and expert had to help his colleagues in many directions. Where there are experts proud of their skill, there is always a danger in ordinary leisurely peaceful times that each will concentrate on his or her own craft, and deny the importance of another's. Evacuation meant the disappearance of any such tendency. Departmentalism was impossible.

But the benefit was also spiritual. If they had stayed in a danger zone, they might have been playing to half-empty houses, which would impair morale and performance, and, ultimately, aim. They would not have known what the majority of people, evacuated and facing heroic problems in the rear, were feeling and thinking. They would, after the war, have been out of touch with the great experiences of their own audiences. They would be giving a theoretic war theatre based on the practice of peace.

As it was, they went where total war was most evident, but where they could have sufficient sense of permanence and continuity to work on the expression of that total war, themselves to develop alongside it. Development is a necessary condition of life in a public art like that of the stage. As it was, thanks to their participation in the life of the rear, in the efforts of production, and in the anxiety of parted families, they created a war theatre that was based on the practice of war, even when much of their packed houses was foreign in speech to their work.

But evacuation had another side ; and let us now turn to the provinces themselves and see its results on their own theatres, both in places where evacuees were received and in places that developed independently their own solutions to their own problems.

CHAPTER VIII

IMPACTS OF EAST AND WEST

WHERE COAL MEETS STEEL

Outside the metropolitan cities by far the most important centre of the U.S.S.R. was the Urals-Kuzbas area. One united area, with a very intimate industrial bond. " Centre " indeed is the wrong word. It was an area so vast and so rich as to be a new country in the world. And if the Fascist advance had not been halted at Leningrad and Stalingrad and before Moscow, the Soviet Union's Government could well have moved thither and still held out till its gigantic war-production could catch up with its gigantic needs.

Nine of the best theatres of Moscow and Leningrad came to this area, nine of the best dramatic theatres, to say nothing of opera, ballet, musical comedy, operetta or young people's theatres, nor those of other nationalities. The flowers of Soviet stage art in all their variety were in blossom in the gardens of the East.

True, the inhabitants of these particular gardens were mainly Russian or Ukrainian or Byelorussian already, and not, strictly speaking, native. Peter the Great had sent gunsmiths from Tula to help the baby war industry of Demidov in the Urals. And it was the comparative prosperity of these Russians which our Polish lady noticed in the early part of the nineteenth century. Two Americans in 1933 took the tale further : [1] " Our trip was like a jaunt through Creation ", they wrote ; but added, " Russians, Ukrainians, Jews, Finns, Tatars, all were moving to help build Magnitogorsk ".[2] Not only Magnitogorsk, but other new places. The advice of the Russian schoolboy to a fellow examinee, that if asked where any mineral was to be found, he should reply " In the Urals ", as they nearly all were, could have applied also to new towns. " Big towns have been built in the Urals since the outbreak of war, where the foot of man had scarcely trodden." And that carries the tale to its final stage so far.

The fused non-local populations set up theatres in these pre-war towns ; and they and their theatres stepped right into the middle of war in its earliest days. Without a break from dawn to dawn they laboured, and because their supplies streamed out to all parts of the Union, their interests were not merely local. When the first evacuees began to arrive, the distant union with the West became a closer, more intimate one, a matter of daily and nightly co-operation and care. Where there were no theatres in the war-built towns, there was need of them.

Let us begin in this area with Sverdlovsk. One of the wealthier Tsarist Russian cities, it had only an opera house. It had no local dramatic company. Nor had it any sanitation or running water. By 1940 it was a city of 450,000 people, with almost every amenity a city of that size could wish. In October 1942, the Sverdlovsk local theatre, then run by Vinyer who had formerly been at the L.O.S.P.S. Theatre in Leningrad, was able to stage a new play about the defence of Moscow (*The Stars Cannot Fade*). The first night of this took place within ten months of the first reverse of the Germans, before Moscow. From which we may judge the interests of the local audience and the alertness of the local theatre. This was the first performance of Boris Romashov's play. It described the intellectuals of Moscow : Professor Kovrigin and his family at home in their little country cottage outside the capital in the opening weeks of the war. The first air-raid sirens work sadly on the nerves of Zhenya Ptashkin, a dreamy, naïve, gawkish young ichthyologist, completely absorbed in his subject, who after a few months volunteers for the Army, and finds that by applying the clear-headedness he has hitherto confined to " his subject " after the fashion of so many University people the world over, he can lead a Red Army unit to success.

Romashov is no new playwright. His *Fighters* was done by the Moscow Maly, the Red Army Theatre, the Yermolova Theatre (to mention only these) in 1934. The Maly did his *Fiery Place* in 1935 on their Filial stage. Petrov produced *The End of Krivolylsk* at the Leningrad Dramatic Theatre in sets by Akimov as early as 1926. Yet here was his first war play, an immediate, direct thing, being presented to an audience like this in a local theatre.

And although it is off the immediate line of this book, it is interesting to note the exceptional success, even in the popular Musical Comedy Theatre of Sverdlovsk, of *Three Encounters*, an operetta specially written for it by the author Tipot and the composer Starokadomsky. The hero and heroine of this are a young Red Air Force lieutenant and a girl country post-woman, with comic relief from a collective-farm watchman. Soviet citizens of all parts enjoy musical comedy, and the war had produced an immense number in many languages. Another to be done at Sverdlovsk was Shebalin's *The Young Man from the Embassy*, which is placed in the Napoleonic Wars and involves Kutuzov.

By March 1943 the population of Sverdlovsk had passed a million. It was humming with the war effort. Side by side with theatre notices on the hoardings, posters clamoured : " Let's Treble the Output for the Urals Plants ! " and " Every ounce of Energy for War Industries ! " Nor was there any contradiction in this statement of war needs and theatre news. Total war affects the spirit, and in the Soviet Union care was taken that an important attribute of the spirit, the theatre-sense, was not impaired.

By February 1943 five new theatres had opened, and a sixth in April. At Sverdlovsk, Chelyabinsk and Molotov, the following star producers of the metropolitan stage had done at least one show each : Popov, Zahava, Baratov, Zaharov and Bebutov. Critics and personalities like Kalashnikov,* Bespalov, Yuzovsky and Nikolay Petrov addressed a conference in Sverd- lovsk which was attended by theatre workers in that town and in Stalinsk, Magnitogorsk, Nizhny-Tagil and Kemerovo. That was in June 1943, and by then there was plenty to occupy the attention. Each of these theatres had done one or other of the new Soviet star war plays.

These were no little provincial Chesterfields or Macclesfields ; they were vital organs in the Soviet industrial system, and their culture was commensurate with their importance. Nizhny-Tagil, for example, was almost as big as Sverdlovsk, although it had started as a mining village in Demidov's time. In the 'thirties, a Raphael Madonna discovered in a palace built for the Demidovs there, but seldom used by their descendants, was exchanged by the Soviet Government for a whole collection of less important paintings greatly prized by the inhabitants at the present time, when the city was a centre of iron, copper, gold and platinum mining and contained a magnesium works and the largest railway-carriage works in the world.

Stalinsk (in 1917 the village of Kuznetsk with 3,000 people) was in 1939 a city the size of Nottingham.†

Their theatres developed strongly. The Molotov Theatre was con- sidered one of the sturdiest of all the provincial theatres. In 1943 its repertoire included *Field-Marshal Kutuzov*, *The Front*, *Invasion*, and Lope de Vega's *Star of Seville*. It had a company of twenty-eight, and a studio- school which was preparing to found a national theatre for the local population of Komi-Perm. Productions to come were *Mudrets*,‡ *Woe from Wit*, Gorky's *The Zykovs*, *Darya*, by Kozakov, and *Long, Long Ago* : also a new play on a Urals theme from a Bazhov story, and possibly also an adaptation from the Komi-Perm national folk-epic *Kudym-Osh*. The ensemble of this small company was very highly developed, and many of their settings were by Peter Williams, rapidly becoming one of the best scene-designers in the Soviet Union.

* Yuri Kalashnikov was appointed head of the Theatre Administration of the Committee for Art Affairs in March 1944.

† Directors of theatres in these towns were : at Molotov, I. Yefremov ; at Chelyabinsk, E. Krasnyansky ; at Magnitogorsk, L. Prozorovsky ; at Stalinsk, V. Torsky ; at Nizhny-Tagil, N. Dobrogin.

‡ Ostrovsky's comedy, *A Bit of a Fool in Every Wise Man* (alternatively in English called *Even a Wise Man Stumbles*), was known to theatre people by the single word *Mudrets* (= " A Wise Man ") as *A Midsummer Night's Dream* is often called *The Dream* by the profession in our countries.

Another strong Molotov theatre was the Musical Comedy, a mobile theatre, whose first season included *La Bayadère*, *Silva*, *The Bartered Bride*, and *On the Banks of the Amur*.

In these local theatres many evacuee directors worked, Bryantsev of the Leningrad Tyuz, Engel-Kron of the Voronezh Theatre, Lyashenko of Oryol, so that this was really a secondary or new theatrical centre of the Union, as it was also a secondary or new industrial one. And the plays given extended not only to the Russian classics, but to non-Russian works like *Pygmalion*, *A Winter's Tale*, *Much Ado About Nothing*, a version of *Oliver Twist;* and even to present-day non-Russian anti-Fascist plays, by Clifford Odets (*The 11th Hour*), Julius Gay (*Cannibal Island*), Friedrich Wolf (*Patriots*) and Stijensky (*Slavic Wind*).

Under the hand of Zahava the Omsk Dramatic Theatre acquired a slight Vahtangov manner. In its *Invasion*, for example, the Gestapo monster became something more than just an evil man ; he had something outsize about him, not supernatural, but more animal than human.

How intensely the theatre took hold of these regions ! and how confident the local theatres were ! In the early part of 1942 the Sverdlovsk theatre was preparing *The Winged Tribe*, notwithstanding that the great Moscow giant, the Central Theatre of the Red Army, evacuated there, was already showing this play. The comparison of the two productions was looked forward to by the critics, because of the great ability shown by the local theatre in its production of *Field-Marshal Kutuzov*, which was also in the repertoire of the Red Army Theatre. It had done, with success, *King Lear*.

Sverdlovsk was the home of a particularly live and militant unit. The local Musical Comedy Theatre was a pioneer. In May 1942 one of the neighbouring factories had been lagging behind its own schedule. The theatre wrote and rehearsed a little revue, which ridiculed the faulty departments and personnel unmercifully. This it staged in the factory club to the discomfiture of the guilty people. Laughter and logic are the only weapons that can defeat a Russian, and in a month the factory had made up for five months' inefficiency.

The Dramatic Theatre followed suit in June. At 08.15 one day at another works it appeared on the factory floor as the night workers were just coming off their shift. It too had written a merciless satire. Where it could praise, it praised ; but in and through its jibes ran such a wire of urgency, and the songs and sketches showed such understanding of the broad issues, that the culprits, laughing with the rest at themselves, felt shame but no resentment, and mended their ways at once. Like the Comradely Courts, which were the first line of Soviet justice in minor matters, it was friendly, informal . . . and effective.

The Kuzbas had become a similar centre of both industry and art. Novosibirsk, for instance, was pleased in May 1943, when one of the " Filials " of the Tretyakov Art Gallery in Moscow, which linked outlying parts of the Soviet Union with the metropolitan art treasures, opened there an exhibition of Theatrical Art.   As a result of her visits from metropolitan theatres, Novosibirsk decided in March 1944 to open a new theatre of the miniature to " show the life of the city and the war work of Siberians ". We have already mentioned the Red Torch Theatre at Novosibirsk, or rather its premises, as having been occupied by the Leningrad " Pushkin " Theatre.   Its proper owners were away on a six-months' tour of the new KuzBas cities, whose names do not appear on all British maps.   Besides Stalinsk, there were Leninsk-Kuznetsk, Prokopyevsk, Zlatoust, home of an ancient precious stone industry and now of a huge open-hearth furnace. When it returned in the summer of 1943, the Red Torch Theatre did not turn out its guest, but built itself a new home in the hall of the Clara Zetkin Club, which seated 700.

As a kind of reward, Rashevskaya of Leningrad directed *Peter Krymov* for them, and Diky *Oleko Dundich*, making strong new additions to their offering of plays which already included *My Son*, *Field-Marshal Kutuzov*, and *A Dog in the Manger*, besides two of the star Soviet war plays.   Vera Redlikh followed with *The Zykovs* and *Romeo and Juliet*.   She had been a pupil of the Moscow Art Theatre, and in 1939 her *Hamlet*, which was still in the repertoire, had been the first in the Soviet Union to use the new translation by Boris Pasternak which was later to be chosen by the Art Theatre.   His was also the version used in her *Romeo*.

In December 1943 this theatre was working on Alexandra Brushtein's new play, *Tristan and Isolde*, which had been accepted by the Vahtangov, though I have come on no reference to its ever having been done there. This is a verse play ; but not quite the story as we know it.   A dying Tristan does not in Brittany await the coming of Iseult from King Mark's Court, as Mallory, Swinburne and Wagner tells it.   A dying Iseult at King Mark's Court awaits the coming of Tristan.   King Mark, a more humane and gentle figure in this version, sees that in her delirium she is mistaking him for Tristan's squire, and he plays up to this belief, assuring her that Tristan has indeed landed and is on his way.   Iseult dies the happier for this knowledge, but her lover arrives too late.

The reversal makes a womanly touch and adds a deeper drama.   But this may be the version with which Soviet listeners are more familiar, since there is a Georgian folk-tale on the subject, which indeed some authorities believe to be the original of all of them.[3]   It may be that the Georgian tale has this ending.

Chelyabinsk, rivalling the largest blast furnace in Europe at Magnitogorsk, was at this time building the largest electric steel-mill in the world, although mammoths have since gone out of design as too clumsy for perfect efficiency. The fare provided by the Chelyabinsk Dramatic Theatre up to June 1943 was of high standard : *Invasion, Nadyezhda Durova, Oleko Dundich, General Brusilov* (all war themes, though covering four different campaigns) ; *A Comedy of Errors* (a difficult play, this), *The Three Sisters, Forma Gordeyev* (after Gorky), and *Last Love*.

From these details we can build up a picture of theatrical work in the Urals and KuzBas. The local units rival the metropolitan ones. They do not fear competition. But, though grateful for help from acknowledged masters brought by war to their district, they use their own local dramatic materials. This is as it was in industry. When any big works were to be constructed, builders and engineers set up their own plant for the material of construction : saw-mills, cement-works, brick-kilns . . . all were thrown up on the spot from virgin soil or forest. Nor had they skilled labour to help, for at least as late as 1943 the extra labour came from Oriental countries, Uzbekistan, Kazakhstan. It had no idea whatever of industrial construction. For mostly country people came. So that war conditions, whether on the job, or in leisure hours, were educating the Uralsmen to educate other nations.[4]

FUSION OF UZBEKS WITH JEWS AND MUSCOVITES

In more distinctly national areas the impact of East and West had more interesting results. Those who have read of the development of national theatres in the Soviet Union since 1933, or in many cases from an even earlier date, need not be told that people remaining in Uzbekistan or Kazakhstan, that is, the non-military working population, did not go without theatre ; they did not suffer a decay of theatre ; they advanced. In some cases a very close inter-relation was set up between themselves and their Western theatrical guests. Particularly was this true of Uzbekistan.

Here, as we have seen, the Moscow State Jewish, the Theatre of the Revolution, the Moscow LenKom, the Ukrainian " Franko " and several other theatres provided an exciting variation for the Uzbek audience. Their presence and example encouraged the Uzbek theatres to further development of their own art. By the summer of 1943 there were thirty-five local theatres in Uzbekistan ; and in Tashkent they had nearly completed the building of a new one, near the Komsomol Lake that was made there some years previously. Not a large building, with a capacity of only 800 ; but precious, because much of the work of building it was given free by collectives from the Farkhadstroy and Uzbek Metal Works. The architectural style was the traditional Uzbek, and it stood as a public building for the workers of Tashkent's " Stalin " quarter. Another building, to

be completed in 1942, was the Academic Theatre, for which the State
Soviet appropriated three million roubles of its funds, and of which A. V.
Shchusev, who designed the Lenin mausoleum in Moscow, was the architect.

In appearance Tashkent was still a double city. The old Oriental
section a maze of cul-de-sacs and narrow, crooked lanes between the low
mud walls of flat-roofed houses, still stood by the European section (for
many Russian families settled here, when Uzbek cotton became profitable
for the moneyed classes of Tsarist days) where wide, straight streets, lined
with tall poplars and mulberry trees, passed along fine white mansions with
heavy doors. But now there was no division between their inhabitants,
although there was still a mixture of dress ; and girls with the traditional
little black Uzbek pigtails, dozens of them, round the backs of their heads
like sticks of liquorice, would be wearing European trousers, or young men
in boiler-suits would wear embroidered skull-caps on their heads, like their
fathers in opulent striped robes. Its peace-time population was 600,000.

In 1942 the orderliness of this city was disturbed. The rapid development of industry, the sudden influx of Russian workers or evacuee families,
caused a shortage of many comforts. Not only Russians, but Jews and
Gentiles from the Western Ukraine and Byelorussia, Bessarabia and North
Bukovina, found work and refuge in Uzbekistan. Crowds besieged the
post offices for news of relatives. Notices appealing for personal information plastered the railway stations. Only the Uzbeks themselves could
sort it out. But they were not unprepared, and they did sort it out, well
and willingly.

A year later the war might be depriving them of luxuries ; but all
was again orderly and determined. And through stress and calm alike
the Uzbek theatres kept open and full.

It was much the same in Samarkand. A play was produced there at
the end of 1942 or early 1943. Its author was the local dramatist, Ismail
Zade, and he called it *Farzand*, meaning, I believe, " The Son ". Well
titled, if so, for it concerned children evacuated from the Ukraine to
Uzbekistan, in both of which countries the action was located. Jurayev,
the Uzbek theatre's director, produced it, to music by Yudakov, in settings
by Zotov. Nor need one limit the picture to Tashkent or Samarkand.
All over the country, not only towns, but farmsteads received and made
homes for the little evacuees. Anyone who has experience (or imagination)
of the problems set up by the evacuation of children will realise what this
must have meant. In Southern England, where London children were
taken to country places only a few miles away, comparatively speaking,
and to people who spoke very nearly the same tongue, problems of unaccustomed food and changes in bodily habits were serious enough. But
here European children were transplanted into Asia, into communities with

utterly different ways of living, different root-language, different basic foods, different relations between people. And yet they settled, in the main, happily. They learned a lot about nations other than their own. And they taught a lot about their own nation. Whether their mothers were with them or no.

This close welcome, this reciprocal interest, was provided by the theatres too. There had been a Russian theatre in Tashkent for years ; now it was joined by the Moscow Jewish Theatre, the Leningrad Jewish Theatre of Operetta, the Kiev Jewish Variety Theatre, in addition to those already mentioned. Faced with this influx of Jewish and Gentile institutions, the Uzbek theatres also taught and learned.

The Tashkent theatres had a varied repertoire. There was, not unexpectedly, the popular patriotic play, *The Sword of Uzbekistan*. The " Hamza " Dramatic Theatre ranged from *Othello* to *The Eagle's Flight*, by the Uzbek playwright Izzat Sultanov. It included *Hamza*, a biographical study of that Uzbek poet-patriot, by Kamil Yanshen and his not so famous collaborator Amin Umara. Yashen was one of the most prominent Uzbek writers for the stage ; he had a straight play, an opera libretto, a music play, and a film scenario already to his credit.

But with astonishing sympathy and readiness the Uzbek theatre, the local Russian theatre, and the Moscow theatres, including the Moscow Jewish, interchanged productions or plays.

The " Hamza " Theatre in the summer of 1943 played the three works mentioned above in the local Russian theatre's premises, while the Russian theatre occupied the " Hamza's " stage. This was not a West-End transfer to a bigger or more central building ; in the close quarters of Soviet theatre life it amounted to an interchange of audiences. That is remarkable enough. (Imagine a similar interchange between Haarlem and Broadway !) But it was soon to be outdistanced by the evacuees themselves in friendship. For while the Moscow LenKom Theatre was in Tashkent, its producer Bersenyev collaborated with the Uzbek producer Turdyev in staging *The Eagle's Flight* and produced it in translation in his own theatre ; and his assistants Serafima Birman and Giasintova helped to stage other plays at the local Russian theatre.

Meantime a yet more vital friendship grew between the Moscow State Jewish Theatre and the " Hamza ". In July 1943 the GOSET produced its first Uzbek play, translated into Yiddish by P. Nister ; this was *Hamza*, directed by Ephraim Loiter to Yampolsky's music in Tyshler's sets, and for it he was assisted and advised by Uigur, head of the " Hamza " Theatre. The dances were arranged by Mukarra Turgunbayeva, People's Artist of the Uzbek S.S.R. On the reverse of the medal, the Uzbek poet Khamid Alimjan, famed for his lyrics and folk-tales in verse, is to be seen finishing his first play, *Mukanna*, a historical work, about the struggle of the Uzbeks more than a thousand years previously, against the Arabs, who were then sweeping over the Levant and Asia Minor toward Central Asia. The first production of this was something of an event, therefore, in Uzbek culture. Consider, then, the importance of the fact that when it took place, at the " Hamza " Theatre in March 1943, it had been produced by People's Artist of the Soviet Union Solomon Mihoels, the great actor and director of the Moscow Jewish Theatre. He had a compatriot for the sets, Tyshler ; but Uzbek composers for the incidental music, in People's Artist of the Uzbek S.S.R. V. Uspensky and G. Mushel. The company was all-Uzbek.

There are very few People's Artists of the Soviet Union, though there are a number of People's Artists of the various Republics, including the Russian. Never was the larger title better deserved !

This play was essentially Uzbek. The dialogue, which was said to be particularly bright and polished, contained many of those aphorisms which I understand to be characteristic of the Uzbek style of popular poetry. This in itself would be a special difficulty for a foreign producer. An aphorism can be enunciated, delivered by an actor, as a jewel can be set in metal. It may be stuck on, and remain a stiff obtrusion. Or it may appear to grow from its surroundings, to give and to receive lustre from them. But only a skilled and knowledgeable craftsman can smoothe it into the whole ; only a producer steeped in the idiom and background of popular speech and thought can give it the weight of a proverb, radiating the right wisdom in any given place. For a foreign producer to do this was very remarkable.

When Professor Mihoels was in Britain on a visit of friendship in the autumn of 1943, I asked him how he had managed to produce a foreign play in a foreign theatre in a foreign language with a foreign cast ; and he replied that he had been studying Uzbek for some time, and found it not so difficult as it might have been if he had had no knowledge of Hebrew.

This was no mere flash in the pan. The Theatre of the Revolution from Moscow, then in Tashkent, accepted a Russian translation of the same play ; and as a result of this three- and four-fold inter-relation of nations, when the time for departure came, the Uzbek Government conferred the title of People's Artist of the Uzbek Republic on Babanova of the Theatre of the Revolution, Bersenyev of the LenKom, and Mihoels of the GOSET, besides lesser titles on other figures in all three Moscow theatres. A very charming gesture ; but also a great deal more than a gesture.

Entente between Uzbek and Ukrainian also was firm. In November 1943 at Tashkent the " Mukimi " Theatre of Musical Drama and Comedy did a translation from the Ukrainian *Natalka of Poltava*, in the production of which Yura of the " Franko " Theatre and the distinguished Ukrainian

ALEXANDRA YABLOCHKINA
of the Maly Theatre, Moscow.
People's Artist of the U.S.S.R.; Stalin prize-winner; President of the V.T.O.

[*facing page* 188.

EAST MEETS WEST.

Actors of the Oirotian Republic present Goldoni's *Servant of Two Masters* in a Western European setting.

[*facing page* 189.

actor Buchma helped the Uzbeks to acquire the true Ukrainian sunniness and exuberance. For the Uzbeks were very fond of musical shows, whether their own (*Hamza* was also made the libretto for an Uzbek opera), or from other Soviet countries, or from the Grand Opera of the West. *Carmen* had been a favourite for a long time.

Many other Uzbek theatres there were; but we cannot follow them all. There was an interesting Theatre of the House of the Red Army in Tashkent which toured the country in 1942. Its most noteworthy production was *The Winged Tribe*, a Russian theme, but one which knitted the cotton-growers with their defenders, especially under the direction of Glekov. Nor was there any fear that the national theatre would be Russified. In conquered parts of an Empire this would be so; social, economic and political forces continually carry it that way, as they did in India. But within the quite unimperial alliance of Soviet peoples, these three forces carried in a contrary direction.

And they are very lively folk, the people of the Uzbek entertainment world. In 1942 they tried in the Tashkent film studios the experiment of mixing sequences from a film with a stage performance on the same theme. The film was *The Spiders*, and showed how Fascist doctors made away with German soldiery when too badly wounded to be easily healed. The director Macharet managed the screen side, and the producer Trauberg the stage side. The script was by Berestinsky, who had knowledge of both arts.

One further facet of Uzbek theatrical life was its attitude to the younger generation. The young producer, Amin Turdyev, did other work for the "Hamza" Theatre. In October 1943 he produced *Mother*, by Uigun, a contemporary play about present-day patriotism, written in verse. And another young producer, Sharif Kayumov, was preparing Lope de Vega's *Laurencia*. This is one of the symptoms of a rich and sturdy dramatic life, that young men or women should be trusted with the direction of plays, an art that cannot be fully developed without much experience of stage and of life, and therefore is liable to be jealously guarded by those that have had both. But this willingness to trust the young was not confined to the Uzbek theatres. The Russian "Gorky" dramatic theatre allowed its young producer Salnykov to do *Mudrets*, and Solovyov to do a new Soviet play, *The Scythe has Struck a Stone*.

In former days the Uzbeks were completely Oriental, knowing nothing more of European literature than an abridged version of *Robinson Crusoe*. There might have been a danger that they would develop a sense of inferiority and backwardness, which would lead them to adopt Russian standards. That danger has been averted. They measure their success by Russian standards of success, but their art by their own tradition, even

12

when they are playing Russian plays. Indeed it may be they are developing a new, or rather old, form of Uzbek entertainment.

All over their country there used to be travelling actor-clowns, called *kyzychi*, who were an evening's entertainment in themselves. They wrote, or made up, either beforehand or on the spur of the moment, scraps of dialogue which frequent repetition in other places refined and polished and adapted. These *kyzychi* had practically died out, but one, Shakirdayev, who had been made a People's Artist for his work, was studied carefully. In the Fergana Valley a number of local traditional interludes and folk-lore farces were noted down and preserved by Uzbek specialists. And out of these it was proposed to build up a repertory of folk plays and performances in a shape that would make them not antiquarian, but organic.

If this can be achieved in a now 75 per cent. industrialised country, so that it remains part of folk consciousness, yet ever new and developing, without need of external stimulus, then in Uzbekistan that impact of East on West and West on East will have produced something new and important indeed.[5]

UKRAINIANS IN THE LAND OF BULLETS

Kazakhstan stretches from the Caspian Sea to China. It is made of minerals. " Nine out of every ten bullets fired at the front ", said the Vice-Chairman of the Kazakh Council of People's Commissars in 1943, " are made óut of lead mined in our republic." New oil fields there were put into production at top speed when the war began ; so were the centres of coal and of manganese. At first these materials had to be sent to the Urals, but soon smelters, furnaces, factories, and with them, whole new towns, were built ; and the production of bombs, mines, hand-grenades and bullets began, as well as lighter essentials like leather and clothes. Thereby a principle of Soviet industrial distribution was adhered to, that the work should go to the metal, not the metal to the work.

The surface of Kazakhstan is as prolific as its lower depths. Millions of head of cattle graze the steppes, increasing 24 per cent. in number during 1942, sheep and goats at the same rate, hogs by 35 per cent. The area under crops was extended by two million acres, with tremendous progress in the south through the growing of " rubber " and sugar-beet. In the north the yield of wheat to the acre exceeded that of the U.S.A. But perhaps most valuable of all Kazakhstan's contributions in war material was its breeds of horses.

New railways and aerodromes had linked together the far, far distant centres of this enormous country, two-thirds the size of India ; and mechanical methods of agriculture had made many of its people machine-minded, but without taking away either the horsemanship or the blood of their mounts for which they were famous. The Eighth Guards Division, which fought so magnificently before Moscow under General Panfilov, contained great numbers of Kazakhs, superb cavalry, fierce and utterly self-regardless fighters, but quite as self-confident in a tank as in the saddle.

At home the war-like Kazakh people were as proud, therefore, of their men-folk as any nationals in the world ; and it is no surprise to find the arts celebrating them with a specific understanding of what they were fighting for : nor that there should be theatres in this up-to-date simple community. By 1943 Kazakhstan had twenty-two permanent national theatres. Most of the purely dramatic ones had performed the prime national play, *Guard of Honour*, by Mukhtar Auezov and Alzhapar Abishev ; for that work celebrates the great Eighth Guards Division, and Panfilov himself is on the stage, with Hero-of-the-Soviet-Union Tokhtarev, who fell in action. The same theme comes into the opera, *Guards, Advance !* to which Eugene Brusilovsky wrote the music. Brusilovsky was not Kazakh-born, but he had been Kazakh-hearted since 1933, when he went to that land to study its folk-music, and merged himself into it thereafter. There are, of course, Kazakh composers too.*

Not all the plays were war plays. The past was explored for native drama. Musrepov wrote a stirring tragedy, which was performed in 1942, about the nineteenth century poet Akhan Sere, a kind of Uriel Akosta of Kazakhstan, fighting religious bigotry and feudalism and other evil powers that fetter human thought ; a drama of ideas. Here and there were heard songs that Akhan Sere himself had sung ; for to be a poet in those days, as in these, meant, for a Kazakh, to be a minstrel. The music of the play was founded on these songs. Perhaps there were too many. Perhaps, to European ears, they held up the action. One critic complained that this was an opera, not a play.

Next year another important work by Auezov, a poetic drama, brought to life *Koblandy the Batyr*, hero and subject of a fourteenth-century poem. This legendary Batyr led the primitive Kazakhs against foreign invaders. A committee of actors, authors and producers, judging this work, found it to have a new direction for Auezov. Hitherto, they said, his work had not been pointed enough, nor lively enough ; but in this, characters, diction, and development of the action, were stage-like and firm. Auezov had turned from poet to playwright. The play was translated into Russian.

The Kazakh Drama Theatre *par excellence* worked in the capital, Alma-Ata ; which city is still famous for the fruit that won its name (=" Father of Apples "). Besides five other local theatres in 1942 there were no fewer

---

* Where, O my Scottish compatriots, are Bridie's play, or Sir Granville Bantock's opera, about the 51st ? And would Inverness go to see Brigadier Campbell, V.C. portrayed in either ? Would Kinlochleven go at all ?

than twelve institutions of higher learning.   So the Kazakhs are no barbarians.   By that year *Othello*, translated by Auezov, had been many
years in the repertory, and was now followed, in the same poet's translation,
by *The Taming of the Shrew*.   It was agreed that as Katharine Honoured
Artist Khadish Bukeyeva gave a subtle performance, revealing a gentle,
wistful femininity under the brusque manner of the Shrew.   So the
Kazakhs are not louts either.

But then it would seem that Bukeyeva spoke beautiful Russian, and
had studied all that was available about the part in that language before
she appeared in it.   And also she had the advantage of frequent attendance
at Russian performances of European plays by one of the best Moscow
theatres.   So much had Zavadsky's Mossoviet productions impressed her
when that theatre was at Alma-Ata, so deeply had she observed them,
that it was the desire of her heart to play Nora in *A Doll's House*.   So the
Kazakhs are not tyrants in their attitude to women any more.

For half a year already the two theatres, Kazakh and Russian, had been
playing under one roof, overcoming, as each occurred, the technical difficulties of sharing one stage, watching, studying, learning from each other's
idiom and methods.   They were of an age, about twenty years old.   Both
had established methods of their own for their own particular audiences ;
neither yielded to the other ;   each expanded.   That, too, was an organic
thing.   For the audience they both served was by now a fusion of Kazakhs
and Russians.

Both elements in this common building had, apart from their common
Socialism, an adventure in common :   the evacuation of industry from
west to east.   Both were pleased, in consequence, when the Kazakh theatre
did Konstantin Finn's *Peter Krymov*.

Peter is head of a foundry in a large Moscow works.   He is 33, and
recently married to Olga, who is ten years younger, and rather romantic.
The enemy is at the approaches to Moscow.   Olga volunteers as a nurse
and is drafted to the front.   Peter, as a good citizen, stays at his job, and is
drafted, with the factory, to the rear.   Superficially, a reversal of the duties
of the sexes and one which the hasty Olga does not understand.   She thinks
her husband, if he had made an effort and been " a man ", might have arranged things in a more glorious way.   Angry, perhaps, with him because
he has failed her belief in him, or perhaps with herself for having been
mistaken in him, she leaves for the front without even saying good-bye.

The factory leaves for the rear.   The difficulties, dangers, humours,
of this operation are made plain.   Peter has foreseen many of them.   He
has a broader view than Olga ;   but it was not without an inward struggle
that he resigns himself to going safety-ward.   A play on an industrial
theme in the Soviet Union is none the less for that a play about human

beings. And even the best Marxist may be unhappy when his wife mis-understands him ! Nor is the safety by any means so great.

He throws himself into the job ; the reassembling takes weeks instead of months ; the production figure leaps up ; shells stream west. But there are others beside Olga who do not realise the desperate need, the real possibility that despite all the well-laid plans, enough war material might not be forthcoming to halt the Fascists where they must be halted. There is carelessness, laziness. As the result, there is a serious accident. Peter who in difficulty, danger and apathy, has been heroic, is injured.

Meanwhile Olga has been wounded in battle, after behaviour just as heroic. She is sent to recuperate, with a decoration for her conduct, to the same town in the Far East. (Apart from the fact that this makes for stage neatness, there is no coincidence in this ; it happened often.) Both have learned from their separate struggles in the war. Each has a firmer under-standing toward the other. The personal problem is solved through the general experience of the community. This happens in many Soviet plays.

British critics might call this play Propaganda. If it had been intended as such, it would have failed. For it was written when there was a cry for plays to celebrate the heroic virtues and importance of the rear ; and surely it is poor propaganda to decorate your heroine at the front but give no sign that your hero is to have any recognition of ardour, courage and self-sacrifice ?

However that may be, it was warmly welcomed by Alma-Ata, Father of Apples and capital of the land of bullets. And in doing it, the Kazakh theatre had the assistance of what one might now call its Russian section. For Margolin produced it, Vinogradov and Lugovsky designed the scenes and Biryukov wrote the music, with Zavadsky himself as a sort of super-visor-consultant. They were all very much taken with the performance of Honoured Artist of the Kazakh Republic Aimanov as Peter.

Quite frankly, this was not the first impact of Russian and Kazakh theatre personnel. For the producers of the Kazakh Drama Theatre for some years back had included Pyzhova and Bibikov. But these two had been specialists in Kara-Kalpakian affairs at the Lunacharsky Institute for some time before, and Kara-Kalpakia is a part of Kazakhstan, the portion south of the Aral Sea. In pre-war days they had given talks and lectures which must have sounded now like theory, preparing for the practical work that the war and the Mossoviet brought them.

But the Ukrainian theatre carries the process in Kazakhstan a little further. " Ukrainian speech sounding from the stage ", said Gnat Yura, describing the work of his national theatre in Semipalatinsk, " is as near and dear to the Kazakh audience as the musical verses of the *akyn* Jamboul are near to the Ukrainian people ".

And when the Odessa Theatre of the Revolution returned to the Ukraine it brought with it a poetic drama of its host Kirghizia, *Sarinji*, by Eshmambetov, translated into Ukrainian.

All the different Central Asiatic peoples were linked together as well, theatrically, by the State Institute of Theatrical Art in Tashkent, where national actors and producers were taking courses for working their own countries of Uzbekistan, Kazakhstan, Tajikstan and Turkmenia.

Here is evidence indeed ! Here is an advance in the friendship of the peoples. So closely were they knit in the common aim of life, the common adventure of war, that the sufferings of the Ukraine became their sufferings, and differences of speech were no barrier. On the contrary they were a bond. The bond of two brother countries in that common aim and adventure.[6]

TURKMENIAN NIGHTS ENTERTAINMENTS

Other countries of Central Asia made similar steps of friendship : Turkmenia and the Moldavians. By the autumn of 1943 the Moldavian Theatre included with their own and their Russian plays a new one by two Turkmenian writers, Mukhtarev and Purlyev, about life on a Turkmenian farm in war-time. This may sound a small thing ; and if the Soviet theatre were mere entertainment, it might be. But the Soviet audience in any country, though they would not sit through any play that did not entertain them (in the wider sense of occupying their attention agreeably), do all the same require some adult degree of truth and good sense in the representation of life. To impersonate foreigners in a foreign play to an audience largely composed of such foreigners with such standards, takes more than good art ; it takes courage.

For the Turkmenians, though their Spain-sized territory was greatly desert, and this had directed their Soviet energies to grandiose and practicable schemes for diverting giant rivers and raising vegetables in dry sand, were not without culture, nor were their arts limited to rug-making. To deal with their natural resources they could produce chemists, hydrological engineers, professors of geology and agronomy ; but to grace life, they also produced painters, poets, architects, actors.

At Ashkhabad, their capital, in November 1941 the premises of the Turkmenian State Theatre of Opera and Ballet were completed ; of Turkmenian opera and Turkmenian ballet, that is. A sumptuous building in the Turkmenian style. And there were several dramatic theatres, of which the first had been opened in 1929, though the scattered population numbered only just over a million. The best known of these dramatic theatres was the " Stalin " Theatre at Ashkhabad, which was the first to produce, in 1942, a play by the Turkmenian Kerbabayev. As in the other Asiatic republics, this celebrated a national Hero-of-the-Soviet Union, in this case Kurban Durdy, most famous of Turkmen soldiery. As in the others, too, there was a biographical drama, in this case a comedy, about a national poet (Kemine). By the end of 1942, this theatre had become quite unrecognisable as the sapling studio of trainees in the Moscow Institute of Theatrical Art. It was a developed national theatre, so wholly and unself-consciously national that it could perform with understanding the arts of other nations, like *Revizor;* and even the contemporary plays of other nations, like *Lyubov Yarovaya.* So national that it is no surprise to this writer, as he types out these words, to hear of a cable from Moscow announcing the publication of the first history of the Turkmenian Theatre, to be translated later into Russian, from the drama studio organised in 1926 by a group of amateurs, with a shepherd among them, now an Honoured Artist of the Republic, to the ten professional theatres of to-day.[7]

SHAKESPEARE IN KIRGHIZIA

A similar double development, without perhaps quite the same degree of co-operation (at least the Odessa Theatre that toured there does not report so), took place in the former nomadic region of Kirghizia near Chinese Turkestan. Nomads indeed the Kirghiz tribesmen were, and without a written language till Soviet times. Now they seemed to be smitten with Shakespeare. By the end of 1941 the local poet Eshmambetov had translated *Hamlet, Othello, King Lear, Romeo and Juliet* and *The Merchant of Venice* for the Kirghiz stage, had just finished *The Merry Wives of Windsor* for the Issyk-Kul Regional Theatre, and started *Twelfth Night* for the Central Dramatic Theatre in Frunze. It was completed in summer 1943 and performed by a sub-company of junior players just graduated from the Moscow Institute of Theatrical Art.

But it should not be supposed that Kirghizia was a pastoral land that had merely settled down to communal herding. Certainly the Fergana Valley is among the most fertile on earth. But a study of fossils had led to the discovery of much-wanted rare minerals ; a study of archæological sites had led to the opening-up of old irrigation systems, and digging the famous Fergana Canal, which in turn led to more archæological discoveries ; and as a result the silk industry, of paramount importance in modern war, made enormous progress.

The Kirghizians, in fact, came to play as big and active part in the war, proportionately to their numbers, of which there are some million and a half, as any other Soviet country. They, too, sent fighters to the front ; and these, too, were celebrated in their seventeen theatres. A new Kirghiz play in 1943 celebrated their most prominent hero of the war. It was called *The Black Cloud.*[8]

GOING BACK WEST

On the border of Europe and Asia lies Bashkiria, between the Urals and the Steppes, above the Caspian Sea. Here the theatrical contact was rather less obvious than the other arts showed. Ukrainian and Bashkirian poets, for example, had translated each other's works. Bashkirian gold miners could read in their own language many of the poems of Byron, many of the plays of Shaw. Burns and Jack London and Upton Sinclair were on sale in the shops. But Bashkiria's three millions were more interested in opera. An operatic technicum was started in the capital, Ufa, in 1924. By 1938 it had become an important cultural factor, doing all the classics of Russia and Europe, *Faust*, *La Traviata*, *Eugene Onyegin* and the rest, but also many by Bashkirian, Kazakh, Azerbaijanian and other national composers. Famous Ukrainian musicians, too, living during the occupation of their own land in Bashkiria, Litvinenko-Volgemut, Zoi Gaidai, Patorzhinsky, had become models of great interest to the local ones. There was again no danger, though, that the national effort would be swamped ; for it was not long before the Bashkir Departments of both the Moscow Conservatoire and the Leningrad School of Choreography were dispatched to their native land.

This does not mean that if the dramatic theatre is backward here, it is non-existent or unimportant. The State Drama Theatre at Ufa had plenty to say. Here a company had been formed in the very heart and heat of the Civil Wars ; and many veterans from those days were still with it in the Fascist War. The repertoire was not very different from those we have been citing. The Bashkir poet Bagazit Bikbaï translated *Revizor*, which was produced in the spring of 1943. But the previous year he had written, and this theatre had performed, two of his own original plays : *Salavat*, celebrating the national hero Salavat Yulayev, and *Kyakhim the Batyr*, about the hero of that name during the war of 1812.

All round here is historical country : Pugachov, Chapayev, Khudai-berdin, Frunze, and other heroes came alive again on the stage in plays written by their compatriots for audiences that either knew them or were brought up in their fame. And the heroes of the present war, who succeeded them as defenders of the people against other tyrants, these are celebrated also on the stage in Mabargahov's *Unquenchable Hearts*, Bikbaï's *The Homeland Calls*.

But Bashkiria, being so near the Urals, had with Ural wealth a Russian population too. These had their own Russian Theatre of Bashkiria, which, by June 1943, had mastered *A Dog in the Manger*, *Russian People*, *Peter Krymov*, *Brave Soldier Schweik*, *The Immortal*, *A Moscow Girl*, and *Twelfth Night*.[9]

Twentieth-Century Tartars are Merry

West flows the River Byelaya (" White ") into Tataria, where it joins the Kama. West flows the River Kama, till it joins the Volga, south of where Kazan the Tatar capital stands. Now we are in country we visited last century. But how it is changed ! The theatre in the capital is no longer for the Russians only. The whole character of the people and the place is altered.

" Nothing ", wrote Laurence Oliphant in 1853, " could be more solemnly dreary, and consequently more genuinely Russian, than Kazan." But then he never went to the theatre there. There was none to go to.

We can. Not to a Russian, but to a Tatar theatre. They are gaily disposing of *The Dog in the Manger*, and about to do an uproarious comedy by the Tatar author Isambet. For the Tatars, descended from the Tartars, are a very high-spirited people, and their stage is strong in rich, fruity, humour. They are a simple people too ; a little too simple for some solemn folk in other parts of the Soviet Union. For it must not be supposed that the unity of the different countries in the Union is so weak and precarious that no voice must be lifted by one national against another, for fear of rupture or racial sulks. If a critic has cause to find fault with a Tatar theatre, he can do so, be he Tatar, Russian, or Ostyak. Only let him beware of falsely generalising into finding fault thereby with *all* Tatar theatres ; or his judgment will be held prejudice, and his reputation fall.

So fault was found in 1943 with Isambet's latest play, *Mariam*. It was a war play. Mariam, a Tatar girl . . . one of those whom Oliphant described as being " tall maidens disclosing the charms " (facial, of course, which had been partly concealed by the shawls drawn over their heads) " which their head-dress was intended to conceal, thus affording an opportunity of observing how far superior they are in personal attractions to the damsels of the country " (i.e. Russia).

But Mariam does not wear a shawl. She is an Army nurse ; a blood donor, whose blood goes into the veins of what seems by the uniform to be a Red Army man, but is in fact a German spy, by name Johannes. Johannes escapes and gets back to his own ranks. Mariam is captured by them, and it is ordered that she be hanged. Johannes is one to carry out the sentence. She tells him that her own blood is in his veins, and a terrible, almost mystical conflict arises in his brain.

This was attacked as mysticism. The fact that so many ounces of red liquid is circulating in a man's body does not affect his brain, they said. But it is questionable whether there is not here material for a fine conflict of dramatic type. We know that captured German, or at any rate pro-Nazi officers, have refused to have transfusions of " decadent " blood, and

one at least preferred to die.   Here ideology has a palpable expression.
And the bodily fusion, at once more impersonal and more intimate than
by an act of sex, would set up in an honest, or fairly honest, German soldier's
mind a self-loathing and a feeling of almost sexual bodily gratitude to the
condemned girl, which to my mind is legitimate drama.   And it must be
remembered also that in simple communities like the Tatar the blood is
regarded as a continuous living link with past and future.   There is a more
real bond between three generations in peasant villages than in more
sophisticated town communities.   And to Tatar audiences this question
would be much more important and intelligible.   Especially if the German
soldier were himself a peasant.

This does not mean, though, that the Tatar theatre only played works
of peasant interest.   An example of topical Russian work done here was
Regiment DD, written by the author Laptyev in collaboration with the
flying ace and Arctic hero Vodopyanov.   Vodopyanov's first venture on
the stage was *The Dream*, which was to be seen in Ohlopkov's Realistic
Theatre in 1937.   That concerned an airman rather like the author himself,
having a dream of making a world famous Arctic flight.   Like the author,
too, his dream came true ; and as a matter of fact Vodopyanov was on a
world famous Arctic flight by the time his play was produced.   When I
was in Moscow the performance had just been broadcast, so that he could
listen to it in the icy wastes.

This play was not quite so topical as that, but its truth was immediate.
It concerned a Red Air Force unit one of whose machines is forced down
in Occupied territory, and by the help of a local girl contacts local partisans,
joining them in a raid on enemy head-quarters and finally making their
base in safety.   But it is not a mere drama of action.   Many of the characters are interesting people, especially one who has been behaving queerly,
so that his comrades are worried about him.   Then he admits that he has
just heard what the Nazis have done to his young wife and children.   The
weight of the action is largely directed on the anger this arouses in unit and
audience.

The Tatars' territory was never occupied by the Germans ; it lay too
far east for that.   But their good luck in geography did not debar them
from losing fighters of their own nation at the front ; nor from suffering
deeply for the women-folk of other nations in the Soviet Union.   For
their natural merriment did not spring from insensitiveness but from a
joy in life and in simple things.   And the sympathy of happy people is
purer, and therefore often more helpful, than that of those who are continually seeing the worst.[10]

CHUVASHES IN RUFFS

The queer Chuvashes, whom Oliphant described weird at their nocturnal tasks, had in Cheboksary, their capital, their national theatre. They had had it for a quarter of a century. In April 1943 it celebrated its twenty-fifth birthday with excerpts from four national plays and *Othello*. This last, which was its first Western European production, had been translated by the local poet Kalgan, helped by Valentine Verigina of Leningrad, an expert on Shakespeare and the theatre of his time. She records that the Chuvashes had some difficulty in mastering the dances, manners and even the gait of Elizabethan English people, but that the result was " an extremely interesting, if perhaps rather original, portrayal of Shakespeare's characters ". Over which gentle speaking of the truth, in the absence of any further information about these almost aboriginal Volga people, the imagination can play very pleasantly.[11]

IN THE CAUCASUS MOUNTAINS

These are weaker vessels. If we turn to the battlefields on this side of the Caucasus and to the parts beyond, we find stronger ones.

The southern flow of the acid of the Fascist advance bit nearer and nearer to its southern objective, the Caspian coast. But it never got there. It was dammed at Vladimirovka and Terek.

It turned southward too, toward the oil of Baku. But it never got there either. It was held in the foothills of the Caucasus. It enjoyed itself, as acid does, destroying, disfiguring, torturing, men, women and children alike. Women especially, the legendary Circassian women, whose beauty was famous down the ages and still is transmitted from generation to generation, in spite of such Fascists and men in similar positions of imperial authority since imperial authority was first appointed.

But in time it had to recede. Soon it was a backward flow, scooped up scientifically as acids must be, though the places they have been in are not as before and can be never.

It did not need this propinquity of danger to bring knowledge of war to the Caucasian peoples. They knew it already. But their knowledge became more immediate ; and when they reflected this on their stages, they did so with depth and seriousness.

Chechen-Ingutia was among the worst hit, being oil country and an enemy objective. In Grozny, its capital, we will not be surprised by now to find a Russian as well as a national theatre. The Russian theatre is named for Lermontov, that exquisite poet who loved and studied and wrote about the Caucasus regions during his periods of exile. In 1942 its repertory included *Field-Marshal Kutuzov*, Perventsev's *Winged Tribe* (a reminder to any Moscow people there) and a play called *The Childhood of the Marshal*.

The national theatre opened its 1943 season with a Russian war play, *On the Eve*, which (see page 240) has a Western locale but an Oriental heroine ; and with a literary-musical interlude by Grin and Bazorkin called *The Word of Hero Khan Pasha Nuradilov*. This latter celebrated the theatre's own eponym, a machine-gunner who exterminated the phenomenal figure of 920 Fascists with his own hand. That is the kind of enemy the Fascists fled from ; for the people of Chechen-Ingutia are remarkable. It gives us the measure of what war meant in the Grozny theatre.

The first full-length Chechen-Ingush war play was given later in that season, *The Birth of Hatred*, also by Bazorkin. Then spirits were relieved with a little Goldoni. And with the arrival of guests from the Ukraine, in the Kiev "Lesya Ukrainka" Theatre showing Leonov and Simonov among a classical repertoire, more than a mere link was formed between two or even three peoples. As the Ukrainian company met and talked with the locals, a link was forged between two Fronts. And the subsequent production of *General Brusilov* by the Kiev theatre at Grozny in November 1943 (for Ukrainians had to stay longer in the East than Russians) recalled the happier relation of two countries since the 1918 conflicts. It was a link between two wars.

A similar link between Caucasus and Ukraine took place between the "Schors" Theatre, which left Zhitomir in 1941, and Ossetia, where it lodged. The Ossetians are an even more remarkable people than the Chechen-Ingushes. Unlike most of the Caucasus peoples, they tend to be blond, with blue eyes, tall, and their hair light-brown or fair. There is a legend that they are connected with the Crusaders, to which colour is lent by the photograph published by George Hume, showing an Ossetian in a much decayed and torn suit of chain armour, an heirloom of his family, as many such suits, breastplates, casques and other bits of mediæval armour have been heirlooms in these parts.

So popular was the Ukrainian theatre that before it left for home the Ossetian Government conferred titles of honour and distinction on some of its members.[12]

IN AZERBAIJAN

More national heroes were celebrated in the Land of Fire. In 1942 the Azerbaijan Dramatic Theatre at Baku presented a new historical play by Osman Saryveli about a ninth-century Babek, followed later in the season by another of the same type, about the thirteenth-century poet and statesman, Prik. This has been written by one of this country's most promising young writers, Tatul Guyan, who had been killed at the Front. Yet another patriotic play, produced for the twenty-fifth anniversary of the Red Army, was *Vefa*, by another Azerbaijanian poet, which moved in time to the present, as did later productions of *Makhabbet* and *Engineer Sergeyev*, whose authors were Ibrahim and Vsevolod Rokk, respectively. The latter describes the scorched earth policy in industry. Other plays that year were a satirical comedy by Mir-Jalil and a study of former days in the now classic Akhundov.

Akhundov's *Tale of Mastali-Shah the Dervish* was to be seen in the Baku Comedy Theatre, with Goldoni's *Servant of Two Masters;* and the Kirovobad Theatre in the following spring put on the stage the first Lope de Vega play to be translated into Azerbaijanian (by Mamelov), *A Dog in the Manger*.

But far across the Volga though Azerbaijan was, it was not peopled only by its own nationals; there lived within its borders Russians, Armenians, Turks, Tats and many another people. The Baku Russian Theatre, doing *Russian People* and *Wait for Me*, glorified the Russians but set up no fiction that they were alone in their struggle and sacrifice nor in any way better than the Tats or the Talyshes, even if they had the advantage of a more developed way of life, any more than *The Front* in Russian implied that the Ukrainians were better than the Russians. Each nation learned from the other. Imagine, for example, the mental and spiritual help given to the Mohammedan maidens by a living representation of Katarina in Ostrovsky's *Storm*.

Indeed the Russian theatres found much to profit them in the local drama; *The Happy Ones*, by Sabit Rakhman, or *Farkhad and Shirin*, by Samed Vurgun, that notable and much honoured poet. These took their place beside Gorky, Lope de Vega and one of the Russian historic-military plays.

Nor was the Armenian theatre at Baku content with only Armenian plays like Guyan's, or *Namus* by Shirvan-Zade; it interpreted the other nations, from Azerbaijanian Jabarly's *Almas*, from Russia, *Invasion* and *Oleko Dundich*, which latter added Serbia and the last war to the triangle of nations in this one.[13]

An Armenian Competition

Armenia returned the compliment. In the war years she had developed fast and solidly. She had good foundations not only for her own development but for relations with other countries. Her statesman, Israel Ori, contemporary with Peter the Great, had taught her that, though Tsarist occupation destroyed her friendship with her freedom of action. In re-enacting on the stage the drama of Israel Ori's life, the dramatist Grigory Chakhiryan implied her ties with her sister republics. Israel Ori, like so many Armenians, who are in some ways like many Lowland Scots, being good business men, was a traveller. In this play modern

Armenia saw herself in the throes of seventeenth-century interventions, but also saw the France of Louis XIV, the building of Peterburg, the court of the Persian Shah Hussein. It was produced at the " Sundukyan " Theatre in Yerevan in 1943 by Ajemyan with sets by Aruchyan. Patriotic in attitude and content, it was in no way chauvinistic. Neither the arts nor the people of Armenia were that ; and the Armenian State Orchestra was heard as gladly when it was doing the Shostakovich Seventh as when it was doing Hachaturyan.

Early in 1943 the Armenian Committee for Art Affairs held a competition for plays on Armenian themes, which would show particularly the part played by Armenians in the war, the help given by them to the Fronts, the struggle of all the Transcaucasian peoples against Fascism, and the way they collaborated in the past against similar threats. The three prizes were large sums, though not so large as the yearly all-Union Stalin Awards : 20,000, 15,000 and 10,000 roubles.

No fewer that 135 original plays were at once submitted, and more followed. Of the first 135 forty-seven were judged good enough for performance, one of the best, by common consent, being *Frenzy*, by A. Gulakyan, which was produced at Leninakan and elsewhere. The theme of this was the exploits and, if need be, the self-sacrifice of young Armenians at the Front. The titles of some of the runners-up indicate their probable contents : *Vengeance, On the Volcano, Second Thoughts, A Son of the Fatherland.*

Virile though this is, it does not show the real solidity of the Armenian theatre. Perhaps *Hamlet* may, as done in the summer of 1943 at Yerevan. A. Fevralsky, reporting on Shakespeare in the theatres of Georgia and Armenia, says that it was an uneven performance, containing " absurd elements of novelty ", fine tradition and the persistence of rule-of-thumb methods. He cites the ghost scene, in which he says there was no note of preparation or warning. By this, I imagine, he means that the ghost was just a stage ghost, speaking in a thin voice and looking fixedly in front of it, not trying to be part of the action, not attaining any fatherly influence over Hamlet. But he approved of the crowd work, especially in the Mousetrap scene, and Burjulyan's handling of Ophelia's funeral. Even he admits, though, that Vagarsh Vagarshyan's Hamlet was a strong character and a fighter against evil ; and this view is upheld by Professor Morozov, the leading authority on Shakespeare in the Soviet Union, in a letter to the present writer. He said that the " Sundukyan " Theatre was famous among other things for its Shakespeare productions.

Certainly it was not without experience. Aruchyan, writing in the *Moscow News* (29.xii.43), said that since its foundation in 1921 his theatre had not let a season go by without including one Shakespeare play. *Othello,*

The Merchant of Venice, *The Taming of the Shrew*, *Macbeth*, and *The Merry Wives of Windsor* are mentioned ; and in the first, three outstanding Othellos and two Desdemonas were found in the Capital. In 1943 *King Lear* was added, with People's Artist of the Armenian Republic Nersesyan, who was also a Stalin Laureate, adding great lustre to the play and his own reputation as the premier Armenian film actor.

In September 1943 the Presidium of the Supreme Soviet of the Armenian Republic recognised this theatre's work by awarding honours to members of the collective for *General Brusilov*, *Field-Marshal Kutuzov*, and *Russian People*, all, be it noticed, Russian plays. It was a great grief that in the same year they should lose their leading lady, Arus Voskanyan, a People's Artist of the Republic. An obituary signed by leading Armenian artists mentioned her unresting war work, and the understanding and distinction with which she had played, especially her last part, that of Haritonova the Doctor's wife, in *Russian People*.

INSET : A SOVIET LUXEMBOURG

Inset into Armenia on the Persian frontier, though it has greater affinities with Azerbaijan, lies an interesting wee country which ought to be mentioned. This is Nakhichevan. It is about the size of Devon in area, and half the size of Luxembourg in population, having about 125,000 inhabitants, chiefly engaged in agriculture and the mining of non-ferrous metals. Its people claim that the chief town, called by the same name as the state, is the oldest town in the world, having been founded by Noah when he stepped out of the ark. Mount Ararat is only 80 miles away. And some of its women have customs that are centuries old, for those who were born before the Soviet way of life was adopted, still have an impulse to cover their faces if men approach. But in war it was no Asiatic survival. Forty-eight per cent. of its budget it devoted to education, and on the outbreak of war it took steps to increase its output of rock-salt, molybdenum, fire-clays, dyes, silk and fruit. One of the smallest republics in the Union it might be, but neither its produce nor its theatre were going to suffer from disorganisation. The favourite play in its State Theatre was *Othello*.[14]

GEORGIA

I doubt if it is any longer necessary to enlarge upon the theatres in Georgia, one of the most advanced of the non-Russian Soviet countries. Tbilisi had always been a centre of the arts. It now had nine theatres, out of the forty-two in the whole country. The others were as permanent, as popular, and as persistently full, at Gori, Poti, Suhum, Batum, Kutaisi, Telavi, Staliniri, Signahi, Chiaturi, Borzhom, Lanchkhut, Makharadze, Velistsikhe, Tskhakaya, places by no means as forbidding as their bristling

consonants seem in English letters to imply. They were ports, watering-
places, centres of tobacco growing, of fruit orchards, oil fields, limestone
quarries, and of a score of industries. The audiences were so keen and
constant that anything up to eight or ten new productions entered the
repertoire of each town each year. Newer theatres like the " Meshkish-
vili " at Kutaisi or the Gori State Dramatic were said to rival in art and
smoothness the older established ones.

The former of these two, which opened in November 1938 (I have
given a short account of it elsewhere), became famous in 1942 for its production of an old play by Yuzhin-Sumbatov, who you will remember
was born in Georgia and became· the leading figure at the Moscow Maly.
This play, *Treachery*, he wrote in 1903. It took an incident from Georgian
history for its theme, the tragedy of the Georgian people ground under the
heel of Shah Abas and led to revolt by the Empress Zeinab, who became
his concubine to save her country. Georgians, like Russians, had learned
to set down naught in malice ; Socialist realism demanded honour paid
even to Empresses where honour was due. More perhaps than honour
—love, understanding and gratitude. These are acquired best and most
easily in the theatre.

The Gori Theatre was established at the time of Stalin's 60th birthday
(1942). Its premises were built specially for it. Of its young producer
Simon Vachandze much was expected after his treatment of *Engineer
Sergeyev*. Another young Georgian producer was Ivan Bochorishvili at
Telavi, whose production of an Ostrovsky play (*Guilty Though Guiltless*)
attracted attention in 1942. At Poti, Teimuz Lordkipanidze did Garcia
Lorca's *Bloody Wedding*, and showed his paces as an actor, too, in the same
Ostrovsky and in the Georgian play, *A Collective Farm Wedding*. The
range and interests of the Georgian theatre can be gauged in plays to be
seen in other places during 1942 : *From the Spark* (Dadiani's study of early
Bolshevik days), *Lado Ketskhoveli*, *Georgii Saakadze* (the seventeenth-century
statesman), Gorky's *Enemies*, *King Lear*, and *Pavel Grekov*, together with
plays about Georgian national figures like David the Builder, Queen Tamara,
Shota Rustaveli. Three different treatments of Saakadze were to be seen
at the same time in different theatres. Two included the figure of Heraclius
the Second. He had a specially topical value, as he signed the agreement
of 1782 whereby Georgia incorporated herself with Russia in return for
protection against the incursions of Aga-Mahmet Khan, and other foreign
conquerors. One of these plays, *King Heraclius*, was particularly exciting
with a feast scene at which the King's enemies offer him a goblet of poisoned
wine. A young poet shoots it out of the King's hands. The other showed
the King grieved at having to evacuate his capital, but confident that his
men will stem the enemy's invasion, as is indeed done by *The Heroes of*

Kartsanisi, after whom the play is titled. There was a splendid crowd scene on the King's return to his liberated capital. Notable, too, for a rare appearance on the Soviet stage of Goethe, was the " Marjanishvili " Theatre's production of *Faust*.

The Georgian theatres had always been interested in foreign classics, but when the war began they looked round for a suitable war-time drama, Georgian, Russian, or foreign. Their first discovery was foreign. The " Rustaveli " Theatre at Tbilisi was perhaps the star theatre of the country, having Vasadze, as fine a producer as Khorava was a fine actor. Indeed the Russian critic and journalist Solodovnikov, in an article in Литература и искусство (27.xi.43) described Khorava's Othello as "a *chef-d'œuvre* of Soviet theatre art ". Between them these two men gave their theatre a high patriotic note. In the years even before the Revolution a playwright Eristavi had taken a Sardou melodrama, *La Patrie* (first performed in Paris in 1869), and turned it into a heroic tragedy of patriotism. This was now revived by Vasadze as a study in the fervour that rids a land of its invaders when everything else seems to favour them. Yuzhin's *Treachery* built up this passion. *General Brussilov* came nearer to actuality by one war. *Oleko Dundich* generalised with a foreign example, and brought back the youth of Voroshilov, Budyonny, and Orjonikidze. But these were all Russian pieces. The blaze came with the Georgian playwright Mdivani. His *Ordered to the Front* was translated into Russian and done by the Moscow Tyuz. His *Moscow Skies*, produced now for the first time on any stage, was just what Georgia had been waiting for : the expression of Georgian admiration for the defence of Moscow. Strictly speaking, perhaps, it was more a series of scenes than a play. It was said to have many faults, by Russian standards. But we are judging by Georgian ones at this time ; and the specially composed songs, the passionate treatment by Khorava's production, the topicality and timeliness of the theme, speaking for a non-Russian nation, made it an immediate success not only in Georgia but in many other lands for which it was translated. As much was owed by as many to as few in the U.S.S.R. as in Britain.

Meanwhile the Russian war plays had come to Georgia : *A Fellow of Our Town*, *The Smoke of the Fatherland*, and more. Mdivani wrote another one, *Partisans*. Doroseli wrote about Kikvidze, the Georgian youth who took part in the defence of Tsaritsyn ; and that was timely, too, when Stalingrad was being watched by Georgia with the same dazed admiration as by the rest of the democratic world. Two other Georgian playwrights joined in, with a play that showed Georgian youth in war, and this was done by both Georgian and Russian theatres for Young Spectators in Tbilisi.

Russian theatres, too, in this country were active. That named for Griboyedov in Tbilisi spent the 1942-3 season touring all the spots in the

13

country where there were groups of Russians old or new. One of their plays was *The School for Scandal*; and in March 1944 it gave the first performance of *The Three Sisters* in Georgia, produced by A. Ridal in sets by V. Ivanov. Relations between Russia and Georgia had been very close ever since the inclusion of Georgia in the Union. Theatrically Georgia gained by Nemirovich's holiday in 1941-2. He helped the " Rustaveli " Theatre with its *Antony and Cleopatra*, discussed with Khorava his forthcoming *King Lear*, as he had done *Hamlet*. Olga Knipper records how impressed she had been on her visit by the fierce hate of the Transcaucasian peoples toward the Fascists. And any dangers that the Georgian theatre might be swept by its characteristically passionate feelings into lack of control or of care for detail would be removed by the example of its premier company, restrained and advised by the wisest theatrical figure in the world.

In Georgia at that time there were three Armenian theatres, one Azerbaijanian, one Ossetian, and one Abkhazian (Abkhazia is the portion of Georgia that lies along the Black Sea coast above Poti). Several of the artists of these received honours from the Georgian Supreme Soviet in 1943. So that the sub-nationalities were not neglected, not even the Ajarians, who live by Turkey, and were given a new play in 1942 by Shervashidze which dealt with General Bagration.[15]

Outside the Soviet Union

The subject of this section is quite irrelevant. It is a country to which no evacuees went, because in fact it was not even part of the Soviet Union. But it is a very interesting example of the impact of East and West ; and until enough material is available for it to fall into its proper place, in a book dealing with the theatres in Mexico and the freer parts of China, and any other countries that were so profoundly and uncompromisingly freed that they asserted their theatres, I make no apology for inserting it here.

It is the Mongolian People's Republic.

Since 1921 this independent and exciting land has maintained an almost family relation with the lands of the Soviet Union. A hot, dry, high country, over 3,000 feet above sea level, it is said to be beautiful, and made more so to the artist's eye by the coloured and picturesque clothes its people wear. A virile, athletic race since the days of Jenghiz Khan, and in no way decadent. They live fully, delighting in music and all the arts. And, as we might now expect, they have a theatre.

Their theatre would appear to have developed as so many of the world's theatres have done, out of burst religious ceremonies, in this case annual ones called Tsam, and encouraged to survive and develop by the Government, which is a People's Revolutionary Party.

Their theatrical history is not unlike that of the Oriental countries inside the Soviet Union, say, Dagestan. An amateur movement, gradually failing to cope with increasing demands and distance, applying for assistance from professionals. There were no professionals in the Mongolian Republic, for as yet there was no theatre. They turned to their friends across the frontier, who had had experience in advising and nursing young Oriental theatres. That was in 1930. In 1931 the first professional theatre in Mongolia opened at Ulan-Bator (Urga).

Two years later it went to Moscow, to take part in the International Olympiad of Revolutionary Theatres. And since then its artists had grown in stature. The actor Tsagan-Tsegmit, the actress Tseren-Dulma (for there is no bar to a mixed company in a free land), and others, were given titles of honour similar to those awarded in Soviet States ; and their faces became familiar to their friends inside the Union through films they made, especially *They Call Him Suë-Bator*, which was shown all over the Union.

They have an extensive repertoire, fifty plays in twelve years. There are many Mongolian plays of national and international life ; but the Russian ones are many, too, including *Revizor* and the Chehov one-acters, and among the European classics, *Fuente Ovejuna*, Goldoni, Molière's *Les Escapades de Scapin*, and the Anatole France short comedy of *The Man who Married a Dumb Wife*. But Soviet plays have always attracted them, especially *Armoured Train 14-69* which, you will remember, showed Eastern Siberia during the Civil Wars.

This country did not declare war on the Axis, but she has always given sisterly help of a non-military kind ; and early in 1943 Tsagan-Tsegmit appeared in Moscow with a delegation bringing gifts for the Front.[16]

TRIPS TO MOSCOW

This was not the only occasion on which far-off lands kept in theatrical touch with Moscow, even in war-time. In July 1943, for example, a Siberian poet from Omsk gave readings from his works in the Moscow Writers' Club ; and many were the single artists who in this way kept the centre in touch with what the provinces were thinking and creating. Whole theatres did the same. As early as August 1942 a company from the Saratov " Karl Marx " Theatre was in Moscow showing their interpretation of *Russian People* and *Nadyezhda Durova*. In April 1943 the theatre from Noginsk, east of the capital, gave the first performance of that superb play, *Invasion*, by Leonov, at the premises of the Moscow Tyuz. In June 1943, at the Central Theatre of the Red Army, the district theatre of Gorky town gave a series of performances of Gorky's *Barbarians* and of *Oleko Dundich* and also a repeat in August, in the Hermitage Winter Theatre. This followed a visit by the Yaroslavl Theatre, named the " Volkov " for the earliest man of the theatre in Russian history ; and the same summer

saw a combined display of acting in Moscow by the leading figures from
the Saratov, Kazan and Sverdlovsk stages.

A complete Festival of Ukrainian Theatre was organised in the summer
of 1942 ; this naturally included opera and ballet as well ; but, owing to
the nature of the component parts, it will be better considered in a later
chapter.[17]

THE WORK OF THE V.T.O.

Each of the national arts we have been considering, and many more
for which we have no space, is a completely independent, self-supporting,
self-developing entity.   They are more than separate organs of a body ; they
are separate bodies.   But in so far as they are all going in the same direction,
they are likely to find common problems and common needs.   The system
which provides them with each other's experience, and co-ordinates their
efforts, if they so wish, so that they need not waste time on unnecessary
research when this has already been done elsewhere, is the All-Russian
Theatrical Society, known by its Russian initials as the V.T.O.

The function of this body was of such importance in helping the
impacts we have been watching, that we must devote a little space to its
history.

It is, in a sense, a survival from Tsarist times though much changed in
character and developed in utility.   It was started in 1884 by a group of
prominent actors and actresses.   Savina was its first president.   Savina
had a great influence over Yablochkina, now the senior actress of the Soviet
Union, who succeeded her and is still president.   Savina drew her attention
in her early years to the conditions under which less well-known actors
had to work, especially in the provinces, unable to help themselves, and
without hope of betterment unless some of the Imperial players interested
themselves in them.   This Savina and Yablochkina, and several others, did.
At first the Society, which was called then the Society for Providing Help
to Stage Workers, was limited to acts of charity, the relief by money grants
of needy professionals.   But the threats to the profession by entrepreneurs
and the police alike (provincial theatres came under the jurisdiction of the
police, like fairs, markets, " public houses ", and were subject to the same
abuses of authority) had to be countered somehow, or the money grants
would just be wasted.   In 1894 a special Bureau of the Society was allowed
to work out a standard contract, arbitration methods, guarantees, and so
on, as a base for further action.

Meanwhile Yablochkina had been taking an ever larger and larger part
in the Maly's own " Corporation of Maly Theatre Artists ", which was
a loosely formed and rather moribund staff association that only woke up
occasionally when the members were specially roused, but otherwise was

purely charitable. Yablochkina was made president of this, and invigorated it to such an extent that she sometimes came into conflict with Yuzhin-Sumbatov, the director.

So she had plenty of experience of social work ; and was a fighter ; and when Savina died in 1915, she was the obvious person to carry on her work. As she once said, she had no personal life and no family, so that all at the Maly were her cousins. From which, she went on, it followed that anyone on the Russian stage was her relative. For them through the wider Society she worked and fought as she did in the Maly. Under her guidance it founded a hostel for actors in Peterburg, a school for actors' orphans, a scheme of family relief, sickness benefit, and other such necessities. The Society grew stronger and stronger. It was recognised by the Imperial Government. It summoned, in 1897, the first Congress of Stage Workers. That year in the Maly premises the Russian actor as a professional person raised his voice for the first time in protest against the conditions of his life. From then on the Society's activities broadened from the charitable to the political, and began to take in questions of provincial repertoire, censored plays, anti-Semitism.

In 1917 the need for its primary function, charitable relief, ceased. With the creation of the Professional Union of Art Workers it seemed as if its secondary, its political function, also was unnecessary. But Yablochkina fought for her Society ; and so great were her prestige and persuasiveness that the new Soviet Government yielded to her, and gave the V.T.O. power to build up and be responsible for a new theatre, a theatre on Socialist foundations.

With Governmental assistance it now built the House of the Actor in the heart of Moscow, with a large hall, conference rooms, reception rooms, library, restaurant and studios. To Savina's Peterburg Hostel it added two " Houses of Stage Veterans " in Leningrad and Moscow (Yablochkina's special pride), two rest houses, in the Crimea and on the Volga, a book shop, and a make-up factory from which it now draws a considerable revenue. It opened branches at Leningrad, Gorky, and Sverdlovsk. It became a huge concern, with an annual budget of $3\frac{1}{2}$ million roubles.

For greater efficiency it was divided into five sections : Acting, Producing, Musical Theatre, Theatre Management, and Amateur Theatre ; and into two departments, one for Ostrovsky, the other for Shakespeare and the Western European dramatists. Professor Michael Morozov was appointed head of the latter, a position in which his scholarship and knowledge of the theatre have very greatly helped the success of the " Classical " European drama in the Soviet Union.

Its functions are not limited to supplying information. Every year on Shakespeare's birthday it holds a conference at which experts and scholars, producers, actors, specialists of one kind or another, read papers on different aspects of Shakespeare's work, life and times.

Other departments examine the work of various theatres, and report back publicly on their findings, as we have already seen with regard to the Mossoviet. In the same way the Yaroslavl " Volkov " Theatre was also examined in 1943. There is a special " Scientific-Creative " department for this purpose, and its methods throw a light on the attitude of the Soviet artist to his work. The identification of the artist, whether creative or a performer, with his work (that is, in stage terms, the identification of the actor with his character in the play), and the secondary importance laid on his personal feelings (always allowing for the artistic temperament in the best sense of that phrase the world over) makes him or her appreciative of honest criticism, not resentful of it, to a degree hard to imagine in countries where the critic has not the same objective attitude. The Society does not jump to hasty conclusions and is not swayed by personal feelings ; so it is greatly respected by theatre people. Its constructive suggestions are generally acted on. Rostolsky, the head of the " Volkov " Theatre, quite sincerely thanked the Society for its criticism after the examination mentioned above.

Nor is the work of the Society limited to the negative function of criticising. It can initiate. In 1942 it held a conference on the question of the one-act play, and the scarcity of good ones ; another on the theatre of the democratic countries ; a five-day session illustrating the first twenty-five years of the Soviet theatre ; another on the same theme for two days in Kalinin. In war conditions the use of such an organisation became tremendous ; especially with the scattering of theatre units through evacuation. Its branches, now numbering twenty in widely distant towns, were of great value to the local and the evacuee organisations. Two new branches were founded, in Sverdlovsk and Irkutsk. These, and the others, placed producers in touch with each other, circulated information about available plays, supplied suggestions for local companies settling to war tasks in the absence of any evacuee theatres in their neighbourhood, and studied the special problems of places like the Mariisk Republic, Udmurt, the Chuvash territory, the Mordovian. More branches and agencies were planted for this purpose.

It also linked the nationalities together. Thus at Kazan in 1943 it organised an Inter-Republic Congress of the four small communities just mentioned, together with the Tatar and Bashkirian Republics, to which came the Presidents of the V.T.O. and of the Russian Committee for Art Affairs from Moscow. Each state displayed photographs, sketches, maquettes, playbills and brochures illustrating work done or in hand ; and to these were added examples of the work of other nationalities organised by the V.T.O. itself, and the "Lunacharsky" Institute of Theatrical Art.

In addition to such big events and routine office work, the Shakespeare Department held twice-monthly meetings at which latest productions in other parts of the world were described, through press-cuttings and photographs ; and the most up-to-date theories or developments of British and American Shakespeare scholarship were discussed. A letter from Iden Payne at Stratford-on-Avon caused much interest in 1942. Alternatively, the development of Shakespeare scholarship and criticism in Armenia, or Azerbaijan, or interpretations by the artists of these lands would be explained. Other classical writers were often included, as in January 1943, when Tihonovich reported on the treatment of Western European works on the Uzbek stage, and Efremov discussed the work of the national theatres in general, with special reference to Molière, Beaumarchais, Lope de Vega and Goldoni. The former had been working in Uzbekistan, and the latter in Mongolia ; so they spoke as men having authority.[18]

It must be remembered that in no sense is the V.T.O. in charge of any theatre. All theatres work to, and are responsible only to, the organisations that maintain them, whether Trade Union, local government unit, or national Soviet. The V.T.O. is independent, advisory, supplementary, whose function is to be ready with the best possible help when help is asked for. It can inform, inspire, advise, criticise ; it can suggest new ideas, or channels of research ; it can recommend the abolition of this or that fault or redundancy. All these things it does, and does readily and fully. The one thing it cannot and does not wish to do, is to dictate.

Part Four

THE WAR : SECOND ASPECT

CHAPTER IX

BRIGADES AT THE FRONT

SPECIAL PARTIES

Perhaps one of the most interesting war development of the V.T.O. was the theatrical " brigades " it organised. These brigades were a universal feature of the Soviet theatres, and provided a further link between East and West. This impinging of the two was not itself a war development ; it had been going on for years, Kipling or no. But war put it in arms against a common threat ; and comrades in arms are the closest and most enduring comrades. Because of international Fascism, Europe and Asia fused ; and that fusion has an importance for us all, if we have only the wit and honesty to see it.

Immediately the war broke out, the V.T.O. began to organise small concert parties to tour the forces, inviting several leading actors from the Maly, Vahtangov, Theatre of the Revolution, the Children's and other Moscow theatres, who were specially released for the purpose. Opera singers too were included. People's Artist N. N. Rybakov of the Maly was placed in charge. These " brigades " as they were called performed sketches, one-act plays, recitations, either solo or in production numbers, popular vaudevilles sometimes so long established as to have become " classic ", songs, dances and so on. Their stages were whatever offered in the shape of lorry platforms, warship decks, forest clearings ; and the scenery was tents or sheets.

Instructional units too were formed, a producer, a choreographer, and a chorus-master, to visit and advise amateur groups in the Red Army and the clubs that were to be found wherever members of any of the forces had a few hours' leisure.

The brigades were such favourites that as the first months passed it became clear that much more was needed. Concert parties were regrouped into companies, capable of taking entire works to the fronts, whether classic or contemporary. Two such companies were in operation by the spring of 1942, one of which had in its repertoire the Ostrovsky comedy, *Not all Cream for the Cat;* ★ a new play by Kaverin, *The House on the Hill*, an evening of Chehov, and a straight concert programme. Its producer was Nikolay Yanovsky a former actor of the Vahtangov Theatre. An abridged version of *Russian People* was added in December 1942, as the company toured the Southern and Stalingrad Fronts up to April 1943. Yanovsky said he was rather doubtful about giving Red Army men a play so near to their own conditions and lives, although before producing it he had spent a good deal of time on the Kalinin and Central fronts getting to know men and commanders, and how they lived, and what they were thinking and feeling. With a gifted company he was thus able to ensure that inner authenticity which Stanislavsky found the essence of a good actor . . . and it is significant that Yanovsky followed the Moscow Art Theatre in giving prime importance to the actor. There can be little doubt that this inner authenticity was largely the cause of the intense emotion roused in Red Army audiences by this play. They appear to have been quite remarkably stirred ; a tribute not only to the actors, and to the author, but also to the sturdy realistic outlook of the audiences.

Put yourself in the position of a commander, resting with his unit somewhere in the rear. Many of your men have been outstanding for an utter absorption in their job . . . to the point of self-oblivion. They have come through alive, so far, by several miracles. Also there may be a particular girl in one of the services whose pluck and resourcefulness in tight corners you and your men have admired, though there is no need to suppose you are unconsciously in love with her, as is the commander in this play. Your mother is back behind the enemy lines in Occupied territory, and you do not know whether she is alive or dead ; but because she is a fine, firm, outspoken old lady who does not count consequences, you are more than doubtful that she has been murdered by the Nazis . . . and in what form of death ? . . .

This will have been a common state of mind among Red Army men whether commanders or not. Yet you will go, and be enthralled by a group of play-actors impersonating yourself in this state of mind, sending the girl on an almost impossible mission because you have to ; your fine soldier going to certain death with song and a light heart ; your old mother losing control and being dragged out to be hanged. You will be moved profoundly to tears ; yet it will not be useless emotionalism. The truer the experience, the more you are made aware that there are millions like you, suffering like you and resolute like you. And the play ends with yourself on the stage, shouting, not in an " effective curtain line ", but in a conclusion drawn by stage logic from the people and the plot, and also in

★ Lit. " Not all Carnival for the Cat ", a title derived, like many of Ostrovsky's titles, from a popular saying.

the only possible climax to your own spiritual experience during it :
" Nothing ! Nothing, Comrade Major-General ; nothing ! Only I
so want to live, to live a long time. To live till the moment when I see
the last of the men that have done this, see them dead with my own eyes.
The very last ; and dead. Dead just here, under my feet ! "

Russian people, like French people, are more directly and expressively
patriotic than the British are ; but only a person viewing life from an armchair on an island could dismiss this as war propaganda. It is the complete
identification of stage and audience.

Yanovsky's qualms were idle. The play was in great demand all through
the winter of 1942-3, as the V.T.O. company went with the advancing
Russian armies through Kotelnikovo to Novo-Cherkassk and Rostov-on-
Don, where performances were given within a few days of the German's
withdrawal.

That was a long road, and hard. In icy winds of the winter steppe on
lorries, to act each evening in villages partially or wholly destroyed by the
retreating Huns ; no food nor water nor even a roofed room big enough
to perform in, and Red Army men rigging up some half-wrecked barn
or store-shed to serve as frosty theatre, with perhaps a few stoves made
from oil drums if they were lucky. But the close relation of stage to audience,
and the skill and spirit of actors and actresses, made such hardships negligible.
Socialist realism made the play important ; and the spirit of the Soviet
peoples shown in it, their hope and objective made its performance valuable. Thinking, as well as suffering, showed them what Nazism means.[1]

THEATRE BRIGADES

If that was the effect of an *ad hoc* company drawn from several theatres,
we can imagine the effect of one composed of fine artists used to playing
to each other. And there was hardly a first-class theatre in the Soviet
Union which did not organise a similar front-line brigade. Nor was this
considered a parergon, or a mere act of " cheering up the boys " ; certainly
not as a means of evading active service in the armed forces. Tarasova,
Zuyeva and Dorohin, in a joint letter to the Press in October 1942, wrote :
" Work at the front must be part of our productive work in the theatre " ;
and again, " We need systematic excursions to the fighting line with the
best examples of our art. We must prepare brigade programmes in the
same way as we prepare first nights. . . . We are bound to show the
front line real high art."

These stars of the Moscow Art Theatre were not writing vaguely.
They were members of an Art Theatre brigade which also included the
violinist Karevich who played principally Dvorak, a singer, and an accordeon-
player. Joseph Rayevsky, an actor attached to the Art Theatre, was in

charge ; and they carried the stars' ideas into practice, by showing excerpts from plays by Tolstoy, Chehov, Ostrovsky and Pushkin, and from *The Lower Depths*. One of the most popular recitations was Lukovsky's topical heroic poem about the defence of Leningrad, delivered by Tarasova with all the power of a skilled actress who had been in touch with audiences for many professional years.

A short tour in the autumn of 1942 was chiefly confined to the Red Air Force, though they stopped at Moscow on their way to the front from Sverdlovsk. In ten days they gave fifteen performances, covering 900 kilometres for the purpose. Often the audience came straight from their machines, clad in the clumsy necessities of an airman's outfit ; and Rayevsky sums up their reactions in the happy phrase : " We were glad that we were able to offer them cultured and joyous relaxation from the strain of battle ".

To this Dorohin added detail : they aimed at keeping " the aroma of Art Theatre productions, their delicate psychological tissue, deep humanity and austere purity of form ". Then it struck them that in the hard, tense atmosphere of war, this kind of thing might conceivably be out of place and their subtle art unwelcome. In most armies discipline necessarily knocks the personal life into an unresponsible, unresponsive anonymity ; peace-time taste is suspended ; fatigue and pattern compel conformity ; there is no time for comment. Of the Red Army the Red actor ought perhaps to have known better ; but the company had none the less that proud self-distrust which overcomes all good stage artists before a first night. And, as if to test them under the most stringent conditions, their first night audience was an uncompromising one, 3,000 men and commanders.

The players put on evening dress, because they wanted to show their respect, and day clothes would have been too ordinary. They had to change in the small bus they had. As the tour continued, they forgot little things, like the confined acting areas, the improvised lighting ; they lost themselves in the art of acting. Hence, whenever they appeared, in hangars, garages, sheds, or simply forest glades, they received an ovation. The audience clamoured for their favourite scenes, something from *Anna Karenina*, or the chief Vershinin-Masha passage from *The Three Sisters*. Dorohin describes how odd it felt to make a stool and an ammunition chest serve for the salon in Princess Betsy's palace, where Anna first meets Vronsky ; or for the Prozorovs' drawing-room. He casts back his mind to the days when the Moscow Art Theatre found difficulty in getting into their parts at the Paris Exposition des Beaux Arts in 1937, because the Théâtre des Champs Elysées had no revolving stage ! But acting triumphed even over cannonade rumble and explosions of land-mines which rattled the window of the tiny " stage ". And when it was over, two planes left an aerodrome, one containing the little company, another visitors from a neighbouring Air Force station who had flown over for the show. Or the little bus would go bumping and grunting over shell-pitted steppe or forest ride.

By such visits, by mixing with the virile, active, cultured, thoughtful men of the Red Air Force who would come round after the show and criticise points that had seemed wrong in the performance and stayed to talk about their own lives and experiences ; by understanding their hatred of Fascism and how it sprang, like Gorky's, from their intense love of life and of individual humanity, and from the system that had made both possible for them ; these fine artists of one of the best theatres in the world acknowledged on their return not only that the venture had been a success, and that they had been wanted, but that they themselves had learned.[2]

The Maly Theatre brigades reported the same. Within nine months in 1942 over a thousand performances were given by various groups of Maly artists. Some in military hospitals, training schools, aerodromes ; others, men crawled through communication trenches to attend. One brigade contained Turchaninova, Shatrova, Fadeyeva, Grigorevskaya, Slobodinskaya, five very gallant women. By September 1943 the Maly had organised and sent out its tenth front-line brigade, which included three prominent actors and a vocal quartet. And to be included in the list of stars who had at least once gone on such a tour were People's Artist Sadovsky, People's Artist Gogolyeva, Honoured Artist Mezhinsky (who played Dr. Mamlock in the film of that name), and Stalin-Laureate Ilyinsky. The first two were in a group that toured near Mozhaisk, Malo-yaroslavl, and Kaluga in the early summer of 1942. Another group was headed by People's Artist Mihail Lenin, one of whose best performances in peace-time was the Shakespeare-spouting old-style strolling tragedian in *The Forest* . . . a subtle study, bringing out the Don Quixote in this character, when he takes the comedian on a visit to his aunt and finds himself in a forest of provincial vulgarity, selfishness and human injustice.

It was not all in the open spaces. Sometimes the area was very cramped. At an exhibition of " The Theatre in Arms " in the foyer of the Maly (December 1942) there was a photograph of Turchaninova reciting to an audience of anti-aircraft gunners in a dug-out. They were sitting on their bunks ; she was standing in the narrow space between them and the log wall. An interesting mental rhythm at this exhibition, one would imagine, as the eye included Repin's portrait of Shchepkin in that very foyer. Or perhaps this had by then been removed for safety.

The reactions of the audience were described by Aksyonov, who headed a brigade early in 1943. On one occasion, he said, the biggest room in a village had been turned into a club. A tent-cloth served as proscenium.

Since the would-be audience could not possibly be stuffed into the remaining space, two consecutive performances had to be given. As soon as Aksyonov announced that the actor Ostuzhev was of the party, the whole of the " first house " rose to its feet and thundered out its appreciation. Apparently more than a sprinkling of Moscow men were among the audience.

If you will turn back in your mind to the same sort of ovation given to the two Moscow actors at Nizhny in 1812, you will see why this reception moved Ostuzhev so deeply that for some time he could not open his mouth. " No triumph ", he said afterwards, " that I have had in playing Othello can compare with the tremendous joy I felt during that brief moment. I felt that the soldiers of my people needed me."

Under these circumstances that was no complacent speech of an exhibitionist, still less the pompous hint of a seeker of honours. Ostuzhev was nearly seventy, and loaded with honours. It was a statement of fact, important not so much to him as to the development of human culture. It was the pride of an artist in a land that loved its artists.

ACTRESSES AT THE FRONT

From the actresses' angle, too, those Maly tours had a wider importance than just personal sensations. Gogolyeva wrote in her diary on International Women's Day : " I want to tell all the women of the world : the Fascists shall pay with their blood for all the sufferings of our women, for all the tears of our mothers, for the anguished yearnings of wives and sweethearts. Our turn will come. We shall make the Hitlerites rebuild our demolished factories brick by brick, the razed villages, the plundered towns."

Was that a mere outburst of general hate, inspired by a figure on a calendar ? No. A day or two previously, after being bombed by a German aeroplane, she had been touring through the remains of a village, and seen bereaved women returning to it ; and not more than a mile off was Petrishchevo, where Zoya Kosmodemyanskaya, " Tanya ", now to all time and to all nations with Joan of Arc and La Pasionaria, was tortured and hanged because though little more than a child she was faithful. And that day Gogolyeva had driven with the others down a road under enemy shell-fire. The brigade leader had hesitated, there being women in the party. But the actresses' only wish was to follow the advancing Soviet Army ; and they drove on, and through.

These are experiences that deepen and impassion a woman of any age. When there is the organic tie between life and art which exists in the Maly Theatre these entries in an actress's diary become events in theatre history.[3]

ACTORS IN ACTION

The Vahtangov Theatre had the honour of being the first central theatre whose brigade visited the Front. Strictly speaking, it collaborated with the V.T.O.'s second company. This brigade went to the Tula, Kalinin, South-Western, Stalingrad, Bryansk, and Voronezh sectors, and followed the advance from Rossosh, Kantemirovka, and Valuiki. Its leader was Orochko. In two months it gave 150 performances, including some within 500 yards of the enemy. One of its most moving experiences was had at Valuiki. There the Fascists during their occupation had closed the school, and planned, if they did not actually contrive, to open it as a brothel. The first time the children re-entered it, a civilised sweetness had been restored to the building by its use by the Vahtangov brigade.[4]

But it was only to be expected that the Central Theatre of the Red Army would bear the honours in some way or other for front-line entertainment. A T.S.D.K.A. brigade holds the record for travel. By June 1942, that is, in eleven months and a half, it had toured the entire Soviet Front, from Bessarabia to Murmansk, giving 855 shows in so doing On one occasion, it is related, they were in a dug-out about 70 metres from the Finnish trenches, and at the request of their invisible audience they included the singing of the " Free Russia " march which was banned in Finland. Indeed the company discovered talents it did not know it possessed, as each member in continually renovating the repertoire on the march found he had a voice, or could dance, or in some other way improve his performance when travelling did not permit new plays to be rehearsed.

Dressed in camouflage capes, often under fire, the six artists and their leader-producer, Shaps, made their way up the map, in any manner they could, on foot, on horseback, hitch-hiking or boarding munitions trains.

As a reward they received decorations from the Karelo-Finnish Government . . . military decorations, not civilian ones. They were the first actors to win them, though later many other members of brigades were so decorated . . . and a military award for war services is not easily won in the Soviet Union. None the less Nina Volodko and Zinovieva, the two acresses in this group, were thus honoured with the men. " For the Fighters of our favourite Central Theatre of the Red Army " said a member of the War Soviet of the Karelian front as he made the awards. It must have been a weird thing sometimes for these Moscow artists . . . driving in sledges through the arctic night under the Northern Lights, and performing sometimes in low earth huts where they could not always stand upright.[5]

Two-thirds of the entire theatre company took part in the theatre's brigades, of which there were eleven in all by the autumn of 1943, regularly visiting the front. Other Red Army Theatres competed with them. At the outbreak of war, the Theatre of the Red Army in the Kiev Special District was playing Lvov and Zholkev. They immediately re-organised themselves as the Theatre of the South-west Front, and mobilised themselves in a column of lorries. They took *A Fellow from Our Town*, *The Keys of Berlin* (by Guss and Finn) and a concert programme. To this they added, by rehearsing anywhere at any time, *The Armoured Train 14-69*, *Unquiet Old Age*, *To be Continued*, *Partisans in the Steppes of the Ukraine*, and a play by Pervomaisky called *Battle Opening*. This was not a first-class theatre ; and it had to acquire its own technique as the months went by. B. Nord reported that it found the way to its technique from the circumstances of playing in the open air by daylight. The audience could follow every move, and the actors, unable to rely much on make-up, had to feel their parts more deeply.

The Red Army Theatre of Central Asia made a three-month tour in 1943 of towns in their region. One of their plays was Rzheshevsky's *Always With Us*, another was *Peter Krymov*, the play that linked front with rear.

The Leningrad House of the Red Army competed too. They sent a party playing mostly Korneichuk's *The Front*, which by January 1943 had reached its 1,500th performance, to the immediate neighbourhood of the Leningrad Front. The figure of performances, which looks unlikely, is possible from the shortness of journeys ; but it implies a high degree of devotion and indeed of physical endurance. Many of the other Leningrad theatres formed brigades for either front or rear, among them the " Pushkin " Theatre, which toured the North-west Front, giving sixty-three shows in a month, which included scenes from *Suvorov*, songs, anti-Fascist sketches, and comedy numbers. The Leningrad " Gorky ", too, gave over fifty shows in much the same space of time to sailors, in submarines, coastal batteries, on battleships' decks, and any other stages they could reach by cart, horse, cutter or boat.[6]

SAILORS' ACTORS

This opens the fascinating tale of the Soviet Navy and its entertainment. Each of the Regional Fleets had its own theatre long before the war, based on a port in each case, but spending most of its time in visits. Some account of them is given in *The New Soviet Theatre*. War meant merely an intensification of this work, and danger in the voyages. Enemy dive-bombers could not differentiate between a travelling theatre and any other form of shipping ; nor would they if they could. But the companies, many of whom were sailors by training, were proud of that danger ; and if I know anything of Soviet citizens, sailor or actor, few will have been content to be passengers during an engagement.

The Northern Fleet had its own tug-boat, in which, laden with props, costumes, simple scenery and all sizes of packing cases, the theatre crept from anchorage to anchorage. Sometimes it landed, was unloaded by marines, and in naval lorries proceeded to the nearest section of the land front, where a marine audience awaited it. *A Servant of Two Masters*, *Russian People*, *The Front*, were played in 1943 ; but there were concerts too. In one trip of nine days, eleven performances and fourteen concerts !

But the Northern Fleet also had its amateur groups, helped by the amateur-dramatic section of Northern Fleet House under Captain Chertygin. One eminent production was Virta's play, *My Friend the Colonel*, acted by commanders, navigators, electricians and men of the lower deck together.

A pleasant photograph of a Fleet concert was shown at the *Theatre in Arms* exhibition. The young actress Ivanova on a skerry sitting and playing the saxophone to an audience so close that their bayonets made steel scenery round her.

In March 1942 the Political Direction of the Navy organised the First Black Sea Front-Line Theatre, including People's Artist Rybnikov of the Maly at its head, B. Filippov as director and political chief, and at least three prominent actors. Besides a concert programme they offered Solovyov's *Belugin's Wedding* and Ostrovsky's " *Truth is Good . . .* ", a new play by Konstantin Finn about the war, *The Ruza Forest*, and other things. All these had sets by the same artist, V. Miller.

The cream of the Fleet theatres, though, was the one belonging to the Red Banner Baltic Fleet. In the summer of 1941, this was already cele-brating its tenth birthday in a ten-day festival. It owed its existence to a chance suggestion of Voroshilov at an amateur Fleet concert, and at first it was amateur. Then it became a branch of naval service, for sailors or commanders, like navigating or engineering. Its range broadened and its standard rose. During those ten years it produced thirty-six classical or Soviet plays and gave nearly 2,500 shows. In 1934 the Leningrad pro-ducer, A. V. Pergament, became its artistic director, and it reached a high degree of skill and experience in dramatic art, though it never abandoned the simple concert as well. Indeed it may well have been the model on which all the brigades were formed. Certainly it began the war fully equipped for its job.

Nor did it lower the standard. Four or five performances might be given in a single day, with hurried transport from point to point by boat, bicycle or plane. By January 1943 its war performances had reached 3,150. It had casualties. One party ran into an enemy ambush and was wiped out. Actors and actresses often did duty as stretcher-bearers and nurses. Distant out-posts were visited in batches of five. On some

FRONT-LINE THEATRE.

The Yaroslavl "Volkov" Theatre performing *A Fellow From Our Town.*

SHAKESPEARE ON THE WESTERN FRONT.

People's Artist of the U.S.S.R. Mihail Lenin gives a Front-Line Brigade performance with Lyubov Merkulova of *The Taming of the Shrew*.

[facing page 205.

occasions inaccessible posts listened-in by field telephone. Often shows were interrupted by enemy land raids or sea attacks, and the company broke off to join in the defence. Fourteen members of it by April 1943 had been decorated for meritorious conduct in action ; and one, Mihailov, won the Order of the Red Star.

Besides touring the Fleet and the Baltic Front, the company spent some time in Leningrad during the siege. Pergament's productions could hold their own with even Leningrad audiences, even in plays like *The Front* and *Oleko Dundich*, which other bodies less specialised and less harassed in their work, had already done there. But primarily it performed its own local, or professional, themes. In July 1942, while in Leningrad, a new play was given its first hearing, *To Meet the Squadron*, by a young writer named Tevelev. (His first name is given as both Mihail and Matvey.) This was a war play basically naval, but including also those fighting the Fascists behind the lines in Occupied zones.

Thereafter quite a group of writers made up a collective with this theatre. Agranenko and Stein wrote a naval vaudeville, *Welcome !* Agranenko collaborated with another war reporter, Ilya Baru, in a more serious work, shown in the summer of 1943, *The Earth Bears Witness*. This was about the Sea Air Arm. Its heroes were two air aces, both Heroes of the Soviet Union. One is a general favourite, and a nice fellow, but hot-headed, ambitious, and always thinking of his own score of enemy machines destroyed. The other is quieter, less self-assertive, but in some ways the more valuable fighter. The central incident is a dog-fight in which the latter joins to keep an eye on his over-daring friend.

During 1943 the Baltic Fleet Theatre added *Wait for Me* and *Admiral Nahimov* to its list. The latter was by Igor Lukovsky. This theatre was also responsible for the reappearance of Vsevolod Vishnevsky as a playwright. Since *An Optimistic Tragedy* Vishnevsky had written several plays, which had been done at the Vahtangov or Meierhold Theatres and perhaps elsewhere, but little had been heard of them. In 1943, however, collaborating with Alexander Kron, the author of the psychological play, *Depth Prospecting*, and with Alexander Azarov, he brought out at this theatre, *Wide Spreads the Sea*, and a new play by himself alone, *At the Walls of Leningrad*. Simultaneous productions were given of these plays by the Kamerny Theatre in Barnaul.

In this way the people of Leningrad and their naval protectors on the Baltic were able to experience what was thought of them in the world outside their areas.

But besides their own special theatre, the Baltic Fleet was visited in the usual way by different brigades. For example, in the spring of 1943 the First V.T.O. Brigade spent six weeks among them doing *Wait for Me*,

The Minor (the most popular play to-day of the eighteenth-century Russian dramatist Fonvisin) and the two nineteenth century plays already mentioned as done by the Black Sea First Brigade.[7]

POLES

Brigades sometimes developed like the theatres of the nationalities, from within. In this case from within regiments. This may happen in any army, even in one of non-Soviet nationality.

In summer 1943 the First Polish Division of refugee Poles, named for Kosciusko the Great Polish democrat patriot, left for the front fully trained and equipped. A few months before it had been a group of would-be soldiers and commanders, anxious to free their country from Fascism of all sorts, but having neither the means nor the knowledge. In early May, during their training, there appeared the nucleus of the Zholner Theatre to be : one Polish literary and artistic stage-manager, one Polish producer, one Polish actress. They had no stage, no costumes, no instruments, no plays. They searched for a company. In the division that was to be, they found two actors and ten musicians. Also a painter, who professed his eagerness to get some materials together and see what he could do. All these worked so hard together that inside one month they had got their first show ready.

Natalia Vilter has described it. "In a big clearing in the forest on the bare grass in front of spectators sitting on the ground, stood a huge semi-circle of plywood with twin borders of red and white, and the inscription театр жолнера. This emblem stood as both curtain and *Décor*. From it appeared a *conférencier*. A soldier. A ne'er-do-weel. A failure. He was greeted with laughter. Enter to him, the Actress. She stood at the crossing of the ways, in front of a signpost bearing a red arrow and a white bayonet, both of which pointed west. They read the direction : ' This Way to Warsaw '. They spoke strong, simple speeches about the struggle before them, and the victory to come. Then they sang Polish songs. The orchestra played selections of Russian songs. The players recited poems about the concentration camps in Poland, till before the audience stood the images of their tortured brethren there. Then they danced the Polish Kuyavyak. A short sketch followed ; and artists and audience joined in a song that had recently been heard in the Division and was well known to it, ' We are the First Division '. In this way the Poles were reminded of dances and scenes familiar since childhood, and felt they were still part of their homeland. They wept. Youngsters and full grown men alike, without being ashamed of their tears. Their emotion was communicated to the actors. The song rang through the forest."

Propaganda ? May be. But what would Ben Jonson not have given for such actual matter, such truthful feeling for the writing and witnessing of his propaganda masques ?

Not a very high dramatic standard, perhaps ; but their task was to find variety in a limited field. Their producer, Krasnovetsky, was alive to this. They kept observant eyes and ears upon the Division, drawing their matter from its daily life and events. In this way they got up four new programmes in three months ; and kept their audience small (and themselves busy thereby) through visiting different portions of the Division and giving three, or often four, performances a day.

Soon a concert brigade was formed. The range of instruments was not great, but happily Chervinskaya, the actress, had a deep, rich voice ; and a solo harmonica player materialised, named Lurye, self-taught but a virtuoso. A jazz band followed ; and a complete and very popular puppet theatre. In this last the favourite puppets were Hitler, Goebbels and their gang, as might have been expected. Their heads were cleverly modelled in stearine (the stuff candles are made of), and said to have been very expressive ! The neurotic Hitler had a fit of hysterics in the course of his usual speech about the greatness of Nazidom ; Goebbels appeared with monkey's tail, hanging mouth, and so on. But other puppets performed themes from popular romances and poems by Vazhik and L. Pasternak.[8] *

PUPPETS

It should not be supposed that puppet theatres were the prerogative and delight only of the Poles, nor that the Red Army, whether Polish, Russian, or anything else, wanted or got only serious shows that would aid their morale. Far, far from it. There was a plethora of light entertainment in the brigades, including plays, puppet shows and whole circuses.

Both glove puppets and marionettes on strings are used in the Soviet Union ; and there had been two permanent puppet theatres in Moscow for years, directed by the puppet masters Eugene Demmeny, and Sergey Obraztsov.

Obraztsov was an Honoured Artist. With his teams of puppeteers (two for gloves, two for marionettes) he had his own new premises in 1938. Till then this theatre had travelled clubs and schools in Moscow and district. It was quite a big concern : ten actresses, nine actors, four pianists, a violinist and three bayanisti, or accordeon players, together with the necessary band of managers, craftsmen, producers, sculptors and such, amounting to twelve more. London readers of this book may have seen a film of Obraztsov's work, including his own most-loved act with a baby, whose life-like noises and movements he succeeds in soothing to sleep with great care and tenderness.

* Not Boris, the Russian poet, and translator of Shakespeare.

They used to give two performances daily at this theatre in peace-time, one in the afternoon for children, the other in the evening for adults, who specially liked *Aladdin's Magic Lamp* and Gogol's fantastic story, *Christmas Eve*.   But alas !   the fine new premises were damaged by bomb blast, and the Obraztsov puppets moved to Novosibirsk.

They took their time on the journey.   Indeed they could not do otherwise ;   for wherever they were discovered, they had to perform.   Even on the waters of a great river, they were able to restore the spirits of two thousand small children, evacuees from Moscow, whom their boat overhauled.   What an encounter for the children !   and how right that a boat of puppets should suddenly draw alongside out of nowhere in strange country, should give them a performance of *The Magic Galosh*, and then putter off downstream ahead, the music of *Moscow Mine* floating behind them from the orchestra as the children waved goodbye, and caught up the tune . . . Moscow mine, land of mine, you are the best !

Five rivers the Puppet Theatre travelled, the Moskva, the Oka ;   past dairy villages, between raspberry fields, by sandy dunes or dense forests of pines or limes or maple-trees, stopping at historic towns, or farming villages, or bright modern mining settlements.   Then down the Volga, as the old Russian actors had done with Burlak, but crossing it now, sailing east of it, over the rampart to a sure welcome in every strange land.   Up the Kama, through Tatar country, and up its tributary the White River, and so into the heart of the Urals.   Surely of all the exodus to the east, this was the most charming and the most acceptable wherever it reached.   Not that it was altogether charming for those in it !   At the heart of winter even these rivers were blocked with ice ;   and the puppet theatre had then to tumble on to railways, and make their way by land.

They toured Bashkiria, Central Asia, parts of Siberia, the Kuzbas.   The tough coal-miners were fascinated by their pit-head performances.   Workers in factories, recruits in Red Army training centres, children and adults in factory areas, of all races, native or evacuees, came crowding and went smiling ;   for it is one of the advantages of puppets that though the ear hears, it is the seeing eye that best appreciates the skill of liveliness in the motions ;   and the eye is international.

But most of all the soldiers.   The four teams split into brigades, touring the outlying rear and the advanced fronts.   There is a tale of a tank corps. One of the shows had a satirical television act, in which " puppets " of another kind were represented by dogs, Pétain, Mussolini, Mannerheim and Antonescu.   Pétain was a mangy hound who whined while " Master " was away.   The big mongrel Mussolini yelped himself hoarse.   The sorely beaten Mannerheim was a very old dog, and groaned in pain all the time. Antonescu, a surly tyke, had his tail permanently between his legs, but most when a certain lean and ravenous Alsatian appeared. However, on this occasion, in the open air as usual, there came a Soviet aeroplane into view during Hitler's speech, and drowning it. The dog with the funny moustache looked up, followed the plane apprehensively with its eyes, and then scratched himself helplessly with his hind leg. The appreciative roar from the tank men drowned the noise of the departing plane.

In spite of lack of time, the theatre in the course of 1943 prepared and put on a new show, set in silver, black and red : *King Deer*, a fantasy by the eighteenth-century Italian, Carlo Gozzi, written for the Sacchi troupe. It was claimed that this had not been performed since on the legitimate stage, and only once by puppets, in Vienna. Certainly it had never been seen in Russia. So it was a real novelty to the men at the Front when it toured there. Another new production was " in the heroic style ", about Dmitry of the Don. As a rule, the music for these shows was written specially . . . in the case of *King Deer* by a woman, Alexandrova. Operettas too were included : *On the Roofs of Berlin* and *The American Linnet*.

The Moscow puppet theatre run by Eugene Demmeny had a rather more sophisticated shape to its shows . . . though no less appeal for spectators old or young. It usually opened with a procession of puppets to a special march round, or through, the audience. It usually ended with a dance of Red Army Man-puppet and Farm-worker Girl-puppet. This theatre favoured the glove form.

A Demmeny brigade in five months on the Leningrad Front gave more than 650 performances. It was a topical show, in the sense that it included pamphlet plays about Nazi leaders and their dupes. Thus for *The Strategists* the Moscow artist Bekleshova created portrait heads in 1943, heads that though they were caricatures, were yet credible, especially because the uniformed bodies below assumed life-like poses. Another anti-Fascist playlet was based on a story by M. Tuberovsky called *Fiddlesticks*. *The Eagle and the Snake* showed mean, inhuman tricks played by Nazi soldiery ; *The Appetite of the Wolf,* their crimes and filthy habits. And so, largely with the help of Tuberovsky and another author called A. Flit, a topical repertoire was built up. This was being extended in 1943 to include a revue by the poet Samuil Marshak, *Young Fritz*, and on another war theme, *Mitza in Spookland*.

Satirical themes like these were popular ; but with puppets fantasy is best of all. *Gulliver's Travels* had been running for years, about fifteen years by 1943. Kipling's *Mowgli* gave opportunity for animal shapes. *The Little Humped-backed Horse*, which had been a tremendous success with all ages on tour, was chosen as the opening play when the Moscow Puppets Theatre returned to the capital in September 1943. But Demmeny told the *Moscow News* that he had found the most wonderful figure for a puppet in Sir John Falstaff, and he was preparing *The Merry Wives of Windsor*, as he thought it had all the necessary features for a first-class puppet theme : sparkling development of action, amusing plot, picturesque settings, and clear-cut characters.[9]

CIRCUSES AT THE FRONT

To those who know the Russians this intense joy in the expressive agility of the inanimate is no surprise. It is a symptom of an unspoilt joy in life, as eloquent as its counterpart, the expressive agility of the animate that is found in the circus. There was always a wide love of the circus in Russia, not confined to children. Alexander Werth, in a despatch from Moscow broadcast from London by the B.B.C. on 30 April 1944, said that children were not allowed to evening performances, as these were reserved for adults, while children could more easily attend matinees. I have not been able to discover whether this was a war measure or not. Nothing is said about it in the 1935 handbook to Theatrical Moscow from which I drew similar information about the Puppet Theatre.

In peace-time there had been two circuses in Moscow, the No. 1 State Circus (Госцирк) on Svetnoy Boulevard seating 2,193 ; and the summer " Shapiro " Circus in the " Gorky " Central Park of Culture and Rest, which seated 5,000. The head of the authority that administers the Soviet circus reported in November 1943 to the Committee for Art Affairs, that there were eighteen separate circus groups in existence, working under acknowledged masters of circus craft and custom. New numbers were being turned out all the time, eleven of the eighteen having created thirty-eight new numbers between them in recent times. Hrapchenko, the president of the Committee, suggested that each unit should carry two complete programmes, so as to be able to stay longer in each town visited.

Circus programmes, like circus folk, are usually international, and do not differ much in different countries ; they are always old and always new. The Soviet circuses may be unique (and in war-time they have this advantage over other lands) in being able to draw upon the skill of so many races within state frontiers. A Russian-looking surname on the bill is no evidence that its owner may not be nearer the Indian, the Chinese, the Turk, or the Eskimo sleight of hand or nimbleness of body than the Russian. But the bills are very much like any other circus's : aerial acrobatics on complicated mechanical constructions (The Kokh sisters) ; Mayatsky's compound illusion-cum-equilibrist act called " The Enigma Ball " ; the Pavlov ensemble, " Giant Strides " ; " Mister Berrouz's Monkeys " ; a grotesque turn by M. Mumjiu ; strong man and athletic displays ; the Russian circus star, Lerri, and his liberty horses ; the Shirman family (three men and two girls) who started as jugglers and switched to musical eccentrics ; and so on. There are clowns too . . . broad, coarse clowns, clumsy, tumbling clowns, nimble, sly clowns, and Karan d'Ash (which is, as we would say, P. Encil), the unique Karan d'Ash, a pathetic, sensitive, subtle figure in the Grock tradition.

But three things separate the Soviet circus from ours. It is owned and run by the whole people. Secondly, it has a training school. Neither of these interferes with the free, atmospheric life without which a circus would be no circus. But the former means that there are no weak turns nor padding ; and one result of the latter is that it is much more easy for children of non-circus families to enter the profession, while fewer rogues and unqualified persons get in. Another advantage, which will ring strangely in British circus ears, is that for the beginners to acquire facility in ringside speech, well-known literary figures like Marshak can provide the texts of practice dialogue !

Both these differences, and indeed all this sub-chapter, would be irrelevant here if it were not for the third ; which is that in August 1943 there came to the newly opened Summer Park in Leningrad, under the management of the well-known ring-master Gershuni, Artist of Merit of the Russian Republic, the first and only front-line circus in the world, organised in order that during leisure moments or convalescence the fighters of the Red Army should see their favourite circus stars as easily as they could see their favourites in opera or drama.[10]

Musical comedies, operettas, theatres of variety, and of what are called miniatures, all these also toured the fronts. Musical comedies and operettas had always been popular in the Soviet Union. Most big towns at least had one theatre specialising in them, and several of the nationalities had written their own, in their own musical idioms. But those of Western Europe had an almost universal appeal. Rose Marie reached its thousandth performance in Moscow in the early part of the war ; nor did it fall from the repertoire. The same artists as act in lighter Shakespeare or classical comedies do not regard musical plays as beneath them ; and there is nothing strange in so distinguished a scholar as Professor Morozov writing an article in Литература и искусство headed : „Мастера веселого спектакль" (Masters of Bright Entertainment), which is largely devoted to a performance of Kalman's Maritza at the Moscow Theatre of Operetta. "Anyone who has seen V. Volodin", he writes, "as Sir Toby in Twelfth Night, has seen the real Falstaff of Shakespeare, and knows what capabilities lie in this actor. The part of Artizak in Maritza he plays with the masterliness inherent in him."

In the same way the brigade from the Stanislavsky-and-Nemirovich-Danchenko Musical Theatre (one of the very best operas in the country) performed The Gipsy Baron, by Johann Strauss. One of the most popular arrivals in sectors containing Ukrainian troops was always the Ukrainian musical comedy *Natalka of Poltava*.[11]

GRAND OPERAS AND MINIATURES

The theatres of miniatures were not unlike the less developed front-line brigades. " One-act plays, carefully chosen to make a harmonious evening, happy-go-lucky satire, a complete unit of entertainment "—that would describe the work of the Moscow Theatre of Miniatures, which remained in Moscow throughout the war. *No Offence*, *Short and Sharp*, are rough renderings of two of its show titles, and indicate the contents. Obviously such would appeal in times of strain ; and obviously they were mobile. Therefore they were in constant demand at the front and touring the farms of the rear, not standing for very much, perhaps, but gladdening the days of those who came to see. The V.T.O. also organised a special front-line minintures-theatre called " Happy Landings ". Its matter came almost entirely from local and topical events and remarks ; which is indeed the essence of such a show.[12]

At the other end of the scale whole operas were taken to the front. The Fifth V.T.O. Theatre was purely operatic. This set out in September 1942 with an all-Chaikovsky repertoire, including *Eugene Onyegin* complete, scenes from *The Queen of Spades* and *The Little Shoes* and a number of songs and light orchestral pieces. Naturally the properties and scenery had to be easily portable. But the show was a complete one, of a high musical and theatrical standard.

This venture was followed within a month or two by brigades from such units as the Leningrad Little Opera, the Leningrad " Kirov " (formerly Mariy) Theatre of Opera and Ballet, the Stanislavsky-and-Nemirovich-Danchenko Musical Theatre, the Byelorussian Theatre of Opera and Ballet, and many others.[13] And just as with the Moscow Art Theatre brigades, the emphasis was on the playing of the drama and the tables and chairs could be left to look after themselves, so in these simplified but still complex shows the emphasis was on the musical tale and not on its trappings. Skill, beauty, understanding, a sweet voice and a good tune in a tale of human feeling, such things made the fighter's life more worth living, and reminded him of the things he was fighting for.

However simple these productions were, they could not be taken right into the firing line. But there were one-man shows that could go any-where, and did, and sometimes met with odd adventures in so doing.

" CHTETSY "

Most people like a good story skilfully told aloud. We British tend to limit our approval to those that are merely funny ; and we will cheerfully endure hearing an old chestnut time and time again as long as it is told with fresh detail and unstumbling words. But we would regard with suspicion, probably with disgust, anyone who paid the same care to telling a good story about an accident or a bereavement.

Simpler people, peasant people, and people with a stronger sense of community do not draw that distinction. If they have had an experience out of the ordinary, whether funny, dangerous or tragic, they wish to transmit the whole thing to the person they are addressing ; and to do that, they seek the right word for a description and the right tone of voice for an impersonation. Hence their speech becomes what we call " dramatic " or even " theatrical ". We would willingly read such a story in print, and admire the skill with which a professional novelist reproduced it. We turn from the same skill in amateur conversation.

The Russians do not so. Hence they admire and have always admired professional men who could assume the necessary feeling toward a story that was not their own. The " recitation " never assumed the drawing-room or charity-concert connotation it assumed in Britain. Nor was their appreciation limited to prose. A good poem could move them as much in spoken as in printed speech. Nor was there any necessity, as I remember seeing done in Chelsea by the Sitwells in the 'twenties, to advertise " Beautiful Readings of Beautiful Poetry ".

The passion of the Russian, and indeed many of the Soviet, peoples for *chtetsy* was not changed by any revolution. Only more people had a chance to hear them, and a regular salary turned them into professionals of a new form of art. At a competition held in Moscow during July 1943 there were present fifty-one professional *chtetsy*, and twenty-four representatives of the big Moscow theatres and dramatic training schools, including also the Radio Committee, which corresponds (in some ways) to the Board of Governors of our B.B.C. Fifty authors' works were used, and the following recitations were regarded as being " classics " for a standard repertoire :

Leo Tolstoy : Passages from *War and Peace*.
Pushkin : *The Bronze Horseman, Calumniators of Russia, Poltava*.
Gorky : *The Storm Petrel, Song of a Falcon*.
Lermontov : *Homeland*.

While favourite passages from contemporary literature, it was noted, included the following :

Simonov : *An Artilleryman's Son*.
Nikitin : *Russia*.
Ryleyev : *Ivan Susanin*.
Tvardovsky : *Vasily Terkin*.
Margarita Aliger : *Zoya*.
Ilya Ehrenburg : *Paris*.

It was found that there were two distinct types of *chtets*. The conversational, intimate, natural type, which was the minority because only a limited number of people had this type of mind ; and the mass-address, declamatory type " with a contemporary style " . . . meaning that though dramatic they were not rhetorical, not in the old-style booming of Karatygin. It is interesting that in this competition a number of amateurs took part, mostly from the Red Army.

In war time these *chtetsy* went often right into the front line. Often before beginning they would wait for silence and then say quietly, " I dedicate my performance to Red Army Man Tsipkin " (for example) " who in nineteen days killed twenty-one Fascists. I will now recite a short story by Maupassant, *The Port*."

These words were actually used by Honoured Artist Kalganov in a dugout, and they were reported by the Battalion Commissar, who (that being before the political instructors were withdrawn) was present. He said that you might not expect a short story by a French writer to mean anything under such circumstances ; but it did, partly, he explains, because " the appeal of true art is all-compelling ".

And, be it confessed, *Le Port* is one of Guy de Maupassant's most moving and terrible studies. It is to be found in that cynical volume, *La Main Gauche*, and tells, in phrases of devastating accuracy, how a French sailor returning home after a four-year voyage, discovers that a girl in a Marseilles brothel is his little sister, and his parents are dead. The dialogue is in lines of little more than four words each, terse, surcharged, a gift to any sensitive *chtets*.

Another most renowned such artist was Sergey Balashov, Honoured Artist of the Russian Republic,* who set off one night through a forest to an advanced field-post. He and his guide wriggled through mud while shells and land-mines exploded all round them. At last they slithered into a damp, dark dugout. It was almost a silent one too ; for no one could speak above an undertone because the enemy lines would hear, locate and destroy them if they did. Balashov had chosen Mayakovsky for his *chteniye* that time, declamatory, exhilarating stuff, meant to be roared at an audience of thousands. He wondered what he should do. The political commissar, who had been his guide, informed him in the opening announcement. " Sergey Balashov ", he said to the men, " for the first time in his life will now recite ' At The Top of My Voice ' in a whisper ! "

The programmes in which these *chtetsy* appeared (for Balashov had four friends with him, and they worked to a plan of the Central House of the

---

* A famous poet, author of *Turksib*, and other poems about Socialist construction. He had given over 500 recitals by March 1943, when an evening was held at the Moscow Actor's House in his honour.

Red Army) were not all recitations. They might contain almost anything, from songs to guitar, violin or other solos, comic turns, conjuring tricks, exhibition dances. But there was no doubt of their usefulness. " You can't imagine ", said a soldier to Balashov, " how we've enjoyed it. It's like a drink of spring water to a parched man." [14]

What the Front Line Brigades Were For

In all armies, after the inhumanity of mechanised battle, during the austerity use of human speech for command and discipline, there is need of words that convey ideas. They may be the humblest and most childlike, in a sentimental story or a funny one ; or they may be the finest poetry or the most comprehensive wisdom. But a book does not always suffice. There are too many distractions, and an inert book cannot stir the attention by itself. Here the live voice wins. When it is wholly identified with the thing read, as a good reader identifies it, coming to each word freshly and in a flash giving its exact position and full meaning by tempo, rhythm, or intonation, then the word becomes alive. The book then can stir and hold the attention, however weary the listener. The something in the voice is then not the personality of the reader, which may differ with the matter read. It is the voice of the thing read. It is a delegate from the culture the fighter is fighting for. So there is nothing wrong in the presence of the word-artist in the firing line. On the contrary, it is right. He was a part of what made the Red Army man fight so well.

With this background to our ideas, we can now consider the vital question, going to the root of all this chapter : what was the best entertainment the Soviet theatre could give to the men at the front ?

A member of a Vahtangov Theatre brigade, A. Gabovich, reported that one time before a performance, a soldier who was obviously speaking for his comrades too, after a discussion as to what sort of show it was going to be, came up and asked, Would it be funny ? Gabovich said he sensed that if he had said No, the soldier would still have come to it, but that he was plainly pleased to be told it would be funny. It was a piece called The Honeymoon, and the audience laughed heartily.

Another time, Gabovich said, an audience of 3,000 had just completed a very long march and were tired out. The brigade was doubtful if their endeavours would be attractive enough to overcome physical exhaustion. But they need not have feared. Nobody fell asleep and everyone laughed to their and the company's content.

Gabovich's article was published in Литература и искусство, January 1943. This paper was intended for consumption by Russian readers interested in the arts. It had no call to be other than topical, and its practice was to be up to date. Gabovich may therefore be taken to refer to events of the late autumn or winter of 1942. From this we may infer that after eighteen months of war those responsible for running these brigades were still regarding each audience as different from the last. No presuppositions or rule-of-thumb methods had become standardised. Each company faced a new problem with each audience that assembled. This is consistent with Soviet theatrical policy in other ways.

Gabovich makes it clear, however, that front-line audiences did not only nor always want funny shows. This fact is confirmed by Kolesayev, producer to a Maly brigade which included *The Blue Scarf* in its repertoire. "The fighting man is as interested in classical tragedy as in light sketches", he was reported as saying to the *Moscow News;* [15] and it should be mentioned that *The Blue Scarf* was a very light comedy. Incidentally, it is amusing to notice that during one performance in the evening the lighting failed. The commander ordered all men who had brought their pocket torches with them to move into the front rows, so that by shining them up on the stage the show could go on. The audience thereupon took charge of the production, and every time a "villain" came on, they light-heartedly plunged him in darkness.

The reason for this readiness to be serious is interesting to speculate about. Front-line audiences are in circumstances of acute emotional strain. They may be listening quietly enough, but they are in full battle-dress and may at any moment be called on to repel an enemy surprise attack. For this they know they must hate their enemy ; and for their own sakes they do not want enervating or nostalgic ideas to be enacted before them. This is a very different thing from singing maudlin, home-sick or ultra-pessimistic ditties, which merely relieve the spirits and do no harm, in spite of the fact that to read the words of such songs on paper might inspire many an unthinking officer to shoot the culprits for spreading alarm and despondency.

There must be no seconds spent in readjustment to the idea and desire for battle. Yet at the same time they do want to be re-familiarised with and reassured about the ideas of home, peace, culture, for these may in the next few minutes be the drive behind their fighting. The extra drive that turns a good soldier into a heroic one.

And how precious these ideas are to the soldier ! Witness the good-humoured attempt which Kolesayev describes, of one detachment in the rear, who heard that a Maly brigade was going to another detachment first, and tried to "capture" it. Others tried all sorts of dodges to keep their visitors with them, by inventing burst tyres, break-downs, and any excuse to delay a departing lorry.

The task of the "entertainers" was not easy. Strong, simple, direct emotions wanted satisfying ; sentimentality must at all costs be avoided.

Gabovich was with a brigade in an area cleared of the enemy. One of the turns was a song about an old mother waiting for her soldier son to come back. Among the audience sat a tough old Red Army General, and by his side an old countrywoman from the neighbourhood. Both were in tears. The General afterwards stated that such a song, with its powerful incentive to clear the whole country of the enemy, was worth more than any number of blank cartridges and stage-easy feats of arms. And the company agreed with him.

At the same time the problem was not quite so simple as the one aspect of it which that General solved. Front-line audiences tended to like any sort of a show, sometimes quite feeble ones. That was natural enough. But any playing down to them, any deliberate or cynical or any careless and scamped lowering of standards, would have had fatal results. A sentimental performer of even this very same song about the old mother would have aroused indirect, sentimental reactions. These reactions are latent in most people, and if evoked would tend to arouse half-formed feelings of pity, not for the old mother (which would lead to action) but for the listener himself, which would lead to nostalgia, inaction, and a weakening of self-discipline.

Further, a dramatic performance of the right kind is a fuller and more satisfying experience than a solo performance of the right kind. If that same old mother were shown in a play, the range of comment, the spread of life, the importance of the experience would be increased. Plays, therefore, must not be excluded, despite the General. But the experience they offered must be a true one, rousing simple emotions and satisfying them by the comment of the play : not indulging feelings of a sentimental kind.

Now two factors enter into every stage performance : the character and outlook of the author on the one hand, the understanding and skill of the performers on the other. Both these factors must be equal to their task, or the audience will not experience, but dream.

The persons on the stage must be convincing as real persons ; and their reality must be enhanced by such surroundings as war conditions, the powers of imagination in the audience, and other factors allow. All front-line performances, like all theatrical performances, draw to some extent on the imagination. But to do so to the very great degree required by formalist productions would at the front be both imprudent and dangerous. It would be imprudent, because even in peace-time to appreciate a formalist production requires a mental effort greater than is required by a straight and deep piece of acting ; the effort of suppressing human sympathy. And front-line conditions require the making of mental recreation as easy as possible for the soldier. (If, in a capitalist

country, the tired business man cannot be bothered with the ingenuities
of La Compagnie des 15, neither, in a Socialist army, can the tired soldier
be bothered with the acrobatics of Meierhold.)

Secondly, it would be dangerous ; because emotions aroused by non-
real productions are whatever the mental state of the beholder happens
to be, like those roused in a child by a toy. They have little direct connection with reality, and are satisfying only as long as reality does not
intrude. But just as when the reality of bedtime intrudes and the toy is
taken away, the child cried and storms, not so much because it dislikes
the reality of bed (where it can have just as good a dream anyway) as because the particular stimulus to a particular dream-emotion has been
withdrawn, so, at the end of a non-real performance, there is left a feeling
not of satisfaction but of deprivation ; and though the adult spectator
does not stamp and roar, he keeps looking back to the dream and resents
the reality. He might particularly resent the reality of battle.

So if the front line is to have plays at all, they must be real experiences.
And that means the consummate art of a well trained, lifelong actor or
actress who knows the world lived in. The better the acting, the fuller
the audience's experience. That is why front rank artists enjoy going to
the front line.

But it also means that the plays themselves must be true and deep. If
they are about the present day, and (as most plays do) show a hero winning
through despite great difficulties, then the difficulties must not just melt
away before the end of the third act because the hero is in a stage situation ;
they must melt away only as and because he copes with them. Otherwise
the event will be worthless to the audience. Reality, and their own
difficulties, will intrude too strongly.

And again, if the hero is to be killed, or if he must be unhappy at the
end (this will evolve by theatre logic from the circumstances of plot and
character), then such a consummation must be related to the real life of
the audience. Just as their own personal lives are in war-time bound even
more tightly than ever with the whole community, so the result of the hero's
personal struggle (and indeed of the struggles of all the persons in the play,
of whom we are merely taking a hero as representative) must be part of the
struggle of the community. Otherwise this experience will be worthless
to the audience.

Again, if the play is about the past, then it must not be a romantic dream,
with the total of several picturesque details making the past seem more
heroic, or more humorous, or more glamorous, than the present. For
the same reason.

But if the past is to be enacted in ways that evoke strong, direct emotions, then in what better way than through plays written in that manner

by great dramatists or writers of the past ?   Tolstoy, Ostrovsky, Lermontov, Molière, Lope de Vega . . . .

Yet the performance, too, must be such that these people are real in their own time.   Otherwise the audience will dream, not experience.

Yet life is complex ; and a mere collection of figures out of the past can be made to bear any meaning.   If they are to be true, then the comment of the author must be studied and made clear ; or else the audience will not understand its own experience.   It will not fit in with what they believe they are fighting for.

So it comes about that the stern demands of the front-line audience can be met only by a Socialist-realist theatre ; and Socialist realism finds a new vindication in battle.

This did not mean that the front-line theatre had to be " educational ", in any narrow sense.   Quite the reverse.   It must be so attractive, so easy, so immediate, that the audience would clamour to come.   Singing, dancing, farces and wise-cracks had as much place there as tears or meditations on the greatness of humanity.   But these must be rich, human, full-blooded, worth-while.   No place there for sentimentality or snivelling, sanctimoniousness nor sneers.

Not every brigade realised this ; and not every group was good enough. There was one group from Novosibirsk which journeyed hopefully west ; but its programme was so bad that it was turned back from Moscow, and ten men who would have been useful citizens in their capacity as militia men, made a journey of 3,500 kilometres in vain.

A filial of the Leningrad " Pushkin " got through to the front with *Forced Landing*. It should have been a bright comedy, full of the joy of life ; but they so overacted that the audience would have none of it ; and back they went.

Sometimes the concert parties were just a *mélange* of turns put together anyhow and rehearsed in trains.   No unity, no harmony.   The audience lost interest.[16]

But these were exceptional.   The majority set out with a sense of the reality they were going to, and what sort of people in what sort of circumstances would want them.   They were, after all, only their peace-time audiences in uniform with some friends.   Where the brigade made adjustments to the experience they gained, they became part of the Army. This happened to the Red Army Theatre group, who used local material in some shows ; and it also explains the popularity of a Vahtangov Theatre brigade.

Such then were the principles on which the troops were entertained. And understanding these things made the performers able to endure what they did.   Splashing through mud that would make an East Anglian fen seem a tennis court, bumped and bruised in cars and carts with broken springs or none at all, over roads that a fenland drover would jib at, crossing rivers on precarious planks, four shows a day and a hundred miles to cover, sweltering in the sun and the dust, losing themselves in forests, arriving on time but to find their audience gone off on a special mission, not arriving on time, afraid of not arriving at all (and any stage person will know what that means to an artist), nevertheless men, women, and stars alike stuck to the job.

They more than stuck to it, they made it phenomenal. Brigades were not, perhaps, quite an invention of this war. Twenty years previously Moskvin had headed a party of actors touring the Caucasian Front. But the figures of this war were astonishing. By August 1942 a hundred and fifty thousand performances had been given ; by December, two hundred thousand. By February 1943 Pokrovsky was able to inform the Plenum of the Central Committee of the Union of Art Workers (R.A.B.I.S.) that 260,000 had been given by 900 brigades composed of 15,000 workers.

NATIONALITY BRIGADES

Not all of these, of course, came from the Central Theatres ; from Sverdlovsk and Nizhny-Tagil, from Omsk and Smolensk they came. It was like a new industry. Nor was the personnel of it confined to Russians. Dozens of nations were fighting beside the Russians. Their theatres, too, sent brigades to them : Byelorussians, Georgians, Tajiks, Buryat-Mongolians, Dagestan actors, and actors from Ukraine, Uzbekistan, Armenia, Kirghizia, Latvians, Lithuanians, Estonians, Karelo-Finns. . . . By August 1942 Georgians and Azerbaijanians alone had given more than 12,000 performances.

The head of the principal Azerbaijanian brigade was a People's Artist of that Republic, with the attractive name of Bul-Bul. It included the world-famous *ashug* Mirza Bairamov, who wrote the major part of the words of the Hymn to Stalin which Hachaturyan the Armenian set to choral music. Its shows were mainly musical and poetic . . . arias from national operas, and recitations, but there were dancers, too, from the national ballet. There were two such brigades on the North Caucasus Front, and a third for service " abroad ", i.e. on the Western or Southern Front, or in the Crimea. Actors, singers, dramatists, who had already helped in the development of the Azerbaijanian theatre, were given titles of honour for their extra efforts in this direction.

The Tajik brigade on the other hand gave mainly choreographic displays and miniatures. The titles evoke agreeable images in default of more information : *A Talking Letter from the Front*, *The Living Piano*, *Soul of a Hero*, *Comrades in Arms*, *A Farewell Song*. There were eighteen performers, some of whom were not Tajik but Russian.   They brought portable scenery from Tajikstan where it had been designed and made.

Chechen-Ingutia sent brigades to the Caucasian Front from her Red Army House, her "Lermontov" Theatre, and the Palace of Pioneers in Grozny.   They gave 1,000 shows in six months, to the troops defending the oilfields, and to the inhabitants of Piatigorsk, Mozdok, Malgobek, as these places were retaken in 1943.

Early in the war the "Rustaveli" Theatre in Tbilisi organised a Georgian brigade to tour the Transcaucasian and North Caucasus Fronts.   It was raised by Vasadze and Khorava, and People's Artist Mjaviy was put in charge.   Their finest actress, Tamara Chavchavadze, went with it ; for, as Khorava said, "We attach to our war-patronage work fully as much importance as to our creative work.   We consider that in the days of the patriotic war the only theatre worth having is one which is connected in every part of its existence with the Red Army."

The Kazakh troops had a brigade of artists mainly from the Kazakh State Opera and Ballet (including People's Artist Turdukolova) and from the "Jamboul" Kazakh Philharmonic.   It came for a short visit to Moscow, as did many another brigade from the nationalities.

Thus, in October 1942, there arrived in Moscow a brigade of Kirghizian players from Frunze, which had set out on a two-month tour of the front giving 123 performances, out of which eighty-nine were in forward posi- tions.   This group included People's Artist Kiizbayeva, three dancers from the Kirghiz Ballet, several artists of merit, the poet Vinikov and the com- poser Vlasov, the last two jointly in charge.   Kirghiz bards gave dramatic recitations.

Moscow also saw a Turkmenian brigade in November of that year. Sona Muradova, a small, dark-eyed opera star, Durdiyev, composer and bard ; Berdiyev, actor ; Seitliyev, poet ; Luka Kolos, playwright ; and others.

In the summer of 1942 Moscow held an exhibition of Ukrainian art, at which the principal theatres were represented, and brigades performed that had been touring the front.   Half the big names of the Ukrainian theatre and opera were there.   In October came a brigade from the "Franko" Theatre, late of Kiev, then working in Central Asia.   Buchma, the celebrated Ukrainian producer was its "brigadier", and it was on its way to the Western Front with programmes of Ukrainian classics.

The Moscow Regional "Ostrovsky" Theatre, after touring the textile mills of Nara-Fominskoye and Orehovo-Zuyevo and the farms about Yegorevsk, came back to Moscow itself with the light comedy *Honeymoon* and *Partisans in the Steppes of Ukraine*.

The Second Byelorussian Theatre played at the Central House of Art

15

Workers in Moscow in December 1943 and January 1944. Others that visited the capital were from Saratov, Sverdlovsk, Kazan, the Leningrad Puppets, the Stalinabad Tajiks, an Azerbaijan company.

Many brigades called in at Moscow, so to speak, for repairs, or to rehearse a new programme, or simply to recover from an unusually exacting spell. May Day made a focus for special brightness and polish ; and many took " time off " to ensure that their standard was high enough. It was by no means a holiday, but it had that atmosphere.

THREE PICTURES

It is manifestly impossible to deal with all the brigades, even if information were forthcoming about each one, as it is not. By August 1943, T.A.S.S. was able to announce that all in all, and including those in hospitals and camps, no fewer than 400,000 performances had been given. One of the groups, a mere concert party of course, with no equipment at all worth speaking of, had actually entertained the guerilas *behind the enemy lines.*

By June 1944 the figure, as quoted by Tarhanov, the Maly actor, was 600,000. By February 1945 it had reached 800,000.

Let us leave them with three pictures in our minds.

In the first, a performance is beginning. The stage is a five-ton lorry with the sides let down. The footlights are the headlamps of another lorry specially backed into a ditch to get the right angle (" as at the Moscow Art Theatre " joked the troops). The stalls are a fruit orchard. The Dress Circle is filled with plums and apple trees, the tops of which have been shorn off by shells, like razors. And in these unaccustomed surroundings the best of artists give their finest studies. This is not because of their superb ensemble, nor their observation of people, nor the plays in the repertoire, though all these contribute to it. It is because their sincerity, their complete unity of purpose with their audience and the usefulness of their work to that common purpose are filling out and inspiring the results of years of craftsmanship. It is because Theatre has in this war justified itself as a human activity to a greater degree perhaps than at any other period of the history of man. That is their direction.

In the second picture the performance has not yet begun. The company is on the road. It is taking Chehov's *The Proposal* to the front. But so bad is the road, that they are continually all but off it. Time is short, they have to be dressing in the springless lorry. They are already in costume, having just given a performance. But make-up needs seeing to ; and the only way is by hand-mirror. You cannot hold on to a lorry that is bucketing about like a dinghy in a storm, and at the same time hold both mirror and grease paint.

Grushetsky has finished adjusting his pompous crêpe hair moustache ;

he is sewing a button on a black frock coat when the lorry bumps to a standstill. It has joined the tail of a lorry column taking ammunition up the line. A German plane has bombed the road. The driver of a leading lorry has been killed. There are no spare drivers.

Grushetsky can drive. Dressed and moustached as he is, out he jumps, runs to the deserted lorry, climbs in and drives on.

The rest of the cast arrive at their destination. No Grushetsky. The curtain is due to go up; or would be, if there were one. Still no Grushetsky.

Anxiously the cast scans the road. A little cloud of dust. A very fast motor bicycle. Grushetsky arrives on the flapper bracket. He jumps off, and the motor-cyclist waves his hand and departs. Grushetsky, still in frock coat but with only half his moustache, walks on to the stage.

The show begins.[17]

That is their spirit.

In the third picture both spirit and direction are united. It was drawn for the writer by Solomon Mihoels when he was visiting Britain in the autumn of 1943.

A Jewish brigade is acting a war play in the front line. They are in the uniforms of their parts, and there is nothing to distinguish them from the real fighters in the real war.

The alarm is given during the performance. A real German attack is taking place. The audience breaks up and meets the enemy at the point of the bayonet.

The actors help in every way they can, but in the ensuing mêlée they get terribly mixed up. Actors in German uniform are taken prisoner; those in Russian uniform protesting their Soviet citizenship are supposed to be spies.

The more loudly they protest, the more angrily they are answered. Blood, heated in battle, threatens danger to them. They in return are roused. They abandon Russian, and pour out violent, vituperative Yiddish.

Their captors are convinced. The real Germans are sorted out and taken away. The company goes back upon the stage. The show continues.

With what added zest, what deeper humour, what more passionate fervour!

If they had not been acting realistically, fully, knowledgeably; if they could not now return to that real acting, how silly and shallow after such an interruption their pretending would seem!

CHAPTER X

BRIGADES AT THE REAR

THE HEROIC REAR

The Soviet peoples in uniform and the Soviet peoples in overalls were one and the same. Whether breaking records and out-achieving plans and schedules of production in factories by skill and endurance, or winning more and yet more food materials in the fields by a skill as great and an endurance even greater, people in the rear were undergoing fully the same degree of nerve strain and physical hardship as those at the front. There may not have been the same danger, nor wounds, nor sudden onslaught, but there was less warm clothing in winter, less of the best in comforts and supplies. If, therefore, the front line was entitled to theatrical brigades, so was what with perfect propriety can be called the " heroic rear ". The function of these brigades was the same as at the front : to entertain, to explain, to inspire.

We begin with Kuibyshev, reserve capital to Moscow, whither were transferred in 1941 the Diplomatic Corps, the foreign Press, and some Government departments. No longer was the Volga a rampart. By this move it was recognised as the real life-stream, not only of Russia, but of all the Soviet Union.

Kuibyshev, rich in artists and theatres of the first quality. The best was the Regional " Gorky " Theatre, starred with People's Artist Vilner the producer, which served not only the population of the town itself (in the thirties of this century, when it was still called Samara, it was the home of two hundred thousand people) but the region round about, the Middle Volga Region. Besides townsfolk gathered for the chemical, textile and heavy engineering industries, therefore, it had to adapt itself also to collective and State farm audiences in the agricultural land to the east and the steppes to the west of the river.

There is an agreeable account of the opening of a quite new theatre in this neighbourhood, at Syzran on the Volga, in November 1943. The opening play was *Lyubov Yarovaya*, and a distinguished company assembled in the auditorium to see it. Telegrams were read from the R.S.F.S.R. Art Administration, the Kuibyshev Oblispolkom, the dramatic theatres at Kuibyshev and Buguruslan, and from other organisations. A red ribbon tied the curtain up. This was cut ; the curtain opened ; the show began. The house seated 650, and the permanent company numbered fifty, with an orchestra.

This region was a reception area, and the increase in population threw a burden on the local theatres. These did not lower their standard, though; they raised it; they widened it. Thus, in the early summer of 1942, new productions at the Regional included two plays from French literature: *Mademoiselle Fifi*, after the short story by Guy de Maupassant, which describes the behaviour of Prussian officers in an occupied chateau during the Franco-Prussian War, and how a girl, brought in for their pleasure, stabs a lieutenant to death; and *The Attack on the Mill*, after a short story by Zola. Then, no less famous an artist than Peter Williams designed the sets for Vilner's production of *Romeo and Juliet* the following July. This was their second Shakespeare, the first having been *Much Ado About Nothing*. The *premières* differed by the distinguished visitors in the audience at *Romeo*; but the abilities of the company were fully equal to the limelight now thrown on them.

Within a year the following were on the stage or in rehearsal: Leonov's *Invasion* and *Lyonushka*, Gorky's *The Lower Depths*, Ostrovsky's *Wolves and Sheep*, Pisemsky's *Bitter Fate*, *Twelfth Night*, and new Soviet plays called *The Emergency Law* and *The Scythe has Struck a Stone*. But perhaps the most celebrated event was the *première* in February 1943 of *The Blue Scarf*, a new play by Valentin Katayev, author of *Squaring the Circle*.

THE BLUE SCARF

This high spirited light comedy centres round a group of lads at the front, who receive a bundle of comforts from unknown wellwishers in the rear. In particular a blue scarf, with an admiring letter signed Shura, causes its recipient much joy and pleasure. In his imagination he constructs a radiant, attractive creature as the knitter and sender of it, and by the time his leave is due, he is completely in love with her, and convinced that she must be with him. On his leave he is able to go to the village from which the parcel came, and after some amusing incidents of mistaken identity, tracks down the sender. But alas for his dreams! "Shura" is short not only for Alexandra, but also for Alexan*der;* and the sender is, in fact, a schoolboy. The other lads have better luck.

Unlike *Squaring the Circle* this play is not meant as a satire on anything. Still less a psychological study. Nor does it preach. It is just a gay, wartime comedy, full of human sympathy, a little sentiment, plenty of light romance. As such it became widely popular among soldiers and civilians alike.

The Regional "Gorky" and the other Kuibyshev theatres formed brigades for the front. It also formed one for the farms during the spring sowing.[1]

IN THE FIELDS OF THE VOLGA

At two seasons of the year those who live near the earth feel a particular elevation, a quickening of the mind and senses on the completion of a job. One is when the harvest is in ; the other is when the spring sowing is done. There is still much work to do on the farm, but a moment is taken for mental breath ; and in an unspoilt and free-living rural community this is a communal experience. In rural communities at these two points of the working calendar since time began, the mumming impulse has been strong. In modern ones, where culture has been reclaimed from the derelict fields of human labour, it finds its expression and satisfaction in Theatre.

Performances may take place anywhere—in club-halls, local theatre buildings, yards, or even during rest hours in the very fields. Big distances must be covered by such brigades ; and not every rural group can have an evening show.

It was the same at Saratov, further down the Volga, a slightly larger town in normal times, but of the same character industrially. The Saratov Opera, having a number of Ukrainian singers as guests for the duration, founded a brigade late in 1942. At the same time the Regional Dramatic Theatre was preparing *General Brusilov*. Out of available talent, both local professionals and guests from Moscow or elsewhere, there came a new, mobile theatre of " Revue and Satire " under a producer called Roshin. We may guess at the material from its titles : *How but Love Moscow ? Our War Magazine* (a different issue every now and then), *Germany To-day*. Much of it was provided by anti-Fascists of German nationality, Brecht, Wolf, Busch, and others. This was as early as February 1942.[2]

It was the same in the upper reaches. Kazan was now rich in theatres, and one of its national plays, Isambet's *Khuzha Nasretdin*, a biographical play about a national sage, had had 300 performances since its first showing in 1940. There were a State Tatar Theatre, a Grand Dramatic (Russian) Theatre, a Musical Comedy, a Mobile Tatar Workers' Theatre, a Tyuz, and a Puppet Theatre, besides four schools. But, in addition, there were four regional theatres permanently touring the farms, centred in three smaller Tatar towns, Menzelinsk, Mamadysh and Bugulma. The standard of the Russian Theatre was demonstrably high : in 1942 it had done *Field-Marshal Kutuzov*, *Partisans in the Steppes*, and Sardou's *La Patrie*, adding in February of that year Fletcher's *Spanish Curate*. *Regiment DD* followed, and, next year, Lermontov's *Masquerade* and Ostrovsky's *Burning Heart*. The producer was none other than the celebrated Muscovite Alexey Diky.

So the Tatar Theatre had a strong rival, with whom it did not fear to compete. Sub-national dramatists like Isanbet and Gizzat were welcomed. In summer the whole theatre became a field-brigade, touring the farms and thereby handing on, in the mutual competitive spirit of all Soviet theatre enterprise, the increased ability engendered by Russian example. So the fundaments of art built upon by Diky in his own little studio in Moscow were made available, through the alertness of local theatres, to the Tatar workers in the fields.[3]

The city of Gorky naturally had an even higher standard, and this was passed on to its regional theatres. It took care that it should be, calling in February 1943 a conference of all the local theatres, urban and rural. In 1938 there were seven theatres in Gorky itself, three at Pavlov-on-the-Oka, Murom and Dzerzhinsky, and four farm theatres at Semenov, Bogorodsk, Sharya and Arzamas. These, through their producers, managers or leading actors, reported on progress and discussed common problems, not excluding general questions like the place of Shakespeare or Gorky in a Soviet theatre's repertoire. Local dramatists and authors also came to this conference.

Two figures stand out from the Gorky landscape. One is, naturally enough in his own birthplace and in the neighbourhood of his exile from Peterburg, the man from whom the city takes its name : Maxim Gorky. The city theatre and the regional theatre may be said to specialise in his plays.

The other was People's Artist N. I. Sobolshchikov-Samarin, whose 75th birthday was celebrated in June 1943. This splendid old man was technically known as a " consultant " ; but he did much producing too, especially his own version of *War and Peace* which he was rehearsing in 1942. In a quarter of a century he had built up a big reputation for *Hamlet* and *The Winter's Tale*, for *Meshchane*, *The Cherry Orchard*, Ostrovsky's *A Dream on the Volga*. But his *chef d'œuvre* was generally held to be *A Noble's Nest*, by Turgenyev. Under his influence the Regional Theatre became so famous that it was invited to Moscow in 1941 to show the cream of its work in the Hermitage Winter Theatre. Its new shows that year were no less successful : *The Rape of Helen*, *Belugin's Wedding*, *La Locandiera*, *A Fellow from Our Town*. Also *Terrible Strength*, a play by the local author, M. Danilevsky. In the 1942-3 season *Oleko Dundich* linked this local thought to that of democracy in general, and *Russian People* bound the provinces into the whole nation. But perhaps the chief production of that year was Gorky's *Barbarians*, with very expressive realistic sets (there is no contradiction) by N. A. Pokrovsky. *Julius Cæsar* was in contemplation next. Meanwhile, the City Theatre, not to be outdone, set to work on *The Taming of the Shrew*, and Gorky's *Enemies*.

From this we can get an idea of the local interest and encouragement of a typical Russian regional theatre and its work, whether in field or town ; and we can also see how, linked by common purpose and interchange of ideas and experience, the theatres that toured the countryside had no mean example to follow.[4]

In the very uppermost reaches of the Volga, north of Moscow, the same story was told. The mediæval town of Yaroslavl, which has been called the Nuremberg of Russia, in the centre of a rich and smiling countryside populous with dairy farms,★ and countless country-houses now used as rest homes and holiday places for the young. . . . Placid, traditional, country like a Southern English meadow in summer. Here, small towns like Kostroma and Rybinsk had their own theatres, two or three in each. The " Nekrassov " Theatre in the latter had the attractive description of Summer Theatre of the Railway Garden. I suppose the Railwaymen's Union had a Rest Home there. And there were two farm theatres as well.

Yaroslavl itself had six theatres, the principal one being the Regional Theatre, named for Fyodor Volkov. Volkov was the adopted son of a merchant of this town who, at Peterburg, started, with the help of a nobleman, the first permanent Russian theatre, during the reign of the Empress Elizabeth in 1756. This " Volkov " Theatre claimed to be the oldest in Russia, for reasons I have not been able to discover. This claim may be challenged by the Kostroma Theatre.

Here, too, was another grand old man of the Russian stage. Pavel Gaibedurov, of whose " travelling theatre " in 1903 I have given a short account in The New Soviet Theatre, was still alive and still active in 1943. After forty-four years on the stage he played the Old Man in Gorky's play of that name, the first revival it had had since the Maly production in 1918. But also, requiring more energy, he played the name part in Selvinsky's General Brusilov, that study of Ludendorff's crafty opponent in the last war, in which Ludendorff, too, was portrayed. Performing these two title rôles he appeared with the rest of the company in Moscow in May 1943, about the time of the 180th anniversary of Volkov's death, and his work in both was much admired, like the production itself, by Rostovtsev ; but the play, as a play, came in for some criticism both in Moscow and in Yaroslavl. Both these pieces had their first production here for the twenty-fifth anniversary of the Red Army in March 1943 ; about the same time two brigades were formed to tour that smiling countryside and remind those who inhabited it not only of their literary traditions but of the threat to these that approached from the west. In April the two brigades performed at the parent theatre's premises. The plays they were to carry forth in eight separate tours that season were Russian People and Fonvizin's The Minor.†

★ The " Yaroslavsky " was a classic breed of dairy cattle.

† Denis Ivanovich Fonvizin (1744-92) was a link between the literary comedies of Sumarokov and the social plays of Ostrovsky. Gorky said of his best play, The Minor, that it was " the first product of a more socially-fruitful line in Russian literature, the ' accusatory-realistic ' ". It attacked the darkest sides of serfdom, the crudeness of the landowners, the corruption of justice, the ugliness of education, or its lack.

Gaibedurov, however, was also a producer, and later that year he put on Leonov's *Invasion* in the Regional Theatre. As if to make a pair, Gogol's *Revizor* was added.[5]

At Ryazan, with the Nazi tide crawling woefully near, at Tula, almost encircled in it, regional theatres went on working their heartening round. In Tula the summer season of 1941 was uninterrupted. In June 1943 *Long, Long Ago* was delightfully inspiring the skeleton determination of the inhabitants, almost within a stone-throw of the German lines. Ryazan, on the woody Oka, was quite a small place ; but it had three theatres. The Regional one in 1942 and 1943 travelled indefatigably round camps and hospitals. It performed *Russian People*, *Invasion*, *Nadyezhda Durova*, and the 1925 Maly classic, *Lyubov Yarovaya*. It denied itself any days off. On nominal days of rest the actors visited aircraft factories. It raised money from its salaries for gifts to former members of its staff now at the front, and for gifts to their families. It formed brigades of actors, singers and musicians to tour places the theatre could not, as a whole, reach. These went to collective farms, clubs, houses of culture, with sketches, songs, short plays, scenes, some specially written on topical matters for the audience to laugh or cry at. Especially at the time of the spring sowing, but at harvest too. State farms, and collective farms, so urgent was the need for growing more food, must outdo themselves. This could be brought about either by giving orders or by showing why. The latter is the wiser, and was the Soviet, way. These brigades showed the farm workers why, both directly by emotional appeal, and indirectly by reminding them what they had to lose. In a sense they might be called " agitational " ; but it was a form of agitation too artistic to be purely practical. A theme like *General Brusilov*, which was in this regional theatre's repertoire too, can hardly be called propaganda.[6]

ROUND LENINGRAD AND MOSCOW

Leningrad and Moscow had their regional theatres too. The Moscow Regional Theatre bore the name of Ostrovsky. During 1943 it was touring the Karelian and Finnish fronts, doing 200 shows in five months. The Commander of the Finnish front gave each actor his personal thanks for their work. But this was not limited to the fronts. The audience in the Moscow Region had changed. As the President of the regional branch of what we would call the Ministry of Information said, in peace-time it had been an audience of mills and factories. Now it included all the incidentals of a war landscape. New conditions required new matter. It not only gave " small form " shows (sketches and so on) ; it took whole plays to war-factory club-rooms : *Russian People* for one, *Rose Marie* for another. It tried to raise the standard of all its performances. It introduced the best literature, the best music.

The Leningrad Region was even better served, though its dangers and suffering were even greater. In January 1943 a conference met of all the regional entertainment industries, radio, performers and composers of music, artists, actors, theatre people. As a result of their deliberations the Regional Board for Art Affairs initiated seven brigades in the spring to serve the rest-hours of the farms. These drew many of their members from the operetta, dramatic and puppet theatres. They toured the front as well as the rear. Actors that went to the centres of supply also went to the centres of resistance. Even young collectives like the Porkhov Theatre of Drama and Comedy, or the Kingissep Theatre, which had been formed only just before the war, came to their maturity under fire.[7]

Local Circles

All over Russia it was the same. Looking at it again from above our animated map, we can now make out a new motion. Besides the general movement eastward and the partial movement westward, threading-in and counter-marching to each other, there are spots in the design moving now in little orbits of their own round hundreds of little points. Reports are not forthcoming about all. To examine even all that are forthcoming would be wearisome to the reader if indeed he is not already surfeited with detail.

But let us at least consider some.

Naturally the Urals and KuzBas districts are the most active. In the Molotov Region in the late summer of 1942, two dozen brigades are out on the farms during the harvest. The Molotov Regional Theatre we have already had up before us ; here it goes the round with an anti-Fascist play on an Austrian theme : *Russia, Help Us !* by Kozakov ; and in the repertoire, *Yegor Bulychov, Field-Marshal Kutuzov, The House on the Hill.* In Novosibirsk the Red Torch Theatre circles the coal-pits and metal combines with sharp satiric warnings to laggards. The Farms Theatre with unceasing zest joins in the agitation. The " Pushkin " Theatre tours both farms and pits, Yuryev talking to the workers after the show. The Omsk Regional Theatre kindles a warlike spirit with *Good Morning, Gun !* and *Suvorov;* and a theatre of miniatures is formed, which runs a Living Newspaper. At Chkalov, which was once Orenburg, Andreyev produces *Krechinsky's Wedding* for the " Gorky " Regional Theatre ; he guides the younger members of the company in *Timur and his Comrades.* A brigade therefrom tours the Omsk countryside. The dramatic theatres of Abdulin and Ponomaryov follow this example, with programmes founded on local material. A group from the variety section of the Chkalov Philharmonium provide lighter fare. At Irkutsk, when a local theatre is to be founded, 200 applicants come from as far away as Buryat-Mongolia and Krasnoyarsk to fill twenty-six vacancies.[8]

Away in the *taiga* to the north of Lake Baikal, to Novy-Ude where Stalin once lived in exile, to Ilimsk where Radishchev was sent, toils the Irkutsk Regional Theatre and the Cheremkhov Theatre, on lorry or on horseback, in carts or by reindeer. For even in the *taiga* there is a spring sowing ; and the farmers gather in the evening for *Russian People*, or *The Front; Long, Long Ago*, or *Anna Karenina;* and there are to be found hospitals too, and camps, where the Red Army's twenty-fifth year is celebrated by such shows. Ostrovsky, too, always gathers a good house. Over on the other side of the great lake, Buryat-Mongolian theatres do the same, visiting over three hundred thousand spectators in the course of a hundred or more performances.

Right in the Far East there are more orbits. From Vladivostok set out the city theatres to the Pacific Fleet, to outposts of the Far Eastern Army, to reading-huts in collective farms and agricultural camps all over the Maritime Province. People's Artist of the Uzbek Republic, Tamara Khanum, is visiting there. She gives "patronage" recitals. The Habarovsk Musical Comedy Theatre is netting a wider audience. The Voroshilov Theatre founds a Filial to tour the front.

At Bodaïbo, in Eastern Siberia, a theatre is founded which plays there and tours the gold mines with Simonov, Pogodin, Ostrovsky and Beaumarchais !

In the *taiga* of Eastern Siberia travels a theatre that has no building. Its company have no houses, flats or rooms of their own. They live, and had lived by 1944, for eighteen years in a train of eleven coaches, seven of which were living quarters, and the rest scene-docks and wardrobe, property-store, dining-room, and so on. Children were born and brought up here. The son of the director, Alexander Fomin, was born on the train eighteen years back. He spent his winters at school in Vladivostok but acted small parts all summer. He volunteered for the front, but was wounded and discharged, and by August 1944 was back on the job in his train-theatre birthplace.

A kind of gipsy life took hold of this company. They rested two months of the year in a special place where they kept cattle and goats and poultry. They hunted their food often with gun and berry-basket. They grew so fond of this open-air stage life that not even an important appointment could tempt Fomin away. He remained to serve the garrisons, the hunters, the fishermen, the peasants of Siberia with Beaumont and Fletcher, and the Russian classics, Soviet plays, war plays, the best of Britain, France and America. Such was the " Transport Theatre of the Maritime Region".

Look north ! There are frozen circles traced in the ice and the tundra. The Norilsk Polar Theatre covers the Taimyr Peninsula from its base in

Dudinka. Reindeer herdsmen gather round to watch. They are fascinated by *Much Ado About Nothing*, by Ostrovsky, by Gogol and Gorky,
by Beaumarchais or Goldoni, or by the latest war play from Moscow.
They understand what they see, for the language is their own. All along
the Arctic Circle this scene may be repeated, as far west as Archangel, where
a fine Russian theatre plays Pogodin or Tolstoy or *Ruy Blas*. This building
seats 1,800, but in 1942 not every seat is full. Perhaps the collective is not
good enough ; perhaps some of the new plays, *A Death for a Death* or
The Station Master, are dull or improbable. Or perhaps there is something in the Arctic climate which even a Soviet theatre cannot overcome ?

On the shores of the White Sea on Kandalaksha Bay, where the Vikings
founded a settlement, other warriors are fighting now. Murmansk Region
raises a mobile theatre for them. It apologises for its smallness . . . only
twenty-one in the company ! But it compensates with the plays offered :
Twelfth Night, *Russian People*, *A Fellow from Our Town*, *Children of the Sun*,
The Siege of Leyden, *Belugin's Wedding*, *La Locandiera*, an Ostrovsky. What
more could they want ? Since the foundation of this unit, it had given
1,145 performances.[9]

From Frunze and Samarkand, from Grozny and Tyanshan, out come
the brigades, circle the towns and fields, and go home. Round Yaroslavl
in the depths of December ten men tramp on snow shoes. Round Voronezh,
with *Kutuzov*, round Stavropol with a Simonov and a Korneichuk, pupils
from the Baku theatre, a mobile unit with a Brushtein play, or a whole
national theatre in the Udmurt A.S.S.R. with a complete repertoire of Soviet
plays, and Chehov, and Shakespeare, Rostand and Ostrovsky, in Bashkiria,
in Chechen-Ingutia, eleven hundred shows in a single Turkmenian year,
one hundred and nineteen groups in Kazakhstan, oil-fields, rice-fields,
corn-fields and cotton-fields, orchard and vineyard and mountain-brae,
even out of the Soviet Union they range, to Teheran, Tavziz, Kazrin, in
Persia.

With them in their orbits go their guests. The Leningrad Dramatic
Theatre, near Kirov, in 1942 gave more than 600 performances at hospitals
and camps. The Ukrainian " Franko ", near Semipalatinsk, gave three
hundred and twenty-two. The " Chkalov " Theatre from Gorky Town
(not to be confused with the " Gorky " Theatre from Chkalov Town)
got as far as Tula with light comedies, *Gardens in Bloom* and *La Locandiera*,
or grim dramas the like of *My Son;* and also with concert programmes
in which the poet-producer, Pavel Antokolsky, helped the actors to write
their own sketches. And among Ukrainian and Russian recruits, and among
the wounded and the convalescent, moved the " Shevchenko " Theatre
with gay Ukrainian plays and musical comedies.

A Theatre of Silence

But of all brigades the most curious at front or at rear, the most startling theatre in the world, comes from Rostov-on-Don. Not a sound is to be heard from the stage. The actors are all dumb. They are all deaf and dumb. So intense is the silence that if any fully-facultied spectator whispers or coughs, the others shush him. Yet the actors have eloquence. The play gets across.

This was not a war-time creation. It started before the war ; started organically and from small beginnings as the best things do in all the arts. It was in a deaf mutes' club, after someone had noticed the dramatic talent of some members in expressing themselves. They found suitable plays, gradually. They acquired their own technique, gradually. So skilful they grew that at last they could hold and move others besides their own afflicted members. They moved out into the world of speech and sound.

The Fascists came to Rostov, and the theatre left. But now it had come into its own. It also had a war-time function, not a sad one, but a fine exhilarating task. Nor were even deaf mutes without their share in the winning of the war. As the tide of war turned, and they could go westward again behind the advancing Soviet armies, it was helping to liberate two worlds at once : the outward audible world of people plundered, tortured and bereaved, and the inward, inaudible world of men in the prime of life who had had their hearing and often their faculty of speech too taken from them, and had thought they were alone for ever on the inside of their eyes.[10]

CHAPTER XI

WAR PLAYS OF FACT, FICTION AND FANCY

A Multitude of Characters

Soviet drama since its beginning about 1925 has developed along paths quite different from those of Western European drama. The difference is not only ideological; it is in treatment as well as theme.

In treatment a representative Soviet play has much in common with the drama of Dekker, Webster, Ford . . . a multitude of characters and a more or less episodic development through a number of shortish scenes. But it differs from Elizabethan and Jacobean drama in two main matters of content; the scenes are less units of plot than units of atmosphere or mood; and the inter-relation of the characters does not, as a rule, build up round a single central figure, but is important in itself. The hero is rather a group, or community, though composed of living, individual people. This is a very rough generalisation, of course, and does not imply, in any case, that the same thing may not be said to some degree with truth about Webster.

The shape and structure of a stage-worthy play of any period are to some extent governed by the stage conditions of the time. Thus neither Elizabethan nor Soviet writers had to consider such factors as the need for a small cast to counterbalance high rents in London or high travel costs on tour, or the limited salary list of a provincial repertory theatre, as our contemporary capitalist playwright must do. Both Elizabethan and Soviet dramatists wrote for full companies, which could handle multiplicity of characters, and indeed welcomed it. But this throws a big strain on the dramatist's ingenuity, since it reduces the cubic area out of which to carve each figure in the round. It reduces time; and time is needed to differentiate character from type. The insight and technical skill needed to cut round figures from minimum marble amount to genius; and I am not sure that such genius has yet appeared in the Soviet Union. But that is not to say the standard of Soviet dramaturgy is not high. It is high. Only it should not be judged by the criteria of C. E. Montague or Granville Barker. If we judge any drama not by what it set out to do, but by what we feel it ought to have set out to do, we will ourselves fall by the wayside, calling it barren seed. First we must establish what it set out to do, then judge whether it has succeeded, or how far, and only then can we, if we wish, fit it into the general picture of world drama.

Out of all the many war playwrights whose names have been mentioned hitherto, three excel the rest in general esteem and in frequency of production : Simonov, with two plays, *Russian People* and *Wait for Me;* Leonov, with *Invasion;* and Korneichuk, with *The Front* and *Partisans in the Steppes of Ukraine.* Of these five plays, two may fairly be described as left in the final round : *Russian People*, which had a hundred and fifty separate productions between July 1942 and July 1943, and *Invasion*, which had eighty-three from the beginning of 1943 to the same date. Many, many other theatres have staged them since.

These, then, we may make the basis of our examination, taking them as plays which Russian theatre people would cite if asked to describe a good play.

To begin with, we must have some disposition to respect their choice. After all, theatrical performance in the U.S.S.R. is a serious thing . . . not that it in any way lacks humour, but actors, producers and audience alike take the theatre far more seriously than they do in any other country I have heard of. A play that satisfied all these three elements of the theatre must be considered to contain something valuable theatrically, especially since the Soviet theatre is under no compulsion to debauch its public for the sake of the box office. The critic's job, then, is to find out first of all what that value is. In the process a number of his old standards cease to apply.

CHARACTERISTICS OF SOVIET PLAYS

First the multiplicity of characters, all of importance, who may none the less share the same fate for quite different reasons, or who, though of equal moral integrity, may yet have different destinies, wipes out the old analysis of tragedy. In *Russian People*, Globa the Army Doctor, valuable, honest, reliable, goes to certain death with a song, while Valya, equally valuable, honest and reliable, shares his adventure but is preserved. In *Partisans in the Steppes* . . . the two mothers, Paraska and Palajka, are in their different ways as wrathful, resolute and faithful as any woman in Soviet territory, but both are hanged by the Germans. Their deaths have the same dramatic effect as the death of the Duchess of Malfi, in that they rouse our grief, pity, and anger against their murderers. But their deaths are not due to any inner weakness of character. They happen because the circumstances causing them are too great for any one person to control. Communities are wrestling with communities. The individual, however deserving, may be destroyed ; but the community can be saved. It can be saved by the very destruction of the deserving individual.

Such a play cannot be called a tragedy within the old meaning of that word ; but neither is it comedy nor " drama ". There is no term as yet to describe it.

Now there is no great drama, no deep dramatic experience unless the moral sense of an audience is stirred and satisfied. Otherwise the suffering becomes merely incidental, meaningless, sentimental. With a community audience such moral sense is undoubtedly stirred and satisfied when the character of the victim in the deepest, moral sense of the word, has contributed to the survival of the community. The more valuable that person, the greater the loss to the community, but also the greater the gain to the community. The value of Globa is greater because of his death rather than in spite of it.

That is the angle of the single person. But the relation of the individual to the community, the inter-relations of all the individuals, the development and change of character because of the community . . . these are much more subtle, more organic and complex in Leonov's *Invasion*, and for this reason among others I find this play quite outstanding among the Soviet plays I have been able to study.

LEONOV'S " INVASION "

This play was first produced at a provincial theatre, in Noginsk near Moscow, Leonov attending rehearsals and explaining it to the actors. When the award of a Stalin prize for the play was announced, Moscow wanted to see it, and the whole company came for the purpose to the Central House of Art Workers.

Inadequate translation in the version published in English (which differs in several respects from the Russian version published in 1942) does not give the subtlety of speech-differentiation between the characters, and tends to read lifelessly and dull. But with the use of a creative imagination, some of the effect of the play can be caught none the less for that.

One of the central features of this fearless and beautiful play is the rape by the Germans of a fifteen-year-old girl, Aniska. (A stage direction mentioning " such a shy freshness gleaming in her movements that you can't watch her without smiling. Fyodor's face softens ", has been rendered in English, " Fyodor's face softens at her awkwardness and extreme timidity"; and her country speech has been turned into the pert sophistication of a suburban tomboy, whereas, on the contrary, she is a very attractive little peasant thing, beautifully and sensitively created.) At the end of the second scene she is carried in, completely shattered and in collapse, having been found in an outhouse after a German officer and some German soldiers have had their will of her . . . a moment that would make even one of Ribbentrop's friends in British High Society rise in horror and rage.

In the following scene she is lying in bed, after her temporary guardian, who is a doctor, has performed an operation on her. Her aunt, Demidyevna, the old nanny, tries to get her off to sleep and forgetfulness of her terror

LEONID LEONOV.
Stalin prize-winner.

[*facing page* 236.

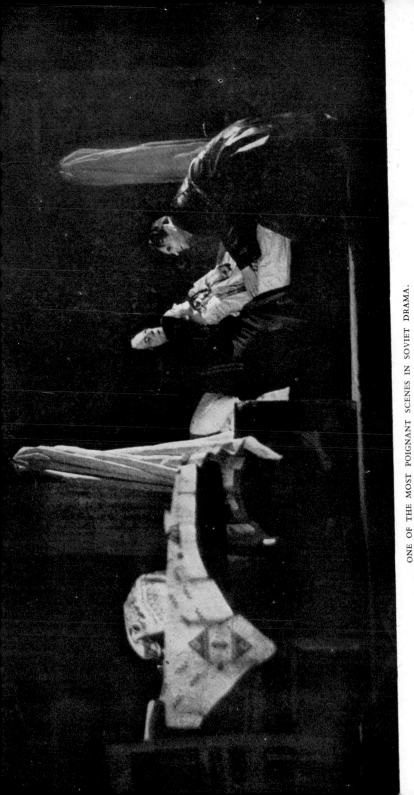

ONE OF THE MOST POIGNANT SCENES IN SOVIET DRAMA.

Aniska's bedside in *Invasion*, as produced by Sudakov at the Maly Theatre, Moscow.

[*facing page* 237.

by telling her favourite story. The reactions of the child to this are beautiful and moving ; but they are not set there in the play just to evoke tears. Nor is the fate of Aniska meant merely to stir the audience to hate the Germans. They affect Fyodor. Fyodor is the ne'er-do-weel son of the doctor, who has returned home after serving a prison sentence for murdering the woman he had married (in the English version this has been altered to the crime of embezzlement). Leonov treats his embittered mental condition with great depth. Fyodor has a sense of wrong against society. It is touch-and-go whether he joins the Germans or not. In fact he tries to join the guerrillas, but is turned down as unreliable. He remains remote from the community and its suffering.

Leonov is a master of psychology ; and in previous plays he has shown particular interest in the return of the delinquent. When the delinquent reforms, Leonov is more plausible and successful in showing this, than Pogodin was. But he does not show any crude change of heart in Fyodor. Much later, when Fyodor is himself up against things, the memory of little Aniska flares up in him, and he passes himself off as Kolesnikov, the local guerrilla leader, so that the Nazis will execute him and Kolesnikov himself be still at large. This recalling of Aniska is shown so subtly that Fyodor himself, before his execution, does not quite understand, and certainly cannot explain what made him do it.

A play cannot be judged by two incidents ; but these two do show the relation of the individual to the community. For in this case the community, faithful to the guerrillas, had to hold out till the Red Army arrived. The conversion of the ne'er-do-weel contributed to that. And so did the rape of little Aniska, as Fyodor's father and the old nanny made it.

Invasion is not a well-made West-End commercial play. It conforms to few of our rules. There is no entrance of the lead (centre back, through french windows) five minutes after curtain-rise and a good build up. It is untidy. We do not know what became of Aniska, nor the nanny. Characters appear as they are wanted, with no need to explain their presence. But it is a good deal tidier than it seems at first sight.

In the first place, it is written with care and those wordless implications that make true and human composition on the stage. The conversion of Fyodor is prepared in his very first appearance, when his father notices his flaunting moustache and the disquiet underlying (and causing) his smart arrogance. It is prepared too in that softening effect of Aniska on him as she runs about. His sister Olga is a true, sensitive person, with an unspoken understanding between her and her parents ; and her question to Fyodor, when he apologises for not knowing that she and Kolesnikov are engaged . . . " Is that all you've learnt, the whole evening ? " is not only subtle writing, it is the gist of the play, relating her to the whole community.

16

This is the striking feature of many Soviet plays, the subtlety with which, not using bombastic or emotional words, but even in their silences sometimes, people indicate their feeling for other people in the community, for the community itself.

Finding these and many other dramatic strengths and symptoms, we must infer that such a playwright is deliberately ignoring our West-End standards, because he has other intentions, which to him are more important ; and it may be through ignorance of this, or haste, that some Sunday paper critics have invented the legend that Soviet plays are bad. The intentions that Soviet playwrights show, and Leonov, Simonov, Korneichuk, Pogodin, especially, are to explore and express that complex relation or series of relations between living individuals and the group they create by their very individuality ; particularly when that group is fighting an all-in, total, life-and-death struggle. In such a struggle the whole people is the hero.

But, in the second place, *Invasion* has a quite definite sweep and plan. The relation of a man to the group he helps to form is not more static or simple than his relation to his friends or relatives. It is organic ; it develops and alters. The hero of *Invasion*, as the whole people, would itself remain a type-figure if it did not develop and alter ; and Yuri Kalashnikov has shown in a fine analysis in the magazine *International Literature*, that the four acts explain and express the four phases of Fascist invasion. These are : approach and arrival, with the various Russian inhabitants deciding what they are going to do ; resistance and retributions under German rule ; the throwing of the occupying forces into confusion and panic of their collaborators, leading to further acts of violence ; and fourthly, liberation and revenge. Nor is this theme a formal framework. The people are real people, their lives and feelings are personal ; but they are subordinated to the common experience ; and this common experience is shown in relation to the war as a whole, not geographically but mentally, in human terms. Behind and under the emotional stimuli, in other words, stand a firm, clear intellectual judgment and comment, which put Leonov high among world playwrights.

Justice cannot be done to any play in a few paragraphs, least of all to this one ; I would refer the reader to the play itself, even in a poor translation, and also to Kalashnikov's article. Personally, I find that beyond any doubt the playwright achieved what he set out to do.

AIMS OF THE SOVIET PLAYWRIGHT

Hrapchenko, in his speech to a playwrights' conference called by the Committee for Art Affairs in May 1942, defined the aim of the Soviet dramatist as follows :—

By the means of art, by the power of their art-forms, they were to actualise the spiritual mobilisation of the people (lit. " to actualise the mobilisation of the people in their ideas ") for the destruction of the enemy, to show the maintenance of the patriotic struggle, to honour the heroic deeds of our country's defenders.[1]

Among established dramatists who might be expected to do this successfully, he cited (though I doubt whether any weight should be attached to the order) Pogodin, Leonov, Korneichuk, Kozakov, Finn, Virta, Simonov, Kaverin and Alexandra Brushtein ; and among new-comers Laptev, and the collaborators Rzheshevsky and Katz.* But, as a whole, he said, Soviet playwrights had not fully answered the people's demands on them ; too many had described guerrilla warfare without knowing anything about it, too few had written of the equally heroic rear, with which they were better acquainted.

Now Soviet playwrights, as Hrapchenko would very likely have agreed, had chosen the more exciting and, superficially, the more theatrical adventures of the front, because they were only human. And we must not forget the quantity with which he was dealing. In the course of 1942 alone no fewer than 200 war plays had been written. And it was stated that out of thirty-seven new productions by Moscow theatres in the 1941-2 season thirty were by Soviet dramatists, and twenty-five were war plays.[2]

But if a playwright's aim is to show the heroism of a people by the Soviet method of many characters and incidents, and he does not do so from personal experience or observation, he will probably fall into one of two errors. He may put his own admiration into the mouths of his characters, and achieve a false heroism ; for the heroes of the U.S.S.R. are simple people, and though perhaps more outspokenly patriotic than the British, nevertheless shrink just as quickly as the British do from bombast about themselves. If he is clever enough to avoid this, he will at best create a " type " hero ; and that, in the strong realistic apparatus which must put his play into action, and in the lively response of a realistic audience, will be immediately exposed as false.

If, on the other hand, he avoids heroics but still has no personal knowledge, his play will become a mere adventure story, of small interest to an audience all too closely involved in the adventure of war themselves ; and he will be lucky if he succeeds in avoiding errors of fact which are not to be picked up in books or newspapers, but which Nord, of the N.W. Front-Line Theatre, said an Army audience was very quick to notice. At best such plays can be mere theatrical tricks and stage effects. Mdivani's *The Battalion Goes West* was often cited in criticism as the classic example of this.

In general, it seemed, playwrights had failed, if they had failed, because

* For a list of war plays and authors, see Appendix II.

they had discovered no medium to carry the new relation and development of the group of the community. The old-fashioned " family play " was too narrow. It could not, in Hrapchenko's phrase, reveal the " All-Union " character of the war in the way it affected people's personal lives. Eugene Schwartz's *One Night* he wrote later, describes Leningrad in the stern days of November and December, but misses out the hero, the people of Leningrad. Consequently it becomes a mere detective adventure story.[3]

Much of the trouble was perhaps due to the difficulty of communication, of producers being too remote to know what plays were available, as A. V. Solodovnikov observed. But it was due also to many dramatists being out of touch with the theatres ; and this was a more serious factor. It was to get worse before it improved.

Plays About Guerrillas

War plays poured out in their scores. Afinogenov's *On the Eve* was among the earliest, being staged in February 1942 by the author's friend, Nikolay Petrov, at the Moscow Railway Workers' Theatre. The curtain rises on Saturday, 21st June 1941. The Zavyalov family in the country outside Moscow is entertaining its friends. The *dramatis personæ* include the old iron-founder Timofey and his sons, Ivan a General, and Andrey an agriculturalist ; a society actress and her son ; a professor and his student daughter ; and Andrey's wife, Jeren, from Turkmenia. Amid songs, talk and flirtations, comes a telephone call. Hitler's hordes have crossed the frontier. Then ensues a picture of the Scorched Earth policy, literally and sadly undertaken by Andrey, who sets fire to 250 acres of ripe wheat, his pride and achievement. Old Zavyalov himself places in position the charges that blow up the foundry to which he had devoted his life, and joins the guerrillas as the Fascists advance. Nor is it without significance that the wife of the hero should be from the East, wounded by a German bullet, and dying in her husband's arms.[4] Afinogenov had never been a deep-thinking dramatist, though he was an able one ; but his loss, killed during an air-raid as he was, deprived the stage of an experienced, if erratic, writer.

Smoke of the Fatherland, by the Tur Brothers and L. Sheinin, we have already mentioned when speaking of the Central Theatre of the Red Army. It carried the theme of the occupied area further. So did *The Immortal*. And with these went a host of others about life behind the Hun lines. One, by Shkvarkin, showed a priest joining a guerrilla detachment after he had seen his son off to the front. (Priests are not celibate in the Orthodox Church, unless they hope to be Bishops.)

The most famous, and one of the very best, was *Partisans in the Steppes of the Ukraine.* This differs from the others as *Invasion* does. It is the work of a man who had already written plays about the same sort of people in peace-time. In Korneichuk's play, in fact, we find old friends out of the previous work, *In the Steppes of the Ukraine.* Chesnok and Galusha, the Montague and Capulet of that country, quarrel, are now firmly united, the former being Manager of the farm, as the end of that play made him, and the latter Deputy-Manager. The rich exuberance of the Ukrainian soil is part of emotional content of this play. Alexander Werth, seeing it in Moscow, called the setting " a trifle muddled " [5] but opulence was the intention, and opulence is not as a rule neat-fingered. The locality is an actor in the play. It is this beloved earth and its bounty of fruit and corn that these simple people by common consent at the opening of the play decide to desert and destroy, rather than yield to the service of the Germans. In a body off they go to the marshes, to hide and fight as guerrillas under Chesnok as leader and Galusha as Second-in-command. Galusha's daughter, Galya, the Juliet of the former romance, is working as a hospital nurse. Gritzko, Chesnok's son, is wounded and in hospital. Alexey and Katarina, who impersonated Budyonny and his adjutant in the former practical joke, are now married ; he is at the front, she still on the farm. She has become even more resourceful and handles grenades with skill.

The second act, of which the willow and lake set, Werth says, was received with applause from the audience, shows in a very human way how careful the ill-trained amateur fighters had to be, despite their knowledge of the local countryside and its ways, and how easily the enthusiasm of a young peasant boy could betray their hide-out. Dutifully he is punished at the request of his great-grandfather, for disobedience. It shows too the very simple souls and feelings of these lovable peasants, young, old, or very old. By a kind of inversion of old Firs in *The Cherry Orchard*, the great-grandfather conceals himself on purpose when the rest leave for another hiding-place, so that he can die, with the skull of an old Cossack for his pillow.

In the third act we meet another acquaintance, Dolgonosik (the name means " Weevil "), the supply agent who nearly sabotaged the prosperity of the farm in peace-time in the previous study. He is now at German H.Q. describing himself as " a poor victim of Bolshevism ". So he is made " Head of the Village ". He betrays Galusha's wife Paraska, but not before she is able to strangle him with her own hands. The partisans arrive too late to save her, though they avenge her death, and will go on doing so. It is the steady, indeflectable revenge of simple people when they are really angered.

The humour, too, is peasant humour, earthy and disconcerting. This is the work of a man who knows and loves his peasantry, through the heart. Werth's reactions to the humour illuminates the social attitude of the author. Two veteran peasants are discussing devils. One tells the other, You can keep devils away by smoking cigarettes wrapped in the writings of Yaroslavsky (the anti-God propagandist of some years back). " The joke ", explains Werth, " cuts both ways. The old peasants are absurd ; but anti-God propaganda is also a bit of a joke." For Werth had bought a copy of the anti-God paper *Bezbozhnik*, and found it full of attacks on the Nazis for their treatment of Catholics and Protestants.[6]

Korneichuk is married to Wanda Wassiliewska, the Polish novelist. After a career as a Deputy to the Supreme Soviet from an unusually early age, he was made one of the Deputy People's Commissars for Foreign Affairs in March 1943, but at his own request was relieved of this post in February the following year. It was generally thought that a big Ukrainian diplomatic post was likely to be his when the war ended.[7] He was then still a very young man.

Konstantin Simonov, author of *Russian People*, also was very young. When only 27 he won a Stalin award in 1942 for his play, *A Fellow from Our Town*. Before that he had been known best as a young poet who had studied Pushkin, Mayakovsky and Kipling. A sturdy young poet, son of a Red Army Commander, working as a turner in a factory. At that time his most famous poem was *The Conqueror*, which described Nikolay Ostrovsky, the Soviet constructional engineer who turned novelist on his sick-bed and in blindness. His first play, by anticipation, showed the psychological effects of war discipline on a not very war-minded young man.[8]

When war came, Simonov went to the front, where he wrote the lyric, *Wait for Me*, the poignancy of which is so great that when the B.B.C. broadcast it as an epilogue to an Alexander Werth dispatch, even in translation, both male reader of the dispatch and female announcer of the broadcast sat staring at each other at the end, unable to speak. This lyric was copied out by hand a thousandfold and sent home by men at the front, so exactly did it catch their feeling ; and its theme is that of his second war play, called by the same title.[9]

MISCELLANEOUS PLAYS DESCRIBED

There are many ways of fighting, and many plays were written about them. Already in March 1942 the Moscow LenSoviet Theatre had staged a play whose title seems to have been *In the Name of Life*, though the *Moscow News* calls it *Victory*. Its action takes place in Occupied France, in a munitions factory working for the Nazis. A new engineer, Dulac, arrives to take charge. He demands the dismissal of Big Pierre Bouvier for sending a consignment of worthless detonators to the front. These detonators bear the works stamp of Marcel Bouvier, leader of the young patriots in the factory ; but Big Pierre takes the blame and is executed by the Gestapo, so that Marcel is preserved to carry on the resistance work. " V " signs appear all over the place ; Dulac begins to understand what he is doing . . . forcing collaboration on workers who will have none of it. Sabotage grows ; and when the curtain falls, a big strike is in progress to delay supplies at a vital point in the Drang Nach Osten. But Dulac is at its head.[10]

In March of the next year, at the Grand Dramatic Theatre in Archangel, appeared a play called *To Those Under Was*, by Yuri Hermann. It describes two merchant ships, one Soviet, one British, in convoy to Britain from a certain North Russian port, and shows the friendship between the Georgian and the English captains, and between the crews. A minor love interest is excited between a British pilot and Irina, first mate of the Soviet ship. An interesting scene takes place when the ships dock at Port of London, and the pilot's aristocratic mother, whose three other sons have been killed, visits the ship and meets Irina. A British captain who was in the audience on one occasion delighted the Russians by saying how perfectly true to life it was.[11]

The defence of Moscow was the theme of Boris Romashov's *The Stars Cannot Fade*. Romashov had written several plays in the 'thirties, his most famous being *Fighters* (1934). His new work was one of the subtler " family plays ". Professor Kovrigin's friends and relations are assembled at his *dacha* near Moscow. One by one they go off to fight. But it is not the dashing major nor the student volunteer who turns out to be heroic, but the gawky, diffident Zhenya Ptashkin, ichthyologist, head over heels in love with his subject, and thrown into confusion by his first air-raid ! This dreamy young man realises what the war is for ; and the discovery galvanises him into an efficient man of action, directing a mind intelligent in other matters toward the tactic of war. One critic, giving the above account in the *Moscow News* added, however, that compared with him the other characters were rather pale and " schematically " drawn.[12]

Boris Lavrenyov, author of *The Break* (1927), wrote *The Oath of Loyalty*, about the siege of Sebastopol and especially the work of the marines there, the " Black Devils ", so much beloved by the Russian people, and so familiar to them in the stories of Leonid Sobolev.

Katayev, mistakenly reported in *Theatre Arts Monthly* to be dead, in confusion with his brother E. P. Katayev (who wrote under the pen-name Evgeny Petrov) came back, as we have seen, with *The Blue Scarf*. Alexander Gladkov's two plays, already described, were followed in 1943 by *A Cruel Romance*, the action of which takes place during a single night in Moscow. Valentin Kaverin, the Leningrad author, had three war plays : *Great Hopes*, accepted by the Maly Theatre on completion in the autumn of 1942, which concerns a battalion of young students, in whose lives the war merely accentuates and protects the things they love, friendship, love, courage, deep questions about life and sex and beauty and virtue. . . . " A person's life ", says the Commander, " during war is worth as much as it can give in the struggle for the happiness of the country. There is no other measure of the value of human life in the war against Fascism." Kaverin wrote the play on the Leningrad Front. The same autumn saw his *House on the Hill*, and the following January, in Molotov, a play called *We Have Changed*. The Tur Brothers and Sheinin in 1934 wrote a work called *The Emergency Law*, in which a serene, undistinguished, simple Soviet father discovers that the happiness caused by his daughter marrying a gifted factory director is being threatened by the wrecking activities of the factory director. It was welcomed as well written and sincere, but somewhat lacking in depth and literary quality.

Another interesting play was by the Left Wing French writer Jean-Richard Bloch, resident in the U.S.S.R. His play, *Toulon*, centred round the family of Admiral Frominoir, a firm supporter of Pétain who, after an inner conflict and bewilderment, gradually comes to realise the betrayal of France and of the French Navy's traditions and finds strength to order the scuttling of the ships in Toulon harbour. France shakes herself free with the victories of the Red Army and the rout of the Axis in North Africa, and the play closes with the Admiral's son in a detachment of franc-tireurs composed of sailors, workers, peasants and students, joining in against the Germans.[13]

POETIC WAR PLAY

March 1943 saw a very delightful play by the poet Victor Gusyev, whose Red Army plays *Glory* and *Friendship* had already won him notice. This was *A Moscow Girl*, produced by Stradomskaya at the Moscow Dramatic, and also at the Nizhny Tagil Theatre. A comedy of a delicious kind, and a tragedy of a heroic one, rolled together The verse is rhymed, but without *enjambement* (not much in favour with Soviet poets) and in conversational style, the rhythm altering in different scenes from iambic to anapæstic and elsewise. It is supple and natural, rising to eloquent passages with metaphor and simile, and punctuated rather after the Rostand manner with gracefully repeated lines to point a situation or raise a laugh.

The Moscow girl is Nastya, a horticulturalist. The action begins in August 1941. She is drafted off to help in the construction of the Moscow fortifications. So is Varya, a young hairdresser's assistant, who finds the work too hard and heavy for her delicate muscles, and tries to desert homeward. Nastya, on the other hand, is a fine Soviet girl, clear thinking, fearless, self-reliant, honest, and more or less heart-whole, much to the disappointment of young Petya, who, convinced she will one day come to love him, seeks her out on his leave, bringing with him a most attractive, vivacious young Georgian lad, Vano. Vano finds, or professes to find, a Georgian legend applicable to almost every event or situation, but I fancy he has made up most of them. He falls in love with Varya, and she with him, slightly under the influence of a game of fortune-telling, which has been floating about in her empty head. Nastya does not fall in love with Petya.

On come the Fascists, and the girls are cut off. Donskoy, an engineer by whom Nastya has been rather intrigued for some time back, is now revealed as a coward if not an actual traitor ; and Petya arrives to look after them till the coming of the Red Army saves the situation. Nastya still does not fall in love with Petya, though she is showing signs. (To write down these very sentences, is like performing a surgical operation on a butterfly with a carving knife.)

In a peasant's hut, where Vano and Petya are quartered, Nastya arrives with some laundry. There also arrives a delightful old actor from the opening scene of the play, now touring the front as a *chtets* in a one-man brigade. He is a real old actor, fond of recalling his great moments, a little vain, with a comic catch-phrase, " As the poet says . . .", but generous and faithful to death ; indeed he dies at the hands of Fascist parachutists, reciting loudly to cover Petya's phoned message to head-quarters. Meanwhile the hut's owner and her daughter have taken refuge in the cellar ; but the Fascists before they are themselves caught by the detachment Petya has phoned for, shoot the daughter dead and wound the mother. When the old woman comes up from the cellar, she is half-crazed and mistakes Nastya for her own daughter, a relationship Nastya promises to make a true one.

In comfortable, and not very much war-touched homes, it might be easy to call this scene melodramatic. To a Russian it is nothing of the kind. Worse derangements than this were to them frequent medical facts from worse causes. At the same time, it is true that this incident does not develop from any logical premiss in the plot, but is incidental. Indeed, all this play is more like a ballad than a drama. But it is a very delightful ballad.

Petya has been very seriously wounded in both legs and is bleeding to death. Nastya now realises she does love him, and characteristically expresses it not in speech but in act, facing a blizzard and the unknown dangers of a war countryside to get medical aid.

In the fifth scene we are back in Moscow, in a barber's shop, where Vano, having grown several weeks' beard for the purpose, comes to be

shaved by Varya.   With adroit tricks he works his way up the queue out
of his turn and takes the astonished Varya off to be married.

Meanwhile Petya, who has answered none of Nastya's letters, arrives,
a cripple with no legs, to say good-bye to her, because now there is no
chance of her ever loving him, except out of pity.   She alters his ideas on
this point, and off they too go to the Registry, only to find it on the point
of closing.   Nastya alters the ideas of the Registry woman on this point
(a tiny part, but like most in this play, carefully considered and having a
depth and life-background of its own) and the comedy would seem to be
complete.   So it is.   But one scene remains.   A short one.   A dusky
spring night in the forest outside Moscow.   Moonlight.   A few traces of
snow still about.   Nearly dawn.   Whispers and lantern light greet Nastya,
who gives and is given sign and countersign.   Life goes on, and the life of
Moscow needs her.   She would not live happily (the comedy could not
satisfy) with her husband until, as he used to say in the first act, " six o'clock
in the evening after the war ".   She has joined the guerrillas.

Here too we see the chaotic coincidences of war, with the principals
appearing where they are wanted ; but the reduction in the number of
characters has given the dramatist a chance to develop them, especially
Nastya, whose gradation from aversion to a very deep and fruitful love
is beautifully and dramatically created.

This is one of the few Soviet plays in which principal women's parts
outnumber principal men's.   Soviet theatre companies have a proportion
of men over women varying from four or five to three.   Soviet dramatists
are following tradition in keeping their women less numerous than their
male characters.

Two other plays of Gusyev's appeared during 1943, *Your Love*, a one-act
play, and *Song of Three Rivers*, to which we have already referred.   Unhappily, it was announced in January 1944 that Victor Gusyev had died
suddenly, at the age of 35 ; and the Soviet Union had lost a popular poet,
a charming playwright, a good social worker and a well-known broadcaster.[14]

Trenyov did little during the first part of the war, but completed *Seeing
It Through* in the late summer of 1943.   This concerned a group of intellectuals, inventors, scientists, and such, engaged on important research
near the frontier in 1941.   The problem of the group was, whether to
abandon their work now near completion, or risk their valuable lives by
staying on.   They chose the latter ; and succeeded in saving their work
as well, but only at the cost of a young scientist's life.[15]

HISTORICAL PLAYS

A marked feature of Soviet dramaturgy during the war was the plethora
of historical plays.   At the head of the authors of these was the now very

large figure of Alexey Tolstoy, whose canvasses had grown bigger and bigger until they began to match the epic measurements of his kinsman the great Leo. On the day war broke out he wrote the last sentence in the third and last volume of his prose trilogy on the war of 1914-18 and the Civil Wars : *The Road to Calvary*, which he had started in 1919. This title is not a strictly accurate rendering of the Russian, and is not altogether satisfactory. The Russian means The Visit to Purgatory, and is understood by all Soviet readers to refer to the legend of the Virgin Mary visiting Purgatory and praying her father to mitigate the suffering she has seen there. It is a humanisation of the Mosaic element in Christianity.

Alexey Tolstoy had also by that time completed two parts of another historical trilogy, *Peter the Great*. In October 1941 he embarked on another huge work, this time a dramatic trilogy, about Ivan the Dread, of which the Maly of Moscow was rehearsing in 1943 the first part : *The Eagle and His Mate*. This shows Ivan in his youth, his marriage to a Circassian princess, and the murder of the Queen by conspirators. The second part, *The Difficult Years*, was given to the Moscow Art Theatre in summer 1943, for Popov to produce, with Hmelyov as Ivan. In this are shown Ivan's struggles with the Boyars in his attempt to unite his kingdom, and the battle of Pskov against the Teutonic Knights who had overrun Livonia ; Ivan laid the foundation on which Peter the Great built.

Simultaneously Tolstoy was engaged on a libretto for an opera about the Decembrists.[16]

Apart from the historical plays we have mentioned in other chapters, here are some of the figures and events staged during the war :

Prince Vladimir (tenth and eleventh century) the old Pagan who became Christian and thereby made Russia a member of the European comity of nations. Alexander of the Neva, Dmitry of the Don, both Russian warriors and statesmen. Suvorov in a new play. Pushkin in two plays. Ivan the Dread in another play, by Smolin. Denis Davydov, hussar, poet and guer-rilla of the Napoleonic wars, on whose character Leo Tolstoy founded Vaska Denissov in *War and Peace*. Nadyezhda Durova ; General Brussilov ; the first Siege of Sevastopol (in the Crimean War) ; the Siege of Leyden.

The last two are interesting for special reasons. *Vice-Admiral Kornilov*, the play about the Crimean War, was written by Sergeyev-Tsensky, who was a man of letters even before the Bolshevik Revolution. He won a Stalin award for this play, the action of which takes place aboard the battle-ship " The Three Saints " at anchor in Sevastopol Bay. A ball is being held on deck in honour of the Tsarevich's birthday, but it breaks up on receipt of news that several hundred French and British ships have been sighted making for the Crimea. The Commander-in-chief, Menshikov, does not trust the people of Russia, and to avoid a sea battle orders half the Black Sea

Fleet to be scuttled and issue to be joined on land.   Vice-Admiral Kornilov
does trust his men, because he knows them ; he pleads with Menshikov
and tears up the list of doomed ships.   For this Menshikov threatens to
remove him from his command, and as such a sentence would mean
Kornilov would no longer be able to defend his country, he sadly agrees
to conform to his instructions.   Miserably the sailors descend to the ships'
bottoms and set about their job.   They are baffled and dispirited.   In rushes
the water, extinguishing the candles they work by.   Shore batteries open
fire to complete the sinking.

Then Kornilov calls the defenders together, including workers that
have been freed from a military prison for the purpose.   Impassionedly
he urges them to fight, and if he himself should ever give an order to retreat,
he now directs them in advance to thrust a bayonet through him.   The
battle begins and Kornilov is mortally wounded ; but before he dies he
hears that victory is with the Russians, and the play ends with his dying
injunction to carry on till all is complete.

The Siege of Leyden is a four-act adventure of Tyl Eulenspiegel, his last
adventure, for he is reported dead in the finale.   The hero, however, is
rather the people of Leyden, pictured in so lively a way that it is sometimes
hard to remember we are not in some twentieth-century town being besieged by Nazis.   There are the same Fifth-columnists, the same sturdy
citizens, the same privations.   And the same resistance, awaiting help
that never seems to come.   There are a romantic love interest, several
songs, and a kind of framework consisting of an *entr'acte* before Act IV,
in which " dozens, hundreds, of voices " speak the feelings of the rest of
the Netherlands, watching Leyden as the Soviet Union watched Sevastopol
or Stalingrad, and an overture, in which after tolling bells and trumpets,
an unidentified voice sets the scene, somewhat *pomposo* and unhistorically,
in " page one thousand five hundred and seventy-four of the book ' A History
of the Planet Entitled " Earth " ' ".   Perhaps some such station-identifica-
tion was needed, for the general atmosphere is not really Netherland, and
certainly not sixteenth century.   But neither is it Russian.   One is tempted
to believe that the author, Isidor Shtok, is a German refugee.

But it is a lively play and the people are all convincingly drawn, even
if their romantic side is a little exaggerated.   It is certainly stage-worthy.
I do not think it was ever accepted for Moscow production.   The Rostov
" Gorky " Theatre did it in 1943.   But as a second-class play (it falls into
that category from its lack of intellectual judgment) it is valuable to compare it with sentimental historical plays of the *Richard of Bordeaux* type,
where important historical figures are played with as if they were just
ordinary people, their personal feelings surrounded in a historical glamour,
like a costume, but their historical significance disregarded.   We may

take this play as no better and no worse than the ordinary run of second-class historical plays in the Soviet theatre. It is much to be preferred to our own second-class historical plays, since it deals only with ordinary people at a historical moment, whose personal feelings are important in themselves.[17]

CRITICISMS OF HISTORICAL PLAYS

Exception was taken to *The Siege of Leyden* on the ground of its inadequacy. But some of this seems to have been undeserved. Press and professional criticism is very rigorous in the Soviet theatre ; perhaps too rigorous. At a conference of producers, playwrights and historians, convened by the V.T.O. in July 1943 at the Moscow Actors' Club, although everyone agreed that there had been a satisfactory increase in historical plays, and indeed that there never had been a time when the historico-patriotic play had occupied so much space in the general repertoire, never-theless there was too much simplification of person and fact in them. Some historians complained that dramatists for conciseness telescoped two figures into one, keeping the name of one of them, and this gave the synthetic stage person much greater power and position than the original historical person ever had, thus falsifying the situation.

Other complaints included the fault of reading more recent history into the remote past. Pankratova, for instance, a Corresponding Member of the Academy of Sciences, and a Stalin Laureate for history, said that Boyajiyev, in writing a play about Prince Vladimir of Kiev, had made him a unifier of the Russian state . . . which was true of later Tsars, but not of Vladimir. Boyajiyev, who was at the conference, argued in his own defence, but after a heated discussion admitted that Pankratova had con-vinced him, and remodelled his play. Krzhizhanovsky, a playwright and critic, gave witty examples of authors not seeing the full sweep of history and splitting it up into watertight compartments, like the portions for the day appointed by the history master when he was a boy. And so on.

If we compare some of the plays with this criticism, the conclusion to be drawn is not that there is a low standard in historical plays written, but that the standard required is very high indeed. No historical play will pass muster, though it may get produced, unless it contains a full intellectual comment as well as being actable and atmospheric.[18]

CRITICISM OF WAR PLAYS

Much the same might be inferred from a bigger Conference on War Plays, held in May 1943 under the direct auspices of the Committee for Art Affairs, from which we will be quoting in the next chapter the re-markable words of a playwright who had escaped from the Gestapo and

joined the guerrillas. " We are not doing full justice to our great epoch ",
cried the authors ; " Give us plays that will really let us stir our audiences
and inspire them ", cried the producers, " with hatred and love ! " This
was not only a Russian conference ; delegates came from all over the
Union.

An improvement in character-drawing was noted . . . this applies to
the rank-and-file, not the Big Three. There was less schematic segregation
into good people and bad people. Full length and one-act plays had been
written in almost all the languages of the Union. The contemporary
writer had first place in most theatre repertoires. (Out of 6,000 first-nights,
4,000 had been of plays by Soviet dramatists.) The Big Three were an
honour to Russia. In short, the report was a good one, and the general
condition seemed healthy.

Yet there was a common weakness diagnosed too. A lack of knowledge of life, leading to a primitive choice of theme, a lack of genuine
thought, too many dramatic clichés, too much sentimentality, especially
in comedies. The Press was deluged with analyses and charges.

Vasily Sahnovsky, of the Moscow Art Theatre, who is certainly entitled to respect, put the theatre's case. Actors were not being given meaty
fare that they could get their teeth into. Only scenes of war and invasion,
such as could be read in any magazine article. They wanted to be real
people on the stage, with something to say to the real people in their
audiences. Drawing pictures or making photo-montage was the job of
the novelist not the playwright. He must have a closer relation with the
stage.

Nikolay Petrov of Leningrad went further. The dramatist had deserted
the stage ; and thanks to that, initiative in the theatre was dropping,
responsibility was declining. Petrov looked back to Trenyov, brought
to the stage by the Maly, Ivanov by the Moscow Art Theatre, Leonov by
the Vahtangov, Simonov by the LenKom . . . each carrying life to the
other partner, and both alive. But to-day, he wrote, it was hard to say
which was the more remote from life, theatre or playwright.

Surely an over-statement, this. But one which did no harm. Serafima
Birman, more quietly and concretely, like the artist she is, raised specific
points. The playwrights were talented people, but they did not write from
any irresistible urge to write ; theirs were true hearts, but not burning
ones. They had the wish to fly ; but where were the " long-distance
pilots " ? All round them were Soviet women, heroic and steadfast ; but
from her point of view, where were the women's parts in the plays ? Many
were the Soviet girl characters ; many were the Soviet grannies ; but the
middle-aged Soviet women, the backbone of the body, were quite ignored.
Even those below 30 and over 60 tended to be typed " from Moscow ",

or " from the woods ", as you might say, " with character, without character ".   So that though they might behave like women, they did not behave like themselves.   And, finally, whatever the talents of the authors, the plays themselves were tame.

Hrapchenko, in his opening speech at the conference, said that historical plays tended to be " anecdotal " and to rely on outward effects.   He realised that, in general, Soviet dramatists did appreciate their position and were acquiring greater depth and social breadth.   But a whole battery of first-class producers rose to attack the material they were being given.   " The playwright must have *wings* "—Ohlopkov's stirring phrase rang through the conference.   Diky said the majority of plays of the day were old-fashioned.   Rather surprisingly he stated, " We have forgotten plays of the ' Agit ' kind, poster plays, publicist plays, which in these days could be shown with extraordinary effect ".   Popov said that the most approachable direction was " hyperbole ".   But the audience was already used to gigantic heroism in its own life.   Stalingrad and Leningrad were epics they had themselves written.   They must be treated homœopathically, by small doses, that is, by deep, accurate, truthful detail, revealing the truth of life by the truth of art.

Popov's attitude to playwrights has always been consistent.   He has always supported new ones, and was largely responsible for the good start made by the young Pogodin.   Popov wrote, in a little monograph published in 1938, that when he first read Pogodin's *Poem About an Axe* he didn't think he wanted to produce it, until he came to the night-scene in the smithy (when the inventor of the blade is trying to recapture his own formula).   This, he said, convinced him that he must do the play.   It showed " the blood of the play ", a thing that had grown together, not been carpentered.   All plays must have this " blood ", this organic, hot, pulsing, substantial flow, or they cannot be worth doing.

Most of those present found the cause of the weakness in a too passive reflection of actuality ; though opinions differed about the cure.   Difficulty of communications was recognised as one contributory cause, and the evacuation of the theatres as another.

But in winding up, Hrapchenko made it clear that the Committee for Art Affairs had no intention of dictating themes or methods.   As Leonov had said, the dramatist writes when he feels he has to, when he can't contain the words any longer.   And the Soviet dramatist must find his own way to express the Soviet hero, that is, the Soviet people.

In an article in Литература и искусство next month, amplifying his views, Hrapchenko praised *Invasion*, *General Brusilov*, *Twelve Months*, *A Far Country*, and *Peter Krymov* as being a fund of good plays, and then criticised several which had the theatre itself for their theme.   He mentioned Faiko's *Actress*, in which the heroine after many doubts and difficulties involving Red Army men and commanders, comes to the conclusion that operetta is necessary for the winning of the war. And that is about all that happens. There were also many bad plays about old professors : *Professor Mamontov*, *The Beauty Secret*, *Moscow Nights*. In the old days the professor had to face up to things like the October Revolution, Mechanisation, Physical Culture ; in these plays it was the same professor, facing up to war, not from any truth to life but from what had become a literary convention. The problems he had to decide on the stage were not the problems of real professors in life.

Other war plays, he complained, were out of date in their form : *The Battalion Goes West*, *My Friend the Colonel*, *The House on the Hill*, *Smoke of the Fatherland*. In these cases the playwright was representing only the outward course of existence, not the human struggle, not the people. Sometimes the theme would be a fine one, family duty, for example ; but ruined by cheap tricks, as in Rzheshevsky's *Always With Us*, in which a wounded officer comes home and finds his wife in another man's arms ; whereupon he feebly goes away again without bothering to find out that the man is his wife's brother whom he has never met. Hrapchenko also dismissed *The Blue Scarf* as irresponsible ; and he reiterated the old complaint about the lack of good plays showing life in the heroic rear.

PLAYS ABOUT THE REAR

This theme had been explored by Yuri Kalashnikov some three months earlier. He analysed them into plays about factories, in which there was no correlation of hero to theme ; and those about collective farms, which were mostly comedies. Kozakov's *Darya*, for instance, attempted to show an innovator in Soviet affairs widening new vistas in the world of gunnery, and the responsibility of every Soviet citizen for the success of the war.

Darya Shmeleva is the director of an ordnance factory evacuated from Leningrad. Prisheltsev is the inventor of a design for an entirely new type of gun. Their lives are complicated by the unhappy course of true love. Before the war Darya had left her husband, a Leningrad actor. She is now sorry for this rupture, for which there were no real causes, and consequently cannot respond to Prisheltsev. Nor does she at first believe in his invention, which he has called the " Darya " and has begun to build a trial specimen at a neighbouring works. Both are lonely people, and indeed Kalashnikov says this loneliness and personal frustration decide the fate of nearly all the characters in the play.

There is no development in the true love theme. " The less they unfold the fundamental conflict, the duller sounds the chief theme about the heroes of the toiling rear, and the paler gets the central figure."

If we compare this play with *Depth Prospecting*, where the personal relationships are bound up both mentally and dramatically with the work to be done, we see what Kalashnikov is driving at.

Dynasty, he says, is about a torpedo-boat builder who alone of his family stays in the rear with his small son and an old nurse. Overcome by this isolation, he spends all his efforts on getting to the front, and is about to succeed in doing so only at the end of the play. At this point, however, he changes his mind, and giving a bronze statuette for salvage in a " heroic " gesture, asserts his determination to stay on his proper job.

Other plays held inadequate for the theme of the heroic rear were : *Deep in the Rear*, *Ivan and Marya*, and *People of the Urals*. The same criticism applied to *Soldiers' Wives*, *When Girls are Left Alone*, and *Islanders*, which were all about collective farms in war-time, and in trying to be light comedies were little better than vaudevilles.

Kalashnikov summed up : " Peter Krymov must be allowed in our plays to work and produce, surrounded by his companions and friends. Then methods of melodrama and vaudeville will become anathema in our plays. Then the bitterness and suffering of their heroes will acquire the necessary virility and seriousness. Then the dead will cease to mask the living."

Conclusion

Maxwell Anderson's war play, *The Eve of St. Mark*, was regarded in the U.S.A. as a deep and moving study of an American boy and girl involved in war. What would have been the Soviet audience's reaction to it was given by a correspondent of Литература и искусство writing from the U.S.A. " The hero inadequately grasps the basic questions for which the war is being waged. He does not arrive at any understanding of what the struggle means, either from the angle of his immediate interests, or of those of mankind in general. Anderson gives us no material for the audience to draw any conclusions from."

That lack of knowledge and understanding itself may be true of American boys and girls. But the author had not said so ; he had not located their going into death and bereavement without knowing why. Consequently, by Soviet standards his play was false. It contained no comment, and to a Soviet audience would be meaningless. In *The Eve of St. Mark*, suffering just happens to people. In the Soviet war it has a purpose and a value.

Such purpose and value has been brought to the audience in most of the plays we have mentioned. It is not to be doubted that the above outspoken analyses of the shortcomings of the rest will bear fruit. It may be that the problem will be solved by an extension of the process already begun, in which, for example, Vishnevsky the naval officer writes plays

17

about the Navy, air aces like Vodopyanov, if necessary in collaboration, write about the air ; it may be that this is a new thing in playwriting . . . a group play written about a group by a member of a group, because life has made their own personal lives depend upon communal forces and directions, conditioning their lives, which can be expressed only through those individual lives and in no other general, or mystical way. Time will show. I have transcribed the criticisms at length, not to show the weakness of Soviet dramaturgy (about which much ill-informed and hasty remarks have been made in our countries) but to show its strength already.[19]

The making of a play demands of an author more than technical ability, more than a knowledge of people, more even than the gift of creating living figures. It demands also judgment. Even when all the other factors are present, when a play is dramatic, the people in it real, the plot true, yet the play may still be false. By the relationship to each other in which the author has placed his figures he must, whether he wishes or not, imply the relationship of those figures to the society from which he has drawn their component parts, outside the theatre. Unless he has studied that society with deep thought, knowledge and speculation, all his sympathy and skill will not save him. The great dramatists of the world are great by reason of this intellectual range, coupled to human imagination and technical skill. In the world there are hundreds, perhaps thousands, of plays which can be called good, because they have an intellectual range, though not perhaps of the widest, the Shakespeare measure. It is a credit to the Soviet theatre, in which are to be included audience, critics and theatre folk, that so high a standard is demanded of the playwright ; and that so many, not so few, attain it.

Part Five

NEW WORLD

CHAPTER XII

WAR AND PEACE

THE IMPORTANCE OF THE PAST

In the first two parts of this book we have seen some of the people and events that made Russian theatre history in the nineteenth century. It did not claim to be exhaustive, but was merely representative. In the third and fourth parts we have seen some of the Soviet theatres and their movements and functions in war. This also was not comprehensive but indicative. There still remains a third aspect of the march across the Volga, created by these two views. There could have been no such war-time function of the theatres if it had not been for the work of the nineteenth-century tradition of pioneering realism the like of which we have been studying ; just as the advance of the nineteenth century Russian theatre could have come to nothing without the social and artistic changes we have traced. Socialist realism, following world events years before the second world war began, kindled in the Soviet Republics an intense and virile national pride toward the first Socialist land and toward the historical past out of which it had come. It would have failed in its purpose if it had looked at and shown the war as anything other than a tremendous, intense, cruel, sacrificial incident in the life of Socialism.

All through that war the more alert of theatre people, especially authors, producers, managers, and those committees of all crafts which decided policy, kept the past and the future of Socialism running before them like a wire along which the war was travelling. The war was not allowed to interfere with those celebrations, for instance, of important dates in cultural or theatrical history, which reminded theatre-goers of their debts to the great names of the past. Let us consider some of these in war-time.

STAGE ANNIVERSARY CELEBRATIONS

The fame of Yermolova dominated the later nineteenth-century Russian stage as, with very great differences in style, that of Siddons dominated

the early years of ours.   The 15th of July 1943 was the ninetieth anniversary
of Yermolova's birth.   When she died, on the 18th of March 1928, she was
75.   On the evening of 11th March 1943, the V.T.O. organised a Memorial
meeting at which spoke Yablochkina, Mihail Lenin, Shchepkina-Kupernik
(the sixty-nine-year-old poetess who had translated thirteen plays of
Shakespeare, besides works of her friend Rostand, Molière, Hugo, Goldoni,
Gozzi, Calderon, Lope de Vega, Tirso de Molino, and Fletcher).   Pupils,
friends and admirers of Yermolova recalled her art, her humanity, her
progressive ideas about the world.   They were in the Large Hall of the
V.T.O. in Moscow.   On the presidium sat senior actors and actresses of
the Maly and the Art Theatre, representatives of the chief theatrical institutions of the Union, delegates from the Union of Soviet Writers,
Moscow University, the Conservatoire, the Literary Museum, and sundry
theatrical studios and schools.   In the chair, and opening the meeting,
was Yablochkina, senior actress of the Russian stage, and president of the
V.T.O.   Speeches were made in honour of the Maly theatre, showing
thus that Yermolova's work lived on ; papers were read about Yermolova
as a national Russian actress, as a heroic actress, as a figure in the development of the Maly's constitution.   In the foyers of the Maly and of the
House of the Actor exhibitions were opened, of photographs, portraits,
drawings and other objects and books that illustrated her life or work.
That night the Filial of the Maly gave a special performance of *Guilty Though
Guiltless*.

In this way not only was the effect of Yermolova on the present displayed
in the middle of Socialism's fight for existence, but the whole life and
personality of a great actress was relit, from the cold January night in 1870
when the prompter's daughter from the ballet school electrified the bored
theatre public as Emilia Galeotti and wrote in her diary when she got home
to the wafer-baker's house where she lived : " I am happy—no ! I'm
the happiest person in the world " ; right on to the series of great heroic
figures she impersonated at the height of her skill and experience, Schiller's
Joan of Arc and Mary Stuart, Lope de Vega's Laurencia, Phèdre, Sappho,
Lady Macbeth, and Katarina in *The Storm*.   But there is a difference between
fame and greatness.   Like many good actresses Yermolova had to learn
after she became famous.   The pretty girl with the quaver in her voice and
her intensely emotional silences could create truthful figures by nature.
But only experience of life, and an evaluation of that experience, could
make those figures valuable.   It is by her values, her understanding of
the life of her times, that you judge the greatness of any actress.

Because Yermolova developed such an understanding and could express
it with a technique and talent rare in the world, she may rightly be called
great.   " Her tragic parts were a call to arms in the reactionary night of

the 'eighties and 'nineties." In relighting her art and rewarming her life
with love and appreciation, the meetings in 1943 relit also the history of
the Russian stage and rewarmed that of the Russian people, of whom she
had always felt herself to be a part.[1]

The 23rd of August 1943 was the eightieth anniversary of the death of
Shchepkin. Again the Maly and the V.T.O. collaborated, calling a
memorial congress with papers read on the Shchepkin tradition in the
Maly Theatre to-day, on his times, and similar themes. There was a
gathering of the classes and students of the Maly School called by his name.
The Maly foyer held an exhibition in which could be seen a playbill of
Shchepkin's first appearance on the 23rd of November 1822, the Service List
of the Imperial Theatres containing his name, a copybook page on which he
wrote his first strokes when learning, adult, to write, his first letter to Gogol,
the Governor of Poltava's signature witnessing his manumission from
slavery. A week later in the Chaikovsky Hall (where all the big Moscow
Symphony Concerts are given) the Maly Theatre got up an evening of excerpts from parts he created in *Revizor*, *Woe from Wit*, *Krechinsky's Wedding*
and other plays, rendered by the cream of Maly talent, Ostuzhev, Sadovsky,
Yakovlev, Mihail Lenin, Ilyinsky, Svetlovidov and their colleagues.[2]

Nearer to their own times was Stanislavsky, whose memory was kept
alive in two ways. First, there is scarcely an actor in the Soviet Union
that has not benefited by the study of Stanislavsky's principles and by
practising them, and scarcely a theatre some prominent member of whose
personnel had not been affected directly or indirectly by the Moscow Art
Theatre, if they had not actually been pupils. Beside names like Vahtangov,
Granovsky, N. M. Tsereteli, Alice Koonen, Meierhold (and his pupil
Ohlopkov), Smyshlayev, even Baliev of the *Chauve Souris* and Mihail
Chehov (both of whom ran away), there stand the new leaders of to-day,
Popov, B. Zon, Bersenyev, Serafima Birman, Zavadsky, Sudakov, Sush-
kevich and many more. To these and others like them a celebration of
Stanislavsky was a re-living of their most precious and impressionable
years, a confirmation of their own methods. For those less fortunate it
was a call to arms, to closer observation, greater sincerity, wider knowledge
of human nature, less guff and more gumption.

On the 7th of August 1943 Stanislavsky had been dead five years. The
street in which he lived, Leontevsky Pereulok, had been renamed Stanislavsky Street, and a plaque placed on No. 6 reading : " Here lived, worked
and on the 7th of August died People's Artist of the Soviet Union Konstantin
Sergeyevich Stanislavsky, founder of the Moscow Art Theatre."

To the theatre specialist that house has a very warm significance. Not
only is it where Stanislavsky lived ; not only is it popularly supposed to
be the original from which Griboyedov took his idea of the setting for

Woe from Wit, when it belonged to the Napoleonic War general Yermolov. But also he can go in and see where and how Stanislavsky lived. He can consult the Curator or the Advisory Bureau if he wants any special detail of Stanislavsky's ideas. For since February 1944 it has been a "House Museum" of the Moscow Art Theatre.

But that plaque is not only of significance for the theatre specialist. It is not like another plaque, fixed over Baker Street Underground Station in London, discovered with astonishment by a few observant eyes from a bus top at a bus stop. Stanislavsky has a deep meaning to almost every passer-by. To the Muscovite he is not just an actor-chap about whom those who know make a bit of a fuss nor is he "a bit high-brow; I like Musicals best". He has made a difference to their personal lives, has opened them up, has widened and deepened their experience of people, and of the world.

So it is no surprise that the tributes should be many. In an article addressed to her fellow-workers in the theatre, Serafima Birman wrote: "We need him. To-day. Here. At this moment. In the days of the decisive struggle against vile and cruel enemies, Stanislavsky is necessary to us theatre people, as necessary as breathing. As a compass. As a father's advice. And if you succeed in doing something better in art, something more humane and useful in life, you are bringing Stanislavsky back to life."

For the essence of Stanislavsky's theory of acting was not that it could be applied to all actors, but that it must be worked out for himself by each actor. Each generation, each separate person, coming into the theatre, brings new problems from life, for life is continually changing. The theatre, therefore, must be continually changing, progressing. The theatre and the actor must combine hard work with inspiration, as Kedrov wrote on the same occasion.

The celebrations were the second method of keeping Stanislavsky's memory alive; they were organised by the Moscow Art Theatre, the Stanislavsky-Nemirovich-Danchenko Musical Theatre, the Stanislavsky Studio and the Moscow State Philharmonic jointly. Excerpts were given of plays and operas he had taken immediate share in: *The Burning Heart*, *Dead Souls*, *Tartuffe*, *Eugene Onyegin*, *The Tsar's Bride*, *The Barber of Seville*, *Madame Butterfly*. Pavel Markov, member and librarian of the Moscow Art Theatre and theatrical historian, spoke of him. That was in the Chaikovsky Hall. A second Evening was held the following day by actors, actresses and singers from the Moscow Art and Musical Theatres.

On the 17th of September these two institutions joined the actors' and producers' department of the V.T.O. in a further celebration at the House of the Actor. This was attended by producers, critics, artists, members of theatre and art schools, and young actors from all over Moscow. Again on this occasion Yablochkina opened the proceedings. Hrapchenko located Stanislavsky in theatre history and called attention to his boldness of innovation and experiment. People's Artist Sahnovsky read a paper on Stanislavsky and his system ; Chehov's widow, Olga Knipper, recalled personal memories ; Honoured Artist Orlov read some unpublished material about him from the theatre archives. Other papers were read on Stanislavsky the Artist, Stanislavsky in Russian Classics, Stanislavsky's Theatre and the Opera.[3]

The life and work of the Moscow Art Theatre itself was the theme of the 27th of October 1943, when it had been in existence forty-five years. The opening play, *Tsar Fyodor Ioannich*, was revived for the purpose. It had never wholly left the repertoire, having reached 789 performances, in which Moskvin had played the Tsar about 600 times. But I. Kruti says that the settings had not been for some time exactly as they were in 1898. The Moscow Art Theatre is no museum of theatrical antiquity, and some of the complex archæological scenery, for Shuisky's Banquet, and other scenes, had been simplified and cleaned of unnecessary detail, if not cut entire. In the course of its forty-five years, the theatre had given 18,000 performances, including a thousand of *The Lower Depths* alone.[4]

Ostrovsky's anniversaries were not forgotten. On the 12th of April 1943 he would have been 120 ; and in honour of his birthday the Maly gave special Jubilee performances of *Truth is Good* on the 11th and 12th, and of *Mudrets* on the 13th. On the birthday itself the Small Stage was used for an additional performance of *Guilty Though Guiltless* During the day there were discussions of his work by the theatre collective and its students ; short introductory talks by Professors Filippov and Durylin ; an Exhibition in the foyer ; and excerpts from the plays broadcast by Maly actors.

The 10th of November 1943 was the 125th anniversary of Turgenyev's birth, and under the V.T.O. his connection with the theatre was remembered. L. Grossmann read a paper on his skill as a playwright, V. Filippov on his debt to Savina, L. Freidkin on the productions the Moscow Art Theatre had done of his plays.[5]

HONOURS TO THE PRESENT

But it is the living as well as the dead whom such celebrations also honour, and a careful account of years of service are kept, so that jubilees can be the milestones they should be. Such was a great day at the Maly in September 1943, when two actresses, an actor and a member of the stage staff all celebrated fifty years' work there. The actresses were Ryzhova, People's Artist of the Soviet Union and Stalin Laureate, and Turchaninova,

People's Artist of the Russian Republic and Stalin Laureate. People's Artist of the Republic Yakovlev was the actor, and the back-stage artist was A. Anarhov, a joiner in the properties workshop. His colleagues presented the last with flowers and a valuable gift, and the management gave him an extra two months' pay.

Naturally, and without any " class " distinctions, but with the homage due to artistic skill and profundity, the players came in for more ostentatious marks of esteem. Both these actresses belonged to what might be called " Maly families ". And though, as we have seen, in Tsarist days such snobbery was founded on financial bases, in that to be the child of a Maly person meant the possibility of a safe career, the advent of Socialism meant that the base for such snobbery had been removed, like the social conditions that encouraged it. But that does not mean that there is no pride and loyalty in the Maly. Doubtless most members of it are convinced, as they should be, that theirs is the best theatre in the country. Naturally, therefore, they are proud of long connections with the theatre. Ryzhova was the daughter of Muzil and grand-daughter of Burozdina (on the Maly stage in 1849). She had been congratulated by the great Tolstoy himself for her Akulina in *The Power of Darkness*. She had played through almost the entire Ostrovsky repertoire. But she had also played in Soviet works, up to the part of the old nurse in *Invasion*.

Turchaninova's father had worked all his life at the Maly, first as an attendant, later in the Box Office. She had played over 300 parts in Ostrovsky, Tolstoy, Gogol, Beaumarchais, and finally as Madame Grandet in a stage version of Balzac's novel. But her war-work, notwithstanding her age, included tours with front-line brigades.

Yakovlev had created more than 350 characters on the Maly stage, including many in Soviet plays, especially Yelisatov in *Lyubov Yarovaya*.

All three were guests of honour at a reception in the Green Room before the evening performance, at which presentations of flowers, gifts, and illuminated addresses were made.

Again, when members of any theatre collective are honoured by the conferring of titles like People's Artist, or by the award of Stalin Prizes, this is made an event for the whole theatre. As it should be, indeed ; for a fine actor on the Soviet stage cannot give a fine performance if his colleagues do not support him. His credit is therefore partly theirs. When six members of the Maly company received Stalin awards in 1943 for outstanding achievements in 1942 (notably for *Invasion*), letters and congratulations flowed, and at a very happy gathering after rehearsal a message of greetings was sent to Stalin himself. The same thing happened at the Moscow Art Theatre, and others.

In November 1943 the whole Soviet theatre celebrated the seventy-fifth birthday of Yablochkina. In fifty-seven years of stage work and fifty-five at the Maly, she had been best liked for her Ophelia, Cordelia, and Desdemona, and in *An Ideal Husband* and *The Silver Box*. During the war she had organised two theatre brigades herself, one for the Army, one for the Navy. Her roots went far back. An ancestor, Ivan Yablochkin, was Court Violinist to Catharine the Second, her father had been actor and stage director at the Alexandrinsky. To her celebration came representatives of the opera, the Moscow Art, Kamerny and other theatres, and the V.T.O., and the president of the Committee for Art Affairs (this made it a major event) ; all made very genuine speeches of admiration for Yablochkina's work both in the past, but relevantly, too, at the present day.

Nor were such events limited to the metropolitan theatres. In the Jewish settlement of Biro-Bijan in the Far East, the " Kaganovich " Theatre was holding in March 1943 the twenty-fifth anniversary of their oldest actor Aarons (twenty-five years from his first appearance on the stage, that is). Moscow theatres held festivities for Lesya Ukrainka at the Moscow Conservatoire, under the Committee for Art Affairs on 1st August 1943. The Ukrainian writer Yuri Smolich opened, and was followed by Pavel Antokolsky, with Margarita Aliger, Mikola Bazhan, N. Braun and M. Isakovsky reading translations into Russian of poems by that remarkable poetess, and the evening ended with a concert.[6]

PUBLIC EVENTS

Public events like the October Revolution Jubilee and the Red Army Jubilee were held by all theatres. The former occurred when most of the principal metropolitan theatres were in evacuation. None the less each marked the day by some special performance. The Theatre of the Revolution gave the recently finished new Pogodin, *Moscow Nights;* the Maly praised Leningrad youth in *Great Hopes; Russian People* was chosen by many, including the Moscow Art Theatre ; the Partisans were the theme for the Mossoviet. National theatres also marked the day. Several of the Azerbaijanian collectives created special " patronage " tours of garrisons and hospitals with *Lyonushka*, for example, at the Baku Russian Theatre. The " Stalin " Theatre of Ashkhabad gave a special performance of a native work ; the Russian "Pushkin" Theatre in the same city did *Invasion*. The " Karl Marx " at Saratov did *The Ferryboat Girl*. At the front some hundred brigades had programmes for the occasion, including three circus troupes, the Vahtangov in Ostrovsky and *Masquerade* excerpts, and the Maly and Moscow Art Theatre brigades.

Quite a valuable cross-section of war-time life was thus depicted, a suitable reflection on such a day. And various nationalities were tied together by Russian producers working for non-Russians. For example, Zahava at Omsk, Zavadsky at Alma-Ata, Bersenyev at Stalinabad. Authors, too, hastened to finish works for it: Gusyev's *Moscow Girl*, Virta's *My Friend the Colonel*. Zoshchenko and Shkvarkin were busy for the Moscow and Leningrad Comedy Theatres.

For the Red Army Jubilee in 1943 theatrical activities took many forms, but most practically, special "patronage" (= free) performances for Red Army men and commanders, or in equipping specially good front-line brigades, joined by as many stars as possible. The Moscow Theatre of Varieties sent out an all-star unit. And all theatres, whether they sent brigades or not, gave Red Army men free admittance from the 20th to the 25th of February.

Sketch-writers had special pieces ready for these special brigades, on the themes of Leningrad, Stalingrad, Odessa or Sevastopol (our enthusiasm for the first two has made us forget the two last. Not so the Russians.) And most brigades bore letters from stars who for any reason could not themselves go to the front, such as Kachalov, Olga Knipper, Moskvin and Tarasova.

Another important anniversary in 1943 was that of the founding of the Lenin Young Communist League. You will perhaps have read of the heroic work, the refusal to speak under extreme and revolting torture, the skill and initiative shown by members of this high-principled and spontaneous organisation. The celebration of its founding naturally centred upon the LenKom Theatre, named in its honour, when this was created ten years previously from the amateur Theatre of Working Youth. Among the many new plays given their first performance here, which included Margarita Aliger's study of Zoya Kosmodemyanskaya, the outstanding one was *The Youth of Our Fathers*, written for this very occasion. And another event in celebration of the peace-time work of the Komsomols was Giasintova's radio production, with a cast from this theatre, of Brushtein's radio play on *How the Steel was Tempered*, Nikolay Ostrovsky's novel. At an evening concert, also, both senior and junior members of the company performed. So vital an element in war and in resistance was of much greater interest and importance than it would sound to a foreigner, and in fact a competition was held for the best play on the subject. Ten writers competed. In 1944 the LenKom accepted one by Bergholtz and Makagonenko about the Young Communists' work in the factories of Leningrad. It was called *They Lived in Leningrad*.[7]

CREATIVE EVENINGS

On ordinary days the " creative evening " continued, and will continue, I imagine, as long as there are Russian mouths to open and Russian ears to hear. Many were held at the House of the Actor, others at the Central House of Art Workers. Honoured Artist Polova, for example, gave an evening in which she performed scenes from Ostrovsky, Trenyov, and a play called *Little Uncle's Dream*, with the assistance of five actors, a pianist and a violin. It was a contribution to the thinned theatrical life of war-time Moscow. In October, when the theatres were back, there came to the House of the Actor Moskvin, Knipper and Kachalov, who after a word or two from Markov gave excerpts from *The Living Corpse*, *The Village Stepanchikovo*, *Ivanov*, *A Month in the Country*, and Tolstoy's novel, *Resurrection*. In the winter of that year Serafima Birman gave a creative evening, during which she spoke of her own theatrical development, and did scenes from Gorky and Tolstoy, supported by other members of the LenKom Theatre and some soloists from the Bolshoy Opera.

Nor did the *chtetsy* suffer by the war. On the contrary, their old-time tradition developed during it. The one-man recitations came to have a theme and a unity beyond that of the solo performer. Yahontov took passages from Mamin the Siberian, Bazhov, and other Urals writers and called the programme " Ural ". Anton Schwartz put together passages of Turgenyev, Blok, Simonov, Tihonov, A. Prokofiev and Tolstoy under the title " The Face of Russia ". Zhuravlev did a " Pushkin " evening. Emmanuel Kaminka dug into American literature, and followed that up with an Evening of English Literature, in which Dickens shared the chief place with a writer reported as V. Jacobs, whom I take to be the late W.W. of the bar and the barge.[8]

APPEALS

The part played by theatres in war-time cannot be wholly limited to the cultural. In the Soviet Union, as in most other belligerent countries, appeals were made to individuals to invest their savings in War Loan, and thus take part of the cost of war off the common funds. The theatres found it their duty to help with this campaign. Most of them held meetings and collected big sums from their members. At the LenKom after a rehearsal V. Solovyov took the chair and Bersenyev made the appeal, as a result of which the 178 members of the theatre collective contributed the total of 93,190 roubles. At the Moscow Art Theatre R. 350,000 was raised, including 25,000 each from Knipper, Kachalov, Moskvin and Tarhanov.[9] That artists should have so much money in a Socialist state is not to be astonished at. Artists are valued in money by their value to art, and not by their ability to benefit, directly or otherwise, the interests or prestige of Big Business. Many composers, like Shostakovich, Katz, Dzerzhinsky, Tihon Hrennikov, Kabalyevsky, Myaskovsky, Hachaturyan, contributed sums ranging from R. 15,000 (the first two) to R. 5,000.

Shebalin found R. 32,000. Solomon Mihoels stated, when in London, that the difference between the salary of a star artist in the theatre and that of an untrained beginner, might be as great as between 6,000 roubles a month and 300. Dramatic authors are paid at a rate of 1 per cent. of the takings for each act at each performance ; or by a lump sum as large, maybe, as R. 20,000, in which case the play belongs to the theatre. If a theatre has commissioned a play, it must pay the purchase price whether the final script is accepted for performance or not. So that authors, too, are paid by the value of their work.

Other objects of generosity included the orphans of Red Army men —not a charity, because the State looked after them—but to give them extras and a sense that people were grateful to their fathers. To this fund artists gave pictures and theatres whole performances.

HERITAGE

But in the main the function of theatres in the war was not only to inspire love of country or to explain the behaviour of human beings, as we have seen it doing in foregoing chapters, it was also to preserve the culture of a progressive civilisation through all the difficulties and personal anxieties of war. To help audiences to attend, to preserve their cultural treasures and the appreciation of them, the Committee for Art Affairs ruled in February 1943 that all Moscow theatres must give at least one matinee every fortnight on a working day. This is an example of the control that this Committee does have. The control functions at the point where theatre practice and public policy coincide.[10]

SHAKESPEARE

War tends to disrupt channels of communication even for ideas. For this reason the Shakespeare anniversaries held by the V.T.O. were of special value to theatre workers, and were held regularly through the war years though it was difficult for producers to attend. In addition, it was decided to hold monthly Shakespeare evenings, with the possibility of opening up an All-Union Shakespeare Society. In the meantime, Morozov's Shakespeare Department of the V.T.O. carried on its arduous and admirable tasks.

In 1942 the celebrations opened on the 20th of April at the Actors' Club with an abridged version of *Othello*, still by far the most popular of Shakespeare's plays. This was directed by a new and young producer, Fotiev. On the 21st, lectures dealt with " Shakespeare and Fascism ", with Humanism as Fascism's natural antithesis (Morozov), " Shakespeare and War " (Timofei Rokotov), and " English Folk Humour in the Works of Shakespeare " (A. Stein).   Radlov came over from Leningrad to discuss the staging of Shakespeare in Elizabethan playhouses.

The Fifth of these annual Shakespeare Conferences was held in Moscow in 1943.   Professor Morozov read a paper showing the great increase in the poet's popularity in war-time by quoting new translations into the Kirghiz, Tatar, Chuvash and Tajik languages.   Vladimir Uzin dealt with *The Tempest*, maintaining that in this work, so far from abandoning the struggle and retiring into a quiet dream, in fact Shakespeare remained as much the humanist, the fighter and the champion as he had been in former works.   Other themes were the ties between Elizabethan and Soviet cultures (O. Litovsky), the Hamlet of the Armenian actor Vagarsh Vagar-shyan (A. Asharuni) and Soviet Actors in Shakespeare generally (Boris Alpers).

This brings us to the question of translation.   We have already heard of Shchepkina-Kupernik.   But besides her work and the very sensitive renderings of Shakespeare's sonnets and lyrics by Samuil Marshak, Russia is wonderfully well served, according to Professor Morozov, by Boris Pasternak.   Of his *Hamlet* Morozov writes :   " When, two years ago, *Hamlet* appeared in Pasternak's translation, many of those who knew the English text of the tragedy were astonished at the unexpected likeness of the translation to the original.   It was not the likeness of a copy literally reproducing outward details, but rather an inner likeness, the likeness of a portrait.   Where we had been acquainted merely with names, there appeared living people.   They breathe, move, speak. . . .   We have never been so intimately acquainted with the real persons (лица) of great tragedy. We had not even known that it was possible to be so closely acquainted with them.   Therein lay the unexpectedness of our impression."

This was partly done, it would seem, through Pasternak's own ability to create people by the correct choice of words.   It was partly due also, as Morozov explains, to his capturing the speech peculiarities of each character, notwithstanding the partial archaicism of the language.

Romeo and Juliet, his next undertaking, was a general advance, but Morozov felt a slight lack of Renaissance lustre in the love scenes . . . his comparison is with the warm light of a picture of the Netherlands School ; but the character parts were notably successful.   With *Antony and Cleo-patra* Pasternak rose to great heights, says this scholar, of both strength and simplicity in the verse and of human understanding in the psychology. Cleopatra was made a woman of tremendous contradictory, yet sincere feeling in the Russian as in the original.   The atmosphere was kept.

Human translation like these was in direct contrast to most of those hitherto available in Russian ;   and it was not achieved without risk.   Morozov locates the risk in over-conversationalising lines which

Shakespeare wrote as aphorisms. But the main thing was that the translation, like the original, had a stage life of its own. "It is more than a translation. It is poet meeting poet."

Incidentally, Morozov at a V.T.O. evening at which Pasternak was reading his translation, stated that this was the fourteenth translation of *Antony and Cleopatra* into Russian since the first one in 1842.

Other languages have similar poets emulating Pasternak's method. At the end of 1942 the Jewish poet Galkin, author of the play, *The Hand of Justice*, had just finished *Richard III*. Indeed, it has been said that Shakespeare translations were a "priority job". The Ukrainian Steshenko put *Twelfth Night* into his native tongue, and the Tajik poet Lahuti was working on *Romeo and Juliet*, even though both would rather have been doing original work for the theatre. To help such national poets, Professor Morozov himself was working on a word-for-word prose version which could be used as either prop or brake when getting the meaning of *Othello*.

Any new turn in British or American Shakespeare scholarship was followed and eagerly discussed in the Soviet Union by writers, critics and producers. A paper read by Professor de Sala Pinto of Nottingham to the Royal Society of Literature in 1943, concerning the importance of Shakespeare in the struggle against Fascism, attracted much attention in many parts of the Union. But ordinary interest is taken from day to day in the twice-monthly discussions of the Shakespeare Study section of the V.T.O.[11]

The tremendous popularity of the English poet in the U.S.S.R. is now widely known in Britain. War-time extensions of that have been shown in various parts of this book. But there was one eloquent testimony to his value for Soviet theatre-goers which ought to be quoted here. It came from a conference of producers, critics and playwrights, held in the Moscow House of the Actor in the summer of 1943. Several hundred attended. The theme was the best way to depict on the stage the war spirit of the Soviet nations. One playwright had been taken prisoner by the Germans, and had been handed over to the Gestapo, but he managed to escape, and fought for ten months with the guerrillas. He may be presumed, therefore, not to be inclined to romantic over-statement in the matter of war spirit. These were his words : " Life gives us Shakespearean images and Shakespearean situations ; but we haven't yet succeeded in giving fit artistic expression to them ".

Further evidence lies in a study of Shakespeare being included in the Red Air Force curriculum ; and from the report of an actor playing Iago to a front-line audience, who heard some of his listeners muttering " Fascist ! " at the character he was impersonating.

In short, the attitude of the Soviet audience is realistic. Starting from respect for the poet as a professional man of the theatre, who did not waste his own time, and as a man of genius who did his creative work for a purpose, they accept his creations as living people in actual situations of time and space, invented in detail but corresponding to actuality. Those people and those situations, by the selection of their creator out of the life he knew, necessarily make a comment on that life ; and inasmuch as the past must have a bearing on the present, they find that comment valuable to them, and they respond to the whole experience alertly and whole-mindedly.

MIHOELS' STUDY OF KING LEAR

The actors approach him with a similar respect, war or no war. Solomon Mihoels has told his own approach to *King Lear* at the Moscow State Jewish Theatre. This dates back to six years before the war, but it ought to be put on record. The production took fifteen months to prepare ; but of course work was not confined during that time to this one production. When the part was suggested to him, he spent three months studying it to see if it came within his capacity. He decided he was not fit to play it, being quite unable to see the motive for Lear's initial act in dividing up his kingdom. Most monarchs in history spent all their waking hours trying to unite theirs or at least to prevent disunity. He found himself, he said, on the point of agreeing with Leo Tolstoy, who hinted that either Shakespeare was drunk when he wrote the play, or he intended Lear to be.

Being baffled like this distressed him, however, though he could find no answer. Then one day, while studying the play afresh, he was struck by the second line Lear utters in Act I, scene i :

" Meantime we shall express our darker purpose."

This plainly referred to the division of the kingdom ; but why " darker " ? The word implies disapproval. That argues a divided mind . . . and in a flash Mihoels had an explanation, helped, as he wittily added, by Tolstoy himself. For was not Lear, in renouncing for a tired old man's whim all that his life had stood for, doing just what Tolstoy himself at the end of his life tried to do in his so-called " flight " and was only prevented by death from doing it ? Lear was betraying himself and his responsibilities, denying life and his duties to it as a man and a king for a childish reassurance. And life, as its habit is, through those nearest to him, wreaked a terrible revenge.

In this attitude to the part Mihoels accepted it, and his rendering has been world-famous ever since.

ORIGINAL HAY IN THE CHERRY ORCHARD

It goes without saying that the same spirit prevailed toward the Russians' own men of genius. It is significant that Chehov's *Cherry Orchard*, first produced in the Moscow Art Theatre on the 17th of January 1904, reached, on the 28th of June 1943, its 900th performance, with Olga Knipper still playing the part she created thirty-nine years previously, Madame Ranyevskaya. Kachalov, who had played Trofimov, now took Gayev ; and Semyonov-Pishchik, first taken by Medvedyev, was now Kedrov. But it was the same production.

I saw this myself in days of peace at the Moscow Art Theatre. It had the original atmosphere, I imagine. It had also the original minor mistakes, as that the moon was still reflected in the second act pond, although it was shining on the actors' faces who were turned away from the pond. The scenery was the same ; now a little fusty, perhaps. But all these things were swallowed up in the spirit of the performance.

How powerful, yet quiet, yet sensitive this performance was, I was well able to judge, having the year before produced it myself in my own repertory company, on one week's rehearsal ! It seemed that I had missed every point, and turned a confidence into a public dissertation. Each motion by anyone on this stage, despite the tatty pine-tree cut-cloth which flapped in the stage draught, was real. Real, in the sense that this seemed no mimed execution, but something that had been going on for years, decades, in some actual existence parallel to ours. When Firs changed the handkerchief in Gayev's pocket, when Trofimov had enough of the manner of a public speaker to make you want to pull his leg for it afterward (and the " afterward " would be somewhere in your life and his), when the shutters were closed on the old house by a peasant, from outside, then you were aware, not only of these acts by themselves, but of the further acts they lead to, off the stage. A life that would go on for ever, were it not for the orchard being sold. And how, I wondered, sitting in my post-revolutionary seat, would this proletarian audience react to the sentimental effect of that sale ? What could it mean to them that this silly old woman and her charming, ineffectual and cracked family, with its entire worthless entourage, had to let their old home be turned into a building estate ? How could it mean anything ? Wouldn't they be bursting their sides with laughing at the pitiable scenes at the end ?

I might have guessed their reaction from Firs's line about the " Great Misfortune ", meaning thereby the emancipation of the serfs. In Britain this had been taken as a comic line—silly, doddering old peasant manservant, not to know that it was a great progressive measure, not a misfortune ! But in Russia !—I think I will never forget the silence that followed the line as Tarhanov spoke it. It was heart-breaking. Not a soul in the audience but knew what the liberation resulted in. In that silence a proletarian audience was offering homage, almost expiation, to the sufferings of their fathers. A whole people breathing a single thought : solemn beyond description.

And then the last farewell. Out, slowly, goes Madame Ranyevskaya. Her brother is about to follow. The quiet of the audience is the quiet of people who can bear no more. There is nothing more to bear. The last word has been said. But Gayev returns, sits on a trunk, and cries. Cries, deliberately, like a child, working himself up, playing a tune with his sobs, like a mournful cadenza on a violin. He really cries ; from the stalls you can see the tears on his grimacing face. But that is easy enough, inevitable, in Chehov. After a very long time, perhaps a minute and a half, maybe two minutes, he gets up and goes out. There is not a dry eye in the house. And somehow it is all bound up with the utter sunshine-joyousness of Anyusha as she went out to a new and a better world. That promise, which was fulfilled to the present audience through her generation up to the war, goes on through the war, through tears and farewells, to the sunshine beyond it. Only this time, there will be no Firs to be left to rot, forgotten. That is how war and peace are telescoped.

Neglect of the Russian Classics : Its Cure

Russian classics have not all the same appeal ; and no theatre collective wants to be doing them all the time. But it was felt at one point during the war that too many theatres were neglecting them in favour of Soviet war plays and Shakespeare. The Committee for Art Affairs studied the situation in the autumn of 1943. It was decided that the V.T.O. should " inspect " the treatment of Russian classics in the provincial theatres and bring the two productions it considered the best to Moscow in the course of 1944. In the meantime it should stimulate interest among theatre committees by a series of exhibitions.

This gave a chance for a competition ; and nothing is more readily welcomed in the Soviet Union in any sphere of life, art, science, industry, or local government. Indeed, in this respect, something of the atmosphere of a Renaissance painter's or Mediæval craftsman's workshop is to be found.

Already by December 1943 reports came in from Kazan, Gorky, Chelyabinsk and other towns in Russia, of special productions of Turgenyev, Gogol, Gorky and Ostrovsky. The Ryazan Regional turned its mind to *The Zykovs*. Gorky was very popular everywhere. Five of his plays were reported in November. Two Chehovs, *Three Sisters* and *Uncle Vanya*, ran them close. Central theatres, too, were stimulated to a revived interest. The newly formed Moscow Studio Theatre under Gotovtsev did a play by Gorky, *Eccentrics*, which had not been produced

18

since its first showing at Peterburg in 1910. It was not a very good play, almost a "water-colour after Chehov", but its revival was interesting. The non-Russian theatres in Kazan, Ossetia, the Udmurt Autonomous Region, did Ostrovsky in translation, although the stimulus was intended for Russian audiences. In Russia alone 574 new productions of national classics were announced, and an unexpected side, healthy in its implication of independence of any prevailing fashion or dictation, was shown in the appearance of works neglected for years, like *A Handsome Man* by Ostrovsky, Gorky's *Eccentrics*, Chaikovsky's opera, *The Maid of Orleans*, to be seen in Siberia or the Volga area. Two Rahmaninov operas were also revived. The Ostrovsky comedy, *Balzaminov's Wedding*, which a large number of Soviet citizens had never seen, was chosen at Sverdlovsk and considered to preserve a perfect blend of ridicule and pathos in its treatment of the central figure.

There were more than 200 provincial productions examined. These had had the assistance of lectures by local professors and *literati*. Local broadcasting stations joined in the campaign by bringing scenes from the Russian masters to the microphone. There were exhibitions in the foyers. Consultants were called in from the metropolitan theatres. Popov went to Ivanovo to advise on Gorky and Griboyedov. Yuon designed sets for *Revizor* at Kazan, and Diky went there to produce *A Burning Heart*.

It was noticed that the best productions came from those areas where first-class metropolitan theatres had been in evacuation—notably *The Girl Without a Dowry* at Saratov, and *Uncle Vanya* at Sverdlovsk, the former under Yefremov, the latter under Brille. But much pleasure was caused by old Gaibedurov in Gorky's study of the old man who believes he has a right to make others suffer because he himself is suffering.

But here again we must be on our guard. The motive was not to exalt national "culture" Hitler-wise at the expense of foreign countries, whether in the Soviet Union or outside it. It was the complement to the international policy which we must now consider. For if it is right for the first Socialist state in the world to encourage the national cultures of all the nations within it, it is also right for the Russians in that union to protect and develop their own past as proudly and faithfully as Uzbeks, Georgians or Tatars. The general direction in the Soviet Union of late months was toward a greater and greater independence of the non-Russian nationalities. It would not be fair to Russia that she should fall behind her sister-republics by any sentimental or shallow internationalism.

Internationalism is only valuable when it springs from a sturdy and healthy nationalism. But that does not mean that the campaign for the Russian classics can be taken as evidence for a slackening of Socialist ideals.

On the contrary, it is evidence of greater confidence and experience in Socialism.

And can there be such a thing as Soviet—as opposed to a Soviet nation's—art ? [12]

INTERNATIONAL CULTURAL RELATIONS : SPAIN

People in the Soviet Union have in their arts a more continuous historical outlook than is the case with us ; and certainly their culture is less obstructed by frontier and language from the other European cultures akin to theirs. In our countries, for example, apart from an occasional revival of a light comedy by Benavente or a sentimental one by Martinez Sierra or the Quinteros, we feel no special kinship with the drama of Spain, classical or pre-war. The Russian theatre, on the other hand, was made familiar with Calderon and Lope de Vega in the second half of the nineteenth century, largely through the enthusiasm of the long-haired stragglebearded prophetic-looking sage and conversationalist Sergey Alexeyevich Yuryev, who translated *Himself His Own Sentinel*, *Fuente Ovejuna* and *The Star of Seville;* and saw to it that the Maly, of which he was the mentor, put them on. " Translated " is perhaps not the right word. Believing in the theatre as an " international cathedral " and, as one of the least subjective arts, as fulfilling to a high measure the mission of all arts, which was, in his opinion, to annul the self-love implicit in all personal feeling, and to replace it with artistic, ideal, communal feeling, arousing nobility in the soul, he re-wrote the plays he translated, and expressed foreign poets' thoughts in terms applicable to Russian society. For he considered that art so orientated should depict intelligibly the life of its own time and place. The same principle underlay his versions of *Macbeth*, *Antony and Cleopatra*, *King Lear*, *The Winter's Tale*, and the *Dream*.

Those who know *Fuente Ovejuna*, with its dynamic Laurencia and its strong protest against tyranny, will not be surprised to hear that its first performance, for Yermolova's benefit, was also its last for a very, very long time. It was so violently successful with the Moscow audience that it had to be withdrawn forthwith, to the great indignation of old Yuryev, indignation being in this case both subjective and ethical.[13]

After the Revolution, however, and specially during the Spanish War, this play found a permanent place in the repertoire, not only of Russian theatres, but all through the nationalities. Others that joined it were *A Dog in the Manger*, *Don Quixote*, *The Star of Seville* and a gipsy story by Cervantes. By seeing these early manifestations of art in a land that has much in common with their own, including a strong peasantry with natural benevolence and an equally strong monarchy with the exact opposite, both surviving into modern times from the feudal past, the Russian and other Soviet peoples acquired a new outlook on that past, and on their present, and, by implication, on their future too ; and their minds were thus prepared for post-war citizenship of the new Europe. Respecting other nations' cultures and self-development.

ITALY

It was the same with Italian plays.   Goldoni necessarily led.   Theatrically speaking, he replaced the stuffed dolls of the Italian Renaissance theatre with human beings.   These earned their living in ways Maxim Gorky would have found the normal as he tramped through Siberia.   But they were full-blooded, and neither the namby-pamby " Gods " of an alien belief, nor the cerebral puzzles of a Pirandello, who was quite unknown in war-time Russia.

FRANCE

With French plays the Soviet theatre far outran our own, finding true dramatic, rich human, and wide social material in playwrights like Scribe and Sardou, whom the most advanced and récherché of our Repertory Theatres have tended to class as mere money-makers of a bye-gone day. They found more historical accuracy in Rostand than we do. On the 2nd of December 1943, the twenty-fifth anniversary of his death, a discussion was held in the Moscow House of the Actor, on the LenKom's production of *Cyrano de Bergerac*.   It is to be noted that it was this theatre's production that was selected and not the Vahtangov's. Professor Morozov opened the discussion by saying that " In the twilight of modern France, the personality of Cyrano is like the cry of the rebellious Gallic cock saluting the dawn.   No wonder French patriots gave the name ' Cyrano ' to one of their underground newspapers published in Occupied France ! "   This aspect was brought out by the LenKom production, by Bersenyev as Cyrano and Serafima Birman as producer.   But, as in all Soviet discussions, dissenting voices were heard.   One critic said that Vladimir Solovyov's translation lacked warmth compared with Shchepkina-Kupernik's, and another found that Bersenyev's Cyrano was more like a brother than a lover !

Soviet theatres can stage Balzac, too, when ours cannot. And how far back their interest in French culture goes ! The Leningrad Ballet, when in Molotov town, revived an old French ballet, *Vain Precaution*, first staged at Bordeaux in 1776.[14] Something of the old gay French laughter from the days of LeSage and from the Comedy of Masks in eighteenth-century Paris, was found by Morozov in the Moscow Operetta Theatre's production of Kalman's *Maritza*.[15] And the more serious side of French literature was brought in with adaptations from Zola and Maupassant. True, much of the traditional French people's spirit was no longer found on its stage, expressly. After the last war, the French theatre having exploited the Chehovian eloquent pause to the point where it became a mannerism, tended to be stodgy or to lose itself in psychological or pathological depths. But that was never the art of the people, only the triviality of the class that had time and money for art. It is the French people that the Soviet audience is interested in, and when the French people is itself again, there is no doubt in Soviet minds that their culture will assert itself in a true, self-determined, national form. When this war is over, that nation will best understand and value the French nation, which is familiar with the roots of its culture.

Meantime Molière, with his superb logic and wit and exquisite skill in words and people, delighted the war-time Soviet audience, even if he did write primarily for a limited class.

Germany

Schiller is the only German dramatist whose works were performed to any extent during the war. The Soviet theatre had little liking for the massive humourless Hebbel, nor the alienist subtleties of Wedekind. The expressionists, Kaiser, Toller and so on, appealed only for a short time and to a limited minority of theatre people. But Schiller, the champion of human rights and decencies against self-appointed or intriguing and inhuman officials and tyrants, served the Soviet citizen as a reminder that there were comrades in Germany who had suffered as much as Ferdinand or Karl Moor, and were outlaws, in concentration camps not picturesque woods. Schiller, with his historical outlook, historically interpreted, established the good that German letters had given the world in the pre-Hitler past, and created a base on which to treat Germany, not by any gentle, gentlemanly or compromise peace, but with the masses liberated and chastened in a wickedly misguided country.

Scandinavia

Ibsen was not so popular as he had been before the war. *The Doll's House* was the only play of his of which I have noted a new production during the war. It is possible that his absorption with the problems of the middle class was not as important to the Soviet theatre as other European dramatists ; but that is a personal guess, and I know no real explanation.

U.S.A. and Britain

On the other hand there were frequent productions of plays out of the English language. Several American film scenarios were turned into stage plays ; Clifford Odets' *Music at Night* was much discussed in book form ; his anti-Fascist play, *The Eleventh Hour*, had a success in the Urals in 1943. Kachalov, when preparing *chteniye* for brigade work, chose passages from Hemingway's *Fifth Column*, and said he regarded him and Richard Aldington as the most distinguished writers of the day in the English language. Toward the end of 1942 the V.T.O. organised a conference on American and British plays with an exhibition of Russian productions past and present, thus centralising the available information.[16]

In this connection, we cannot ignore the remarkable popularity of *Rose Marie*, the musical comedy, which was first produced by the Moscow Operetta Theatre in 1928 and reached its 1,000th performance in 1942, rivalling Kalman's *Silva*, and the most popular of the many Soviet musical comedies, Alexandrov's Russian *Wedding at Malinovka*, or *The Girl from Barcelona*, about a Spanish girl who finds a second home in the U.S.S.R.[17]

Of contemporary British and American playwrights Shaw heads the list, seventeen of his plays having been done since the Revolution, and some many times. During the war *Pygmalion* seems to have been the favourite, which we have seen on the lists of Tajik, Moscow, Urals and other theatres. At the Maly it was not considered necessary to do this as a costume play, but in the period of the 'thirties. This to us may sound strange ; but maybe we have not changed to others as greatly as we think we have to ourselves. In a way it was the correction of a tendency to play it as a farce, as was almost done in some theatres. Mark Bryansky, attending a rehearsal, picked up a book lying on a small table at the approach to the stalls. It was a handbook on English dialects, which had been studied by the translator Nina Konstantinova and by the actress playing Eliza Doolittle. All the workers in the theatre were invited to attend a lecture by Morozov on " Bernard Shaw and the struggle against Hitlerism ". For the play was being done, explained the producer Zubov, " not only as a lively, witty comedy, but also as a serious play, based on knowledge of the English intelligentsia and representatives of various strata of the London population ".

The changes in London society which to us may seem so big since 1915, are perhaps imperceptible except to ourselves. The middle classes may not be quite so outrageously stuffy nowadays in public ; but there are still plenty of families to-day who would behave in the same manner when it came to marriage. At least there is this stratum in English, and in British, society ; and that fact runs out at both ends of the war emergency.

Other angles on English life were found in Priestley (during the war *They Came to a City* followed the list of those done in peace-time) and by a publication of *Poison Pen*, though I do not know where, if anywhere, this last was put on the stage.

The classics of British drama were staged more than once in many cases : *She Stoops to Conquer*, *The School for Scandal*, *The Duenna*, Wilde,

Ben Jonson, Fletcher, and *Oliver Twist*. A number of Elizabethan plays were translated in 1943 and performed to Red Army Units.[18]

The translation of such Western European plays was scrutinised by the Shakespeare and Western Dramaturgy Department of the V.T.O., which in July 1943 held yet another conference, at which reports were made on the standards attained in rendering French, Spanish, Italian and English classics. When things are undertaken in the Soviet Union, because they are considered worth undertaking, there is always an interest to know whether the undertaking was successful or not, and what people thought of it. Anyone who has been in touch with Soviet artists will confirm that, like all creators, they enjoy being praised, but they respect only praise that is reasoned, and expect judgment to be genuine.

INTERNATIONAL DEMOCRACY

Cultural ties with other countries were tightened in the summer of 1942 by an exhibition of the theatres of all the Slavonic Peoples, got up by the V.T.O. and the All-Slav Committee. Photos of famous productions at Warsaw, Prague, Belgrade, Brno, Zagreb, Kiev, Minsk, and Moscow lined the walls, with books and documents in show cases giving the histories of the countries in which these cities lie. Karel Capek, Wladislaw Wanchura, Mickiewicz, and Wysznianski were celebrated. Balakirev's first production of Glinka's *Russlan and Lyudmilla* in Prague in 1867 was an interesting exhibit. Another Slavonic tie was the election of Yuzhin-Sumbatov of the Maly as Honorary Producer to the Serbian Royal Theatre. At the time of this exhibition *Oleko Dundich* had aroused interest in things Serbian.

The democratic peoples generally were explained to Russian culture at a Moscow congress of producers, playwrights and critics in August 1942, mainly devoted to Britain and America, the themes being translations and their effects, the influence of the Moscow Art Theatre on British and American theatres, Shaw, Priestley, Odets, Lilian Helman, Cronin, Ernest Hemingway. There was a big exhibition of photographs, sketches and designs.[19]

Knowledge so acquired was passed on by performance. And in this way the theatre fulfilled a deep and wide war-time function. People coming into it from battle, from air-raids, from industrial fatigue ; on leave or holiday ; people with a divine curiosity to know more, feel more, experience more than any single life suffices to give them, people, too, with a wish merely to be entertained and forget their anxieties and losses ; all kinds of people, coming into such shows, not only lived the revived past of their own land, they travelled abroad, relived the past there, felt how it resembled or differed from their own. In this way, amused, thrilled, intrigued, studying, their own lives developed. They became more fully aware of their place in history and the way the world was going. "A spectator " (recalls Serafima Birman in her little book on acting) " comes to the theatre not only to hear the text of an author, but also to see the depths of the hearts of the figures on the stage." [20] Perhaps that is truer of women than of men, but it is true of both. You cannot understand the world of any time unless you understand the people of that world ; and the human mind is keen to know how it has come to stand where it does, as can be seen in all folk-lore, in the popular sayings of all peoples that are not wholly crushed.

But the war could not be a mere incident in the U.S.S.R. It was a crisis of events to which the world had been working since 1918, and long earlier. Its successful end would mean a new step in human relations. The Soviet Government's policy was toward that step. So that a mere continuum of international culture was not enough. There must be interpretation. " Realism "—again Serafima Birman—" reflects life ; Socialist realism re-forms it."

For unless you are understanding the implications of past and present, you are failing in your duty to the future, your own, your children's, your world's. In the Soviet Union the future belongs to the people, and they know their duty to it.

We must now consider that future.

CHAPTER XIII

THE YOUNG

THEATRE YOUTH AND WAR SERVICE

Enough has been said in preceding chapters to make plain how important the theatre was held to be as a war-time activity. It would have been contradictory if such organisms had been kept going only by their pre-war staff, entry to the profession closed, and all young people diverted to other war work. In the Soviet Union contradictions are avoided ; and organisms are regarded as what they are, organic, and therefore liable to decay if not allowed to develop.

Vladimirsky, chief of the Education Board on the Committee for Art Affairs, reported in October 1942, " Scores of young actors have graduated this year at theatre schools and studios of the Soviet Union ". Including operatic and ballet schools, the figure for 1942 was nearly 3,000. That for 1943 was 1,000. Not content with graduating, some of them set up on their own. Students from the Moscow City Theatrical School formed a new studio with *Twelfth Night* as its first public production in 1942, followed by *Mudrets, the Break* (a pre-war play by Lavrenyov), and in 1943 *Russian People*. They took the Bauman Theatre premises and appeared three times a week. Their producer's name was Titushin.

Twenty others from the " Lunacharsky " State Institute, working at that time in Saratov, formed a brigade in the same year to tour Red Army Units. Eight groups materialised in this way from among young beginners in 1942.[1]

Evacuation did not interrupt the curriculum for such students. The " Shchepkin " School, attached to the Maly, accompanied its motherorganism to the Urals in 1941, and next spring twenty young actors were launched on their professional careers, one in particular being the envy of the rest, Konstantin Nazarov, who was given a good part in the Maly production of *The Front*. Others got minor parts ; yet others joined local theatres which had no pool of their own to draw recruits from ; and a few went with the front line brigades. A group touring the Urals showed prowess with pitchfork and binder as well as buskin.

Such students found their war work not in something to which their talents must be sacrificed, but in getting those talents fighting fit. Some of them even fretted at delay in getting to the front ; like a group of senior students who sent in a petition that a brigade should be formed at once to tour front and rear.

But this did not mean that no young players went into the fighting forces. Many did. Vera Pashennaya, Maly actress, teacher, and herself a graduate of the " Shchepkin " School, stated that several of her favourite pupils had been killed on active service. One of the most promising, Boris Gusyev, graduated just before the war. He volunteered immediately it broke out, and in October 1943 was a Lieutenant. Vladimir Golovin had got further, having been taken into the Maly company ; he too volunteered, and fought at Stalingrad. But because of his exceptional gifts as an actor, and the Maly being in urgent need of him to play a lead in *Invasion*, his Army Command at their request released him from further military service, and he returned to the company. It cannot be doubted that experience at the front, from the inside, improved his performances in military parts.

Others had been wounded, though not incapacitated from stage work. Vera Pashennaya mentions a Tatar lad who on convalescence returned to his Third Year at the school.[2]

TRAINING THEATRE YOUTH

When the Moscow State Jewish Theatre was evacuated to Tashkent, some of the senior pupils were taken into the company, but others went to the theatre in the Jewish Autonomous Republic of Biro-Bijan in the Far East. The future of the national theatres was carefully nursed in this way by those looking after cultural matters from the administrational angle. The " Lunacharsky " Institute in 1942 was training a number of Latvian refugees, for instance, who had stage ambitions and abilities, so that when Latvia was liberated her culture would revive as quickly as possible. Artistic education in this institution was a high and wide one, for in addition to theatrical history, technical stage training, and other specialised subjects, courses were given in the history of music, painting and literature.

The period of training varied with different schools, but the most usual was two years. The " Azizbekov " Theatre in Baku gave a two-year course to students, which included the same wide artistic range, and subjects like movement, speech, gesture, plastic, on its technical side. After graduation the students formed junior companies to tour the neighbourhood. Similar two-year courses were given at studio-schools organised in Habarovsk, Sverdlovsk, Saratov, Vladivostok, and the Harkov Russian Theatre in evacuation at Ulan-Ude. The Leningrad " Gorky " Theatre gave its two-year students a chance to act on the main stage after their first year. For twenty-five vacancies in 1943, there were 250 entrants.

Co-operation was evident in this too. A combined studio was organised in Novosibirsk for the pupils of the Leningrad " Pushkin ", the Leningrad Theatre Institute and the Moscow Theatre Institute, all in the neighbourhood. And similar studios were opened about the same time, autumn 1943, by the LenKom (with Bersenyev at its head) and by the Red Torch Theatre.[3] An advertisement in the Moscow Press in November 1943 announcing the existence of a MosSoviet Theatre studio under Zavadsky is interesting for the following credentials required of candidates for admission :—

(1) Birth certificate,
(2) Education certificate,
(3) Medical papers,
(4) Three photographs,
(5) Papers showing candidate's position in regard to war service.

Such a studio-school had long been the dream of Nemirovich-Danchenko for the Moscow Art Theatre. Plans were being made for it at the time he died. There were to be two groups, senior and junior. As the juniors joined the seniors, they would come more and more fully into the backstage atmosphere of the theatre, equipping themselves thus not only technically and temperamentally, but also in the mind, ethically, to take their personal places in the progress of the theatre and become true " M.X.A.T.-ists ".

The scheme was realised and the school opened in August 1943, the " advanced " group being formed from pupils out of other dramatic schools. Sahnovsky was made head of it. The course was fixed at three years.

Both this Moscow Art Theatre School and the Maly " Shchepkin " were formally recognised as institutes of higher education. Each had a mandate to undertake scientific research in theatre matters as well as theatre training. But their work was also practical. The kind of plays on which it was done may be exampled by the latter's billing in 1943 : *The Cherry Orchard*, *The Storm*, *The Stone Guest* (the one-act play by Pushkin), *The Immortal*.[4]

At the other end of the scale, the junior members of the Vahtangov Theatre company, who had recently left its school, gave a production of their own at Omsk, Dyhovichny's *Honeymoon*.

Young actors and actresses of different institutes and outside them were encouraged to keep in touch with each other. At Kuibyshev, for instance, in the summer of 1943, there was a reunion of students from several schools and junior players from the Moscow Opera, " Gorky " dramatic, Musical Comedy, and Theatre for Young Spectators. They gave a joint show.

YOUNG PRODUCERS

But young talent directed only by old caution would never do. A careful watch was kept for producers who, when experience of life had

made their young institution sound, or who had a definite flair that anticipated the results of experience, would be able to put a scientific training
to good use. In the summer of 1943 the Committee for Art Affairs decided to hold a Review (смотр) of the work of young producers, and
appointed commissions for the purpose. These consisted of heads of theatres
and presidents of local parties and comsomols and other such organisations
in each region. They were to adjudicate the first round, so to speak ; and
every part of the Soviet Union was included. The terms of reference
embraced any independent production by anyone who had finished a
course of instruction in the subject within the period 1936-42, or who,
without having had any special education for the purpose, had been system-
atically practising production inside that period and could show productions
of their own. They had to have chosen the plays themselves, and the
leading players of the theatre in question had to be performing in them.
In other words, it was made a strictly professional and serious study.

The talented amateur was thus excluded. But there seems to have been
no specific bar against amateurs as such. The purpose was to see what the
young producers were doing, and what they were capable of. How they
happened to be earning their living was immaterial. The point was that
they must be serious and have some experience of the highly technical
craft of production.

The Review was to take place between the first of October and the
first of December. Uzbekistan found itself admiring the talents of the
young Amin Turdyev in his work on Uigun's *The Mother* at the " Hamza "
Theatre.[5] The young producers of three theatres in the Novosibirsk
area decided to do plays not previously seen there : Alexandra Brushtein's
King Spider was chosen by Andrushkevich for the Leningrad New Tyuz
at Novosibirsk itself ; S. Ivanov of the Novosibirsk Tyuz, then at Auzhero-
sujensk, took *A Far Country;* and S. Korostynev of the Red Torch gave
Oleko Dundich over to young Gintsborg with very successful results. In
Armenia, *A Lucrative Post* was chosen ; in Turkmenia, Gogol's *Wedding*.
In Georgia no fewer than thirty-two young producers appeared. In
Russia itself the following districts were represented : Ulyanovsk (Radun
producing *Oleko Dundich*), and Tyumen (Davydov with *A Moscow Girl*).
The Mordovian, Bashkirian, and other small nations found candidates.
In Cheboksary a young man just out of G.I.T.I.S., who had already tried
his prentice hand on *Othello*, did a play called *Lisa Kovatkova*.

An interesting example of the quality of the work of the young is given
by Professor Morozov in an article in Литература и искусство (20.xi.43).
It should be remembered that these are not dilettantes who come into the
theatre because they " have ideas " about production. But nor are they,
like most producers in other countries, actors who have found a special

branch of stage work better suited to them than others. They have been selected for the apparent bent of their talents and mentality, and have been trained by the cumulative experience of an organised and scientific theatre body. Thus equipped, they go out into the world of art. They still have to conquer that world by achievement. And training by itself will get them nowhere.

The production Morozov describes is *The Taming of the Shrew* at the Gorky (town) Dramatic Theatre. M. Kurabelnik, the young producer of it, had barely finished at G.I.T.I.S. Apart from productions he had done in working for a diploma, it was his first. Morozov says the young artist had profited by the productions of Popov and Zavadsky ; and humanity was his key-note ; but the rendering was quite his own. The idea running through it was that Katharine marries the man, and not the clothes.

Like Popov, Kurabelnik cut the Sly prologue, opening direct in Padua, a sunny southern atmosphere ; but the people as English as possible, with Gremio very far from the usual Pantalone, in fact so English that he reminded Morozov a little of Sir John Falstaff.

The scene with the tailor in Petruchio's country house was like a comedy written by Petruchio and produced by Gremio, Morozov says. The clothes had almost a symbolic value, and Petruchio's speech at the end of it made this a key scene, almost the *dénouement*. The return to Padua, though, the road scene, extended the play further, almost Morozov says into heroic comedy. The horses were placed right down by the footlights and the countryside streamed past, projected on a screen. The essential comradeship of man and woman on a joint adventure, as Shakespeare portrayed it, had a bearing on the men and women of Gorky town in war.

Morozov did not think the production was perfect. Korabelnik, he said, had not done enough work with the players about the words they were using, and he advised him to try *Romeo and Juliet* or some other play where Shakespeare's words are more fully charged. Indeed, being the good scholar he is, Professor Morozov suggested that many theatre schools might pay more attention to Shakespeare's words. For, as he says, with the theatre knowledge he has, " Shakespeare productions are not only created by producers and actors ; they also create producers and actors ".

The element which principally affects theatre people in this way is perhaps most of all the audience, and that brings us to the most delightful and picturesque side of this chapter, the Young Audience.

YOUNG AUDIENCES

A children's theatre in the U.S.S.R. could not exist without its audience. Not only its actual performances, but its organisation, structure, policy, its production methods, its acting, singing, dancing and *décor*, in short the whole of its meaning and art are wholly determined by the wants and tastes of the children. These are neither assessed nor assumed, either by the childhood memories of an adult (at best adult-coloured, and at worst adult-dimmed) nor by the whims of any single child whether advanced or " representative " ; still less are they made to conform to supposed mental condition of an " average child of that age ". Least of all do the managers take instructions from political party members, though of course morality and ethics are important. The proper assessment of the audience's requirements, and thereby the success of the children's theatres, are made possible through the triangle of theatre, school, individual child. The actor is the child's personal friend ; he talks to him in the theatre and in the school, and they get to know one another. The teacher, too, is the child's friend, a helper and almost elder relative to a degree difficult to imagine outside the Soviet educational system, and indeed inseparable from it and from the Soviet way of life. As far as possible actor and teacher are in close contact too. For to entertain a child is both a picturesque and a serious matter, and the actor profits by the seriousness of the teacher as much as the teacher profits by the picturesqueness of the actor.

The basis of each new entertainment is the individual child's reaction to previous ones, expressed in general comment, in letters, essays, or drawings. Often the children go to the same play more than once, and their reactions differ at each visit. These are taken into account. They are made the basis of action by trained child-psychologists (very human and unpresumptuous people) who also observe the audience during performances ; and in this way an apparatus is built up on which by trial and error Soviet children's actors and children's producers can work.

Now, as Obraztsov the puppet-master said in the nineteen-thirties to Alfredo Gomez de la Vega,[6] " A show for children must not be purely imaginative ; on the contrary, one must begin from a firm base of reality, to unfold better the wings of fantasy ". The U.S.S.R. is still in construction, and that construction has affected, often magically, the lives of even the smallest children. So Obraztsev went on, " The Children's Theatre in its field of action shares the big problems of the adult theatre, both in the enormous importance it has as an educational factor, and in its own really remarkable development ".

One tremendous fact in the construction of the U.S.S.R. was its partial destruction and partial postponement of construction because of war. That fact could not be hidden from the children, nor, therefore, from their theatres. To have tried to hide it would have made a children's theatre, or indeed an adult theatre, conflict with the reality of the life of the audience. In peace-time children's theatres, like adults', were charming, attractive, fascinating, but, or because, they were truthful. The persons on the stage were real people, not dummies, even when they were fantastic. And so, too, they continued in war.

In peace-time children's theatres served audiences in particular localities, apart from summer tours. The children of another district in the same town, if they could not get to the premises easily, had the theatre brought to them. Hordes of small persons must not at any given hour occupy all the transport of the streets and put a strain on their guardians, whether teacher or policeman, if it could be otherwise arranged. So, in war, the theatres went to the children. Without their audiences they would have ceased to exist, anyway.

CHILDRENS' THEATRES IN EVACUATION

The Central Children's Theatre, which is the Rolls-Royce of young entertainment, moved to Stalinsk in the KuzBas. Only one children's theatre was left in Moscow, the one which in peace-time had played largely to those in the country round about. Life and space in that countryside had narrowed and contracted. Its theatre stayed in the threatened city, and was packed out. For most performances tickets could be got only through schools. But it had a duty to others than children too. It played to the troops defending Moscow, and to the men and women who built the city's fortifications. During air-raids it played in cellars.

Yet its real audience was a country one, and back to the country it had to go. The men in the company felt their place was in the city, in the People's Guard ; they would not evacuate. In fairy tales animals could be played by women, but there were male parts men were needed for ; so there had to be an official order issued for the evacuation to proceed. Then, like good citizens, they went.

There was no transport, not even for them. They did their own carrying. All through the 1942 spring sowing they played to the farmers and their children ; and when they returned to base in Moscow, there were wounded in hospitals to play to. 1,007 performances in two years, besides 156 concerts. And what did they play ?

Here are some specimens : Goldoni's *Servant of Two Masters*, Ostrovsky's *Poverty No Crime*, an anti-Fascist play by Alexandra Brushtein about Czechoslovakia, fairy tales. One of the fairy tales was *Puss in Boots*, founded on Perrault by the Soviet playwright Malyarevsky, but depicting Puss's determined struggles (aided considerably by the audience, child or adult) against the cruel autocrat, the Marquis Blue Beard, and with a few other characters straying in from elsewhere. Another was a Chinese one, called *The Sword of China*, about a boy who fought against the evil oppressing his people.

When you come to think of it, most children's tales are about boys or girls who outwit evil monsters or tyrants oppressing a people. That is the moral essence, the real content of all the classic fairy tales. A folk memory, a folk conscience, a folk community, precious to us all and most precious when we are children. Why do we in our adulthood forget the gist and meaning of these stories, and dwell as we used not, on the picturesque or sentimental detail? It is partly because they are presented to us sentimentally. And partly also from the reason for that presentation; because we are trained by the circumstances we grow up in to ignore the oppression that we encounter ourselves; so we forget the truth of the story. "A fairy tale!" we remark with a contemptuous smile, ridicule being the best reply when no answer can be found to the truth. In the Soviet Union they do not so.

Young Spectators' Theatres

The adolescents' theatres moved too; Theatres For Young Spectators, or Tyuzes. But in one way their task was more difficult. Adolescence in war needs a brake more than an accelerator pedal; and rarely is it possible for a theatre to be a brake. Let us follow the fortunes of two Tyuzes from Moscow and Leningrad.

A very large proportion of the Moscow Tyuz's audience was gone to the Tatar Republic. The Tyuz arrived at Zelyonodonsk with thirteen new plays and seven revivals. Soon it moved to Murom in the same republic. Truly it needed a new repertoire. Old favourites like *The Bayonet*, in which a gang of bad young boys led by a problem child of a young thief, were shown the pleasures of Army discipline in their own ranks by a young Army Lieutenant, may have been very popular in its day, but its truth had faded. Military action in the Far East was nearer the mark. *Lyubov Yarovaya*, for the Red Army Celebrations in 1942, with its reminder of what it had been like to be young in the Civil Wars, made a man, or a woman, of the young listener. Gogol's *Wedding*, *The Marriage of Figaro*, *Guilty Though Guiltless*, *Kremlin Chimes*, *Depth Prospecting*, the building up of culture, the facing of problems of the day, these show how the minds of the young adolescents were directing themselves in their temporary exile. Simukov's *Native Soil*, Mdivani's *Ordered to the Front*, added at-home-ness and heroicism to their growing up. The former was a folk-play (rather like Marshak's *Twelve Months*), in which a brother and sister protect a magic tablecloth against foreign enemies trying to steal it, and the forest protects them.

Children's Plays in War-Time

But writing children's plays is an art in itself, learned only by actual contact. "These playwrights", said Diana Levin in an interview broad-

HANS ANDERSEN FOR THE CHILDREN.

Gerda asks a reindeer in Lapland to guide her to the Palace of the Snow Queen.

[facing page 284.

cast by the B.B.C. in ' Ariel in War-time ' (23 January 1943), " go about from one school to another lecturing on their work, and having discussions with the children. They invite suggestions on what kind of plays the children want, and what themes they wish to have dealt with."

A kind of actuality is thus possible. Perhaps the most interesting of actuality plays was *A Far Country*, by Eugene Schwartz, a subtle and fanciful playwright. The hero is a 15-year-old Leningrad lad evacuated to the east who makes up his mind to run away home to excitement and " war service ", but changes it when he realises the need for evacuated children to help with the harvest. The first night of this took place in March 1943. . . . Its heroes and heroines being the schoolchildren of Leningrad, many of them were also its audience. Local schools visited the theatre in turn to see it, and after one performance the management had a letter from a Leningrad school in the Mamadysh area close by, saying they wanted to do the play themselves and would the theatre help ? The Tyuz became patron to the young amateurs. Incidentally, as an appendix to our Brigade news, a group from this Tyuz joined the Fourth front-line brigade of the V.T.O.

At Murom the audience included Red Army men ; but it was hard to say whether they or the younger folk more enjoyed *Russian People*, *Intrigue and Love*, *Spring in Moscow*, the new play *Finist, Bright Falcon*.

By October 1943 this Tyuz was back in Moscow. It was the better for its tour. Partly, as the Director Krichko said, because the enforced " laconicism " of work on tour had improved its skill and ingenuity. Partly, too, because it had been among an audience, its own audience, struggling with the war as it could not have imagined them doing if it had stayed in Moscow. And in that case, after the war, the returning audience would be separated for ever by a great experience not shared, and the theatre would not have known a great period in the life of young Russia.

But it had also linked up three quite separate audiences : little children, adolescents, and adults. It had kept its plays for these separate, but the same company (the Moscow Tyuz company numbers sixty) had performed them. This was necessary, and not altogether a bad thing, in war.

It reasserted reality ; and the same thing happened in other Tyuzes, whether Russian or belonging to other Soviet nationalities. The Regional one at Ryazan, for example, early in 1943 gave *The Immortal;* so did the Leningrad New Tyuz, evacuated under B. Zon to Novosibirsk. The most successful new Armenian play in 1943 was *Fury*, first done by the Yerevan Tyuz. *Romeo and Juliet*, in a new translation by Pereteli, was done with Italianate-Georgian music in Tbilisi. And among others in the burst of Shakespeare were Novosibirsk's *Comedy of Errors* and the State Central Children's *Merry Wives of Windsor*. Among new Soviet plays was the Uzbek Children's Theatre with *Daughter of Moscow*, showing the loved figure of the girl guerrilla Lisa Chaikina, and *Gulkhan*, about the war work of Uzbek children. The Novosibirsk Tyuz chose for its first 1942 show, *Timur and his Comrades*, an excellent choice, as the thrills got by these young men from the help they gave to the whole countryside through their self-made gang, was an inspiration to the young men and women of all ages in the audience, and like the book from which it was taken, helped to spread an unofficial movement that caught the imagination of Soviet boys as scouting did that of the Edwardian and inter-war British boy. Tula and many other Tyuzes copied Novosibirsk.*

The plays that Tsenterovich followed this with were strikingly different : *Professor Mamlock*, *Little Red Riding Hood* (a version by Eugene Schwartz), *Ilya Murometz* (a Russian legendary hero), and to come, a Goldoni, a new play about an acrobat in a front-line brigade, and another Brushtein anti-Fascist play.

The Leningrad Tyuz told the same tale. Under its chief, People's Artist A. A. Bryantsev, it went to Beryozniki in the Urals. A number of young people were in lumber camps on the Kama and Vishera Rivers ; but the adults, too, the lumbermen, their appetites whetted by the Moscow Dramatic Theatre, the Leningrad Opera and Ballet, and a local opera-and-dramatic, gave a big welcome to their Ostrovsky (*Poverty no Crime*), their Afinogenov, *Mashenka*, and *To Be Continued*. In December in that region the Tyuz gave *The Little Hump-Backed Horse* in honour of B. V. Beier's 75th birthday. Besides *Puss in Boots* and other children's plays this Tyuz was doing *Fruits of Enlightenment* (Leo Tolstoy), *Tartuffe*, and warlike plays called *Childhood of a Marshal* and *A Hero's Brother*. The nature of another play with the curious title of *Visiting a Miser* (or *Skeleton ?*) I have been unable to discover.

But there was need of more and more plays for the young. In July 1943 the Committee for Art Affairs gave a recommendation that Tyuzi be established in Rostov-on-Don, Grozny, Saratov, Tashkent, and Frunze ; and additional ones at Molotov, Chelyabinsk, and Alma-Ata ; and made it clear, too, that the job of a children's or young person's theatre was to serve children and young people, and not grown-ups. Where there were no young people's theatres of any kind, the local adults' theatres were urged to include productions for children, with not less than two matinees a month, half of the tickets to be available to schools. Some regional theatres were already doing this. That at Ivanovo had a special production of Alexey

---

* An English translation of Gaidar's book was issued by the Pilot Press in London, 1942.

Tolstoy's *Golden Key*, a Russian version of the tale of a puppet that comes alive.

By this time the war emergency may be said to have been over. Evacuee children's theatres and tyuzes were on the point of going home. Local theatres had learned much from them, of the scientific attitude and methods needed. It was unthinkable that children in these neighbourhoods, having once tasted of the delights and benefits of theatres for them, should be left theatre-less with the war still raging. Hence the need for this directive.

The effect was immediate. In October 1943 the Kuibyshev Tyuz, reorganised under Honoured Artist Komarovskaya, drew up a schedule for children only. It had earned the reproach that out of five recent productions only one had been for young people. Kuibyshev also opened a puppet theatre, run by a woman puppeteer called Karatozova. In their opening season, 1943-4, they showed *The Circus*, *Petrushka* (= The Puppet) *Beats the Fascists*, and *Gulliver in Lilliput*. The scripts for all these were written by Helen Danko. The puppet-sculptor and the scene-painter were both men.

But a more significant note can be struck to end this chapter on the theatrical care of the young. The Central Children's Theatre, now directed by Volkov, the Leningrad New Tyuz, and the two tyuzes at Tbilisi, Georgian and Russian, were to open studios of their own ! [7]

Truly the organisms were developing.

CHAPTER XIV

ODDS AND ENDS

PROPAGANDA

No account of the Soviet theatres in war would be complete if it did not take notice of the many smaller organisms attached to the main body and travelling with it. Nor would it be correct to say that there was no more propaganda on the Soviet stage. There was. In special propaganda theatres.

Before the war the Moscow Planetarium had a small staff theatre called "The Star", which did plays on astronomical themes, like Kochelnikov's dramatic biography of Copernicus in ten scenes. The object was to popularise and stimulate general interest in astronomy.

In May 1942 the Institute of Hygienic Enlightenment at Moscow opened a similar theatre for one-act plays. These were not like the poster-plays of the Revolution, wherein microbes spouted monologues. These presented similar themes with similar intentions ; but the problems were treated from the human angle, as a list of some of the twenty plays they produced in the first year will show. The blood of a girl donor saves the life of a badly wounded sailor ; a little boy catches an infectious disease by playing with somebody else's fluffy teddy-bear ; a girl finds a way of breaking her boy friend of certain unhygienic habits ; a German scout in the Russian front line tries to evade capture by pretending to have typhus ; an old peasant woman persists in using old wives' cures instead of going to a doctor.

Other plays were biographical, about Louis Pasteur and the boy bitten by a mad dog (not the Guitry play), or about Horatio Wells, the Boston doctor who first used narcotics medicinally in 1857, or about Pirogov the nineteenth-century Russian, and others. There were also songs, dances, variety turns, mimes, on the subject of malingerers or quacks. And a special section for children had a whole "opera" about little bears gobbling too much and too quickly.

The *décor* was simple and portable, because the theatre travelled about among Army units, base hospitals, factory-clubs and schools.[1]

There was also a definitely agitational travelling theatre, designed to foster and maintain the war spirit in the militia of Moscow by the use of satire. It was called "Yastrebok" . . . the Sparrow Hawk. This was a theatre of the miniature, springing directly from the war. It gibed at the Gestapo, the "Fifth Columnist", the White Russian *émigrés* with their dreams of another empire. It celebrated heroism and nobility, of the resistance movements, of British airmen and gunners. Lench's grotesque "Jumpy Jerries" was based on a "Nerve Economy Campaign" in the Reich. A comic interlude by Dyhovichny concerned a poet writing verses in praise of the great feats of a certain airman who continually outpaced his celebrator. And besides such sketches and playlets it did a Soviet oratorio, a short comedy, a dramatic "study". There were two producers and a permanent scene designer. It toured towns in the rear.

From this in turn came regional theatres of the same sort, at Saratov, for instance ; and one that sprang up in Tbilisi, staffed by actors from the Harkov Theatre of Miniature, and called "Mig" in honour of one of the best types of Soviet aircraft.[2]

ONE-ACT PLAYS

Some few have been translated, but there was quite a large output of one-act plays during the war. In March 1942, in the Maritime Province (Far East), a competition was held for this type of play. A hundred and eighty-six were sent in, forty-six of them from as far away as Tomsk, Ulan-Ude, Chelyabinsk and Gorky ; but the majority from the Maritime Province itself. Nearly all were about the Front Line. Ten were about Tanya. Seventeen only were on local themes. The standard was reported to be disappointing on technical grounds, and no first prize was awarded, but the second prize was won by a local dramatic unit.[3]

A more important competition was held the following year in Moscow, by decision of the Committee for Art Affairs. Big prizes were offered, because more and more small units were forming and there was a dearth of good, short plays. The prizes were ten thousand, seven, and four thousand roubles, and among those judging the competition were authors of the calibre of Vsevolod Ivanov (author of *Armoured Train*), Trenyov, Alexandra Brushtein, Zoshchenko the humorist, Konstantin Paustovsky, Pogodin, Nikitin and Romashov. The specific theme was to be the war ; but it was noticed with approval that now quite a number placed their locale in the rear, in factory or farm.

The outstanding author of comic one-act plays was Leonid Lench, an evening of whose work was given in the Moscow House of the Actor in summer 1943. Lench had the reputation of being funny not by shutting his eyes to the more serious side of life, but, like the classic wits, by finding unexpectedly comic situations and shafts in quite ordinary circumstances . . . life in a town flat, a dressmaker's *atelier*, a Public Services Combine. Doubtless his wit lost nothing that evening from the fact that his stories and playlets were read or performed by actors from the Moscow Theatre of Miniature, which regularly did his work. One of Lench's longer plays was *Thrice Murdered*, described as a "comic melodrama" (the Russians being more honest in their publicity than we are toward spy plays), founded on Clare Booth's *Margin for Error*. This was accepted by the Radlov and Comedy Theatres of Leningrad and by the LenSoviet of Moscow (1942). The action takes place in the house of a German consul in America. The consul hates all Slavs by order, and is in the unhappy position of being guarded and protected in his home by a policeman of Czech origin.

But the genius of Russian literature does not take kindly to the one-act form. Somehow the ghosts and eternity caught by the great novelists seem to haunt short works, and they leave a sense of incompletion. Life goes on before and after the little scene, and it feels as if it were only a portion of a big play. Even the admirable *Watchmaker and Doctor* in the eleven one-act plays published in English by the Pilot Press (1944) is not a unity but an incident.[4]

FOLK-LORE POET

The quality of satirical fantasy in the war was sharpened in a man hitherto known and loved as a children's author, Samuil Marshak. His poems about toyland, animals, the bird world, which, though full of quaintness and attractive invention, had never been wholly subconscious, never surrealist, but always with one foot and the weight of the body on reality, now became sharp, indignant, bitter. That is the healthy reaction of a Beautiful soul to the mad depravities of Hitlerism among and on the bodies of the bairns that were Marshak's public. In his pre-war poems and fairy tales, "wicked" animals were given the quality folk-lore gives them. The wolf, the bear, the rat, hateful to the serf-folk they menaced. In war these took on the attributes of the Fascist, the mad kitten who thought he was a lion, the cringing curs of Finland or Rumania, the monkey on the Italian barrel-organ . . . folk-lore of Soviet folk.

Many such poems were illustrated and issued as posters by the Kukriniksy. The Kukriniksy were a small syndicate of cartoonists and book-illustrators who signed their work by the first syllables of their names : Mihail Kuprianov, Porfiri Krilov, and Nikolay Sokolov, all three young men, though the first two had been in partnership since their schooldays nearly twenty years ago. It was this syndicate which designed the settings for Mayakovsky's futurist-satirical play, *The Bug*, and they worked at the Theatre of Satire for some years. Since 1933, however, they had been known for their black-and-white cartoons in *Pravda*. Their wit was pungent, accurate and pictorial. The nearest thing to them in our countries is Low. They spared nobody ; and their brilliant draughtsmanship rewards long scrutiny of most of their pictures. There is liable to be a sting in apparently unimportant strokes. When the Fascists invaded Russia, therefore, it was only to be expected that their wit would be savage. And it was because they were available that the TASS window posters reappeared on every hoarding and notice-board. Like Marshak, they received a Stalin award in 1942.

Marshak is an English scholar, and has made translations of poets from Shakespeare, Milton and Blake to Browning, Kipling and Yeats. Also of Burns. Some of these last were set by Tihon Hrennikov.* He is thus much more than a mere grown-up child. And when he was preparing a play-story for the children's theatres in 1943, so much truth and thought went to the making of it, that he was invited to give a reading to the Moscow Art Theatre company, in November, as a result of which it was at once accepted for performance there.

This was *Twelve Months,* a three-act verse play with prologue and epilogue. It was described by one critic as having a beauty that is not *recherché,* but is " the deep beauty of folk-consciousness, caught by a poet in an age-old ' wanderer ' theme of Slav story ". The wanderer is a young girl, sent by a wicked stepmother into the woods to gather snowdrops in winter. In the wood she meets all the twelve months together, brewing over a magic fire the mysterious sap that makes vegetation. They know her. She is a farm girl and they have often seen her working in the fields at all seasons, and have noticed that she worked well because she loved the soil. (Russian science was ahead of all the world in making an analytical classification of soils.) One by one they approach her, giving her each the product of the soil that belongs to the month, showing her their secrets, and sheltering her. She does not return. The wicked stepmother sends her own daughter to the forest. She does not love the soil. The months do not shelter her. She freezes to death.

That is the bare bone of it. But the forest is filled with animals and birds, their joy and abundance, their directness and willingness contrasting with the empty vanities of court life, subject to frowsty conventions and the whims of a young queen. An idle fancy to-day ? Fanciful, perhaps ; or imaginative. But not remote ; and in no sense out of tune with the war. The Moscow Art Theatre did well to accept it. It had so much that the war-time theatre wanted. Picturesque, like a fairy tale, it showed the honesty of those that live near the land, and the dishonesty of artificial society, as all good folk tales always do ; it also showed as fairy tales do, how nature responds to those who study and work with and use her aright.

---

* Shostakovich also has set several Burns songs, less simply perhaps, but with exquisite musicianship. Scottish popular songs were a speciality of Lyudmilla Glasgova, the radio soprano, who toured the Urals in 1942. Some Soviet music-ologists, compare Hrennikov's work with the English ballad-operas of the eighteenth Century, or the "dialogue operas" of the seventeenth.

But set it truthfully, as the Moscow Art Theatre can, with no " modern-isation " of the months ; and those in the auditorium are those who have withstood the Fascist advance, sniped the Fascist forces, from nature's secure places, and watched with derisive country eyes the Fascist nerve giving way, just because those defenders knew their country as the little stepdaughter did. Knowing their land they trusted it, and because they were well pre-pared and well led in human matters, they could and did take full advantage when nature responded to that trust.

No place there for mysticism, whether of sentiment or stylised gesture ! Marshak had written no fairy pantomime nor allegory. He had taken a folk tale and breathed on it with a modern scientist's creative breath. If the figures spoke delicate, accurate verse, yet it was the verse of actual speech. The Soviet folk tale lived by the finest of Soviet actors and actresses.

And served by the finest artists. The Art Theatre was right not only to accept this play, but to secure for it the best brains in the Union to help in the final perfection of the show : Shostakovich with music, Peter Williams with poetry of colour and form.[5]

PAINTERS

Peter Williams had been known as a painter both in the theatre and outside it for years. He graduated at the Moscow School of Art in 1924, and designed the setting of *La Traviata* for Nemirovich-Danchenko in his experimental opera studio in 1934. He was a nephew of the eminent Soviet authority on the nature and use of the soil, Academician Williams, of British descent.

Those who saw in pre-war days his sets for *The Pickwick Club* at the Moscow Art Theatre Filial, will not need to be reminded of his daring craftsmanship, high spirit and subtle fancy ; for they are not likely to forget them. He exactly caught the spirit of Stanitsyn's Dickens. But how particularly theatrical they were only came out in performance. The subtlety of a fancy that placed a huge painting of a mirror across the back of Mr. Pickwick's lodging, and then produced at the bottom of it a re-flection of the candlesticks on the real table in front of it ! The boldness that used a painted background of clouds and birds lyrically flying behind the café scene, and then in a brief black-out with Mr. Pickwick tumbled into the hogshead and the carriage horses impatiently pawing the ground, martial music suddenly changing to vile cacophony as the lights came up on a quite new back-drop . . . a military review, with guns firing, spec-tators looking, officers saluting, horses curvetting, and ranks and ranks of soldiers stretching away to the camps and manœuvres in the distance, stiff and serried as reeds in a reed-bed, while overhead two epauletted cherubs blew their trumpets, moustachios on their cheeks and bearskins on their heads ! Or the daring with which, in the Prison scene, painted figures of larger-than-life people on the walls vied with the moving three-dimensional people on the stage, yet did not interfere with their reality, as by all the laws of stage *décor* they ought to have done. The reason being, I thought, as I marvelled in the stalls, the designer's skill alone ; for the painted figures are in vigorous motion and the composition of their grouping made an actual frame for the actors' action.

The brutal reds and blues of that scene contrasted with the autumn hues of the inn scene, the moonlit garden. And that is another character-istic of Peter Williams, his firm but not obtrusive change of mood to suit that of the acting scene, yet not losing the style, the location, of the play.

So it does not surprise us to learn that Williams was also a serious canvas artist, and by summer 1942 had started on a big series of war-time pictures, expecting them to number about fifty, one of the earliest and most striking being " Spring 1942 ", a woman in a flaming village who held in her hands all that was left of her family and home, a child's doll.

Among the sets for which Williams made a reputation before the war were the Vahtangov *Don Quixote*, and *Mary Stuart* at the Theatre of the Revolution. He was also liked for opera, *Boris Godunov* at the Bolshoy being done in his sets. He became one of the favourite designers for the Bolshoy, and when it was evacuated to Kuibyshev, he designed Rossini's *William Tell* and Yurovsky's ballet, *Red Sails*. The set for the ballet was so successful that critics commented : " As usual, the settings by Peter Williams evoked a burst of spontaneous applause each time the curtain rose ". The theme of this ballet was a story by A. S. Grinevsky (" A. Grin "), about a sailor's daughter whose widowed father leaves the sea and takes to making toy boats for a living, while his daughter grows up dreamy and alone. An old bard tells her the folk tale of a handsome prince in a magic ship with scarlet sails, who will one day come and carry her off to happiness. A schooner, commanded by a handsome captain, does put in to the little port, and he and she fall in love with one another. Hearing the story, he puts out to sea, hoists sails of the right colour, and returns ; so her dream becomes true, and she wakes to life.

While in Kuibyshev, Williams also worked for the local " Gorky " dramatic theatre, one of the best in the provinces, and set in 1942-3 their *Romeo and Juliet*. Previously he had done *décor* for the Prokoviev ballet on the same subject in Leningrad. For the Shakespeare he was reported to have made stately use of the spaciousness of the Renaissance. But he does not need only big jobs. He was asked to do staging and costumes for " Fatherland ", a song and dance ensemble sponsored by the People's Commissar for Home Affairs in 1942. These costumes included almost every national dress in the Soviet Union, whirling, and flashing under back-drops that depicted Leningrad majestically and Moscow from the Kremlin Tower with the night sky ribboned by searchlight beams.[6]

There is not a great deal of information about the war-time activities of the best-known pre-war Soviet scene designers. Rabinovich, Shtoffer and Dmitriyev lectured on their work at Saratov and Sverdlovsk to a conference of national and provincial theatres held in Moscow in the winter of 1942-3, to discuss the best way of using folk-lore on the stage. Shifrin, besides doing the important Popov productions, exhibited some front-line sketches he had made. Later in the same year, 1943, Ryndin also held an exhibition of work at the Vahtangov. So did Fyedotov of sets and costumes for *Long, Long Ago*, at the Red Army Theatre, and for *Invasion*. E. Lanser, besides being a stage designer, was like most theatre artists, also renowned for his canvases. These were monumental in conception. A " creative evening " in his honour took place in Moscow in March 1944. He was a Stalin laureate.

Dmitriyev, a Leningrad man, was a direct descendant of the Benois-Bakst-Golovin-Serov-Korovin group in pre-revolutionary days. At the Revolution he followed Meierhold through various theoretic extravagances, the result of which he consolidated, when the time came, into Socialist realism. A lively, alert mind, open to the essence of any author's work, and a fully practised skill, he made a name for catching the atmosphere of a play. His favourite theme was Leningrad, and two operas gave him an opportunity to compose variations upon that theme, Chaikovsky's *Queen of Spades* and Dzerzhinsky's *Nadyezhda Svetlova*, which was dedicated to the defenders of Lenin's city. In drama, his most notable war-time settings were for *The Storm* when Zahava produced it at the Vahtangov, and for Hmelyov's production of *Russian People* at the Moscow Art Theatre.

In parenthesis to the Bakst group, it is interesting that the V.T.O. in Leningrad and the Theatrical Museum in Moscow in 1943 showed an album of some eighty-six illustrations in colour of sketches done by Golovin in the last hours of Old Russia for the Alexandrinsky *Masquerade*. This volume had been assembled by Lanser. Golovin died in 1930.[7]

POET, ARTIST, PRODUCER

Among the many new figures that emerged in war stood Pavel Antokolsky, a young writer and man of the theatre coming from the same family as had produced, in the nineteenth century, a well-known sculptor of that name. In 1943 his most recent volume of verse coincided with a verse play he had written about the Soviet Air Ace Chkalov and which he had himself produced in one of the best front-line theatre units. Of this unit he was director. Another poem of his, *The Ballad of an Unknown*

Boy, was taken as text for a cantata by Prokofiev. He is described in 1942 as having been helping members of the " Chkalov " Theatre in Gorky (town) to compose their own sketches for front-line performance. Also he was the translator of Jean-Richard Bloch's play, *Toulon*, and had a deep love for the Ukrainian classics.

But an article he wrote for Литература и искусство on " War and Culture " shows even more than that. " To-day ", he wrote, " when there is being decided the fate both of Russia and of the whole world, we must search round us and into the byegone, and if possible into to-morrow . . . search in company with all fearless folk who believe in their own historical existence." Urgently, therefore, he examines Soviet culture. " Culture is the result and total of the efforts that man puts into his society." And this is indestructible, so long as that society is indestructible. Let the Germans with their fallacious race-creeds try to destroy Tolstoy's home and manuscripts, as the origin of the art of slaves ! " Yasnaya Polyana ", cries Antokosky, with no rhetoric, " is in our hearts. We have seen many things in our time. We have seen the growth of people, their admirable hunger after work and knowledge. We have seen the potent outcome of the construction schemes in the Stalin Five-Year-Plans, hydro-electric stations that give light and current to regions hitherto deprived of the elementary blessings of civilisation, a whole body of new factories, new university halls, schools, libraries, Pioneers' Palaces ; the creation of bold thinking and exact calculation. We have seen the stage of the Bolshoy Theatre flung into a rapturous whirl of dancing by Caucasian Highlanders, and have heard the intricate tonalities of the Central Asian shepherds. . . ." And he considers the collective farms, the amateurs. " We have seen how talents are born, so shy at first, and so objective in their initial purity. And everywhere and everywhither we have seen how rich our country is with its finest gold, its most primary wealth, People ! Youth ! "

This youth, he affirms, is strong because in its hands are firearms ; and in its heart, hate. A hate that is born of humanism, a hate that seeks the destruction of all that threatens its culture, because it knows that that culture is its life. " When our youth returns to the tasks of construction, returns in victory to the home which bore it, there will be tales to tell for future generations to learn. And, who knows ? already somewhere to-day, in some advanced position, in some mud-hut by the light of a flickering oil-lamp, there may be shaping the conception of an Iliad that people will listen to for centuries. Youth is beginning to tell its tale. To-day we can only sense the stillness of the watch in which it will sound forth. But that is the to-morrow of our culture. The thought of it cannot and must not ever leave us. The thought of it is the thought of the immortality of a people. And in it many things are involved : memory and hope, love for our homeland, and the self-awareness of individual man. On the bright banner of our culture there is written : " Herewith Shalt Thou Conquer ".⁸

And with that rapturous but firm greeting to the new world ringing in our ears, let us now consider how the old one was already being rebuilt, and youth was back in its home about the tasks of construction, before the last ruin had ceased to fall.

CHAPTER XV

REGENERATION

STALINGRAD

The Fascist advance swept across Russia, till by the beginning of 1943 its farthest edge lay in a north-east to south-west beach of desolation from Leningrad to almost Grozny, and back due west to the Black Sea coast : Kalinin, almost Moscow, Tula, Yelets, Voronezh, along the Don, over the Don, to the Volga, the heart of Russia now, the last river bastion, Stalingrad.

Stalin said the city of steel must not fall ; and the world listened breathlessly. The city of steel rivalled Malta in the admiration of the whole progressive world. It outrivalled Sevastopol. For five months it was bombarded from hour to hour and from minute to minute. But Stalin's call was answered. The Fascists never crossed the Volga. At terrible cost to both sides, but worse to the Fascists, Stalingrad did not fall. The citizens, the women and the children, and Ukrainians, Tats, Uzbeks, Georgians, Tajiks as well as Russian fighters, defended it. At last, on the second day of February 1943 its liberation was completed. And the defeat of the Germans at Stalingrad was no local reverse ; it was the beginning of utter defeat, taken up by the British, Americans, French and patriot Italians in other countries. The run that the Germans started did not stop till they reached their own country. They could hold their own no more. Back across the Don they were swept, back to the Black Sea coast, back across the Donets and across the Dnieper. Back from the Oka, back to the frontier. Across the frontier. Across the Ingul and the Ingulets, across the Bug, across the Dniester ; back into Byelorussia and Poland, Lithuania, Latvia and Estonia. As the months passed, Harkov, Kiev and Odessa were cleared of them. The last invader was driven from Russian, from Ukrainian and Byelorussian soil.

It would have been surprising, in view of the part the theatres had played hitherto, if they had not followed closely on the liberating armies, if they had not immediately set out for the regeneration, spiritual and material, of the places and people devastated by Fascist occupation. What is surprising is the speed and thoroughness with which they did so.

By May 1943 the Stalingrad "Gorky" Regional Dramatic Theatre, which had been evacuated up the Volga to Syzran, near Kuibyshev, returned and started rehearsals. But already in April concert brigades had been performing and a show given by the Astrakhan "Kirov" Theatre. By June 1943 the Stalingrad Variety Theatre was back ; and the Comedy

Theatre expected any time. Four theatres were active in the immediate neighbourhood, two centrally, the others round Astrakhan and Kamyshin. The "Gorky" Theatre's building had been destroyed by the Fascists. Until it could be rebuilt, shows were given in a just useable hall belonging to the Stalgres (Hydro-electric Station) Workers' Club. On the 24th of August an advance group of the theatre had begun to give shows. The play was the *Russian People*, which though written with Sevastopol in mind might well have been taken from the recent lives of the Stalingrad people themselves.

By that date the city was already alive again. Crowds of stone masons, plasterers, carpenters, engineers, and technicians of all kinds had poured into it. Bricklayers were vying with each other to break records day after day, men and women. Maria Sagaidak from Kremenchug laid 7,445 in six hours. Lida Babkina, her mate, beat this by 42 bricks.* Brigade challenged brigade. Factories and houses rose at miracle speed, while demolition of unsafe walls and girders was still being started. Suburban trains began running. The Volga ferry service became normal. Markets opened again, and collective farmers from the district sold fruit, fish, butter, eggs and milk. Queues formed as of old at newspaper kiosks. Shops opened, and restaurants, and libraries. Even cool drinks were on the streets again. For rebuilding, in August, is dry and hot work.

Eight cinemas showed Russian films, *Lermontov*, *Masquerade*, *A Son of Tajikstan*, and the old American semi-historical, *In Old Chicago*. The Shapito Circus returned. Actors' brigades arrived from all over the Union. Local amateurs started up again, coached by graduates from Moscow. A competition for singing, dancing and recitation had 200 entries. Life, indeed, was urgent, but normal ; and most significant of all symptoms, the Defence of Stalingrad had become not only a legend of the world for ever, but also a favourite children's game in débris not yet cleared.

How the Regeneration Began

Even in a Socialist State rebuilding costs money. Piles of rubble have none. Money is stored labour, and takes time to accumulate. Further, materials were hard to obtain locally, whether steel for frames or cloth and wood for stage purposes. So help was welcomed from any source. The response of other theatres was as immediate as that of other towns with materials for rebuilding. With the approval of the Committee for Art Affairs in May 1943, the Kuibyshev Theatre of Opera, Ballet and

---

* An enquiry for the British record for comparison was answered by the Brick-layers' Union by the information that there was none. "On rough work a man can lay from 900 to 1,000 bricks per day, but on good work the average is probably about 300." The Russians evidently use a different system.

Musical Comedy opened a fund with the State Bank. It did so with a gift collected by itself which amounted to a hundred thousand roubles. The Gorky Theatre in the same town contributed 50,000. The Molotov Regional Dramatic Theatre paid in 16,000. The " Gorky " Grand Dramatic of Leningrad gave the proceeds of a performance and organised similar gifts from other Leningrad theatres. The Urals-KuzBas theatres did the same. The Ufa Bashkirian Academic Theatre gave the entire proceeds of a special show (R. 35,000) for the relief of battle-scarred Voroshilovgrad when touring that region. There was scarcely a theatre anywhere which did not help in some way the theatre of Stalingrad to work in that heroic place.

That is the first thing that strikes the student of the regeneration of theatrical life in the devastated areas : it became at once and without question the part concern of every theatre in luckier neighbourhoods. The Fascist advance had affected these reception areas closely. So did the Fascist retreat. For varying periods of over a year hostess-stages had served evacuees, or evacuee theatres had served hosts. A friendship had been established, which was the closest expression of communal feeling—the theatre. When the evacuee theatres returned home, or the country of the evacuee theatres had been restored to them, it was as proper as it was natural that the luckier ones should want to help in the reconstruction of buildings and equipment. Metropolitan artists now had a concern in distant parts.

As a result, a group of architects and engineers arrived in Stalingrad with plans by the architect Aurenn for a fine new theatre, seating 1,000. As work on the structure began the theatre company opened its first full post-invasion season at home on the 24th of October, 1943 with the following repertoire : *Invasion, Meshchane, General Brusilov, Wide Spreads the Sea*, and two Shakespeare plays in immediate preparation. They were *The Taming of the Shrew* and *Much Ado About Nothing*. Nor was it very long, as theatre seasons go, before the people of Stalingrad saw themselves as others saw them, in the play by Yuri Chepurin which Popov in Moscow had commissioned. This occurred in February 1944. The difficulties were immense, but Maierov overcame them, and the spirit of preparation was much like that of rebuilding the city itself. Periodic bulletins were issued to answer enquiries as to how the preparation was getting on.

As if to strengthen this theatre, on which the eyes of the theatre world were now turned, the Committee for Art Affairs directed ten Moscow actors, from the Art Theatre, the Maly, the LenKom, and elsewhere, to join the Stalingrad company, which was further implemented by eight beginners just graduated at G.I.T.I.S. It was also a tribute to the theatre on the Volga ; and it was also part of the general policy of the Communist Government. Local cultures were akin in their general direction ; let

them feel and express this kinship in act. These players were really am-
bassadors. Out of this, and out of the war, there was bound to be a deeper
understanding of that community ; and that would have importance not
only for the future of the Soviet Union, but for the future and peace of the
whole world. This explains why, though monetary credit could easily,
and in fact was, provided from Government sources, these money gifts
and these technical aids were accepted and encouraged.[1]

The Tajik play, *Nadir's House*, was significant, as the East's tribute to
Stalingrad. Written by a Tajik and a Russian author in collaboration,
Jalol Ikrami and Alexey Faiko, it showed a Tajik, a Tatar and two Russians
holding an important building against Fascist assault. Nadir, the Tajik
commander, knows that in stopping the invaders at Stalingrad he is stopping
them from reaching Stalinabad, his home. And when the play was produced at the " Lahuti " Theatre in the Tajik city, the theatre was crowded
night after night with Tajiks who knew that this was just what the defence
of Stalingrad had done for them. Their experience was deeply emotional,
and not just that of people going to an exciting war play.

IN THE CAUCASUS

Stalingrad was not the only hero city. The peoples of the North
Caucasus had been badly hit. Evacuation was not for them. At Nalchik,
for instance, the capital of Kabardino-Balkaria, in the woody valleys of
the Black Mountains midway between the Black Sea and the Caspian,
not only was the theatre burned down by the Fascists, but every concert
hall and club room, except one cinema for children. Casualties included
the president of its Committee for Art Affairs, who was killed in action ;
and two of its principal actors and the chief scene designer, were murdered
by the Nazis. When the hateful tide had receded, the one cinema was
taken jointly by four theatres, the Russian Dramatic, the Kabardinian
National, the Balkarian National, and the Song-and-Dance Ensemble.
Also there returned a group of G.I.T.I.S. students, who had been training
under Tarhanov since 1941. To set these theatre units up, surviving as
they were without any accessories whatever, the V.T.O. and other bodies
provided make-up, paint, wigs, cloth for curtains and costumes, and the
nucleus of a theatre library.

At Pyatigorsk, the mountain watering-place just to the north, always
associated with Lermontov, the Fascists sacked and burned the Lermontov
Gallery and Museum, and the Pushkin Gallery at Zheleznovodsky near by,
and all the libraries and cultural institutions they could find. (And in a
Socialist State a Gallery and Library are not the dreary official places they
tend to be in our midland cities, but realise rather the dreams of the founders
of those august and often rather remote institutions. They are places to

which the workers go as naturally and with as keen an interest as to a football match.) Over fifty artists of one kind or another were tortured and shot in these inoffensive spas. But thanks to the arrival of the Red Army, the theatre buildings at these two places, as at Essentukh and the " Gorky " Theatre at Kislovodsk, were all saved intact. In less than a month after the liberation, they were in full working order. The Leningrad Comedy Theatre under Akimov came on tour from Stalingrad. Circuses arrived. The parks were open for symphony concerts. Only now their audiences were mostly convalescent soldiers.

Farther north still, Stavropol, which had been inundated by invasion, saw its regional theatre rebuilt at a cost of 650,000 roubles. The district theatre company returned from Minusinsk in Siberia whither it had managed to escape. At Krasnodar, chief town of Adyge, or Circassia, the dramatic theatre worked in a cinema till its premises could be rebuilt. The Krasnodar Regional Theatre had been playing at Sochi on the Black Sea coast beyond the Fascist high tide. It had a company of fifty, and was doing *Russian People*. At Armavir, too, rebuilding was necessary. In August 1943 the Adyge Theatre had begun work in Maikop. And meanwhile brigades from Baku and other parts of Azerbaijan had been holding the audiences of Orjonikidze (Vladikavkaz), Mozdok, Malgobek, and other places, either occupied or within days and miles of occupation.

In Dagestan, last defence before the Caspian, which had not in fact been forced, reorganisation and new birth took the place of liberation. The Kumyk National Theatre transferred to Mahach-Kala (formerly Petrovsk, and the chief town), and was regrouped as the National Theatre of Dagestan. And there appeared and began work, Avar, Lezgin, Highland-Jewish,* Lak and other theatres. In North Ossetia's chief town, Orjonikidze, which had been similarly threatened, Russian and Ossetian dramatic theatres, a national musico-dramatic theatre too, began work and opened an opera studio. Meanwhile brigades and travelling theatres circled round the stricken towns like animals round their injured mates. Three brigades in Kabardino-Balkaria from Georgia and Azerbaijan, two regional theatres, six from Russian towns. Six brigades from Stavropol, Kursk, Kislovodsk, Pyatigorsk, Rostov and Krasnodar. Circuses to Stalingrad, Orjonikidze, Grozny. And these were followed or accompanied by other cultural things, travelling art exhibitions, musical programmes, which for space we must leave out of our survey, though they all bear out what Antokolsky said.

* The Highland Jews of the Caucasus live in scattered rural communities centred round Dag-Chufut. There were nearly twenty-six thousand of a total population in 1926. They had retained their Hebrew religion and Semitic facial characteristics, but spoke the Tat language.

20

Half-way between these places and Stalingrad stood Yelista, capital of the Kalmyk steppes. Not a theatre building of any kind was left there. The Kalmyk Dramatic Theatre's company had to remain at Astrakhan till their premises had been re-raised entirely, at a cost of some 760,000 roubles.[2]

ROSTOV-ON-DON

Rostov lies due west of Yelista, some 250 miles. Sad was the tale of this seaport. Before the war it had been one of the most theatrically-minded cities of the Soviet Union. In 1935 the "Gorky" Theatre had opened there a noble building, with a capacity of 2,200, equipped with the finest lighting and stage plant of the time. Besides that there was a big Musical Comedy Theatre, a Tyuz, and a LenKom Theatre built on the model, though to smaller scale, of the Moscow Bolshoy Opera. The Germans closed all these houses to the local population, and seldom used them for their own purposes. Free speech was forbidden ; national songs were forbidden. The old Tsarist imperialism had returned in a new guise. The local population did not particularly want to go to a theatre where neither of these things were to be heard. But from time to time, usually at precisely 6 o'clock on a Sunday evening, a van would drive up to the square in front of the Gorky Theatre's closed and padlocked doors, and a German soldier would produce a gramophone. Grimly the Russian people would listen to the sound of a banal German military march. That was culture, entertainment enough by the standards of these degenerate compatriots, these landowner-class-cum-Nazi-party-ridden serf-compatriots of the genius Goethe and the rebel Schiller. For seven months the Rostov people had to endure such vulgarity.

Then came signs of retreat. The Red Army was advancing. The Nazis prepared to run. Before they did so, they blew up the "Gorky" Theatre, stage, fittings, and all. Practically nothing stood but the foundations. With the one exception of the LenKom every other theatre and hall were looted and then blown up or set on fire. And with them, all libraries and places of culture or history. These were not the spontaneous acts of drunken soldiers, unable to appreciate either art or what they were doing. They were the acts of savages, who thought that all things of the arts and of the spirit which a civilised race holds dear, were only fetishes of another tribe no higher than their own ; and that by destroying the fetish, they would in some mystical way destroy the soul, and therefore the will to resist, of a people in every other way too strong for them. To blow up a theatre, to throw flying bombs at civilian cities, rather than to produce aircraft to outwit armies, these were similar acts from the same fallacious theory . . . that any one group of mankind must necessarily be better than another by nature, by the blood in their veins. It is the *reductio ad absurdum* of aristocrats of all kinds in any country.

But it took more than the aristocracy of the neurotic to daunt the Soviet people of Rostov. The day after the Red Army marched in, there was an open-air concert in the central square (it could be nowhere else, for there was nowhere else) with singing and dancing and variety turns. Quickly the Rostov Theatre, which had been since 1941 in the Ivanovo region, north-east of Moscow, returned. It had been kept intact under Lukovsky, and Brill as artistic director. It had learned to make and make do with its own home-made props and costumes, and to act on tiny and non-equipped stages. Perhaps it was the better for that . . . always assuming it would soon have its fine equipment restored somehow. The war-time productions of *Field-Marshal Kutuzov*, *Wait for Me*, *Pygmalion*, Zavadsky's staging of *La Locandiera* as Levitsky revised it, may not have had the luxury of their show-place stage, but they had an immediacy, an urgency, especially the first two, which no amount of imagination without stern factual experience could have achieved. And when the theatre returned, it was these two plays to which the people of Rostov flocked, and to *Russian People*, too, even nearer their own experience.

The theatre now had no premises at all. It used a repaired workers' club. So did the other theatres quickly returning home, a medical workers' club, a tobacco factory club, the soonest ready and handiest. The Musical Comedy Theatre, returning from Penza, even gave birth to a Filial, which staged gay, tuneful entertaining shows like *Silva*, *Rose Marie*, and *The Wedding at Malinovka*. And all in the region roundabout came and went two more such musical comedy theatres, and a puppet theatre, and others to the number of seven. The LenKom set to work on its own building, and by October was playing at home.

Meanwhile, four principal architects were on plans for rebuilding whole sections of the town, theatres included ; and work began at once. It began, too, in neighbouring towns, Shakhti, and Salsk, and Novocherkassk, where the theatres had been burned down in the same way, and companies came home to nothing, but with plays by Simonov and Leonov and Ostrovsky and Goldoni.

By October 1941 the Fascists in their swoop had reached Taganrog, Chehov's birthplace, and a city founded by Peter the Great, with a great oak, believed to be the one he planted, in one of its parks. Its little Town Theatre was as well known as its rich library ; and it had a Tyuz, and another theatre called the Theatre of Popular Creation. The Fascists failed to destroy all of these. The Town Theatre was kept intact. And as soon as the Red Army had driven out the last Nazi, a company was on its stage, performing Prut's play, *The Secretary of the District Committee*, and the

Regional Theatre of Comedy and Miniatures arrived on tour. The Rostov
Musical Comedy Filial which we have mentioned also gave shows here.[3]

IN THE UKRAINE

How can the pen or the typewriter do justice to the Ukraine ? That
joyous earth pulped with blood and spilt human brains, that radiant people,
more musical than the Italians, more gay than the Andaluces . . . tortured
and bereaved, and treated like insects by men with minds of metal. Yet
how resilient they were ! What reassurance of human dignity and will
was found in the rebirth of the Ukraine after its crucifixion. Poltava,
Harkov, Kiev, Dneipropetrovsk—drop a finger on the map and find a
theatre. But not, after the Fascists had gone, a theatre building. The
Ukrainians did as the men of Stalingrad and Rostov. Where no building
was left, club halls were repaired and adapted. Where no club halls were
left in adaptable condition, brigades and concert parties held their audiences
in any place where an actor could be seen or an audience could sit or stand
to listen.

Above all, the theatres were mobile. For the whole liberated district
was their audience. A theatre looked upon itself as an itinerary unit, able,
liable, and keen to go anywhere inside that audience. Most of them had
been doing this very thing to foreigners during their evacuation. It was
adding welcome to routine to keep on doing so now. This is yet another
way in which the stage was helped to develop both for and by the war.
And just as in the North Caucasus, new units sprang up to meet new conditions, so in Taganrog, Kamenskoye and elsewhere, new dramatic theatre
companies welded themselves together, at Rostov a new Tyuz (especially
new theatres for the young), at Kursk a new children's theatre, and at Stalingrad ; and a new puppet theatre in the North Caucasus. The Leningrad
Puppet Theatre gave a course to no fewer than thirty intending puppeteers.

KIEV

The history of each place differs. Kiev, for instance, the Holy City,
second Constantinople, historical heart of the Russian body, had a deep
humiliation : theatrical occupation by Nazi art. The Kiev Opera, by
common consent the finest in the Ukraine, was evacuated to Irkutsk. The
Germans, finding the noble Opera House empty, filled it with singers from
Berlin. A certain Wolfgang Brückner was sent as " Intendant ". A rise
for him. Previously he had been the leader of a café band in Koenigsberg.

During the twenty-five months of their occupation, the Germans were
not getting quite the music they expected. Brückner, a typical Prussian
brute, could not understand the evacuation scheme. He was convinced
the singers and musicians of the Opera must still be in the city, hiding.

So he had a register of occupations made, saying he wished to form a new Ukrainian opera unit. Of course there were some people in Kiev who were musicians, and it was difficult to escape from registering. They were listed. Then Brückner called his victims together, stating that they were to start work at once, but all Russian and Ukrainian music would be forbidden. Rehearsals of German opera began. Now most of those brought in were at best second-class performers, and many of them were old and ill from privation and apprehension. One asked Brückner's permission to go home, and was at once handed over to the Gestapo. Another, elderly, musician was accused of playing wrong. When he pointed out that that was how his part was written in the full score, Brückner started screaming and slashed the old man's face with his baton. His behaviour at rehearsal was often revolting.

But in time the relieving Soviet forces approached, and this little beast of an official packed up all the scores, scenery, costumes, props and library books, and sent them off to Germany, telling the company to get ready to follow, as he was about to blow up the opera. But the Red Army got there too soon, and foiled that purpose. A few days later an all-Ukrainian concert was held. The emotional value of this, when after more than two years of Nazi-Junker " art " at last national songs and the rhythm of the Gopak sounded again from a stage, can well be imagined ! Ukrainian opera was not to be killed by such creatures as Brückner.

Nor could Kiev be killed by the treatment it had taken. Maurice Hindus reports that at least a hundred thousand people had been murdered in the horrible ravine of Babii Yar. Out of a million inhabitants, only one-tenth remained, when Hindus went there. Out of two hundred thousand Jews, only five Jews. The Germans removed all the birchwood and mahogany furniture for which the city was famous ; all the fittings and furnishings of Soviet workers' flats and houses. They destroyed deliberately six million books. It is easy to imagine what liberation meant after that ; and in safe and, despite bumble-bombs, comfortable Britain, one has almost a feeling of shame as one writes of these people. The things of the spirit, of which we seem so careless, so ignorant, were the things that showed them they really had been liberated. The re-assertion of humanity.

Tutyshkin, who was in charge of the Vahtangov brigade following up the advance of the Red Army, wrote a description of their entry by lorry into the ruins of this once beautiful city on the 15th of November. They came in by the Kreshchatik, a famous avenue. The ashes of the burned buildings were still smouldering ; the pavements littered with glass. Back from neighbouring hamlets and woods, with packages and sacks on their shoulders, or pushing barrows, trudged the former inhabitants of Kiev, greedily asking for news, news of Moscow (how significant that is !), news of the way the war was going, begging for Moscow newspapers. Next day a loudspeaker fixed on a car patrolled the streets to announce a meeting that night in the Central Cinema, at which a statement would be made on the international situation, and that would be followed by a show from the Vahtangov theatre brigade. There was no electricity yet in the city. And then suddenly the chandeliers in the cinema lit up. Every new sentence was received with applause. "Soviet actors", ends Tutyshin, "are fortunate in that by following up the Red Army, they carry to our brothers as they are liberated, the light and happiness of Soviet culture, Soviet art."

Of the dramatic theatres of Kiev, one by one as they came in, perhaps the most interesting was the "Franko" Theatre with its new translation into Ukrainian of *Twelfth Night*. By the end of 1943 three theatres were again permanently open in this remarkable city.[4]

HARKOV

If Kiev held the sentiment of the Ukrainians for its antiquity, Harkov held their pride for its modernity. Not that it was not old as well ; for much of the old town was built in the eighteenth century. But it was the outstanding example of Soviet Ukrainian enterprise . . . a huge tractor factory, schools, flats, works, and particularly the vast and beautiful House of State Planning, a special treasure of modern architecture and town design, the concrete and steel shell of which mercifully still stands. Before the war a world-wide competition was held for a huge theatre to seat 4,000, meet companion to the giant Stadium already planned.

The story of Harkov is horrible. A double occupation by the Fascists, with all that implies of the cruelty of injured triumph and of beastlier revenge than before. The Red Army finally liberated this city on the 23rd of August 1943. Many of the inhabitants, unable to bear the Nazis any longer, abandoned even the remains of their twentieth-century life and fled to the woods and ravines, or lived day and night in cellars. The intellectuals who remained had been particularly oppressed. Professors, doctors, engineers, artists, were avoiding starvation by selling matches and cigarettes and cheap lighters. Here the electric lights did not come on so soon ; for the plant had been utterly wrecked and had to be rebuilt entirely. But the day after the re-entry, shops and markets and hospitals and clinics were open again. Country products were sold. The local newspaper *Socialist Ukraine* appeared. A cinema showed a film about Stalingrad.

By aeroplane arrived a brigade of the finest Ukrainian actors and actresses and singers : Litvinenko Volgemut, Kozlovsky, Patorzhinsky, Shumsky, and Lepeshinskaya. This had been specially organised by the Committee for Art Affairs and the Artistic Administration of the Ukraine.

Another brigade from the " Shevchenko " Theatre came two days later with scenes from *Partisans in the Steppes of the Ukraine* (what is the sturdy mentality which immediately after its own suffering is over can bear the vicarious suffering and heroism of its compatriots ?), and a Ukrainian comedy called *Shelmenko the Batman*. With them came singers from the Kiev Opera ; and brigades soon from the " Franko " and " Shchors " Theatres, to prepare in advance for the hurriedly returning theatre collectives as a whole. Two travelling Ukrainian theatres followed.

The great circus building had been demolished. But in the early months of 1944 the circus was restored, with a special opening prologue called " Clowns' Landing ", and a great pantomime (in the French sense) in preparation. But even in the circus reality was wanted by the sturdy population of this famous centre of resistance ; and the name of the " pantomime " was *Avengers of the People*.

The " Shchors " Theatre had already been in the liberated portion of the Ukraine for a little while. It was playing *The Wreck of the Squadron*, *In the Steppes of Ukraine*, *A Night in May* (after a Gogol story) and other shows. But besides their own theatres, the Ukrainian towns and villages were visited by brigades from other nations, like a Tajik brigade which toured in June 1943 Smolyensk, Kursk, Yelna, with songs, dances and sketches.

Odessa suffered like Kiev and Harkov. Here the Rumanian Fascists were as bad as the Germans, or possibly worse. Maikan, director of the Rumanian National Theatre, carried away all the theatrical property he could to his own theatre in Bucarest. The " Ivanov " Dramatic Theatre was robbed of costumes, props and scenery ; so was the Opera and Ballet, which lost the scores and parts of 109 operas and sixteen ballets, and a whole music library. The Fascists mined the opera house, but were prevented from blowing it up before the Red Army got there. The big Musical Comedy Theatre and the Summer Theatre were both blown up, together with many other cultural institutions, after Rumanian professors had sent all the treasures of science and art they wanted to their own homes. The casualty list of cultural and intellectual figures was tragic in its length and wantonness.[5]

THE LITTLE PLACES OF THE UKRAINE

Little towns like Starobyelsk and Kupyansk set about repairing their theatres as quickly and quietly as they could. Brigades and travelling theatres served them till this could be done. For it is an extraordinary angle on the popularity of the theatre in Soviet Ukraine that almost every little place, before the war unknown, but now pronounced all over the world as one after the other they came into the war news, had their own theatres : Vinnitsa, Berdichev, Zhmerinka, Mogilyov-Podolsk, Tulchin, Zaporozhe,

Dnyeprodzershinsk, Krivoy Rog, Melitopol, Berdyansk, Mariupol, Konstantinovka, Kramatorsk, Makeyevka, Lisichansk, Kamenets-Podolsk, Proskurov, Shepetovka, Voznyesensk, Pervomaisk, Kremenchug, Chernigov . . . some little more than villages, the Horshams and Huntingdons of the Ukraine, yet each with a permanent theatre and its permanent company, the capacity ranging from Mogilyov-Podolsk's 437 seats to 1,200 at Herson. Many, indeed, had more than one theatre, an opera theatre, which would be much bigger, or a circus, which would be bigger still. Kiev had nine permanent theatres.[6]

The same tale is to be told of the towns between the Ukrainian border and Moscow. Smolyensk had five dramatic theatres including a Lettish and a Jewish Mobile. A young actor who had been fighting with collective farmers in a partisan unit returned from the occupied areas and formed a sixth, a new Young Spectators' Theatre. He became head of it, with the declared policy of working at the front as much as possible. He hoped to have a series of plays that would show young manhood down the ages. His series would include Ostrovsky and Shakespeare.

Vyazma and Karachev had a theatre each ; Rzhov had two, both small. Kalinin, as a manufacturing city, had three, the principal one seating over 1,000. When its company returned on the 13th of February 1942, its favourite actors had a big welcome. They showed *A Fellow from Our Town, The House on the Hill, Partisans in the Steppes, etc.,* and *Kremlin Chimes.* They were preparing an Ostrovsky. Kaluga, Noginsk, Kolomna had small theatres ; Orehovo-Zuyevo, an industrial centre, had a big one and a Tyuz and two alternative buildings. Oryol, Bryansk, Yelets had at least one each. Kursk had four. Immediately on liberation it received a visit from the Moscow New Theatre, followed by the Byelgorod Theatre. Its own principal premises had to be rebuilt entirely. Meanwhile the Morshansk Regional Theatre entertained the town with *Invasion, Russian People* and *Nadyezhda Durova.*

Lipetsk and Borisoglyebsk had small theatres. Voronezh, their big town, had not made all the headway that Yermolova might have expected of her favourite provincial date, could she have returned to the burst of theatre art that Soviet conditions have given rise to. It had only two permanent theatres, though, like most of the bigger towns above, it also had a large circus and a summer theatre. One was the " Young " Theatre, the other the Grand Soviet. The last was utterly destroyed and an estimate of 1,200,000 roubles made for its replacement. Meantime, as at Kursk, a concert hall was repaired, and some seven or eight hundred people were enabled to go to the play every night.

This account of the little places and their loss of theatre buildings has not included Kolkhoz or Mobile Workers' Theatres. Many of these little towns had three or four collective farm touring theatres, with central premises on which they were based, although most of their time was spent in the country. Most of these base buildings were destroyed. But the rehabilitation of the countryside through the theatre units went on.

Some measure of the task of rebuilding can now be seen. The Sovnarkom of the Russian S.F.S.R. when it assigned a huge sum for rebuilding the Stalingrad Theatre together with repairs to the Musical Comedy and the Tyuz there, also provided 250,000 roubles for the Kursk Regional Theatre to be restored. And much of the cost naturally fell on the national budget. But other, happier theatres contributed not only funds, but also costumes, scenery, lighting plant. Yet with all the help in the world, and all the assignments of State money, the reconstitution of the theatres would be as hard and as exhausting work as the regeneration of the spirit of the occupied areas was easy and exhilarating. Although in the Soviet Union the destruction of a theatre building does not destroy a theatre, and though audiences were crying out for them long before they could return, nevertheless the creation of those theatres had been the work of devoted, eager, gifted and patient people over a period of many years. How sturdy that theatre had become, how true to life, we have seen.[7]

We have seen the countryside of Russia at first static, held so by officialdom and ownership ; then loosening up into an unwilling liberalism, and the players free now but poor, wandering aimlessly in all directions inside the ramparts of the Volga. We have followed some of them up and down that river, and to different places inside its line but rarely venturing beyond it. Then with the liberation of 1918, theatres sprang up in outer places. Life became good and there was need for more and more of it. But War and Death came instead, blowing up theatres, disrupting homes, bereaving and disfiguring and violating and annihilating. The actors went east, across the Volga.

The Germans followed east, but not across the Volga. And towards them we saw the counterflow, parties going from east to west across the Volga, like the tanks and shells and bullets that sped to the front, bringing up reserves of mind and life. The Volga became the point at which resistance was too tough for the Germans, and knowing they could never wear down that resistance, they retreated.

As they retreated the westward flow became immense. Dozens, scores, hundreds, thousands of actors and actresses crowded homeward to the ruins of the old life ; to ruins that were foundations for the new. There, at the time of writing, they remain, with rebuilding, rejoinings, rejoicings, and regeneration before them.

A process that can have no end in a world that will always be new.

This is a chapter that can have no end. So let us stop here. Watching them.

July, 1944.

SOME THEATRE MEMORIAL NAMES

Town and Location	Name	Description of Eponym	Century
Moscow Art Theatre (Russia)	Maxim Gorky	Russian author and dramatist (and founder)	20
Leningrad Grand (Russia)	,,		
Chkalov Regional (Russia)	,,		
Tula (Russia)	,,		
Rostov-on-Don Regional (Russia)	,,		
Kuibyshev (Russia)	,,		
Stalingrad (Russia)	,,		
Kislovodsk (N. Caucasus)	,,		
Vladivostok (Far East)	,,		
Krasnodar (Russia)	,,		
Pavlov-on-the-Oka (Russia)	,,		
Shuya (Russia)	,,		
Orenburg (Russia)	,,		
Mahach-Kala (Dagestan)	,,		
Simferopol (Crimea)	,,		
Kiev Children's (Ukraine)	,,		
Dniepropetrovsk Russian (Ukraine)	,,		
Tiraspol (Moldaiva)	,,		
Baku Tyuz (Azerbaijan)	,,		
Tashkent Russian (Uzbekistan)	,,		
Voroshilovsk (Russia)	Lunacharsky	Russian author, playwright and educator	20
Vladimir (Russia)	,,		
Kaluga (Russia)	,,		
Tomsk (Siberia)	,,		
Sverdlovsk Opera (Urals)	,,		
Tambov (Russia)	,,		
Ufa Summer (Bashkiria)	,,		
Sevastopol (Crimea)	,,		
Kramatorsk (Ukraine)	,,		
Odessa Russian (Ukraine)	,,		
Moscow Regional (Russia)	Ostrovsky	Russian dramatist	19
Kostroma (Russia)	,,		
Kineshma (Russia)	,,		
Leningrad (former Alexandrinsky) (Russia)	Pushkin	Russian poet and playwright	19
Krasnoyarsk (Siberia)	,,		
Grozny (Chechen-Ingutia)	Lermontov	Russian poet and playwright	19

Town and Location	Name	Description of Eponym	Century
Rybinsk " Railway Garden " (Russia)	Nekrassov	Russian poet	19
Stalinabad Russian (Tajikstan)	Mayakovsky	Russian poet	20
Tbilisi Russian (Georgia)	Griboyedov	Russian playwright	19
Borisoglyebsk (Russia)	Chernyshevsky	Russian author	19
Kolomna (Russia)	Vorovsky	Bolshevik author and diplomat	19
Maly Theatre School (Russia)	Shchepkin	Maly actor	19
Yaroslav (Russia)	Volkov	Russian actor	18
Yermolova (Moscow)	Yermolova	Russian actress	19
Maly Filial (Moscow)	Safonov	Russian actor	19
Igarka (Arctic)	Pashennaya	Russian actress	20
Harkov (Ukraine)	Shevchenko	Ukrainian poet	19
Dnyepropetrovsk (Ukraine)	"		
Kiev Opera (Ukraine)	"		
Odessa Farms (Ukraine)	"		
Chernigov (Ukraine)	"		
Kiev (Ukraine)	Lesya Ukrainka	Ukrainian poetess and playwright	19
Kiev (Ukraine)	Ivan Franko	Ukrainian author and playwright	19
Yerevan (Armenia)	Sundukyan	Armenian author	19
Tashkent Armenian (Uzbekistan)	Abelyan	Soviet architect	20
Yerevan Turkish (Armenia)	Jabarly	Armenian dramatist	20
Baku Opera (Azerbaijan)	Akhundov	Azerbaijanian dramatist	20
Stalinabad (Tajikstan)	Lakhuti	Tajik poet	20
Tbilisi (Georgia)	Rust'veli	Georgian poet	12
Tbilisi (Georgia)	Marjanishvili	Georgian producer	20
Kutaisi (Georgia)	Meshkishvili	Georgian actor	20
Kazan (Tatar Republic)	Kamal	Tatar dramatist	20
Ashkhabad (Turkmenia)	Stalin		20
Voroshilovsk (Russia)	Lenin		20
Samarkand (Uzbekistan)	"		
Saratov (Russia)	Karl Marx	German Socialist author	19
Leningrad Opera	Kirov	Leningrad Bolshevik	20
Astrakhan (Russia)	"		
Birobijan (Far East)	Kaganovich	Jewish Soviet administrator	20
Kuibyshev (Russia)	Chapayev	Civil War Leader	20
Zhitomir (Ukraine)	Shchors	Ukrainian Civil War Hero	20
Konstantinovka (Ukraine)	Artem	Ukrainian Bolshevik	20
Gorky (Russia)	Chkalov	Soviet Air Ace	20
Nikolayev (Russia)	"		
Tashkent (Uzbekistan)	Sverdlov	Russian Bolshevik	20
Grozny (Chechen-Ingutia)	Nuradilov	Chechen Hero	20
Grozny	May Day		

Town and Location	Name
Zlatoust (Urals)	10th Year of October Revolution
Sverdlovsk (Urals)	15th Anniversary of Urals Komsomol
Zhitomir Mobile (Ukraine)	Regional Professional Unions
Blagoveshchensk (Far East)	The Amur Reservoir
Tyumen (Urals)	17th Anniversary of the Red Army
Tbilisi Armenian (Georgia)	The 26 Commissars
Baku Workers' (Azerbaijan)	The Revolution
Uzbek Farms	The Socialism of Gulyubasa

APPENDIX II

SOME SOVIET WAR PLAYS

This list is not exhaustive. Few historical plays are not included.

Title	Author	Subject
Actress, An	Faiko	Stage life in war-time.
Always With Us	Rzheshevsky	Officer on leave.
At the Walls of Leningrad	Vishnevsky	Defence of Leningrad.
Battalion Goes West, The	Mdivani	(Georgian) Spiritual serenity.
Beauty Secret, The	Finn	Spiritual serenity.
Birth of Hatred, The	Bazorkin	Chechen-Ingush patriotism.
Black Cloud, The		Kirghiz play about a Kirghiz war hero.
Blue Scarf, The	Katayev	Soldiers on leave, a comedy.
Brave Soldier Schweik, Further Adventures of the	Slobodskoy	Czech comic figure in occupied country.
Brothers, The	Dyhovichny	Twins in occupied land.
Cottage at Cherkizov, The	Arbuzov	Moscow Young Communists.
Cruel Romance, The	Gladkov	New Year's Eve in Moscow.
Darya	Kozakov	Heroic rear.
Daughter of Moscow, A		Uzbek tribute to Russian girl partisan.
Deep in the Rear	Churkin and Kruglov	Heroic rear.
Dniester's Banks, On		Gipsies in war.
Dynasty	Staboy	Heroic rear.
Eagle's Flight, The	Sultanov	Uzbek fighters.
Earth Bears Witness, The	Baru and Agranenko	War correspondent's first play, about Fleet Air Arm, Leningrad.
Engineer Sergeyev	Rokk	Destruction of plant during Nazi advance.
Emergency Law	Tur Bros. and Sheinin	Sabotage and family crisis.
Family Drama, A	Pantaleyev	One-act play.
Far Country, A	Schwartz	Leningrad children evacuees.
Farzand	Ismail Zade	Uzbek play about Ukrainian children evacuees.
Field Post	Mints and Pomeshikov	Love on a farm and at the Front.
Forced Landing	Vodopyanov and Laptyev	Famous Soviet airman's comedy of State farm occupied by Nazis and liberated.
Fortress, The	Diakov and Penkin	Stalingrad actors' play about defence of Tsaritsyn, written in siege of Stalingrad.
Frenzy	Gulakyan	Armenian war heroes.

Title	Author	Subject
Ferryboat Girl, The	Pogodin	Stalingrad.
Front, The	Korneichuk	Inefficiency and its cure in the Army.
Great Hopes	Kaverin	Students' battalion.
Guard of Honour	Auezov and Abishev	Kazakh play about Panfilov and 8th Division.
Gulkan		Uzbek play about Uzbek children in war.
Hand of Justice, The	Galkin	Jewish poet's psychological play.
Homeland Calls, The	Bikbai	Bashkirian patriotism.
House on the Hill, The	Kaverin	
Immortal, The	Gladkov	Guerrillas and Moscow youth.
In the Name of Life	Alexandrov	Occupied France.
Invasion	Leonov	Occupied territory.
Islanders	Buranova	Collective farm comedy.
Ivan and Marya	Permyak	Heroic rear.
Kikvidze	Doroseli	Historical Georgian play about Tsaritsyn.
Knights of the Starry Sky	Paustovsky	Red Air Force.
Krestovsky Island	Stein	Comedy of Convalescent Home for naval officers.
Kurban Durdy	Kerbabayev	Turkmenian play about Turkmen war hero.
Land of My Birth	Simukov	Patriotic.
Long, Long Ago	Gladkov	Poetic comedy of Napoleonic Wars.
Madelaine Mine	Rzheshevsky	Occupied France.
Mariam	Isambet	Tatar play about Tatar girl heroine.
Meet the Squadron, To	Tevelyev	Navy and occupied land.
Missing	Zhalkin	Poet and guerrilla's play about guerrillas.
Moscow Girl, A	Gusyev	Poetic play about defence of Moscow.
Moscow Nights	Pogodin	Intellectuals in war.
Moscow Skies	Mdivani	Georgian tribute to defence of Moscow.
Mother	Uigun	Uzbek patriotism.
Nadir's House	Ikrami and Faiko	Tajik and Russian tribute to Stalingrad.
Naval Officer	Kron	Soviet Navy.
Northern Lights	Levin and Metter	Partisans.
Oath of Loyalty	Lavrenyov	Marines at Sevastopol
Observation Post	Tur Bros. and Sheinin	Red Army.
One Night	Schwartz	Siege of Leningrad.
Ordered to the Front	Mdivani	Georgian war response.
Partisans	Mdivani	Georgian partisans in the Crimea.
Partisans in the Steppes of Ukraine	Korneichuk	Heroic collective farm.
People of the Urals	Slonimsky	Heroic rear.
Peter Krymov	Finn	Evacuation of factories.
Ploughed Field on the Black Sea, A	Umansky and Olenin	From the German. Mind of Nazism.

Title	Author	Subject
Professor Mamontov	Marienhof	Intellectuals in war.
Quiet Little Town, A	Bela Ballash	Hungarian.
Regiment DD	Vodopyanov and Laptyev	Red Air Force.
Russian People	Simonov	Red Army and occupied territory.
Salavat	Bikbai	Bashkirian play about Bashkirian war hero.
Seeing It Through	Trenyov	Intellectuals in war.
Smoke of the Fatherland	Tur Bros. and Sheinin	Occupied territory.
Soldiers' Wives	Virta	Collective farm comedy.
Song about the Men of the Black Sea	Lavrenyov	Soviet Navy.
Sons of Three Rivers	Gusyev	Poetic fantasy of war mothers.
Spring in Moscow		
Stalingrad, People of	Chepurin	By one who was there.
Stars Cannot Fade, The	Romashov	Intellectuals in war.
Tea Talk	Furmansky	" A lyrical etude."
They Lived in Leningrad	Bergholtz and Makagonenko	Young Communists during siege.
Timur and His Comrades	Gaidar	Children's war work.
To Those Under Way	Herman	Anglo-Soviet sea convoy.
Toulon	J.-R. Bloch	Sinking of French Fleet.
Town " N "	Malyarevsky	Intellectuals in war.
Twelve Months, The	Marshak	Poetic nature play.
Unquenchable Hearts	Mabargahov	Bashkirian patriotism.
Valya Sokolova	Gogiashvili and Makhviladze	Georgian youth in war.
When Girls are Left Alone	Kloss	Collective farm comedy.
While the Heart Does Not Stop	Paustovsky	Actress-mother.
Wicked Rival, The	Shestakov	One-act play about an officer's love.
Wide Spreads the Sea	Vishnevsky, Kron and Azarov	Baltic Fleet.
Winged Tribe, The	Perventsev	Soviet Pilots
X and Y	Pogodin	
Your Love	Gusyev	One-act romance.
Youth of Our Fathers, The	Gorbatov	Part of larger work on Young Communist League.

LIST OF SOURCES AND ADDITIONAL NOTES

CHAPTER I

1. Laurence Oliphant : *The Russian Shores of the Black Sea in the autumn of* 1852 (Edinburgh and London, 2nd edn., 1853), p. 78.
2. *Ibid.* p. 77.
3. „Письма о путешествии его имп. выс. гос. великого князя Владимира Александровича 1870 г" (St. Petersburg, 1871).
4. Oliphant : *op. cit.* p. 313.
5. George Hume : *Thirty-five Years in Russia.* London, 1914 (written much earlier), pp. 112-13.
6. Ф. Булгарин: „Пантеон", 1840. I. стр. 81-7. Reprinted in „Хрестоматия по истории русского театра XVIII и XIX веков". Leningrad-Moscow, 1940, pp. 7-8.
7. В. Г. Белинский: „Александринский театр". Reprinted in Хрестоматия, pp. 70-2. Byelinsky began his literary career when a student with a tragedy that contained tirades against serfdom and got him into trouble with the pundits of Moscow University. (See N. Boguslavsky : *International Literature*, 1944, v. p. 54.)
8. „Сто лет. Александринский театр—театр госдрамы". Leningrad, 1932 ; Брянский стр. 3-78; Марков стр. 180-208.
9. From the diary of an inspector of repertoire, А. И. Храповицкий. Reprinted in Хрестоматия, pp. 77-8.
10. E. Bradlee Watson : *From Sheridan to Robertson* (Harvard, 1926), p. 206.
11. Литература и искусство: В. Всеволодский: „Премьера в Костроме". 23.ii.44. А. В. Луначарский: „Сборник: Малый театр.", 1924. Reprinted in „Статьи о театре и литературе". Moscow-Leningrad, 1938, стр. 113-21.
    A. Maximov : " Russian Natural Science ". Voks Bulletin, 1943, viii, 35-45.
12. " Speaking of Bannister, Leigh Hunt informs us that the stage appears to be his own room, of which the audience compose the fourth wall ; if they clap him, he does not stand still to enjoy their applause." Allardyce Nicoll : *A History of Late XVIIIth Century Drama* (Cambridge, 1937), p. 40.
13. In a letter Lermontov called it a " Hurrah for Patriotism " play. See Б. Нейман: „Драматургия Лермонтова", in collected edition of Lermontov's works, Искусство, 1940, pp. 26-7.
14. Quoted in Campbell's *Life of Mrs. Siddons* (London, 1834), Vol. I, p. 290.
15. С. П. Жихарев: „Записки современника". Reprinted Хрестоматия, pp. 26 and 34. This is the contemporary spelling. Varneke calls him Dmitrevsky. D. made a special hit in the " lachrymose comedy " which found its way to Russia, as to most countries. See Варнеке, *op. cit.* pp. 72 and 109.
16. Campbell's *Life of Mrs. Siddons*, Vol. II, p. 35.
17. С. Т. Аксаков. Хрестоматия, p. 35. I am obliged to the English Department of V.O.K.S. for the following information derived from an Imperial Order of 1827. Imperial Theatre personnel were grouped for the assessment of pensions in four grades, which repay close consideration. Grade I included artists of " first-class *emploi* ", decorateurs, machinists, chief *regisseurs*, and directors. Grade II included artists of 2nd class *emploi*, musicians, and machinists' assistants.

Grade III included artists taking parts of third importance, prompters, painters, "teatr-meisters", and wardrobe and property staff. Grade IV included small-part artists, the chorus, supers, dancers, assistant-painters, and flower-women. Grade I received a maximum pension of 4,000 roubles after 18 years ; Grade II a maximum of 2,500 after 20 years ; Grade III 1,500 after 22 ; and Grade IV 750 roubles after 25 years. The actual pension received depended on the salary or wages during service.

18. Авдотя Панаева: *ibid.* p. 114.
19. Аксаков: *ibid.* p. 54.
20. *Ibid.* p. 66.
21. А. А. Стахович: *ibid.* p. 84.

CHAPTER II

1. Details from Laurence Oliphant : *Russian Shores of the Black Sea* (Edinburgh and London, 1853, 2nd edn.).
2. И. М. Долгорукий: „Хрестоматия по истории русского театра", pp. 222-5.
3. Н. Ф. Юшков: *ibid.* pp. 225-30.
4. И. А. Гиляровский : „Люди театра". Искусство, 1941, pp. 82-3.
5. W. J. Lawrence : *Old Theatre Days and Ways* (London, 1935), p. 193.
6. Quoted by Н. Ф. Юшков, *loc. cit.*
7. И. С. Жиркевич, *ibid.* p. 232.
8. *Ibid.* p. 235. Most of the Imperial Theatre actors had been slaves, and were still subject to corporal punishment for misbehaviour. Varneke notes laconically, " The singer Butenbrok was beaten with rods before her wedding-day " (*op cit.* p. 141).
9. Ф. Ф. Внгел: *ibid.* p. 234.
10. *Ibid.* p. 221.
11. D. S. Mirsky : *Russia, a Short Cultural History* (London, 1931), p. 225.
12. И. М. Долгорукий: „Хрест. по ист.", p. 230.
13. *Revelations of Siberia by a Banished Lady* (London, 1853, 2nd edn.), Vol. I, *passim.*
14. From Северная пчела, 1843, quoted, „Хрест. по ист.", pp. 257-8.
15. See Allardyce Nicoll : *A History of Late XVIIIth Century Drama* (Cambridge, 1937), pp. 21 and 24.

CHAPTER III

1. П. А. Стрепетова: „Хрестоматия по истории русскою театра" стр., 259-63.
2. В. Н. Давыдов: *ibid.* pp. 268-9. Miloslavsky's real name was Baron Frideburg.
3. М. Савина: *ibid.* p. 315.
4. Н. Н. Синельников: *ibid.* pp. 266-7
5. М. И. Велизарий : *ibid.* pp. 264-5.
6. *Letters of A. P. Tchehov to O. L. Knipper* (London, 1926), p. 160.
7. Хрест. по ист. : p. 277. V. N. Davydov was a fine actor who died in 1925 at the age of 78. The stipulated inclusion of Russian plays in a Ukrainian performance was often a hardship financially, as it meant engaging extra players. But it was often minimised by the Russian plays being mere five-minute vaudevilles. Sometimes an enlightened local Russian governor would give permission for there to be only one of these " quota quickies " ; and this was frequently not heard by the audience, who retreated to the buffets and cloak-rooms, or whistled it down in the auditorium. The Ukrainian plays, on the

other hand, which were usually written by Ukrainian actors, were enormously popular, although whenever the well-established Russian critics of the day were asked to take note of this " cultural renaissance ", they handed the request from one to another, and ended by agreeing that the whole thing was the work of a " mere clique (сект.) ".   Saxagansky gives a personal account of the successful tours of at least two companies, especially in the South, during the 'eighties and 'nineties.   („Из прошлого Украинского театра".   Искусство 1938.)   He made an eloquent plea for better conditions and fairer treatment for Ukrainian and other provincial companies at the 1st Conference of Actors (1897) in which he was helped by the author-actor Karpenko-Kary, his cousin.

8. George Hume : *Thirty-five Years in Russia* (London, 1914), p. 115.
9. *Ibid.* p. 125.
10. Хрест. по ист. : p. 307.
11. Robb Lawson : *The Story of the Scots Stage* (Paisley, 1917), *passim.*
12. E. K. Chambers : *The Elizabethan Stage* (Oxford, 1923), Vol. I, pp. 255 and 263.
13. Литература и искусство : 31.vii.43.
    Труд : 1.viii.43 (*bis*).
    Лев Озеров : „Леся Украинка".   Труд : 1.viii.43.
    Павел Антокольский : „Леся Украинка".   *Лит. и иск.* : 31.vii.43.
    Moscow News : 6.viii.43.
    Б. Варнеке : „История русского театра XVII-XIX веков" стр. 249, 262.
    Малая советская энциклопедия.   X. 134-5.

CHAPTER IV

1. D. S. Mirsky : *Russia, A Short Cultural History* (London, 1931), p. 227.
2. Хрестоматия по ист., p. 142.
3. Ю. Юрев : „Записки", Искусство : 1939, p. 31.
4. В. М. Дорешевич.   Хрест. по ист., p. 143.   At this time the censorship was relaxed towards the Press.   See Sir B. Pares, *History of Russia*, 3rd edn., p. 345.
5. Вл. А. Гиляровский : „Люди театра".   Искусство, 1941, p. 170.
6. А. Р. Кугель. Хрест. по ист. : p. 153.   She said there was a " kind of fog " round the character, but added seriously, " As a rule I don't feel a mother's heart at all well ".
7. Н. Н. Ходотов : *ibid.* p. 163.
8. *Ibid.* p. 160, and А. Глама-Мещерская : „Воспоминания" Искусство, 1937, p. 68.
9. *Ibid. loc. cit.*
10. „Семья Садовских" : V.T.O. 1939, p. 36.
11. Quoted *Soviet Theatre Chronicle*, 1943, iii, 4.
12. For a short account, see *The New Soviet Theatre.*
13. B. Romashov Лит. и иск. : 10.iv.43.   The novelist was Goncharov.
14. „Семья Садовских", Вл. Филиппов : V.T.O. 1939, pp. 12, 21.
15. Глама : *op. cit.* pp. 79-84.
16. Э. Бескин : „А. И. Южин-Сумбатов".   Искусство, 1936, p. 8.
17. *Ibid.* p. 11.   Some did have full sets and costumes, but, as Brenko said, " under a Damocles' sword ".
18. Глама : *op. cit.* p. 130.
19. Юрев : *op. cit.* p. 14.
20. Глама : *op. cit.* pp. 128-68 ; and notes by Носков : p. 348.

21. Б. Варнеке: Ист. русск. театра : p. 345 ; and Глама : *op. cit.* p. 85 ; and Б. А. Горий-Горяйков: „Кулисы," (Leningrad, 1940), p. 78.

22. Глама : *op. cit.* p. 133.

23. Юрев : *op. cit.* p. 71.

24. Бескин : *op. cit.* p. 12.

25. „А. А. Яблочкина" : p. 55.   When Burlak died, in 1888, his personal possessions were auctioned for the sum of 9 roubles, 60 kopeks. See И. Груздев : „Горький и его время" (Leningrad 1936), Vol. I, p. 411.

26. Юрев : *op. cit.* pp. 75-7.

27. *Ibid.* p. 226.

28. „А. А. Я лочкина" : p. 100 and n. 28.

29. Юрев : *op. cit.* pp. 94, 147.

30. Семья Садовских : pp. 40-61.

31. *Ibid.* p. 184 (О. Дурылин).

32. Юрев : *op. cit.* pp. 186-7.

33. Бескин : *op. cit.* pp. 35-55 and 112.

34. Горий : *op. cit.* p. 168.   It should not be assumed, from the prominence I have given to Ostrovsky, that he stood absolutely alone.   The following plays at the Alexandrinsky, even in Peterburg of the 'fifties, are reputed to have had considerable reality and contact with the way real people lived :

The World is Not Without Kindly Folk (1857) by N. Lvov, showing up the bribery prevalent among the *chinovniki*. *Chinovniki* (1956) by Count Sologub, on a similar theme.   Dyachenko's *Victim for Victim*, about the way " justice " was administered.

Chernyshev's *Paterfamilias*, about the position of women.

V. Krylov's *Against The Current*, about the lot of the serfs.   (This was not Ivan Krylov, the Fable-writer, but Victor Krylov, who was on the staff of an Imperial Theatre.)

It is interesting that the inclusion of the first-named play was due to the Director's wish to increase his receipts ; but the Tsar banned it unless it was given without any advance publicity ; in Moscow it was banned absolutely.   See „Сто лет", pp. 90-92.

35. „Сто лет. Александринский театр—театр госдрам." (Leningrad, 1932), p. 81 ; and several references *passim* in this chapter.

CHAPTER V

1. Б. Варнеке : *op. cit.* p. 349.

2. *A Narrative of the Life of Mrs. Charlotte Charke,* by Herself.   1755.   Reprinted, London, 1929.

3. Вл. А. Гиляровский ; „Люди театра" (Иск. 1941), p. 39.

4. George Hume : *Thirty-five Years in Russia* (London, 1914), pp. 127-8. Гиляровский, *op. cit.* p. 49.   The great nineteenth-century actor, W. C. Macready, wrote that in the early years of his century when our stage was at as low a level as the Russian, a " theatre was considered indispensable in towns of very scanty populations ".   The audiences were primarily middle-class, because there were too few seats at prices accessible to the others, as Saxagansky says was true also of the Russian provinces.   But " the larger towns were centres to which the country families resorted for the winter season, or crowded to the public weeks of races and assizes, when the assembly

rooms and the theatres were the places of fashionable meeting ". These provincial theatres were linked in circuits that could occupy a company for a whole year, so that they felt " at home " with their audiences and made quite a decent living. Macready himself did so well that he hesitated to take the risk of going to London. (*Macready's Reminiscences* (London, 1875), Vol. I, pp. 37, 124, etc.). A close-up account of provincial theatres in our own countries, so like in many ways to those of Russia, can be had in the admirable records of Brighton and Worthing now being compiled under the Worthing Art Development Scheme.

5. Гиляровский : *op. cit.* p. 53.
6. *Ibid.* p. 57.
7. *Ibid.* p. 59.
8. *Ibid.* p. 112. There were many settlements called " Communes " in Peterburg at this time, where poor students lived who could not afford lodgings. They were suspect to the Tsarist police.
9. *Ibid.* p. 110.
10. *Ibid.* pp. 83–5.
11. *Ibid.* pp. 140, 251–2.
12. *Ibid.* p. 81.
13. *Ibid.* pp. 254–5.
14. *Ibid.* p. 62.
15. *Ibid.* p. 50.
16. Ник. Ряжский : „Оборудование клубной сцены“ (Moscow, 1935), p. 11.
17. Гиляровский : *op. cit.* pp. 209, 54, 81 ; and А. Глама-Мещерская : *op. cit.* pp. 85–106 ; and Б. Варнеке : *op. cit.* p. 347.
18. Гиляровский : *op. cit.* pp. 194, 210, 212, 216.
19. Sir B. Pares : *History of Russia*, 3rd edn., p. 385.
20. Гиляровский : *op. cit.* pp. 28, 38, 43, 52, 71, 85, 95, 110, 185, 257–8.
21. *Ibid.* pp. 70–1.
22. *Ibid.* pp. 142–160.
23. *Ibid.* p. 63.
24. Глама-Мещерская : *op. cit.* p. 111.
25. Гиляровский : *op. cit.* p. 253.
26. Глама-Мещерская : *op. cit.* pp. 119–25.
27. Гиляровский : *op. cit.* p. 266.
28. *Ibid.* pp. 260–3.
29. L. W. Shklovsky : *In Far N.-E. Siberia* (London, 1916), pp. 50, 186, 202–3.
30. G. Hume : *op. cit.* p. 196.
31. „Самарсая Газета,“ 24.viii.1895. Reprinted in „Горкий об искусстве“ (Искусство, 1940), pp. 9, 10, 17, 18–19, 22.
32. С. Дурылин : „Н. М. Радин“ монография (Искусство, 1941), Chap. I.

CHAPTER VI

1. А. Фрейдкин : „Новатор-реалист“ ТЕАТР. (1938), x-xi, p. 137.
   В. Я. Виленкин : „Вл. И. Немирович-Данченко“ Муз. Теат. им. Н-Д. (1941), p. 39. As author, Nemirovich-Danchenko partly produced his own plays at the Maly. He avoided superficial tricks like the gunshots, faints, and face-slapping, so popular with the official producers, Victor Krylov, Spazhinsky and others.

2. Вл. И. Немирович-Данченко : „Из прошлого" (1936), pp. 13, 71.
Komissarzhevsky : *Myself and the Theatre* (London, 1929), pp. 23-4.

3. Виленкин : *op. cit.*

3a. Material has arrived too late, unfortunately, for the detailed examination I had hoped to give in this chapter to the influence of the Art Theatre on the provinces. Suffice it to say here that its tours drew crowded houses, especially during the 2nd decade of its life. These tours were mostly of " the South ", Kiev, Harkov, Rostov-on-Don, Odessa ; in short, the centres of the more enlightened bourgeoisie of the early twentieth century. The most popular authors in these circles were Chehov and Ibsen (by contemporary account), but Hauptmann, Maeterlinck and Leonid Andreyev were also sure of a hearing. Plays written in the old style, according to a Peterburg writer describing the provinces in 1909, " met sour looks not only on the critics' side, but the public's too ". And he calls the Art Theatre " a kind of Table of the Covenant, on which are inscribed the Sacred Words of the Law ". Even in a small place like Lubny in Poltava district (a place so small that it is barely mentioned in Baedeker's *Guide to Russia*) a performance of *Children of the Sun* in 1906 was given " after the Moscow Art Theatre Production ".

4. *Ibid.* p. 106.

5. Немирович-Данченко : *op. cit.* p. 154. Out of twenty-six rehearsals for *The Seagull*, N.-D. took fifteen, Stanislavsky nine, and Luzhsky two. (Freidkin, *op. cit.* p. 143.)

6. К. С. Станиславский : „Моя жизнь в искусстве." 3rd edn., p. 339. The Art Theatre, being a subscription Theatre, could do Chehov's plays as he wrote them without conforming to the censor's demands in regard to public performance.

7. 10.iv.1904. See *Letters of A. P. Tchehov to O. L. Knipper* (London, 1926), p. 380.

8. Notes quoted by S. Baruhaty in „Чехов и Московский Художественный Театр.", ТЕАТР. (1938), x-xi, pp. 109-23.

9. A. I. Adashev's school was taught entirely by actors of the Art Theatre : Adashev, Alexandrov, Luzhsky, Kachalov, Leonidov. A springboard for young aspirants to leap into the company. See Н. Зограф : „Вахтангов" (Искусство : 1939), p. 151, n. 5. Vahtangov had been a friend of " Suler " in Paris, and learned much from him before joining the Art Theatre in March 1911 after eight years' work with amateurs.

10. Quoted by Фрейдкин : *loc. cit.* p. 145.

11. Ю. Юзовский : „Враги" Горького на сцене „МХАТ." ТЕАТР : (1938), x-xi, p. 75. Yuzovsky in his searching book, „Драматургия Горького" (Искусство, 1940), Vol. I, p. 163, notes that Gorky always shows distinct and usually conflicting groups among the intelligentsia—working or idle, progressive or conservative, humane or selfish, cultured or crude—never in a schematic fashion, but as individuals. Even Nil, the first proletarian-revolutionary on the Russian stage, was no doctrinaire figure. It is to this burning truthfulness, so characteristic of Gorky, that Yuzovsky ascribes the success of his plays, especially *The Lower Depths*, at a time when the Russian middle class wanted to know the truth.

Gorky had little direct and intimate connection with the stage itself. He has left a little-known but amusing sketch of his experiences when walking-on as a super in the spectacular melodramas at Nizhny-Novgorod in his youth. These generally required a large number of supers in several guises ; as, in

Christopher Columbus, both Indians and Devils. Gorky recalls that he could recall no mention of the latter in Prescott, but that in any case the Stage Manager could instil no sense or discipline into his charges, and ended by losing his temper and calling the Indians " pigs " and the devils " bears ". Burlak was in the company at this time. He told stories, slightly drunk, from the fore-stage in the intervals. (See И. Груздев : *op. cit.* Vol. I, pp. 404-13.)

I feel I should add that in writing up Gorky, I do not seek to write down Chehov, who certainly had the same moralist's and satirist's intention of inspiring people to *change* their way of living, though I do not think he succeeded so well in his intention with his plays. But neither do I wish to underrate his influence on Gorky, which, as upon most dramatists of Europe and America since his day, was great. Our own Shaw and Priestley have confessed as much in letters to Литература и искусство (15.vi.44 and 1.vii.44).

12. It was performed in a translation by Laurence Irving at the Kingsway Theatre, London, in December 1911, with Holman Clarke, Frances Wetherall and Haidee Wright in the cast. I fancy this was the first Gorky play to be done in our countries and few of his pre-Revolutionary plays seem to have been done here.

13. М. Горкий : „О пьесах" (1932). Published in the collection of articles and speeches „Горкий о литературе" (Moscow, 1935). The reason for Gorky's dissatisfaction is brilliantly explained by Yuzovsky (*op. cit.* Chapter II). Luka is not a saint, but very much a sinner ; at the same time he is not altogether unlikeable. His " elevating illusion of the Blessed Land " is something that each of these unfortunates deeply needs ; and if his comfort inhibits them from action against the causes of their misery, it also inhibits them from suicide. He is not a Tolstoyan, nor a Dostoyevsky type. He may be a liar and a deceiver, but he is not himself a false figure within the " truth of fact " (a conception at the root of Gorky's thinking as at that of Carlyle). The correct interpretation of him, and therefore of the play, consists, Luzovsky says, in showing the two sides of him. In the same way the play itself is on two planes : " the obvious and the concealed ; the talk of the principal figures that goes on before the audience's eyes, and the processes that go on in the depth of the play ". This latter process might be called " a journey from past to future ".

14. Ю. Соболев : „Московский художественный театр." (Иск : 1938), p. 54.

15. Quoted by Д. Тальников : „Комиссаржевская" (Иск : 1938), p. 194.

16. Л. Малюгин, in a review of the play at the Leningrad Grand Dramatic, ТЕАТР : (1939), vi, pp. 76-84.

17. M. Gorky in the article quoted above. An important article, as it is largely the inspiration of the idea of Socialist Realism, p. 148.

18. Vol. III, p. 555.

19. = " Way of Living ". What Government Reports and Statistics denote but cannot describe.

20. Виленкин : *op. cit.* p. 170. Gorky was not objecting here to Dostoyevsky in books, where an intelligent reader can weigh up the figures he is reading about and compare them with what he knows of life ; but on the stage, especially with the realistic talents of the Moscow Art Theatre, no such comparison was possible. " The stage transfers the spectator from the realm of thought, of freely permitted discussion, to a realm of suggestion, hypnosis, to a shadowy realm of emotions and feelings—what is more, to peculiar,

'Karamazovish' feelings, which become malignantly stressed and thickened. . . . On the stage the spectator sees humanity created by Dostoyevsky after the fashion and in the likeness of a savage and evil beast. But humanity is not like that. I know."

This consequence of naturalistic performance, and the responsibility it would throw on a dramatic author, are of great importance in assessing socialist realism.

See Gorky's second letter on Karamazovism, printed in Горький об искусстве, pp. 163-6.

21. Б. А. Бялик : „Горкий в борбе с театральной реакцией" (Иск. : 1938), pp. 21-34. The phrase properly referred to movements of " Free " Verse and " Free " Art which replaced accuracy with a misty impressionism, devoid of social contents.

22. *The Life of Klim Samgin*, published in American as *The Bystander*.

23. M. Gorky : *Reminiscences of Tolstoy, Chehov and Andreyev* (London, 1934), p. 108.

24. *Ibid.* p. 110.

25. A letter to Русское слово, 27.x.13. Reprinted in „Горкий об искусстве" : (1940), pp. 163-6. Nemirovich-Danchenko gave *When We Dead Awaken*, his first solo Art Theatre production (1900), realistic not symbolic treatment. (Freidkin, *op. cit.* p. 143.)

26. Юзовский : *op. cit.* pp. 44-77.

27. Вилинкин : *op. cit.* pp. 214-15.

28. M. Gorky : " Tasks and Times of the B.D.T." (1919), No. 1. Quoted in „Гос. Большой Драматический Театр им. М. Горкого 1919-1939" (Leningrad, 1939), pp. 11-12.

CHAPTER VII

1. *Moscow News* : 4.i.43 ; 27.ii.43.

2. *International Literature*, 1942, vii-viii, p. 116. Литература и искусство : 13.i.42 ; 6.vi.42 ; 15.viii.42 ; 30.i.43 ; 10.vii.43 ; 13.xi.43 ; 10.vi.44. The Sardou play was *La Patrie* (1869), known in the U.S.S.R. as *Flanders*. Another play was by the Byelorussian producer Golovchiner. N. Loiter (not E. Loiter of the GOSET) is the chief producer of the second Byelorussian Theatre. Late in 1943 Litvinov, his opposite number in the first Byelorussian Theatre, produced another Lope de Vega play, *The Dog in the Manger*, and a new play about his compatriot partisans by another Byelorussian, Romanovich. In 1944 this theatre was rehearsing a new one. When it performed the comedies of the national poet Yanka Kupala, informal lectures were held in which the Director acquainted the audience with the poet's other works.

3. *Soviet War News* : 8.iv.42.

4. *Moscow News* : 7.iv.42 ; 24.xi.43. Лит. и иск. : 27.ii.43 ; 14.viii.43 ; 18.xii.43. Many Ukrainian miners evacuated to the Urals, where they carried on their mining. The two regions had different methods, and learnt much from each other industrially, as the theatres helped them to understand each other culturally.

5. *Moscow News* : 16.ix.42. Лит. и иск. : 13.i.42 ; 18.vii.42 ; 24.x.42 ; 22.v.43 ; 21.viii.43 ; 20.xi.44 ; 25.xi.44. Ivan Franko is perhaps best known for the play here mentioned,

whose title is sometimes rendered *Stolen Happiness*. It is a study of a sturdy old Ukrainian peasant who, after the vicissitudes of a strenuous life, settles down peacefully to happiness with a young wife, painfully stolen from him by a handsome young rural policeman. In the above production, which was not a new one, Gnat Yura had splendid acting material to direct in the persons of Buchma and Krivitskaya, both stars of the Ukrainian stage. In 1944 this theatre was rehearsing a new play by Dmiterko about the Soviet hero, Marshal Vatutin.

6. *Ibid.*: 27.vii.42 ; 25.xii.42 ; 30.i.43 ; 21.viii.43.

7. *Soviet War News*: 8.iv.42.
   Moscow News: 9.vi.42.
   Лит. и иск.: 19.i.42 ; 14.ii.42 ; 21.iii.42 (*bis*) ; 4.iv.42 ; 25.xii.42 ; 13.ii.43.

8. *Moscow News*: 29.viii.43.

9. *Ibid.*: 10.iii.42.

10. Лит. и иск.: 30.v.42 ; 18.vii.42 ; 12.xii.42 ; 10.vii.43 ; 11.xii.43 ; 1.v.44 ; 8.iv.44. In the course of 1943 this Estonian collective toured the Estonian sections of the Red Army with a play by the Estonian author Paul Rumm, called *The Brown Plague*. It was then under the direction of People's Artist of the Estonian Republic Paul Pinn.

The literature of agrarian Latvia developed healthily during the war, in all shapes from lyrics to historical novels. Several war plays are mentioned as being as good as any other Soviet war play, especially *The Daughter-in-Law* (V. Lapis), *A Latvian Partisan* (A. Upits), *Latvians Go To War* (F. Roktselnis), and some one-act plays by A. Kupshe. Those Latvian performers who managed to escape East were formed into a single collective early in the war.

11. *Soviet Theatre Chronicle*, 1943, iv, p. 26.
    Moscow News: 8.ix.43.
    Int. Lit. 1944, vi, 76.
    Лит. и иск.: 3.vii.43. There were 277 theatres in the R.S.F.S.R.: that at Oryol being reputed for passionate, full-blooded shows.

12. *Moscow News*: 8.ix.43.
    Лит. и иск.: 21.viii.43 ; 28.viii.43.

13. Material for M.X.A.T. from :
    Ю. Калашников in Лит. и иск.: 4.ix.43.
    A. Novikov: "The M.A.T. in Saratov", *Int. Lit.*, 1942, iii-iv, pp. 109-12.
    H. Rovich: *Moscow News*: 7.vi.43.
    N. Militsyna, *ibid.*: 28.x.42.
    N. Vladimirova, *ibid.*: 21.vi.42.
    Prof. Gorchakov: *Soviet War News*: 7.i.43.
    Ibid.: 13.iv.42 ; 17.ix.42 ; 26.ix.42 ; 28.iv.43.
    Int. Lit.: 1943, viii, pp. 79-80 ; 1944, vii, 78.
    Moscow News: 9.ix.42 ; 2.viii.43 ; 27.x.43.
    Sov. Th. Chron. (in Russian), 1943, i, p. 1. (In English), 1943, iv, 5-10.
    Лит. и иск.: 19.i.42 ; 4.iv.42 ; 12.xii.42 ; 13.ii.43 ; 6.iii.43 ; 31.vii.43 ; 17.vii.43 ; 28.viii.43 ; 25.ix.43 ; 25.xii.43 ; 12.ii.44. Another interesting production was that of a play by Bulgakov about Pushkin (*The Final Days*), in which the central figure, the poet himself, never appeared on the stage. It was written as a tragedy, but was considered a weak one, and the sets by Peter Williams were said to be the best thing in the show (Дурылин „Театр," 1944, p. 93).

Other Shakespearean productions in view were *Julius Caesar*, *Othello*, and *Antony and Cleopatra*.

The School for Scandal was produced by Gorchakov. Critics linked it with a production about the same time, in the Stanislavsky Opera and Drama Studio, of *The Duenna*, with music by the Soviet composers Kreitner and Gin, in place of the music by Linley for which Sheridan wrote it. This was produced by Kedrov.

The 1000th performance of *The Blue Bird* took place on 11 February 1944. The 900th performance of *The Cherry Orchard* on 28 July 1943, with Olga Knipper-Chehova still playing Ranyevskaya, her original part, and Kachalov (the original Trofimov) as Gayev.

Simonov wrote of *Russian People* " If my play is acted in such a way that it does not call for revenge, then it is not serving its purpose (*Moscow News* : 9.ix.42).

Teleshyova had helped with the production of Ostrovsky's *Last Sacrifice* which Hmelyov directed in its first Moscow Art Theatre performance on 27 June 1944. A certain amount of improvisation was encouraged among the company in this tragi-comedy of a nineteenth-century wedding.

Nemirovich-Danchenko's house with all its contents has been declared a National Museum.

During the rehearsals for *Kremlin Chimes* at Lenin's favourite theatre, the text altered a good deal. Pogodin's additions swelled it by about 10 pages. It became a deeper and broader study of Lenin. Leonidov, joint producer with Knyebel, took his task so seriously that he asked Nemirovich-Danchenko himself to help. Unfortunately, Leonidov himself also died shortly before the theatre left for Saratov ; and the first night took place without him, on the 22 January 1942. Four workers of the Moscow Art Theatre received Stalin Awards for their part in this play.

Theatre, 1944, v-vi, 5-9.

14. Material for Maly :

M. Bertenson, *Moscow News* : 13.ii.43.

G. Corner, *ibid.* : 17.x.42.

Prof. Durylin, *Soviet War News* : 7.i.43. Правда, 11.x.42.

Moscow News : 26.v.42 ; 9.vi.42 ; 2.ix.42 ; 17.x.42 ; 20.viii.43.

Soviet War News : 26.ix.42 ; 7.i.43.

Sov. Th. Chron. : 1943, i, p. 2 ; iv, p. 18.

Правда : 28.x.42 ; 30.x.42.

Труд : 9.ix.42 ; 17.ix.42.

Лит. и иск. : 12.xii.42 ; 30.i.43 ; 5.vi.43 ; 19.vi.43. ; 4.iii.44.

Известия : 30.iii.43 ; 2.iv.43 ; 29.iv.43.

Театральный справочник С.С.С.Р. : 1937-8, pp. 108-16.

Огонёк : 11.x.42.

Boris Pasternak's translation of *Romeo and Juliet* was to be used. There should be an interesting comparison for Moscow playgoers between *Antony and Cleopatra* at the two leading theatres.

Other plays being done by the younger generation were *The Cherry Orchard*, *The Storm*, and Pushkin's Don Juan play, *The Stone Guest*.

The general attitude of evacuees seems to have been as shown in that otherwise rather personal and limited book by Margaret Wettlin, *Russian Road* (London, 1945). Life and people in evacuation were interesting, but the heart yearned for Moscow, even in the days of its danger and destruction and grim living.

I. Kruti in Литература и искусство, 5.vi.43, says that the Maly was at that time playing *Invasion* " for the first time ". This does not mean, however, that the Maly production was the first in Russia.

Uspensky's first book, *The Morals of Rasteryayeva Street*, implies in the street name confusion and despair.

15. Material for Red Army Theatre :

Г. Бояджиев, „Алексей Попов", Лит. и иск. 21.iii.43.

С. Герасимов, „Театр Красной Армии", *ibid.* : 19.vi.43.

John Gibbons, *Daily Worker*, London : 17.v.44.

Moscow News : 3.iii.43 ; 11.vi.43.

V.O.K.S. Bulletins, 1942, i-ii, pp. 65-6 ; vii-viii, pp. 63-7.

Лит. и иск. : 5.vi.43 ; 11.ix.43 ; 18.xii.43 ; 11.xii.43.

Театральная Москва : 1935, pp. 156 and 161.

Театральный справочник : 1936, pp. 150 and 289.

The new play by Gerassimov was called *The Great Land*, and had to do with wartime production in the Urals. It was not a very profound or original play, but frank and in many passages, moving.

The Stalingrad play was produced by Ivan Voroshilov under Popov's direction.

16. Material for LenKom :

A. Kocharyants, *Moscow News* : 10.ii.43.

Alfredo Gomez de la Vega : *El Teatro en la U.R.S.S.* (Mexico, 1938), p. 143.

С. Раджинский : „Сирано де Бержерак," Лит. и иск. 2.x.43.

Moscow News : 14.iii.43.

Sov. Th. Chron., 1943, iii. pp. 33-5.

Лит. и иск. : 15.iv.42 ; 6.ii.43 ; 6.iii.43 ; 17.vii.43 ; 31.vii.43 ; 18.ix.43 ; 23.x.43 ; 30.x.43 ; 2.iii.44 ; 20.v.44. Комсомольская правда, 16.xi.43.

The Day of the Living was produced by Sofya Giatsintova, another leading LenKom actress, and wife of Bersenyev. The LenKom production of *The Eagle's Flight* was the first occasion on which an Uzbek play was done in Moscow in the Russian language.

A later show was *The Duel* (see Chap. XI, note 5) by the Tur Brothers and Sheinin. This, although produced by Bersenyev, remained a rather ordinary detective-story play of intrigue, adventure and " situations ". More interesting in theme was to be *They Lived in Leningrad*, a story of heroism among the young Communists in Leningrad war-factories during the Siege. It was written by O. Bergholtz and G. Makagonenko. Another Komsomol play was Arbuzov's *The Cottage in Cherkizov*, in preparation late in 1943. Giatsintova was at this time working on a production of Turgenyev's *Month in the Country*.

Konstantin Simonov has accepted the post of literary consultant to this theatre.

17. Material for Mossoviet :

Sov. Th. Chron., 1943, i, pp. 10-11 ; iii, p. 35 ; iv, pp. 19-22.

Moscow News : 24.xi.43 ; 18.x.44.

Театральный справочник : 1937-8, pp. 310 and 356.

Лит. и иск. : 16.v.42 ; 8.v.43 ; 7.viii.43 ; 23.x.43 ; 23.ii.44 ; 13.v.44 ; 15.vi.44.

Soviet War News : 20.xii.44.

While in evacuation the Mossoviet Theatre celebrated its 25th birthday. It was originally the M.O.S.P.S. Theatre, which served Trade Union Clubs in Moscow. Zavadsky had been a pupil of Stanislavsky and of Vahtangov. His style might be described as " selective socialist realism " since, although it gives full opportunity to the actor, it also takes heed of "accuracy in furniture and accessories, but few in number ". Zavadsky has been building up a reputation as a teacher of young actors.

In 1944 he produced Goldoni's *An Amusing Situation* and a new play by Knorre, *Encounter in the Dark*, the story of a young Soviet girl behind the German lines. Maretskaya, whom British filmgoers will remember in that moving film, *No Greater Love*, is said to have given another wonderful performance in this play. At this time the Mossoviet was using the Winter Theatre at the Hermitage, as its own premises were being occupied by the LenSoviet Theatre. The Goldoni inspired Boyajiyev to write his approval of Zavadsky's "journey to truth ".

18. Material for Vahtangov :

П. Новицкий, „Рубен Симонов", Лит. и. иск. : 21.iii.43.

Moscow News : 21.x.42 ; 8.ix.43.

Soviet War News : 25.i.43 ; 3.v.43.

Int. Lit. : 1942, v-vi, p. 110.

Sov. Th. Chron. : 1943, i, pp. 9-10 ; iii, 17-18 ; iv, 29-32.

Лит. и. иск. : 7.viii.43 ; 28.viii.43 ; 4.ix.43 ; 25.ix.43 ; 32.x.43 ; 13.xi.43 ; 4.iii.44 ; 8.vii.44.

Although there is no " grading " of Moscow theatres, and it is difficult to choose between the importance of the Vahtangov and Revolution Theatres (the latter is slightly bigger than the former in its capacity, 1,320 to 1,197), Ohlopkov's transfer implies promotion, in that he is now sole Director. I am told he has since returned as a guest producer on occasion to the Vahtangov Theatre. Simonov took over the part of Hamlet.

The 1944 productions, *A Servant of Two Masters* and Osctrovsky's *Storm*, do not seem to have impressed the critics very greatly. In the former the producer, Tutyshkin, is said to have somewhat spoiled an intended gaiety and lightness by too many pauses and a lack of rhythm ; the latter, according to Boyajiyev, lacked that "optimistic tonality" which socialist realism finds in Ostrovsky, and merely plunged the spectator into a kind of historical gloom.

On the other hand, Simonov's production of *The Front* was taken by the same critic as an example of the difference between Truth and mere Versimilitude (see Театр, 1944, pp. 98-102). This was performed without front tabs ; and the scene for Staff Headquarters consisted of an oval table, with a red cloth, a big green armchair, and a few smaller chairs ; no maps, heavy doors or bookshelves. A non-realistic use of the forestage. All most unverisimilar, commented Boyajiyev ; but the audience got to know these characters intimately, from the intensity and breadth with which the actors conceived them. A deeply realistic production, Boyajiyev concluded.

19. Material about Theatre of the Revolution :

„Планы театра революции," Лит. и иск. : 9.x.43.

Soviet Home Front : 1943, Oct.-Nov.-Dec.

Театральный справочник. : 1936, p. 124 ; 1937-8, p. 136.

Лит. и иск. : 31.vii.43 ; 9.x.43 ; 23.x.43 ; 20.xi.43.

20. Moscow Theatre of Drama :

    Sov. Th. Chron. : 1943, i, pp. 3-4.

    Театр. справ. : 1937-8, p. 145.

    Moscow News, 24.x.43.

    Лит. и иск. : 4.ix.43.

    Other plays done during the war to the citizens of Moscow were *A Moscow Girl* (Victor Gusyev) and *Wait For Me* (Simonov). All, it will be noticed, current drama. I have no information that this theatre attempted the classics.

21. Moscow Theatre of Satire :

    Alexander Werth : *Moscow ' 41* (London, 1942), p. 120.

    Moscow News : 14.vii.42.

    Sov. Th. Chron. : 1943, iv, pp. 23-4.

    театральный справочник : 1935, pp. 135-6.

    Лит. и. иск. : 13.i.42 ; 9.v.42 ; 15.v.43 ; 28.viii.43 ; 25.ix.43 ; 23.x.43 ; 20.xi.43.

22. Kamerny Theatre :

    С. Дрейден „На сцене Камерного театра" Лит. и иск. : 21.viii.43.

    Moscow News : 9.vi.42 ; 24.x.42 ; 9.ix.44.

    Int. Lit. : 1942, iii-iv, p. 122. 1944, iii, 72 ; vii, 74.

    Sov. Th. Chron. : 1943, iv, pp. 22-3.

    Известия : 2.x.43.

    „Камерный театр." (Moscow, 1934), p. 9.

    Лит. и иск. : 8.iii.42 ; 14.iii.42 ; 1.viii.42 ; 28.viii.43 ; 25.xii.43 ; 1.v.44 ; 2.xi.44.

    In 1944 Tairov was preparing Ostrovsky's *Guilty Though Guiltless*, a pathetic play about a mother seeking her lost son. During that year *Adrienne Lecouvreur* reached her 750th performance. Later, Tairov gave *Wide Spreads the Sea, Admiral Nahimov* (a historical play about the Battle of Navarino and the independence of Greece), *L'Avare,* and for the Chehov celebrations a " concert " performance of the *Seagull.* This last was a remarkable affair. Music by Chaikovsky, vocal, instrumental, and orchestral, was performed off-stage. An open stage was draped with grey cloth and a grey back-drop. A horse-shoe rostrum, with armchairs and round tables at its horns ; and during the second half of the entertainment, a black grand piano with a stuffed seagull on it, was placed in position. Across the grey back-drop passed misty visions of a purplish colour while Nina and Treplev listened to part of a Chaikovsky Symphony. These visions reappeared in old gold during the performance of the play-within-the-play. Even the B flat minor Concerto was brought in, when Treplev flung away his MS. and sat down at the piano, the invisible orchestra taking over from him like film music. The final touch of visual " interpretation " was added at the end, when to a Chaikovsky Nocturne a single spot picked out on the darkened stage the symbol of a seagull soaring. No make-up was used, and the players appeared in evening dress.

    In 1945 the Kamerny Theatre held its thirtieth anniversary. Tairov received the Order of Lenin, and Alice Koonen the Order of the Red Banner of Labour.

23. GOSET :

    Soviet War News : 8.iv.42.

    Moscow News, 15.i.44.

    Лит. и иск. : 4.vii.42 ; 28.viii.43 ; 9.x.43 ; 23.x.43 ; 18.xii.43.

24. G. Grigoryev, " The Gipsy Theatre ", *Soviet War News* : 21.i.43.

    Sov. Th. Chron. : 1943, iv, p. 24.

    Moscow News, 10.vi.44.

    Int. Lit. : 1944, vi, p. 75.

    Лит. и иск. : 21.viii.43 ; 23.x.43 ; 4.iii.44.

The Gipsy Theatre still tended to rely more on colour and music than on depth of character or truth of dramatic life. For that reason the full-scale Cervantes show tended to get a little boring, one critic noted, in spite of the colour and rhythm and dances. This fault was removed in *The Cobbler's Fair Wife,* by Garcia Lorca, in which the gipsy actress, Lyalya Chornaya, gave a fascinating study of the bewitching, taunting, tyrannical, scintillating, flighty, but loyal and beautiful young wife of the staid old cobbler.

It will be noted that there is a close connection between Spain and Russia by way of the gipsies. The Spanish writer, Cesare Arconada, now resident in the Soviet Union, made the stage adaptation of the Cervantes. Where Spanish characters were on the stage, the dialogue was in Russian ; where Gipsies only, in Romany, the usual language of this theatre. Similarly, in these plays Bugachevsky, the theatre's musician, studied Spanish folksong and dance idiom before writing the music.

25. G. Boyajiyev, " A Theatre on Wheels ", *Sov. Th. Chron.* : 1943, iv, pp. 15-17.

    Moscow News : 12.i.43 ; 13.v.44.

    Sov. Th. Chron. : 1943, iii, pp. 35-6.

    Огонёк : 25.x.42.

    Лит. и иск. : 25.iii.44 ; 1.v.44 ; 11.xi.44.

One of the most popular of this Railway Theatre's productions was Shakespeare's *Comedy of Errors.* I must confess to some confusion about the " Transport " Theatres. In 1937 there existed a Moscow Theatre of the Railway Centre, and also a Moscow Central Theatre of Water Transport. The former had premises on Komsomol Square ; its administrator was Nikolay Petrov. On the other hand, by 1934 there was already in existence a Moscow Railway Transport Theatre, without fixed premises, the aim of which was that alluded to in the text paragraph I am at present annotating. Petrov is not mentioned as being connected with this ; but he is mentioned in the Directory of Theatre Workers in Театральный справочник, 1937-8, as being resident at the " Theatre of Transport ", although no such theatre is listed in the Theatre Directory in the same book. On the other hand, a theatre called the Moscow Central Theatre of Transport is mentioned in Огонёк (25.x.42) as having been to the Mongolian Republic, and it is not likely that two such theatres did this. I conclude that the " Theatre of Transport " was a popular name for the Railwaymen's Theatre ; but in that case *Soviet Theatre Chronicle* must be wrong in saying that Petrov had been at the head of this theatre since its founding in 1938.

    References to such a theatre in 1944 all call it the Central Transport Theatre, and Petrov is mentioned as producing *Balzaminov's Wedding* ; also a children's play written by Vladimir Goldfeldt from folk tales, on the old theme of the adventures of the youngest of three sons, and called *A Tale of Prince Ivan, His Homeland, and His Beloved Mother.* Goldfeldt himself produced *The Girl Without a Dowry.*

26. Yermolova Theatre :

     Театр. справ. : 1935, p. 157 ; 1937-8, pp. 153-6.

     Alexander Werth, *loc. cit.*

     Лит. и иск. : 6.vi.42 ; 27.ii.43 ; 10.iv.43 ; 17.vii.43 ; 18.xi.44.

     The obituary of Teleshyova mentions her work at the little Yermolova Theatre.

     Hmelyov seems to have been maintaining his connection in addition to his duties at the Moscow Art Theatre. At the end of 1944 he produced a play by John Fletcher (1579-1625), author of *The Spanish Curate*, popular at the Second Moscow Art Theatre in the nineteen-thirties. This was *The Woman's Prize*, or *The Tamer Tamed*, called by its sub-title in the Russian production.

     The chief producer now is A. Lobanov, who was at work on Ostrovsky's *Crazy Money.*

27. *Sov. Th. Chron.* : 1943, iii, pp. 38-9.

     Лит. и иск. : 8.iii.42 ; 4.vii.42 ; 15.viii.42 ; 12.vi.43 ; 25.ix.43 ; 25.xii.43.

     Soviet War News : 3.v.43.

28. *Moscow News :* 1.x.42.

     Int. Lit. : 1943, iv, p. 80.

     Soviet War News : 24.i.44.

     Sov. Th. Chron. : 1943, iii, p. 37.

     Правда : 4.vii.42.

     Лит. и иск. : 16.v.42 ; 22.viii.42 ; 27.iii.43 ; 5.vi.43 ; 19.ii.44.

29. *Moscow News :* 24.x.42.

     Soviet Home Front : 1943, July-Aug.

     Лит. и иск. : 13.vi.42 ; 20.vi.42 ; 30.i.43 ; 7.viii.43 ; 29.i.44 ; 19.ii.44.

     Int. Lit. : 1944, x, p. 71-2.

     The Comedy Theatre remained in Leningrad through the winter of 1941-2. The company lived on the premises, like many office workers in London, and slept for weeks on any kind of bed in the dressing-rooms and offices ; for street traffic had stopped, and siege conditions made everyone husband their strength, particularly in a job like acting, which makes heavy demands on the nervous system.

     Sirens often interrupted rehearsals ; and present-day explosions mingled with eighteenth-century noises off in *Long, Long Ago*. At the end of December the company left for Magnitogorsk by plane.

30. *Soviet War News :* 28.iv.43.

     Лит. и иск. : 23.v.42 ; 17.vii.43 ; 23.x.43.

31. *Soviet Home Front :* 1943, Aug.-Sept.-Oct.

CHAPTER VIII

1. R. A. Davis and A. J. Steiger : *Soviet Asia* (Eng. edn., London, 1943), p. 34. Use has been made in this chapter of material in Chaps. III and IV.

2. *Ibid.* p. 39.

3. Hugh MacDiarmid : *A Golden Treasury of Scottish Verse* (London, 1941) : Introduction, p. 9.

4. Material on Urals and KuzBas :

     Сим. Дрейден: „Сибирь театральная", Лит. и иск. : 8.v.43.

     Boris Agapov, *Moscow News :* 10.iii.43.

А. А. Бартошевич: „Акимов", (Leningrad, 1933), p. 103.

Moscow News: 24.ii.42 ; 26.vi.42 ; 17.ii.43 ; 6.v.43.

Soviet War News: 20.x.42 ; 28.iv.43.

Труд. : 29.viii.43.

Лит. и иск. : 27.ii.43 ; 15.v.43 ; 5.vi.43 ; 12.vi.43 ; 3.vii.43 ; 10.vii.43 ; 25.xii.43 ; 11.iii.44.

Sov. Th. Chron. : 1943, iv, pp. 25-8.

Soviet Home Front : Feb.-March 1943.

V.O.K.S. Bulletin, undated, received by the writer September 1942.

5. Material on Uzbekistan :

Лит. и иск. : 14.ii.42 ; 4.iv.42 ; 27.vii.42 ; 30.i.43 ; 6.iii.43 ; 13.iii.43 ; 5.vi.43 ; 26.vi.43 ; 10.vii.43 ; 9.x.43 ; 23.x.43 ; 7.xi.43 ; 13.xi.43 ; 11.xii.43 ; 28.x.44.

Moscow News: 7.iv.42 ; 14.iii.43.

M. Yufit, *ibid.* : 17.iii.43.

Sov. Th. Chron. : 1943, iii, p. 35.

Soviet War News : 4.x.43.

Int. Lit. : 1942, x, p. 79.

Soviet Home Front : 1943, July-August.

Three new theatres were opened in Uzbekistan in 1944 : the Tashkent Theatre for Young Spectators, playing Gogol's *The Wedding;* an Uzbek musico-dramatic theatre with a new version of *Farshad and Shiriya;* and a Russian theatre at Andizhan, which opened with Lavrenyov's *Song of the Black Sea Sailors.* The Hamza Theatre was preparing *The Girl Without a Dowry.* I imagine *Laurencia* is *Fuente Ovejuna.*

6. Kazakhstan :

M. Bursky, :*Moscow News* : 8.viii.42.

Lina Voitolovskaya, *Soviet War News* : 14.i.44.

Moscow News : 2.x.43 ; 30.i.43 ; 14.vi.43 ; 16.x.43 ; 25.iv.42 ; 30.v.42 ; 25.xii.42 ; 8.v.43 ; 22.v.43 ; 5.vi.43 ; 24.vii.43 ; 4.iii.44 ; 11.iii.44.

Another striking example of fusion is to be seen in the Tajik play, *Nadir's House*, produced at the " Lahuti " Theatre, Stalinabad, early in 1944. This was written jointly by a Tajik, Ikrami, and a Russian, Faiko, and described the battle that centred on a famous street block in Stalingrad, defended by a Tajik, a Tatar, and two Russians under the command of the Tajik Junior Lieutenant Nadir Hakimov.

The Tajik theatre followed those of other nationalities in 1944, when it staged a patriotic-historical play about a national hero, Takhmos of Hojent, written by the actor Kasymov and the author Mitelman. By that year Tajikstan had 27 theatres, and a number of regional and children's theatres were planned to start touring in 1945. A Tajik Theatrical Society was founded in 1944.

7. Turkmenia :

Cable received via *Soviet War News* : August 1944.

M. Аннакурдов: „Искусство солнечной Туркмении", Лит. и иск. : 31.vii.43.

Moscow News : 4.i.43.

Лит. и иск. : 6.vi.42 ; 21.xi.42. *V.O.K.S. Bulletin*, 1944, iv-v, pp. 76 *seq.*

These amateur founders of national theatres did not impose themselves from above. They developed under the stimulus of a national, social-political-economic freedom, and drew their forms from two sources : the folk-bards and the religious or pagan processional-plays ; thus adding another chapter to the history of the world theatre, similar in movement to those of the

Classical Greek, Chinese, Japanese, and Mediaeval European theatres.   The folk-bards had a different name in each country, shakhir (Turkmenia), ashug (Azerbaijan), akyn, or lyrniki or bakhshi ; but their functions were very similar.   The kyzychi of Uzbekistan were more like clown or tumbler than bard, but the same element of impromptu celebration entered into their performance too.   There still exists in Kazakhstan the entertainer Haji Mukan, almost the last of his kind.   He sings, recites, cracks jokes to his " feed ", ranging in theme from folk-lore to a local topical gag ; but he juggles and conjures as well ; and old, fat and bald as he is, the show never ends without a challenge to wrestle any spectator to a fall.   For the past forty years nobody has thrown him.

Turkmenia, it might be mentioned, was in former times so dry a country that wealth was assessed in water.   " He has fifteen minutes of water every twelve days."   Water was given as part of a dowry ; and the withholding of it was a method of fine.

8. Kirghizia :

Moscow News : 27.i.42 ; 9.ii.44.
Soviet War News : 1.xii.42.
Int. Lit. : 1943,vi, p. 80 ; 1942, iii–iv, p. 122.
Лит. и иск. : 20.v.44.

The principal Kirghiz theatre is at Frunze, the capital—formerly Pishpek, but renamed for the revolutionary leader Frunze who was roasted alive in a locomotive furnace by Japanese interventionists.   Although the Kirghiz stage's operatic achievements have been better known than its purely dramatic ones, several interesting shows were given in 1943.   Of Russian plays, Pogodin's *Kremlin Chimes* showed the silk-workers how much they owed to Lenin ; and Anna Karenina was to follow.   *Mashenka* and *Wait for Me* were the contemporary plays.   Western Europe gave them a Goldoni and Shaw's *Pygmalion.*

9. Bashkiria :

У. Усманов : „Искусство Башкирии в дне войны", Лит. и иск. : 30.i.43.
Moscow News : 18.ii.42 ; 14.iii.43.
Лит. и иск. : 15.v.43 ; 26.vi.43 ; 25.iii.44.
Известия : 7.x.42.
Театр, 1944, p. 143.

Among the most prominent drama theatres in Bashkiria are to be included also five collective farm theatres, three puppet theatres, a Musical Comedy, the dramatic theatre at the mining town of Beloretz and a travelling theatre centred in Belebeye.   The Russian repertory included Ostrovsky, Gogol, Chehov, Gorky and Pushkin ; but local dramatists had arisen with plays about great national figures, remote or recent, including the Bashkirian writer Gafuri, kept under the surveillance of the Tsarist police.

10. Tataria :

L. Oliphant : *op. cit.* pp. 60 and 63.
Int. Lit. : 1942, iii–iv, p. 122.
Лит. и иск. : 24.iv.43 ; 23.x.43.
Soviet War News : 13.i.44.
Театр, 1944, p. 144.

Other Tatar productions in 1943–4 were *King Lear*, a new comedy and a dramatic poem by Isambet, a tragedy by Nur Zahit, a war play about the partisans, another about collective farmers, and *Daughter of Her Country*, by a woman writer, Yelizarova, which celebrated yet again the heroic life and death of Zoya Kosmodemyanskaya. A play about the national poet Tukay was done in several places besides Kazan, notably in Ufa.

11. Chuvashes :
   Moscow News : 18.ix.43.
   Лит. и иск. : 10.iv.43.

12. Chechen-Ingutia :
   Лит. и иск. : 18.iv.42 ; 16.i.43 ; 10.iv.43 ; 21.viii.43 ; 20.xi.43.
   The Lesya Ukrainka Theatre was also showing *Pygmalion*. An interesting theme of an Ossetian play, written during the war years, was that by the young dramatist Muhtar Shavlov, about the semi-historical love-story of the Nart, Batradz. The "Narts" seem to have been ancient heroes or nobles, the Formorians or Homeric chiefs, of Ossetian folk-epics ; but their womenfolk were as warlike as the men ; and in the central incident, Batradz's wedding, women and men together drive out unwelcome guests from rival clans. This play was first staged at the Kosta Hetagurov Theatre at Staliniri in 1943-4.

13. Azerbaijan :
   Soviet War News : 5.x.42.
   Лит. и иск. : 23.ii.43 ; 10.iv.43 ; 10.vii.43 ; 29.i.44.

14. Armenia :
   B. Krinitsy, *Moscow News* : 5.xii.42.
   Sergey Aruchyan, *ibid.* : 29.xii.43.
   Soviet Home Front : July-Aug. 1943.
   Лит. и иск. : 27.ii.43 ; 22.v.43 ; 5.vi.43 ; 26.vi.43 ; 25.ix.43 ; 1.vii.44.
   For the Chehov celebrations in 1944, the Yerevan Theatre produced that not very remarkable early work, *Ivanov*.

15. Georgia :
   Int. Lit. : 1943, vii, p. 80.
   Alexander Fevralsky, *Soviet War News* : 17.viii.42.
   Ibid. : 17.ix.42 ; 26.ix.42.
   Лит. и иск. : 8.ii.42 ; 21.iii.42 ; 16.v.42 ; 25.vii.42 ; 27.ii.43 ; 3.iv.43 ; 8.v.43 ; 19.vi.43 ; 28.viii.43 ; 11.iii.44 ; 28.x.44.
   Moscow News : 4.iii.44.
   The Gori Theatre opened its recently completed new building which was designed, by the Georgian architect Tavadze, on traditional lines of Georgian architecture, adapted for the purposes of an up-to-date theatre. Its administrative head is People's Artist of the Georgian Republic Prangishvili. Vachandze was invited from Baku as its chief producer ; and with him works Alexishvili, a former pupil of the Moscow Art Theatre. They have produced many plays from "brother republics", Turkmenia, Armenia, as well as Russian and Western European classics. Like most Soviet theatres, this one spends some weeks every year in touring the country districts.
   Mdivani's play, *Partisans*, was about guerrilla warfare in the Crimea.

16. Mongolia :
   Г. Уварова: „Искусство Монгольского народа", Лит. и иск. : 16.i.43.

17. *Ibid.* : 22.viii.42 ; 12.vi.43 ; 3.vii.43 ; 28.viii.43.
   Известия : 21.iii.43 ; 1.iv.43.

22

18. V.T.O. :

    Sov. Th. Chron. : 1943, i, pp. 13-16.

    Лит. и иск. : 29.v.43.

    А. Э. Ашанин : „Яблочкина и ВТО.“ in the symposium, „А. А. Яблочкина к пятидесятилетного сценической деятельности“ (Искусство-ВТО., 1937), pp. 210-26.

CHAPTER IX

1. Лит. и иск. : 8.iii.42 ; 16.v.42.

    Soviet War News : 8.vi.43.

    Sov. Th. Chron. : 1943, i, p. 4 ; iv, p. 12.

2. Н. Дорохин : „В землянке“ Литература и искусство. : 4.xii.43.

    Soviet War News : 17.ix.42.

    Sov. Th. Chron. : 1943, iii, p. 27.

    Лит. и иск. : 24.x.42 ; 6.ii.43 ; 11.iii.44.

3. *Moscow News* : 16.i.43 ; 3.iii.43.

    Soviet War News : 7.i.43.

    Int. Lit. : 1942, iii-iv, p. 116.

    Лит. и иск. : 4.ix.43.

    Огонёк : 28.vi.1942.

    Sov. Th. Chron. : 1943, iii, pp. 28-30.

4. *Moscow News* : 26.iv.43.

    Sov. War News : 8. vi. 43.

    Sov. Th. Chron. : 1943, iii, pp. 30-1.

    Лит. и иск. : 4.vii.42 ; 20.vi.43.

5. *Moscow News* : 3.vii.42.

    Лит. и иск. : 16.v.42.

6. *Ibid.* : 21.iii.42 ; 30.i.43 ; 8.v.43.

    Int. Lit. : 1942, xi. p. 84 ; 1943, viii, p. 78.

    Moscow News : 14.xi.42.

    Nord's account is interesting. My own experience of playing in the open is that the tendency is the other way ; the bigger scale, the lack of resonance, the sensation of being a small speck of humanity on show, rather than an assumed personality living in the life of the audience, incline the actor to a " poster " performance. But then I was never trained in a Socialist Realist theatre.

    Nord is corroborated by other writers. L. Zhukov, writing of the Moscow Front Line Dramatic Theatre under Rayevsky, which was formed in 1942 from graduates of Rayevsky's and Teleshyova's classes at G.I.T.I.S., says (Литература и искусство, 12.viii.44), " The voice has to be forced, a ' close-up ' technique has to be adopted constantly, certain details have to be forgone. . . . But this kind of thing does not decide the fate of the show. A front-line theatre, which is a special form of our contemporary people's theatre, makes a definite demand on one thing only : that there should be a relationship of creativeness between the actor and his work, a realistic exactness and vividness in the figure created."

7. *Sov. Th. Chron.* : 1943, iv. pp. 12-13 ; iii, pp. 31-2.

    Moscow News : 16.i.43.

    Anglo-Soviet Journal : 1941, July, pp. 268-9.

Лит. и иск. : 21.iii.42 ; 22.i.43 ; 29.v.43 ; 14.viii.43 ; 28.viii.43 (*bis*).
Известия : 7.vii.42.
8. Лит. и иск. : 4.ix.43.
9. Т. Куляковская : „Чудесный спектакль кукол.“   „Искусство“ — 20.xi.43.
   Moscow News : 4.ix.43 ; 2.x.43 (*bis*).
   Int. Lit. : 1942, x, p. 79. 1944, vi, p. 77.
   Лит. и иск. : 20.vi.42 ; 23.ii.43 (*bis*) ; 22.v.43.
   Театральная москва : 1935, p. 198.
10. Виктор Эрманс : „Сила и ловкость“, Лит. и иск. : 13.ii.43.
    Ibid. : 5.vi.43 ; 10.vii.43 ; 14.viii.43 ; 11.ix.43 ; 13.xi.43.
11. *Moscow News* : 16.i.43.
    Лит. и иск. : 23.ii.43 ; 14.viii.43.
12. Известия : 21.iii.43.
    Лит. и иск. : 30.i.43 ; 13.iii.43 ; 14.viii.43 ; 2.x.43.
    Sov. Th. Chron. : 1943, i, p. 6.
13. *Moscow News* : 25.ix.42.
    Лит. и иск. : 6.ii.43.
    Sov. Th. Chron. : 1943, i, p. 14.
    The Little Shoes (*cherevichki* = high-heeled court-shoes) was the name
    Chaikovsky gave to his revised version of *Vakula the Smith*, an opera of
    witchcraft and demons, founded on a Gogol story. Outside Russia it
    was sometimes known as *Oxana's Caprices*.
14. Лит. и иск. : 22.v.43 ; 17.vii.43 ; 12.ii.44 ; 11.iii.44.
    Int. Lit. : 1942, iii–iv, pp. 112–16.
    Moscow News : 10.vii.42.
    Виктор Эрманс : „На конкурсе чтецов“, Лит. и иск. : 24.vii.43.
15. *Moscow News* : 3.iii.43.
16. А. Габович : „Театр на фронте“, Лит. и иск. : 16.i.43.
    И. Любинский : „Боевое содружество“, *ibid.* : 28.viii.43.
    M. Bursky, *Moscow News* : 25.xi.43.
    Ibid. : 16.i.43.
17. М. Загорский „Отелло“, Лит. и иск. : 19.ii.44.
    Mihail Tarhanov : *Soviet War News* : 24.vi.44.
    M. Dolgopolov, *Moscow News* : 12.viii.42.
    И. Любинский : „Художественные бригады на фронте“, Лит. и иск.: 20.xi.43.
    С. Преображенский : „Фронтовые бригады“, *ibid.* : 23.ii.43.
    Moscow News : 9.vi.42 ; 14.x.42 ; 18.xi.42 ; 27.i.43 ; 26.iv.43.
    Soviet War News : 11.xii.42 ; 28.ii.45.
    Int. Lit. : 1943, vii, p. 80.
    Sov. Th. Chron. : 1943, iv, pp. 11–13.
    Лит. и иск. : 16.v.42 ; 4.vii.42 ; 6.ii.43 (*bis*) ; 23.ii.43 ; 27.iii.43 ; 8.v.43 ;
    22.v.43 ; 31.vii.43 ; 21.viii.43 ; 4.ix.43 ; 18.ix.43 ; 18.xii.43 ; 25.xii.43.
    Известия : 14.vi.42.
    Труд. : 29.viii.43.

CHAPTER X

1. General information from Театральный справочник, 1937-8, under regions.
   M. Luchansky, *Moscow News* : 10.vii.42.
   Sov. Th. Chron. : 1943, iv, pp. 14 and 28.
   Лит. и иск. : 16.v.42 ; 21.ii.43 ; 8.v.43 ; 10.vii.43 ; 23.x.43 ; 27.xi.43.

2. Лит. и иск : 14.iii.42 ; 23.ii.43 ; 27.ii.43.

3. *Ibid.* : 14.ii.42 ; 14.iii.42 ; 15.v.43 ; 19.vi.43 ; 7.viii.43 ; 25.xii.43.

4. Илья Груздев : „Горьковские спектакли,“ *ibid.* : 11.ix.43.
   Ю. Головащенко : „Варвара,“ *ibid.* : 6.ii.43.
   Ibid. : 4.vii.42 ; 13.ii.43 ; 12.vi.43 (*bis*) ; 7.viii.43 ; 2.x.43.

5. *Int. Lit.* : 1943, vii, p. 80.
   Лит. и иск. : 6.iii.43 ; 8.v.43 ; 29.v.43 ; 7.viii.43 ; 9.x.43.
   Г. Фалковский : „Спектакль о Брусилове“, *ibid.* : 8.v.43.

6. Б. Варнеке — *op. cit.* pp. 115-19.
   Лит. и иск. : 19.i.42 ; 27.ii.43 ; 8.v.43 ; 22.v.43 ; 19.vi.43 ; 28.viii.43.

7. *Sov. Th. Chron.* : 1943, i, pp. 4-5 ; iv, pp. 18-19.
   Лит. и иск. : 8.v.43 ; 10.vii.43 ; 28.viii.43.

Besieged Leningrad was by no means without theatres. Like many others, Akimov's Comedy Theatre was evacuated ; but its premises gave birth to a new " Civic " Theatre. It happened like this : the Leningrad radio had done a performance of *Russian People*. The scratch company was so successful that they decided to do it " live " on a stage. Rough in production, it was nonetheless welcome to besieged Leningrad, and the public asked for more. A young producer, Morshchinin, just out of hospital, with his arm still in a sling, took rehearsals. More players joined, some well-known figures from the Grand Dramatic Theatre who, for various reasons, had stayed in the city. Dancers and singers came too. Three companies were soon using the stage for plays, operas, and ballets. Often the alert would sound during performance, but the act would be finished, even by the light of torches and lanterns when the current was turned off.

8. *Moscow News* : 22.viii.42.
   Лит. и иск. : 14.ii.42 ; 14.iii.42 ; 18.vii.42 ; 15.viii.42 ; 12.vi.43 ; 8.v.43 ;
   14.viii.43.

9. Yuri Nagibin, *Soviet War News* : 17.iii.43.
   Лит. и иск. : 14.ii.42 ; 25.iv.42 ; 1.viii.42 ; 30.i.42 ; 23.ii.43 ; 27.ii.43 ;
   6.iii.43 ; 10.iv.43 ; 17.vii.43 ; 7.viii.43 ; 25.ix.43 ; 5.ii.44.
   Nikolay Virta : " Theatre on Wheels ", *Soviet War News* : 11.viii.44.

10. A. Morozov, *Soviet War News* : 12.ii.44.
    Moscow News : 16.ix.42 ; 1.x.42 ; 18.xi.42 ; 20.v.43.
    Int. Lit. : 1942, iii-iv, p. 122.
    Лит. и иск. : 4.iv.42 ; 15.iv.42 ; 16.v.42 ; 30.v.42 ; 4.vii.42 ; 24.x.42 ; 8.v.43 ;
    26.vi.43 ; 3.vii.43 ; 31.vii.43 (*bis*) ; 28.viii.43 ; 25.xii.43.
    Правда : 4.vii.42.

CHAPTER XI

1. Лит. и иск. : 16.v.42 ; 24.vii.43.
   Yuri Kalashnikov : " Invasion, Leonov's New Play ". *Int. Lit.* : 1943, ix,
   pp. 57-62.
   D. Saskovsky : " Invasion, a New Play by Leonov ". *V.O.K.S. Bulletin*,
   1943, i-ii, pp. 33-6.
   S. Radzinsky : " Leonov's ' Invasion ' ". *Soviet War News* : 8.vii.43.
   (English translation of play published in *Int. Lit.*, 1943, vi. Also in " Four
   Soviet War Plays " (London, 1944), which includes *Russian People*, *The
   Front* and *Partisans in the Steppes of Ukraine.*

2. *Soviet War News*: 5.vi.43.
   Ushakov, in Лит. и иск. : 9.v.42.
3. *Ibid.*: 30.v.42.
4. *Sov. Th. Chron.*: 1943, iv, pp. 16-17.
   Moscow News: 10.ii.42.
   Лит. и иск. : 19.i.42.
5. Alexander Werth : *Moscow ' 41* (London 1942), pp. 59-60.
   Soviet War News: 5.vi.43.
   Int. Lit.: 1944, v. 72 ; ix. 75.
   Лит. и иск. : 20.v.44.

   The Tur Brothers and Sheinin produced two new plays after the above was
   written. *Emergency Law* had a success at the Moscow Theatre of Satire
   in the early part of 1944. This was founded on an actual case of embezzlement. The leading part was a rather flashy, but quickwitted sales department manager in a canning factory, who does a number of shady deals in
   rationed goods. It was played with biting humour by the theatre's leading
   comedian. The slight detective-story atmosphere that usually clings to
   the work of this syndicate of authors was more pronounced in *The Duel*
   performed at the LenKom Theatre later in the same year. The German
   Secret Service is trying to kidnap the inventor of a new field gun. A
   Rumanian spy and his assistants, disguised as collective farmers, parachute
   into the front line where the inventor is working. He, however, has
   as his chauffeur a man who is in fact a member of the State Security, and
   this figure re-disguises himself and gets intentionally captured in mistake
   for the inventor. There is the happy ending usual in plots of this kind.
   That Bersenyev should have produced this play shows his versatility. The
   more intellectual Soviet dramatic criticism accepts the type as interesting,
   entertaining, and useful in its way, but asks for a bolder approach, with the
   problems encountered by the State Security less simplified. Quite a reason-
   able request ; and an adult one.

6. Werth, *op. cit. loc. cit.* and p. 33.
7. *Soviet War News*: 24.iii.43.
   Times, London : 3.ii.44.
8. *V.O.K.S. Bulletin*, 1942, v-vi, pp. 47-51.
9. Лит. и иск. : 5.i.44.
10. *Moscow News*: 13.iii.42.
    Правда : 27.vi.42.
11. *Moscow News*: 13.iii.43.
    Times, London : 20.iii.43.
12. N. Militsyna, *Moscow News*: 14.x.42.
13. *Ibid.*: 1.x.42 ; 25.xi.42 ; 12.i.43 ; 3.iii.43 ; 16.x.43.
    Известия : 11.ix.42.
    Soviet War News: 11.i.43.
    Б. Ростоцкий: „Заметки о комедии", Лит. и иск. : 2.x.43.
    An English translation of *The Blue Scarf* was published in *Moscow News* during
    January 1943.
    Лит. и иск. : 11.ix.43 ; 23.ii.44.
    Int. Lit.: 1944, xii. p. 76.
    Литературная газета ; 2.xii.44.

Similar in theme to *The Blue Scarf*, less farcical, but more sentimental, was *Somewhere in Moscow*, by Vladimir Mass and Mihail Chervinsky, which was done by the Vahtangov Frontline Brigade. In this a young lieutenant on leave seeks, seems to miss, and finally locates a girl who had saved his life at the Front. Collaboration in dramatic authorship does not seem to breed profundity in the Soviet Union any more than elsewhere.

Another comedy, of a more satirical kind, was Korneichuk's *Mr. Perkins' Mission to the Land of the Bolsheviks*, produced by the Moscow Theatre of Satire in December 1944. This was reported to be of more robust quality, but no further particulars are to hand.

14. *Moscow News*: 17.ii.43.
     Лит. и иск.: 27.ii.43 ; 29.i.44.
15. *Int. Lit.*: 1943, vi, p. 80.
16. Interview with Alexey Tolstoy, *Int. Lit.*: 1943, iv, p. 4.
     Olga Voitinskaya, " A Visit to Alexey Tolstoy ", *Soviet War News*: 30.x.43.
     Konstantin Fedin, " A Story of the Russian People ", *Int. Lit.*: 1943, x, pp. 65-8.
     Moscow News: 20.viii.43 ; 23.ix.43.
     Лит. и иск.: 31.vii.43.
17. Prof. Morozov, " A Debate on the Historical Play ", *Int. Lit.*, 1943, ix, pp. 65-7.
     Г. Фалковский: „Спектакль о Брусилове", Лит. и иск.: 8.v.43.
     Moscow News: 28.v.43.
     Soviet War News: 5.vi.43.
     Лит. и иск.: 5.vi.43 ; 10.vii.43 ; 28.viii.43.
     V.O.K.S. Bulletin (typed), received September 1942.
18. M. Morozov, *loc. cit.*
     Moscow News: 23.ix.43.
     Лит. и иск.: 22.v.43 ; 10.viii.43.
19. Вас. Сахновский: „В поисках современной пьесы", Лит. и иск.: 22.v.43.
     Ник. Петров: „Драматург и театр", *ibid.*
     Серафима Бирман: „Штурманы дальнего плавания", *ibid.*
     М. Храпченко: „Проблемы советской драматургии", *ibid.*: 5.vi.43.
     Ю. Калашников: „Живое и мёртвое", *ibid.*: 27.iii.43.
     Moscow News: 4.vi.43.
     Лит. и иск.: 8.v.43 ; 22.v.43 (*bis*) ; 29.v.43.

CHAPTER XII

1. Ю. М. Юрев: „Записки" (Искусство, 1939), pp. 51-3.
     Лит. и иск.: 13.iii.43 ; 10.vii.43 ; 17.vii.43 ; 29.i.44.
     Int. Lit.: 1944, iii, p. 77.
     Shchepkina-Kupernik was herself the object of a celebration in 1944, when she was awarded the Order of the Red Banner of Labour and fêted on her 70th birthday. Shchepkin was her great-grandfather, and she herself had been on the stage in her youth, notably at Korsh's Theatre.
2. *Ibid.*: 14.viii.43.
3. С. Бирман: „Живой Станиславский", *ibid.*: 7.viii.43.
     Кедров: „Труд и вдохновение", *ibid.* Also B. Livanov in the same issue.
     Ibid.: 31.vii.43 ; 7.viii.43 ; 18.ix.43 ; 12.ii.44.
4. *Ibid.*: 23.x.43 ; 30.x.43.
5. *Ibid.*: 3.iv.43 ; 13.xi.43.

6. *Sov. Th. Chron.* : 1943, iii, *passim*.
   Moscow News : 27.xi.43.
   Лит. и иск. : 13.iii.43 ; 21.iii.43 ; 31.vii.43 ; 18.ix.43 ; 20.xi.43 ; 6.v.44.
   In 1942 the Birobijan Theatre presented a play called *Bolsheviks*, in which for
   the first time on the Jewish stage great Russian historical figures like Lenin,
   Stalin, Sverdlov, and Gorky were impersonated.

7. *Moscow News* : 30.x.43.
   Sov. Th. Chron. : 1943, i, pp. 5–6.
   Лит. и иск.: 13.ii.43 (*bis*) ; 23.ii.43 ; 30.x.43 ; (*bis*) ; 7.xi.43 ; 11.iii.44.

8. Among favourite Americans were O. Henry and Ambrose Bierce.   *Chtetsy* often
   group their recitations round a single theme, Pushkin, London.   The majority of the contemporary Soviet works used were poems, sketches, reportage,
   short stories about the war.   Some of the poetic fables of Krylov were
   the subject of a competition at Kuibyshev in 1944.   The reciter, Balashov,
   (see p. 214) contributed from his savings an entire tank to the Red Army,
   and was delighted to hear at the end of 1943 that this tank, bearing his name,
   had already destroyed five panzers, many guns and a hundred Germans.

9. Solomon Mihoels, at an informal gathering of British actors and actresses,
   Claridge's, London, 22 November 1943.
   Лит. и иск. : 5.vi.43.

10. *Ibid.* : 6.ii.43.

11. М. Морозов: „Шекспир в переводах Б. Пастернака." *ibid.* : 7.viii.43.
    Moscow News : 21.iv.42 ; 28.xi.42 ; 26.iv.43 ; 6.v.43 ; 4.vi.43 ; 26.vii.43 ;
    18.ix.43 ; 18.ix.44.
    Лит. и иск. : 8.v.43.
    Sov. Th. Chron. : 1943, iv, pp. 33–4.
    Soviet War News : 3.v.43 ; 14.i.44 ; 13.x.44.
    Int. Lit. : 1942, v–vi, pp. 101–5.   1944, viii, p. 71 *seq.* ; x, p. 73.
    Solomon Mihoels, at gathering above.
    V.O.K.S. Bulletin, 1943, iii–iv, p. 57.
    Theatre : 1944, v–vi, p. 14.
    The sixth annual Shakespearean conference was held in 1944 at Yerevan.
    Naturally the work of Armenia on Shakespeare was the chief object of
    attention.   The delegates were entertained to Shakespeare in the local
    theatres in Armenian, Russian, and Azerbaijanian, including a special pro-
    duction of *Twelfth Night*.
    Professor Morozov has now done a literal prose translation of *Hamlet* for the
    same purpose as he did *Othello*.
    Much Ado About Nothing in its rhythmical form at the Vahtangov Theatre,
    reached its 500th performance in 1944.

12. В. Городинский: „Женитьба Бальзаминова", Лит. и иск. : 4.xii.43.
    Moscow News : 15.xii.43.
    Лит. и иск. : 31.vii.43 (*bis*) ; 7.viii.43 ; 7.xi.43 ; 13.xi.43 ; 4.xii.43 ; 11.iii.44 ;
    (*bis*) ; 18.iii.44.
    The fortieth anniversary of Chehov's death was celebrated in 1944 by per-
    formances of his works throughout the Soviet Union, and by articles and
    reminiscences printed in dozens and scores of newspapers and magazines.
    Ninety-three theatres were performing him, in Russian, Ukrainian, Armenian,
    Azerbaijanian, Kazakh, Acar, and other languages.   Besides the great plays,

and the little one-act plays, entertainments were made out of many of his stories ; as at the Moscow Theatre of Drama, and the Mossoviet. Every important Moscow theatre showed a Chehov of some sort or another. A theatre in Taganrog was founded and named for him. The side of Chehov which received most notice during these wartime celebrations was the way in which he tried to make people see what miserable lives they led, not that they should weep, from pity for themselves, but that they should improve their lives, and the firm faith he had that the Russian people would one day do this for themselves. Soviet writers and actors joined in evenings in his honour, and reciters included his short stories in their programmes at the front.

13. Ю. М. Юрев., *op. cit.* pp. 50–4.
14. *Moscow News* : 2.viii.43 ; 4.xii.43.
15. М. Морозов : „Мастера веселого спектакля", Лит. и иск. : 14.viii.43.
16. *Moscow News* : 23.ix.42 (*bis*) ; 17.ii.43.
    Int. Lit. : 1942,x, p. 79.
    Лит. и иск. : 7.x.44.
    The "Stanislavsky" Theatre at Yerevan (Russian speaking) opened its 1944 season with the historical Ibsen *Lady Inger of Ostrat*.
17. *Moscow News* : 4.x.42.
18. *Ibid.* : 13.ii.43 ; 17.ii.43 ; 23.ix.42.
    Soviet War News : 28.iv.43 ; 21.vi.43 ; 12.i.44 ; 4.i.45.
    Лит. и иск. : 21.viii.43 ; 7.x.44.
    Int. Lit. : 1944, iii, p. 70 ; ix, p. 78 ; x, p. 74.
    Among the nationalities *Pygmalion* was a special success, as we have already noted, in Kirghizia. Latest reports say that the Kamerny Theatre is to do a translation of Kaufman and Hart's *The Man Who Came to Dinner*. A class of G.I.T.I.S. students tried out Dickens' little-known farce, *The Strange Gentleman*. The Mossoviet accepted a translation of Terence Rattigan's *Flare Path*, the preliminary announcement of which trailed it as having been written by an English airman who had taken part in many raids over Fascist Germany, and as picturing "daily life on an English aerodrome" with the personal problem of the airman Teddy Graham, his wife Patricia, and a Hollywood film-star.
19. *Soviet War News* : 17.viii.42.
    Moscow News : 3.vii.42 ; 10.vii.42.
    Int. Lit. : 1942, x, p. 78.
    Лит. и иск. : 24.vii.43.
20. Серафима Бирман : „Труд актера" (Искусство, 1939), pp. 62, 123, 130–1, 134.

CHAPTER XIII

1. *Moscow News* : 3.vii.42 ; 21.x.42 ; 15.vii.44.
    Лит. и иск. : 4.iv.42 ; 30.i.43.
    Soviet War News : 20.xii.44.
    Советское искусство, 19.xii.44.
    In 1944 no fewer than eight new theatrical schools were opened, two of them being the first of their kind in Armenia and Uzbekistan ; and in the same year fifty-four new theatre-studios were opened, twenty-three in the Russian Republic, their purpose and function being much like those of a

theatre school. Zavadsky, Tarhanov, Bersenyev, and Popov were among the big names that taught in them. Applications poured in. In 1944 at the Nemirovich-Danchenko studio of the Moscow Art Theatre auditions were given to two hundred and thirty candidates for thirty vacancies ; in the Shchukin School to one hundred and fifty-four for twenty-five vacancies. One hundred and twenty-five new students were enrolled at G.I.T.I.S., ninety for acting, twenty for production, fifteen for theatre management. Of the one thousand new pupils that year, one hundred and eighty were to train for the ballet.

The Chehov Theatre at Taganrog was largely composed of a number of young Russians who had attracted attention by their end-of-term performance of *The Three Sisters* at G.I.T.I.S. A Ukrainian class there having similarly proved themselves with a translation of Gorky's *The Last*, became an independent unit in their own country. The Filial of the Vahtangov Theatre, in this case a separate ensemble, mostly from the Shchukin school (Boris Shchukin was a fine Vahtangov actor, the first of his profession to impersonate Lenin) gained much praise for its interpretation of *Somewhere in Moscow* at the front.

2. *Moscow News* : 20.v.43 (Nina Vladimirova).
Vera Pashennaya, *Soviet War News* : 4.x.43.
3. *Moscow News* : 15.xii.43.
Лит. и иск. : 12.vi.43 ; 3.vii.43 ; 28.viii.43 ; 4.xii.43 ; 13.xi.43.
Sov. Th. Chron. : 1943, i, p. 13.
4. Москвин, Хмелёв, Месхатели : „Ближайшие работы Художественного театра“,
Лит. и иск. : 31.vii.43.
Soviet War News : 6.i.44.
Moscow News : 8.ix.43.
Огонёк : 10.iv.43.
Sov. Th. Chron. : 1943, iv, p. 18 ; 1943, viii, pp. 9-10.
Лит. и иск. : 12.vi.43 ; 3.vii.43 ; 4.ix.43.
5. *Ibid.* : 22.v.43 ; 19.vi.43 ; 23.x.43 ; 13.xi.43 ; 20.xi.43 ; 4.xii.43 ; 11.xii.43.
6. A. Gomez de la Vega : *El Teatro en la U.R.S.S.* (Mexico 1938), p. 134.
7. S. Radzinsky, " Moscow's Children's Theatres ", *Soviet War News* : 26.vi.43.
Ibid. : 17.viii.42 ; 25.x.43.
В. Эрманс : „Кот в сапогах“, Лит. и иск. : 6.ii.43.
Sov. Th. Chron. : 1943, iv, pp. 24-5.
Moscow News : 25.ix.42 ; 27.x.43 ; 15.i.44 ; 2.xii.44.
Лит. и иск. : 14.ii.42 ; 4.iv.42 ; 9.v.42 (*bis*) ; 20.vi.42 ; 13.iii.43 (*bis*) ; 10.iv.43 ; 8.v.43 ; 26.vi.43 ; 14.viii.43 ; 28.viii.43 ; 23.x.43 ; 30.x.43 ; 4.xii.43 ; 18.xii.43 ; 23.ii.44 ; 1.vii.44 ; 7.x.44.
Литературная газета : 2.xii.44.
The opening play on the return of the Moscow Tyuz was a dramatisation of Simukov's story, *Native Soil*, in which an inseparable brother and sister and their aged grandfather are protected by a magic table-cloth. Wicked foreigners try to steal this but, as they approach, the forest comes to life, saves the family, and punishes the robbers. A real parable of the war.
When the Grozny Tyuz was re-opened after nearly three years, at the beginning of 1944, the senior children's actor in the Soviet Union, People's Artist of the R.S.F.S.R., A. Bryantsev, was present. In the repertoire were an Ostrovsky, *King Spider* and *The Twelve Months*.

In 1944 a special Variety Theatre for children opened in the Colonnaded Hall of Union House.

In all there are about one hundred and forty children's theatres in the Soviet Union, of which half are purely dramatic, and half puppet theatres. (*Soviet War News*: 20.x.44 ; *Soviet News*: 18.x.45). Over fourteen languages are used.

The Central Theatre for Children, Moscow, had a good selection of plays planned for 1945. Gogol, Dickens, Jules Verne, were seldom neglected. Mark Twain's *The Prince and the Pauper* (always a popular play with these audiences) was to be joined by *A Yankee at the Court of King Arthur*. In a version specially made by Lev Slavin, author of *Intervention*. There were to be plays about Pushkin, Lomonosov, Peter the Great, the revolutionary Bauman. A particularly interesting historical play was to be *Two Volunteers*, about a small Russian naval squadron sent to the American Civil Wars in 1863 to help the North against the Southern States. In December 1944 appeared *Craftsmen's Town*, otherwise known as *A Tale of Two Hunchbacks*. This, written by Gabbe, with music by no less a composer than Dmitri Kabalyevsky, was founded on a Flemish fairy-story. There was a town of jewellers, clock-makers, armourers, lapidaries, goldsmiths and pastrycooks. In this town lived Gilbert, a hunchback with a happy disposition, whose nickname was Karakol, which means a snail. He was a street sweeper. Foreigners had taken possession of the town, and one of the worst of them was its governor, the Count de Malicorne, also a hunchback, but of an evil disposition. He and his crony, Big Guillaume, who had magic powers, oppressed the free townsmen, till they combined against him under Gilbert's guidance. Even the animals, who were Gilbert's friends, protected and helped them. So the town was liberated, the Count was killed, Gilbert lost his hump magically and married the beautiful Veronica who had long loved him for his sweet nature, and whom I do not doubt, though my informant does not say so, he had himself passionately doted upon for years in despair of her ever looking at him.

Trenyov was preparing a play for this theatre about the boyhood of Peter the Great. The poet Mihalkov had written a Soviet version of Gozzi's *Love for the Three Oranges*, called *In Coupon Kingdom*. Marshak was writing a play on a fairy-tale theme. A musical comedy was already in performance, on a story by Jules Verne with music by Offenbach, called *Doctor Ox*. Three new plays already written and delivered to the theatres were *I Can Work Miracles* by A. Ginsburg, *Knights in Green Forage Caps* by M. Tevelev, and *Son of the Battalion* by M. Svetlov. So the Children's Theatre was not being neglected.

CHAPTER XIV

1. Лит. и иск. : 23.ii.44.
    Int. Lit. : 1943, v, p. 77 ; vi, pp. 77-8.
    Moscow News : 2.ii.44.
2. Лит. и иск. : 26.i.42 ; 8.ii.42 ; 15.iv.42 ; 9.v.42 ; 30.v.42.
3. *Ibid.* : 4.vii.42.
4. *Moscow News* : 7.vii.42.
    Лит. и иск. : 31.vii.43 ; 2.viii.43.

5. В. Виленин: „Сказка для театра", Лит. и иск. : 28.viii.43.
    Moscow News : 23.ix.43 ; 13.x.43.
    V.O.K.S. Bulletin : 1942, v–vi, pp. 52–4 and 66–9.
    Лит. и иск. : 4.xii.43 ; 25.xii.43 ; 11.iii.44.
6. Mihail Dubson, *Moscow News* : 8.xii.43.
    Ibid. : 3.vii.42 ; 17.xii.42.
    Лит. и иск. : 16.v.42 ; 10.vii.43.
    Int. Lit. : 1943, v, pp. 79–80.
7. А. Я. Головин: „Встречи и впечатления" (1940).
    Nikolay Volkov, " A Soviet Scenic Artist ", in *Soviet War News* : 19.v.43.
    Moscow News : 15.ix.43.
    Лит. и иск. : 13.ii.43 ; 24.vii.43 ; 28.viii.43; 25.ix.43 ; 20.xi.43 ; 25.xii.43 ;
    11.iii.44.
    It is interesting to note that Deineke, one of the outstanding Soviet painters,
    has entered the theatre. The new Central Red Army Theatre production,
    Birthday, by the Tur Brothers, was to have sets designed by him.
8. П. Антокольский: „Война и культура", *ibid.* : 19.vi.43.
    Int. Lit. : 1943, iv, p. 73.
    Лит. и иск. : 4.iv.42 ; 25.ix.43.

CHAPTER XV

1. В. Ульев : „В Сталинграде", Известия : 13.viii.43.
    Moscow News : 26.iv.43 ; 7.vi.43 ; 29.viii.43 ; 8.ix.43.
    N. Militsina, *ibid.* : 6.v.43.
    Sov. Th. Chron. : 1944, viii, pp. 3–4.
    Лит. и иск. : 15.v.43 ; 22.v.43 ; 7.viii.43 ; 28.viii.43 ; 2.x.43 ; 19.ii.44 ;
    23.ii.44 ; 10.vi.44.
    In the course of 1944 the Stalingrad Theatre did a remarkable thing. It pro-
    duced for the anniversary of the Relief the Chepurin play, *Men of Stalingrad*.
    This was remarkable technically, not only in the speed of its rehearsal (one
    month only), nor for its surmounting of difficulties (it is a complex, spec-
    tacular " epic " play and had to be put on in makeshift premises with re-
    building going on all round) ; it was far more remarkable in its results.
    For it meant that Stalingrad people were acting Stalingrad people to Stalin-
    grad people ; the recent heroes were being glorified by their survivors to
    their survivors.
    This was followed by *La Locandiera*, *Encounter in the Dark*, *Belugin's Wedding*,
    Le Chandelier (Alfred de Musset), *A Month in the Country* and *A Great
    Sovereign*.
2. М. Б. Храпченко, *ibid.* : 28.viii.43.
    Ibid. : 27.ii.43 ; 13.iii.43 (*bis*) ; 3.vii.43.
    Within three months of returning the Stavropol Theatre was touring the
    neighbourhood with *Russian People*, again a new thing in theatre history ;
    for here were the heroes of just such scenes as were enacted on the stage,
    now sitting in the audience.
    The Krasnodar company set to the task of improving the ruins of their theatre.
    Everyone helped. But even so the accommodation in the cinema was so
    limited that they looked about for plays with only a single set, chafing
    the while at such a silly limitation to their choice of play. They decided

to do costume plays, and were delighted to receive 400 costumes as a gift from the Moscow Maly Theatre, and furniture from the Moscow Theatre of Satire, and wigs from the Sverdlovsk Theatre.

3. А. Григорев : „В Ростове", *ibid.* : 2.x.43.

     В. Беляев : „В возрожденном Ростове", *ibid.* : 4.ix.43.

     Л. Сейфуллина : „Ростовчане", *ibid.*

     Ibid. : 29.v.43 ; 21.viii.43 ; 28.viii.43 ; 11.ix.43 ; 25.ix.43.

4. В. Ардаматский : „Возрождение в жизни", *ibid.* : 4.xii.43.

     М. Михайлов : „Советское Шескпироведение", *ibid.* : 18.xii.43.

     А. Тутышкин : „В Киеве", *ibid.* : 20.xi.43.

     Maurice Hindus : " Kiev To-day ", *Moscow News* : 4.xii.43.

     Лит. и иск. : 25.ix.43.

5. З. Липавский : „Харков севодня" Труд. : 29.viii.43.

     Евгений Кирилюк : „Город великих традиции" Лит. и иск. : 28.viii.43.

     Moscow News : 8.ix.43.

     Лит. и иск. : 28.viii.43 ; 18.ix.43.

6. *Soviet War News* : 16.vi.44.

     Искусство : 20.xi.43.

     Лит. и иск. : 13.ii.43.

     Театральный справочник : 1937-8, pp. 440-52.

7. *Int. Lit.* : 1942, x, p. 79 ; 1944, xi, p. 76.

     Театральный справочник, 1937-8, pp. 420-1 and 397-8.

     Sov. Th. Chron. : 1943, viii, pp. 3-4.

     Известия :11.ix.42.

     Лит. и иск. : 21.ii.42 ; 7.viii.43 ; 28.viii.43 (*bis*) ; 11.ix.43 ; 23.x.43 ; 21.ix.44.

The town of Lvov provides an example of an underground theatre. Three performances were given, with the Germans in occupation of the town, of a play called *They Were Four*. It was written by Gabrielle Zapolska, a native of Lvov ; written in Polish and performed in the attic of a big house. Three weeks after the town had been liberated, the Polish Dramatic Theatre opened with it.

Other works in reviving Lvov were the operetta *A Zaporozhe Cossack Beyond the Danube* and Maeterlinck's *The Burgomaster*, reminding the brave citizens of Lvov how brutal the Germans were in Belgium in an earlier war, and showing the national heritage of their savage governor, the butcher Steiner, who with Nazi-like gloating used to remark, " When I see blood, I feel good ".

A small part of the material of this book has appeared in articles by the author in the *Spectator* and the *Anglo-Soviet Journal*, in a Cantor Lecture to the Royal Society of Arts, and in short talks broadcast in the Home and European Services of the B.B.C.

INDEX TO PRINCIPAL NAMES AND SUBJECTS

Figures in italics refer to the additional notes

Children's Theatres : 131, 138 n., 196, 281-7, *vii* 25, *viii* 6, *xiii* 7.

Chimkent : 143.

China : 283.

Chinovniki : see Officials.

Chkalov : 230, 232.

Chtetsy : 212-5, 263, 274, *xii* 8 & *12.*

Churkin (author) : 313.

Chuvashes : 183, 265.

Circus : 73, 86, 210-12, 298, 301, 307.

Cloches de Corneville, Les : 118.

Collective Farm Theatres : 308.

Collective Farm Wedding, A : 188.

Comedy of Errors, A (Shakespeare) : 169, 285, *vii* 25.

Committee for Art Affairs : 194, 210, 238-9, 249-51, 261, 264, 269, 277, 280, 286, 289, 298, 299, 300.

Commonwealths : 43, 66-9.

" Contemporary " Theatre, Moscow : 137.

Corneille : 20.

Costumes and Properties : 44, 67, 70, 77, 85, 124, 153, 157, 294, 300, 303, 307.

Cottage in Cherkizov, The (Arbuzov) : 162, 313, *vii* 16.

Craig, Gordon : 99, 129.

" Creative evenings " : 262-3.

Cruel Romance, A (Gladkov) : 138, 243, 313.

Cyrano de Bergerac (Rostand) : 141, 145-6 272.

Czechoslovakia : 115, 141, 283.

DACHNIKI (Gorky) : 102, 105-6.

Dadiani (author) : 188.

Dagestan : 12, 124, 158, 220, 301.

Dalmatov (actor), 64, 81.

Dalsky (actor) : 71.

Darya (Kozakov) : 166, 252, 313.

Davydov (actor) : 26, 44, 45, 55, 56-7, 62, 145, *iii* 7.

Days of the Living, The (Brushtein) : 141, 159, *vii* 16.

Days of the Turbins, The (Bulgakov) : 112.

Dead Souls (after Gogol) : 258.

Deaf-and-Dumb Theatre : 233.

Deep in the Rear (Churkin, &c.) : 253, 313.

Demidov (producer) : 122.

Demmeny (puppeteer) : 209-10.

Depth Prospecting (Kron) : 126, 205, 253, 284.

Desire Under the Elms (O'Neill) : 154.

Diakov (author) : 313.

Dickens : 167, 263, 275, 292, *xii* 18, *xiii* 7.

Difficult Years, The (A. Tolstoy) : 247.

Diky (producer) : 133, 145, 147, 168, 226-7, 270.

Dmitrevskoy (actor) : 22, *i* 15.

Dmitriev (designer) : 294.

Dmitry of the Don (Ozerov) : 21, 154.

Dniepropetrovsk : 122, 304.

Dniepropetrovsk " Gorky " Theatre : 119.

Dniepropetrovsk " Shevchenko" Theatre: 118, 232.

Dobrushin (author) : 155.

Dobrzhanskaya (actress) : 136.

Dog in the Manger, A (Lope de Vega) : 121, 148, 168, 180, 181, 185, 271, *vii* 2.

Doll's House, A (Ibsen) : 106, 121, 122, 140, 176, 273.

Don Juan ((Molière) : 132.

Don Quixote (after Cervantes) : 89, 159, 271, 293.

Dorohin (actor) : 198-9.

Doroseli (author) : 189, 314.

Dostigayev and Others (Gorky) : 114.

Dostoyevsky : 10, 46, 56, 83, 109, 145, *vi* 20.

Drama, Moscow Theatre of : 150, *xii* 12.

Dramatic Clubs and Societies : 94, 109, 153.

Dramatic Theatre, Moscow : 150, 244.

Dramatis Personæ : 156.

Dream, The (Vodopyanov) : 182.

Dream on the Volga, A (Ostrovsky) : 227.

Dreiden (author) : 152.

Duel, The (Tur Brothers, &c.) : *vii* 16, *xi* 5.

Duenna, The (Sheridan) : 154, 274, *vii* 13.

Durylin (critic) : 259.

Duse (actress) : 72, 132.

Dyhovichny (author) : 138, 161, 279, 289, 313.

Dynasty (Staboy) : 253, 313.

Dyukov (manager) : 42-3.

Dzerzhinsky (composer) : 294.

EAGLE and His Mate, The (A. Tolstoy) : 247.

Eagle's Flight, The (Sultanov) : 142, 171, 313, *vii* 16.

Earth Bears Witness, The (Baru) : 205, 313.

Eccentrics (Gorky) : 269-70.

Ehrenburg (author) : 213.

Eleventh Hour, The (Odets) : 167, 273.

Elizabethan drama : 234.

Emergency Law (Tur Brothers, &c.) : 244, 313, *xi* 5.

GEORGE ALLEN & UNWIN LTD
LONDON: 40 MUSEUM STREET, W.C. 1
CAPE TOWN: 58-60 LONG STREET
TORONTO: 91 WELLINGTON STREET WEST
BOMBAY: 15 GRAHAM ROAD, BALLARD ESTATE
WELLINGTON, N.Z.: 8 KINGS CRESCENT, LOWER HUTT
SYDNEY, N.S.W.: BRADBURY HOUSE, 55 YORK STREET